Whole Life Asset Management

[L4M7]
Core
Study Guide

Level 4
Diploma in Procurement
and Supply

Printed and distributed by:
The Chartered Institute of Procurement & Supply, Easton House, Easton on the Hill, Stamford, Lincolnshire
PE9 3NZ

info@cips.org
www.cips.org

Every attempt has been made to ensure the accuracy of this study guide; however, no liability can be accepted for any loss incurred in any way whatsoever by any person relying solely on the information contained within it. The study guide has been produced solely for the purpose of professional qualification study and should not be taken as definitive of the legal position. CIPS cannot be held responsible for the content of any website mentioned in this study guide. Specific advice should always be obtained before undertaking any investment.

ISBN: 978-1-86124-294-5

A CIP (Catalogue in Publication) catalogue record for this publication is available from the British Library.

All facts are correct at time of publication.

Authors: Adrian Bettinson FCIPS and Jim Goodhead, CEng, FCIPS

First published in 2019 by CIPS

Editorial and project management by Haremi Ltd.
Typesetting by York Publishing Solutions Pvt. Ltd., INDIA
Index by LNS Indexing.

Every effort has been made to trace all copyright holders, but if any have been inadvertently overlooked, the Publishers will be pleased to make the necessary arrangements at the first opportunity.

Contents

Chapter 3

Your qualification

CIPS qualifications are regulated internationally to ensure we offer a recognised, professional standard in procurement and supply. CIPS Level 4* Diploma in Procurement and Supply is a vocationally related professional qualification. Formal recognition is included within the regulatory frameworks of an increasing number of countries such as the UK (England, Wales and Northern Ireland), UAE (including Dubai) and Africa (including Zambia). Further information on this recognition and the details of corresponding qualifications levels for other international qualifications frameworks are detailed on our website. CIPS members can have the confidence in our regulated qualifications, which reliably indicate the standard of knowledge, skills and understanding that you, as a learner, are required to demonstrate.

A step up from the Level 3 Advanced Certificate in Procurement and Supply Operations, the Level 4 Diploma in Procurement and Supply is a stepping stone to study on the CIPS Level 5 Advanced Diploma in Procurement and Supply. The content has been written using the CIPS Procurement and Supply Cycle as its focus, which presents a cyclical process of key steps faced by those procuring goods or services. The Diploma offers the most common entry route to the profession and should be used by learners to develop a professional 'tool box' which learners can apply in the practical environment and further develop at Levels 5 and 6.

In this way successful learners will possess transferable workplace skills, developing their operational and tactical abilities as they strive for managerial roles and responsibilities. It is aimed at those in the profession who have procurement and supply activity at the heart of their role. Learners will be expected to provide advice and guidance to key stakeholders on the performance of organisational procedures and processes associated with procurement and supply and will aspire to manage developments in and improvements to the related functions. Transferable skills are those such as communication, teamwork, and planning and completing tasks to high standards, all enable the learner to add value to the organisation.

Entry level — Level 2 Certificate in Procurement and Supply Operations

Entry level — Level 3 Advanced Certificate in Procurement and Supply Operations

Highest Entry level — Level 4 Diploma in Procurement and Supply Operations

Level 5 Advanced Diploma in Procurement and Supply

Level 6 Professional Diploma in Procurement and Supply

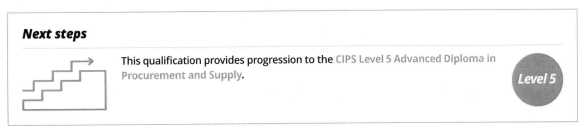

Next steps

This qualification provides progression to the CIPS Level 5 Advanced Diploma in Procurement and Supply.

Level 5

*Refers to levels within the UK RQF. Other regulatory bodies may have different corresponding levels

Based on the Tactical competency level of CIPS Global Standard

Guide to qualification content

What will I study?

Eight CORE modules make up 60 required credits

60 Credits required for completion

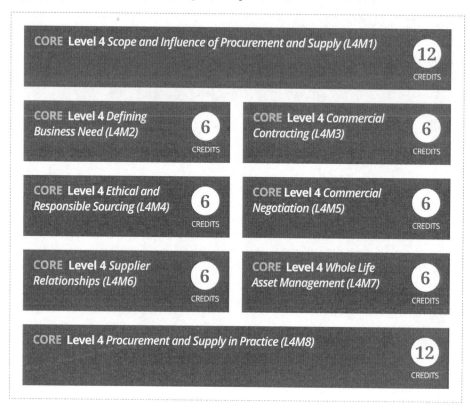

CORE **Level 4** *Scope and Influence of Procurement and Supply (L4M1)*
12 CREDITS

CORE **Level 4** *Defining Business Need (L4M2)*
6 CREDITS

CORE **Level 4** *Commercial Contracting (L4M3)*
6 CREDITS

CORE **Level 4** *Ethical and Responsible Sourcing (L4M4)*
6 CREDITS

CORE **Level 4** *Commercial Negotiation (L4M5)*
6 CREDITS

CORE **Level 4** *Supplier Relationships (L4M6)*
6 CREDITS

CORE **Level 4** *Whole Life Asset Management (L4M7)*
6 CREDITS

CORE **Level 4** *Procurement and Supply in Practice (L4M8)*
12 CREDITS

Who is it for?

This qualification is the essential toolkit for anyone planning a career in procurement and supply. Developed and written using the Procurement and Supply cycle** as its focus, it is at the same level as the first year of an undergraduate degree course. It's suitable for those in operational roles or those managing or supervising the procurement and supply function who want to develop their career and work towards MCIPS Chartered Procurement and Supply Professional.

What will I learn?

You will learn about making procurement and supply happen within an organisation, and you will be equipped with an essential range of knowledge and tools that you can apply immediately in your workplace. Learn how to apply practical, theoretical and technical knowledge, gain a clear understanding of procurement and supply and develop the ability to address complex, non-routine problems.

On completion, you will be able to analyse, interpret and evaluate relevant information and ideas and have an informed awareness of differing perspectives and approaches within the profession. You will also be able to review the effectiveness and appropriateness of methods, actions and results.

Entry requirements

This is the only entry point onto our Diploma qualifications. A minimum of at least two A-levels (or international equivalent) or a CIPS Level 3 Advanced Certificate qualification is required. Alternatively, you will need a minimum of two years' relevant experience in a business environment.

Credit values

To gain a qualification you are required to complete a total number of credits. This is a way of quantifying the required number of study hours. 1 credit is equivalent to 10 hours of study. Each module is given a credit value of 6 or 12 credits.

*** The Procurement cycle is the cyclical process of key steps when procuring goods or services.**
www.cips.org/en-gb/knowledge/procurement-cycle/

Total credits required for completion 60

About our exams and your study commitments

Objective Response exam format (OR)

These questions allow you to select a response from a list of possible answers. You will find these types of exams across all our qualifications levels and they are marked by computer and then moderated by CIPS examiners.

Constructed Response exam format (CR)

These questions require you to create or 'construct' a response to the question such as an essay or case study. You will find this type of exam in our diploma level qualifications and they will be marked by subject expert examiners.

Your total qualification time (TQT)

The TQT indicates the overall number of guided learning hours, additional self-study and assessment time that is required.

Guided learning hours (GLH)

It is expected that you will undertake 250 GLH. The definition of guided learning hours is: 'A measure of the amount of input time required to achieve the qualification. This includes lectures, tutorials and practicals, as well as supervised study in, for example, learning centres and workshops'.

Self-study requirement (SSR)

Additionally, we recommend that you also commit to at least 335 SSR hours. This includes wider reading of the subject areas and revision to give yourself the best preparation for successfully achieving the qualification.

Total exam time

All the modules in CIPS qualifications are assessed by an examination.

How to use this book

Welcome to this study guide for Whole Life Asset Management. It contains all the information needed to prepare you for the assessment in this module.

This study guide follows the order of the module specification and each chapter relates to one of the learning outcomes below. You can also see the assessment criteria for each learning outcome.

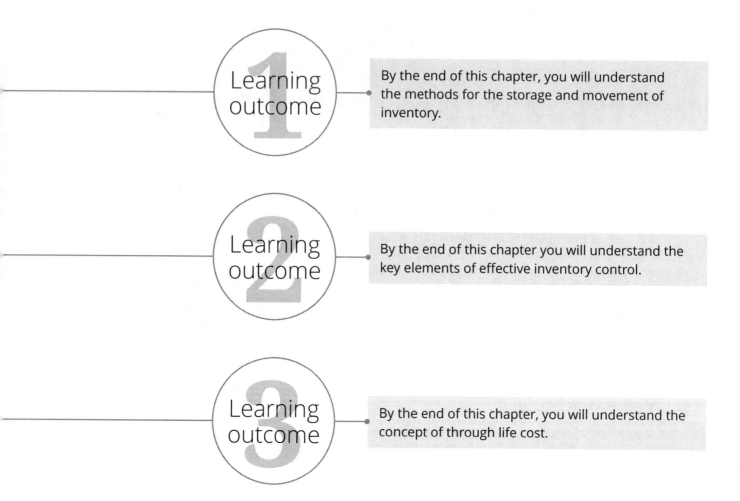

Learning outcome 1

By the end of this chapter, you will understand the methods for the storage and movement of inventory.

Learning outcome 2

By the end of this chapter you will understand the key elements of effective inventory control.

Learning outcome 3

By the end of this chapter, you will understand the concept of through life cost.

Book features

Throughout this book there are a number of features to aid your learning and simplify your revision. Take a look at the different features you will find in the book below.

Glossary
These are the key terms and their definitions

Remember This information is important, so you should make a note of it.	
Check These revision questions give you a chance to check you understand the content in this chapter.	
Apply These tasks give you a chance to test out your knowledge and understanding.	
Recap This information will summarise sections from previous chapters.	
Case study These case studies will relate the content you have learned to real-world examples.	
Recommended reading These books can give you more understanding on the subject.	

Link to CIPS knowledge where members will be able to access additional resources to extend your knowledge, plus links to online eLearning content including videos, audio and interactive quizzes to recap and test your knowledge and understanding.

End of chapter assessments

At the end of each chapter in the book there is a set of exam-style questions to prepare you for your assessment.

End of Chapter Assessment

IDENTIFY

1. The National Health Service (NHS) in the UK is an example of an organisation from which sector?

   a. Public
   b. Private
   c. Third
   d. Primary

Whole Life Asset Management [L4M7]

CORE MODULE

CIPS GLOBAL STANDARD 4.2 • 4.3

Module purpose

On completion of this module, learners will be able to explain methods of inventory storage and control and analyse the concept of whole life cost from concept through to disposal.

Module aim(s)

Whole life costing takes into account the total cost of a product or service over its lifetime, from concept through to disposal including purchase, hire or lease, maintenance, operation, utilities, training and disposal. Hence, it is important for those involved in the procurement and supply function to take all these elements into consideration when making decisions and comparing the costs of buying, renting or leasing equipment. In most cases the purchase costs are a small proportion of the cost of operating it. Although costly, there are numerous reasons why organisations elect to hold inventory. The management and control of such inventory is therefore vital to organisational success. This module is designed for those who will have responsibility for the whole life management of assets and enables learners to analyse methods for inventory movement and control and to analyse the concept of whole life cost.

OR

OBJECTIVE RESPONSE EXAM

1.5 HRS

EXAM DURATION HOURS

60 HRS

MODULE LEARNING TIME

Credit value

6 CREDITS

CHAPTER 1
Understand methods for the storage and movement of inventory

 **By the end of this chapter, you will understand the methods for the storage and movement of inventory.**

Chapter overview

1.1 Identify the principles, purpose and impact of stores and warehouse design

You will understand:
- Location of stores and warehouses
- Stores and warehouse design
- Factors that influence stores and warehouse layout
- Flow, space utilisation and flexibility

1.2 Explain the use of product coding in inventory operations

You will understand:
- Systems for product coding
- Bar coding
- Order tracking technologies
- The use of RFID technologies

1.3 Contrast the impact of the use of different warehousing equipment

You will understand:
- Materials handling equipment
- Palletisation and unit loads
- Packing and packaging
- Environmental standards for packaging
- The use of automation in warehousing

Introduction

In this chapter you will consider the wide variety of situations that require the storage of raw materials; part-processed materials; manufactured products; and maintenance, repair and operating supplies. At first glance, this may seem technical or abstract, but storage is seen in our day-to-day lives as customers in shops. At work, even if stock cannot be seen, we are often affected by the storage decisions of suppliers and experience the cost of delivery – and delivery delays.

This chapter also looks in detail at some of the decisions made and systems used by organisations in the supply chain that also contribute to the availability and speed of delivery of stock. These include decisions of location, design and layout which can aid, or hinder, everyday operations.

Identify the principles, purpose and impact of stores and warehouse design

Principles of stores and warehouses

Stores
Small, local storage facility for immediate-use items

Warehouse
Large-scale storage facility – can be 'stand-alone' (for example, not connected to manufacturing, assembly, retailing) or 'integrated' (for example, on the same site products are either used or retailed)

Distribution centres and distribution hubs
Warehouses that are intended to be a focal point for a specific activity for a geographic area

Stockyard
An open area (which may have a canopy or some protection) often used to store bulky stock items, vehicles and appropriate materials

Stores are small, local storage facilities for immediate-use items.

Warehouses are larger scale storage facilities. These may be the following.

- **Stand-alone**: for example, not connected to manufacturing, assembly or retailing
- **Integrated**: for example, on the same site that materials or products are used by or sold to external users

Distribution centres and **distribution hubs** are terms used to describe warehouses which are intended to be a focal point for a specific activity for a geographic area. Because the term is often used loosely, most of this text and examples that refer to warehouses also apply to distribution centres and distribution hubs.

Stores and warehouses may contain the following.

- Raw materials
- Partly processed materials
- Part or fully assembled components
- Spare parts
- Items returned from customers or users (reverse logistics)
- Items used as part of processing and manufacturing
- Equipment stored for hire or use by the organisation in various sites

They may well have a combination of these items.

Stockyards are open or semi-covered areas that are used for the following.

- Bulk loose or packaged materials
- Bulky or oversized items that may be difficult to move inside
- Materials that may require specialised handling, loading and unloading
- Equipment suitable for outside storage, for example, earth-moving machinery

Some warehouses handle large volumes of bulk items and make these available to retailers or commercial customers. Some warehouses receive these bulk items but then make smaller amounts available to customers. Other warehouses may specialise in smaller volume, non-bulky items.

1.1 LO1

Purposes of stores and warehouses

The purposes of stores and warehouses are listed below.

- To make stock available to internal and/or external customers in alignment with the stocking decisions of the organisation
- To maintain a safe environment for workers in the stores or warehouse
- To maintain a secure environment to avoid stock losses
- To maintain a suitable environment for stock, minimising losses from damage and deterioration

To fulfil these purposes, store and warehouse managers and staff need to do the following.

- Receive, inspect, record and store stock received
- Retrieve, record and release stock to authorised persons, providing documentation and packaging as required
- Report and liaise internally and externally on stock availability, re-ordering and future stock levels
- Minimise stock losses and damages to stock
- Manage and account for returned stock inwards and stock returned to suppliers

Volumes of stock and locations

Organisations must make decisions regarding the volumes of stock that are required for immediate use – they also must consider an appropriate timescale for making stock available. In each case, physical stock needs to be stored.

Organisations must also consider the supply chain involved.

- In some cases there may be a long delay – or long **lead time** – involved in obtaining stock, meaning that larger stock volumes need to be kept.
- In other cases there may be near-zero stock held as items are available in hours, or overnight.

The impact of low stock in the supply chain can be the following.

- Stock is not available at times of higher than expected demand.
- There are delays and additional costs to achieve supply.

But a lower stock results in lower overall costs to the supply chain.

Organisations also have many issues regarding costs. As will be seen in chapter 2, higher levels of stock incur higher costs of storage to the organisation.

Organisations often select a structure of storage and distribution that is best suited to its combination of requirements and costs. Types of storage and distribution structures include the following.

- **Centralised warehouse**: at a single location that can be used to supply a whole country
- **Regional warehouse**: can be used to supply an area of a country

Lead time
The time delay between placing an order and the availability of the item in the required location. There may be an internal lead time in creating an order and another between receipt of goods and making them available to a user

- **Local warehouse or stores**: storage at many locations situated close to the users or customers

- **Warehousing in another country**: this is useful when servicing multiple countries

- **Outsourced warehousing**: storage may be outsourced to a specialist organisation

- **Partnering**: warehousing can be achieved by partnering with other organisations in the same industry or other industries

Unfortunately, many organisations make compromises on their structure owing to cost limitations and changes of priority over time – they may be left with a 'legacy' structure that no longer matches the 'best solution'.

Case study

Toilet rolls (toilet tissue) supply chain

In the UK, most home-consumer users obtain supplies, such as toilet tissue, from a local supermarket. There are different manufacturers of toilet tissue, but the following simplified example shows the warehouse and storage pattern for one manufacturer.

Manufacturing centre

Manufactures to predictions based on sales reported by the supermarket ensuring sufficient raw materials are available to meet the production plan. Finished goods are stored on pallets ready for bulk delivery (each of the stacked boxes contain 144 rolls, the inner packs in this case having four rolls each). Raw materials, packaging materials, manufacturing machinery spare parts, cleaning and maintenance materials are also required.

Supermarket regional warehouse

The warehouse receives the bulk delivery. Some whole pallets and boxes are prepared for larger store delivery. Most whole pallets are broken down for smaller stores and the required volumes of inner packs are delivered to retail shops in steel cages.

Supermarket retail shops

The supermarket receives the pallets, boxes or steel cages. It breaks down the pallets or boxes and places the packs for sale on shelves in the supermarket.

This process is shown in figure 1.1.

Figure 1.1 Typical supply chain for a supermarket

Each stage has storage requirements. At each stage there is an attempt to provide the volume required to the next-in-line within the timescale required. Each organisation in the chain also tries to limit storage volumes to avoid additional costs.

Apply

Using the simple supply chain model for a supermarket shown in figure 1.1, suggest five reasons for a supermarket running out of toilet roll stock.

Factors influencing locations of storage

There are many different factors that must be considered when assessing warehouse and stock locations. Some of the following may conflict with each other.

- **Cost of location**: in many countries there are areas of low-cost land and buildings and higher-cost areas. There may be local or government grants or other incentives available. Staff costs will also be lower in low-cost countries. It is tempting to have warehouses in cheaper areas, but this may mean higher transport costs to supply customers or transfer stock to the point of use.

- **Availability and suitability of the building**: the desired size and layout requirements of a warehouse may be affected by what is available. In some cases, this could result in a 'new build' which may be affected by land availability and higher costs. Alternatively, a compromised specification or multiple, smaller warehouses may be required.

- **Availability and suitability of staff**: all warehouses require staff for the operations outlined earlier. The location of a warehouse may not attract skilled staff to move to a new area and there may be limited suitable staff.

- **Nature of the items to be stored**: for example, items required for emergency use would need to be stored close to where they are to be used. Some food items may have a one day 'shelf life' – in which case a location requiring more than one day's transport would be unacceptable. Some products require special handling and storage.

- **Access to transport infrastructure**: the ability to get to efficient transport links may affect the cost of the building and may affect operational lead times and transport costs. This could therefore include the following.

  - Access to ports and airports for internal transport, import and/or export
  - Access to inland waterways (particularly useful in some countries)
  - Access to a good road network (perhaps with links to continental road networks)
  - Closeness to suppliers – this could consider the relative importance of geographic clusters of suppliers and projected volumes of stock ordered
  - Closeness to customers – this could consider the relative importance of geographic clusters of customers and projected volumes of stock ordered

The impact of not considering some of these factors is likely to be that customer service is reduced. Higher costs may be incurred and/or loss of business may result.

Remember

Decisions regarding stores and warehouse locations involve a complex range of issues that are unique to each business. The solution is usually an optimisation (or 'best overall result') of multiple factors.

Deciding on storage facilities and locations

Qualitative analysis
Analysis based on opinions and statements (which are often non-quantifiable) rather than numerical or statistical evidence

Quantitative analysis
Analysis based on numerical or statistical-based information rather than opinions and statements

Inventory
Alternative term used for stock held in a facility or organisation

Organisations should first analyse and assess their current requirements, facilities and performance. Future needs are then added, based on projections and any change or development of the organisation.

A **qualitative analysis** involves a series of opinion-based statements, resulting in the identification of existing strengths and weaknesses and the future requirements. These may include statements from management, staff, suppliers and customers with opinions regarding, for example, stock levels, locations, transport issues and time to supply.

A **quantitative analysis** uses numbers-based factual statements. This may include the following.

- Cost analysis for the current premises and future predictions based on current premises: these costs can be calculated as overall figures and, for example, 'costs per cubic metre' or 'cost per order' (these are featured in detail in section 3.1).

- Cost analysis for routine operations: these are costs which are not premises based. These costs can be calculated as overall figures and, for example, 'costs per product', 'cost per order' and 'cost per operating hour or day' (these are also featured in detail in section 3.1).

- Current **inventory** performance measures: these are current measurements and future requirements, such as lead times, service levels, rate of stock turn, stockouts in a given period and stock cover (see section 2.3).

Remember
Most storage facility and location decisions are based on a combination of qualitative and quantitative analysis.

How many storage facilities should an organisation have?

It is tempting to just think that 'more store facilities' must be better. However, this may resolve the supply requirement, but it will come at a cost, as shown in figure 1.2.

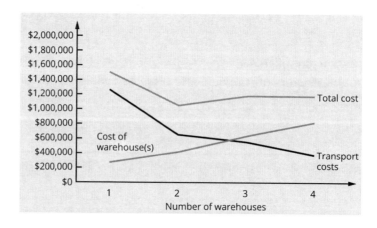

Figure 1.2 Example of a cost comparison of adding warehouses

Figure 1.2 shows a situation with worked figures representing the following.

a) **The cost of warehouses**: each one has a different cost, and each has a cost of stockholding and stock management included.

b) **The transport costs**: in this case, the total transport cost reduces as further warehouses mean shorter final delivery to the customers.

c) **The total cost**: simply the cost of warehouses plus the cost of transport.

In this case, the lowest total cost is achieved by having two warehouses. There is also no gain but no apparent loss in terms of the costs of having three or four warehouses. This does not, however, place a value on the improved customer service or other advantages and disadvantages, which would be understood by further quantitative or qualitative analysis.

Generating options for storage location

Further analysis will help to assess potential options. Options generated can be variations on a single concept, but it is beneficial to explore other choices as each option will have advantages and disadvantages. There are also likely to be differences in costs. Look at the following illustrations to see how this works.

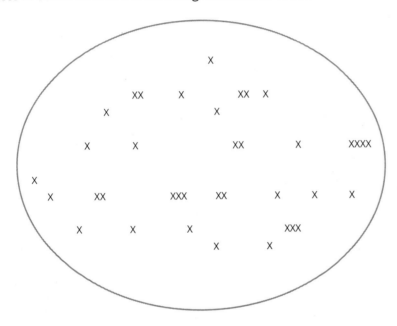

Figure 1.3 Requirements for customer deliveries

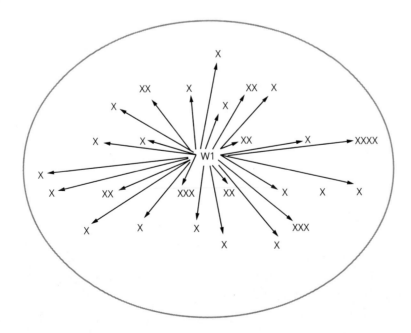

Figure 1.4 Impact of a single warehouse solution

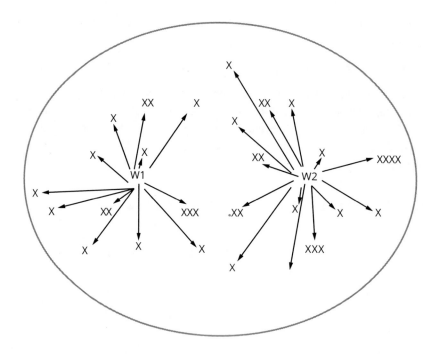

Figure 1.5 Impact of a two-warehouse solution

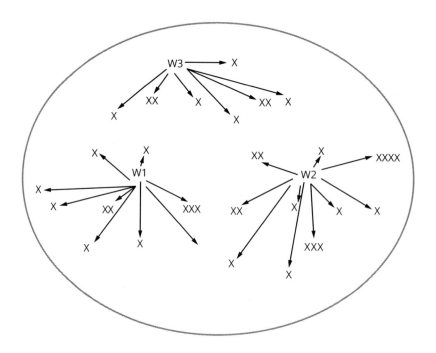

Figure 1.6 Impact of a three-warehouse solution

In figure 1.3 each customer location has been identified (x). The multiple 'x' locations may have more than one customer. In each of the diagrams that follow, the customer locations are unchanged.

Figure 1.4 shows the impact of a single warehouse (W1), roughly in the middle of the customer grouping. It would also be possible to locate the warehouse closer to the customers with a higher frequency of deliveries or higher spend. The single warehouse would require enough stock levels to meet the demand of all customers. The distances between the customers on the opposite sides of the area suggest the potential for long journeys.

Figure 1.5 shows the impact of two warehouses (W1 and W2). It would be possible to locate the two warehouses closer to the customers with a higher frequency of deliveries or higher spend. The two-warehouse layout allows each warehouse to have fewer customers which suggests lower stock can be held in each location. It also shows that shorter delivery distances are expected.

Figure 1.6 shows the impact of a three-warehouse solution (W1, W2 and W3). Again, the exact location of each warehouse could reflect higher customer frequency or spend. The three-warehouse layout allows each warehouse to have fewer customers which suggests lower stock can be held in each location. The more localised customers again reduce delivery distances.

Multiple warehouse locations can significantly help organisations where long delivery distances are involved. They can also help where transport links and delays are encountered.

Remember
Deciding the optimum number of warehouses in any situation and their location(s) involves a systematic approach where multiple options are considered and evaluated.

The following case study uses the concept of multiple options and evaluations. It also includes the concept of including the future direction of the business.

≪ Case study

Optimising warehousing in drink supply (DS)
This case shows a simplified view of a real decision faced by a major drink manufacturer (DS) for a specific country (B) which was an export market for DS.

DS bought a long-established drink manufacturer (R) as a means of gaining a much larger market share in country B, which is some distance from its manufacturing base. It was already importing products by sea prior to the takeover, using a warehouse located in the port of entry.

The new owner had analysed the situation, and this provided the following simplified overview.

- There was an objective to sell more brands in country B.

- The traditional location of former site R was very important to maintaining sales in country B.

- Former site R had spare production capacity and space for storage.

- Distances from site R to deliver to distant sales locations in country B would take a full day.

- 'Inland' areas were not well served by transport links despite cheaper land and availability.

- Sales in country A were very low as brands developed and sold in country A were dominant.

Figure 1.7 shows the key locations.

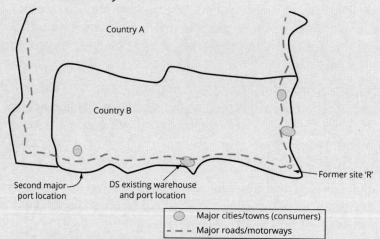

Figure 1.7 Country A and Country B key location map

The following four options are possible here.

- Option 1: maintain former site R for the existing brand; maintain existing DS site for imports.

- Option 2: develop former site R to include warehousing of imported brands; close existing warehouse.

- Option 3: maintain former site R; develop existing DS warehouse to a national distribution centre for all brands including those from former site R.

- Option 4: develop a new single manufacturing site for all products; closing former site R.

Each option has multiple advantages and disadvantages. Although the detailed reports and cost comparisons are not available, the following table presents a summarised qualitative analysis and option comparison.

Option	Cost of development	Delivery	Maintain production tradition	Future development	Other comments
1	Low: uses existing locations	Unchanged, some long journeys	YES	Limited	Still means customers require multiple deliveries for other brands
2	Low/Medium: uses existing locations but warehouse close-down required	Imported brands now have increased transport movements	YES	Very limited after site use expanded	Gains from single site and multiple brand deliveries to customers
3	Medium: Some new development needed	Some extra transport movements, in the 'wrong direction' for some deliveries	YES	Yes, but distribution point now further away from some customers	Gains from single distribution point and lower total transport costs
4	High: new location and close-down needed	Depends on location, could be 'best location'	NO	Dependent on location, could be designed in	Uncertain value of old site and reuse. Gains from latest production techniques. Could manufacture other brands on site

1.1 LO1

DS chose Option 1. The reasons were linked to the pace of change that the company wanted. It was soon decided to increase production at former site R and to use the DS warehouse to stock products from site R for export. This strengthened the role of site R which was well received by locals and the government. Later, other DS brands were produced in former site R for distribution in country B, avoiding the long journey times from other production sites.

Notice in this case that the structure of warehousing and location decisions were affected by changing ideas within the company. Any of the options could have been successful, but DS avoided potential disruption and initial costs by maintaining existing facilities. Notice also the importance of major infrastructure features in country B – major populations are also connected by the major road network.

Apply

Using the location principles, provide your own 'summarised qualitative analysis' for:

Option 5: Maintain former site R, close down existing warehouse and port location; build new production facility for other DS brands in the second major port location.

Record your findings in table form using the headings as above.

Stores and warehouse design

Organisations vary widely in their approach to the design of stores and warehouses. In many cases design is driven by limitations on cost and location, both of which are linked to availability. There seems to be a common view that stores and warehouses are an unwelcome cost, but a questioning of what is required, and a drive for efficiency and effectiveness linked to design, can improve an organisation's performance and lower costs.

In many cases, organisations are limited by what they already work with. The following investigates some common design elements of buildings and how these affect storage and warehousing operations.

Structural features

Single floor design/layout

A single floor layout means that there is no requirement for higher-level access via lifts and stairs. It should also mean that weight loading issues are far less important provided a suitable solid ground floor is in place. A single floor layout may allow full use of the height of the building, subject to appropriate racking and equipment. A flat floor throughout allows maximum use of handling equipment and reduces operating risks.

The locations of doors, lifts, stairs, ceiling heights and structural columns will all affect the usefulness of a building and introduce limitations for layouts.

Multiple floors design/layout

Multiple floors maximise the use of the available land and each floor can be allocated different products, creating zones. The construction of the floors needs to be considered and full stock weight loading, the equipment weight and racking weight also all needs considering. Although lifts, conveyors and hoists are commonplace, these add to costs and require maintenance. Some high-volume locations may need to duplicate access equipment and methods to avoid breakdowns causing operational delays.

Light, temperature, humidity and ventilation

The design of a building should consider the advantages of natural light as this can reduce the cost of artificial lighting and improve the environmental performance of the building. Daylight entering the building can also help reduce heating costs. Unfortunately, some stock reacts badly to direct sunlight, and some stock reacts badly to extremes of temperature or may require a specific temperature for storage. Some stock may require a warmer temperature than the ambient temperature and other stock may require a cooler temperature. Some specific stock may require through-flow ventilation to avoid deterioration. All these factors require design consideration as modern construction techniques can all support specific environmental control equipment.

Warehouse equipment requirements

Heavy-lift cranes may be required to move weighty items or finished products. These may require integration within the structure of the building and this may affect the design. Other equipment may have safe operating requirements or space limitations.

Getting goods in and out

This is an obvious issue, but the actual requirements can vary from organisation to organisation and will be dependent on the expected role and movements for the facility.

The sizing and positioning of both external and internal doors need to be considered (see figure 1.8). This often requires the use of automated access doors and/or curtain screening.

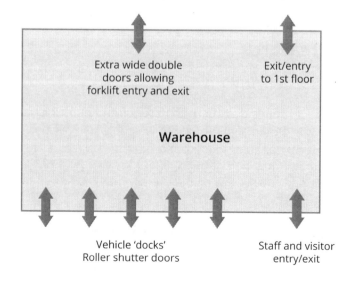

Figure 1.8 Building design – typical access requirements

Access roads need to accommodate vehicles, and vehicles passing each other.

Some warehouses have very small numbers of very large volume and quantity deliveries; others have very large numbers of small deliveries. Similarly, some may have small numbers of large volume and quantity despatches, and others may have very large numbers of small despatches. The bays and spaces allocated within a design should take this into account. Having 'dual use' in and out **docks** increases flexibility as there may be a requirement to have many collections at particular times during the day. Having 'sole use' docks ensures that a minimum number of docks are available for specific transport.

Docks
A feature of warehouse design – used for unloading and loading vehicles (i.e. loading and unloading bays)

It is not efficient for supplier delivery vehicles to be queuing for a delivery bay, but all space has a cost and could have alternative uses. It is a similar situation with goods-out – courier and transport companies try to ensure they maximise their usable time, so waiting time should be kept to a minimum.

'Goods-in' and 'goods-out' bays should be designed to allow vehicles to safely position themselves – so the exterior space for manoeuvring becomes important. The design also needs to allow for appropriate equipment to unload and load.

In many cases efficient and effective loading and unloading is achieved by a **dock** design that places the loading and unloading vehicles' rear platform at the same height as the warehouse floor (see figure 1.9). Alternatively, loading and unloading vehicles with side access (either rigid panels or curtain sides) will require equipment access at the sides (see figure 1.10). The design of the doors area needs to protect the warehouse interior but allow easy access for the equipment used to load and unload the vehicles.

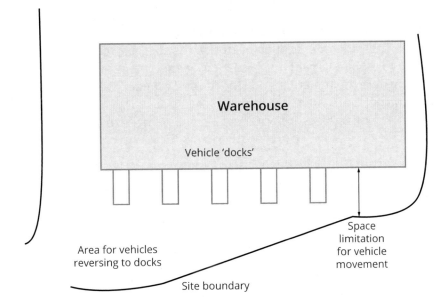

Figure 1.9 Example of external constraints on goods-out and goods-in

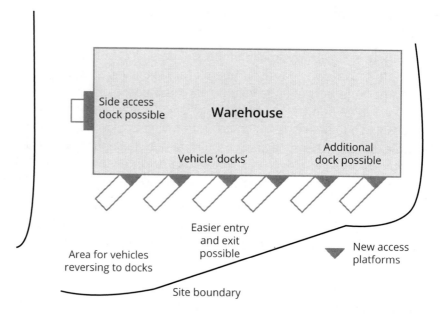

Figure 1.10 Example of external redesign to allow more docks and side-opening vehicle use

> *Check*
> What 'structural' factors have an influence on warehouse design?

Zoning
An arrangement in a stockyard, warehouse or stores facility where areas are determined based on requirements for different access, or the characteristics of different types of equipment or stock

Stockyard design

Stockyards need to have enough allocated space for stock storage and movement. The earlier description of stockyards suggests that the bulky items are more likely to require larger lifting and moving equipment. A flat ground area that is resilient to the materials and stock stored is beneficial as uneven ground can make movements difficult and may make stock storage unstable. Good drainage is essential to ensure waterlogging and damage to the surface do not occur.

Some covered areas may be beneficial to reduce climate impact and allow some stock protection. **Zoning** is also appropriate, but this will depend on the items to be stored, the frequency of movements and the equipment needed.

Health and safety

Alongside efficiency and effectiveness, stores, warehouses and stockyards must all comply with any health and safety regulations. In practice, compliance with regulations will help contribute to smooth running – organisations will find that the designing of safe working practices will reduce or eliminate risks and therefore reduce or eliminate any delays caused by problems. Examples include the zoning of the warehouse, particularly where forklift trucks are operating, and areas permitting or excluding staff and equipment can be allocated (see figure 1.11).

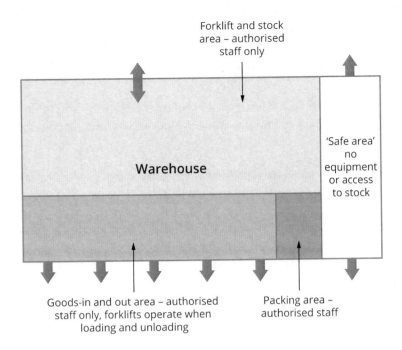

Forklift and stock area – authorised staff only

Warehouse

'Safe area' no equipment or access to stock

Goods-in and out area – authorised staff only, forklifts operate when loading and unloading

Packing area – authorised staff

Figure 1.11 Zoning for security and health and safety

Security

Security of both staff and assets within the premises should be considered as part of the design. Accessibility for the public should be restricted on-site where possible. The external structure should resist attempts to gain unauthorised entry and designs accommodating higher risk stock should reflect a higher standard of security (see figure 1.12). It is good practice to isolate delivery and collection vehicles from materials and products. Stockyard security can be particularly difficult, so the location of the stockyard and perimeter security are important design elements.

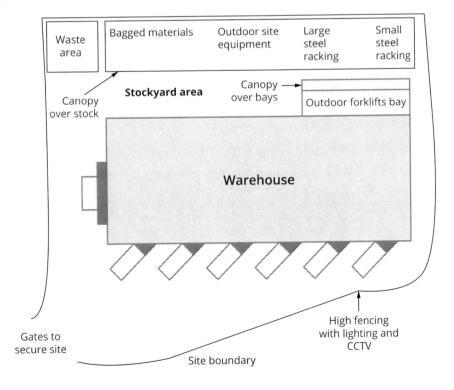

Waste area

Bagged materials

Outdoor site equipment

Large steel racking

Small steel racking

Canopy over stock

Stockyard area

Canopy over bays

Canopy over bays

Outdoor forklifts bay

Warehouse

Gates to secure site

Site boundary

High fencing with lighting and CCTV

Figure 1.12 An example of stockyard integration with a warehouse

Factors that influence stores and warehouse layout

Warehouses tend to be large scale and handle a wide range and large quantity of items, but the same issues affect warehouses as stores and stockyards.

What is required?

Stores tend to work based on immediate-use requirements. Some items will be more critical to continued operations than others. There may also be long lead times for some items. Irregular or highly variable demand can cause difficulties establishing stock levels needed. There may be cost efficiencies in bulk buying which may also need to be considered.

What items must be available for immediate use or supply?

This question forces an organisation to consider whether there is a need to store stock at all – there may be business-to-business (B2B) suppliers that can offer a following-day delivery service, and many offer a local 'collection on demand' capability. Although time could be lost in waiting for stock, this could be weighed against the cost of holding stock (and the cost of disposal should the item(s) have a limited 'use by' lifetime). Some retailers are merely 'order takers' and the manufacturer or distributor is passed the order for processing and delivery to the end customer rather than the retailer.

There has been much work undertaken in some organisations to reduce or eliminate the storage requirement. Some warehouses may receive goods-in and hold them in an area for same-day collection. Others which have outbound deliveries going to customers or other warehouses may use cross-docking, with a goods-in delivery being transferred to one or more goods-out bays ready for onward journeys.

Items that require stocking could still vary widely by how often they are required. In a kitchen, it is most likely that the most often required items are very easy to retrieve. A favourite cup is likely to remain on a worktop but a 'New Year' celebration banner is likely to be much more time consuming to find. In warehouses, stockrooms and stockyards, there is a potential for time and labour saving by reducing the total distance travelled by positioning high-use items close to the point of entry or exit (see figure 1.13).

Business-to-business (B2B)
Commercial trade transactions between businesses (as opposed to business-to-consumer, B2C)

Cross-docking
Activity in a warehouse or stockyard where a delivery is unloaded but then prepared for despatch without being stored. In some cases, a vehicle may be awaiting loading

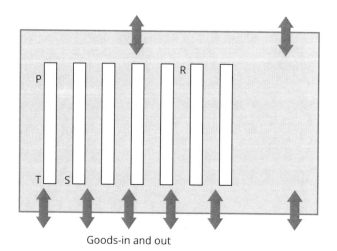

Goods-in and out

Figure 1.13 Positioning of high- and low-usage items

In figure 1.13, imagine the distances travelled if, for example, items in positions P and R were required 20 times per day, but items at positions S and T were only required once a day. If these positions are reversed the savings in distances travelled and time to retrieve in total are significant – consider if this was a typical weekly and annual pattern. Repositioning like this means the items are unlikely to be in product number order, so a 'location' chart or look-up becomes necessary.

> *Check*
> How does the frequency of demand of an item influence the layout of a store or warehouse?

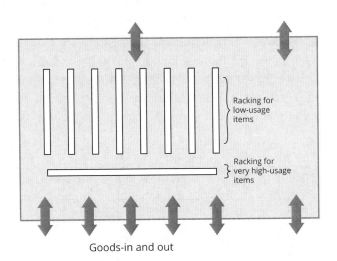

Figure 1.14 Layout for high-usage access efficiency

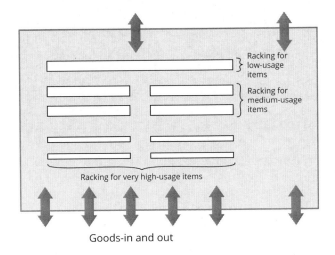

Figure 1.15 Alternative layout for high-usage access efficiency

Figure 1.14 and figure 1.15 show alternative layouts working on the frequency of requirements and location closest to the point of use or entry/exit point. The principle of location by frequency of use requires an analysis and judgment regarding both the layout and the question of 'what frequency makes it high/medium/low use?'

What are the characteristics and storage requirements of stock items?

The size, shape, weight and volume of stock items need to be considered when planning or changing layouts.

Tote box
Reusable storage box. These can be open or have lids or flaps to close them and come in a large variety of sizes and weight loadings

Pallets
Platform structures designed to support a load and be lifted using the forks typically seen on forklift trucks and other equipment. These are in a variety of standard sizes and can be made of many materials including plastic, resin, board or timber

Drum
Container for stock, which is usually cylindrical and can be made from a variety of materials. Contents are usually loose material or liquids

Picking
The activity of retrieving stock from storage

Stock might be on convenient pallets or in **tote boxes**, or even standard-sized cardboard boxes. Some organisations have arrangements with suppliers for delivery in appropriate **pallets** or containers – and return these after the items are used. In other cases, an organisation will open a delivery and transfer it to a pallet, tote box or cardboard box.

Pallets are available in a variety of sizes and there are European and international standard specifications. These allow standard lifting equipment to be used.

Tote boxes look like household storage boxes. They come in a very wide range of sizes (two litres or smaller, or up to 160 litres). They are available as removable-lidded, hinged-lidded, open-fronted and open-topped. There are versions that comply with different standards, and ones that have spaces for forklift or pallet truck use. Many are stackable when empty, taking up very little space.

Space in the stock area is also required for empty pallets, packaging and tote boxes which will be returned to the originator, retained for future use or removed for recycling. There is a recent trend for organisations to shred packaging with the end result being used as an internal 'void filling' packing material.

Stock can also be in **drums** or loose. Individual items may be very large or very small. It is good practice to store similar types of items in the same area – this allows specific racking or space allocation. Weight is important as floor loading can become an issue if a solid floor is not available or racking is used.

Stock should not be stored directly on the floor. This is because it becomes more difficult to lift, and also it is much more vulnerable to damage caused when cleaning the floor, spillages and leakages.

Special racking is available to maximise the space usage for a wide range of items and the layout of the area needs to allow for this.

- Pallet racking has the capability of taking multiple pallets so that they can be removed without the need to unload other pallets – they sit on shelves. The appropriate weight loading needs to be selected for the stock expected.

- Tote racking is spaced to allow easy access to boxes for **picking** or whole box storage retrieval.

- Bar, sheet and rod racks are all designed to allow safe storage, easy access and efficient space usage. Racks often separate sizes or types either vertically or horizontally (the choice depends on the length of item(s), weight and the degree of support required along its length to avoid bending).

- High-value items may benefit from isolation and additional security measures – common tactics are to keep these away from outer doors and walls, sometimes in cages and requiring specific staff access or even dual control.

Cable spools are often mounted on dispensers allowing lengths to be cut. They can also be flat-stored on very narrow-set shelving.

Stock cages are available in many sizes and can hold single items or groups of items. Cages with wheels offer flexibility as they can be moved around the warehouse without the need for other handling equipment.

Specific products may have environmental considerations.

- Bulk paper is vulnerable to damp and can also be damaged by heavy compression (for example, storing at the bottom of a large stack).

- Many food supply chain warehouses and stores need careful consideration of the temperature control to maintain product condition (see figure 1.16). Many products may be 'ambient' and can be stored within a range of temperatures. Some require lower 'chilled' conditions, and some require a 'cold' environment.

By zoning the areas, different temperatures can be maintained in an efficient way. The 'doorways' in the zoned areas often have strips of plastic 'thermal curtaining' to help preserve the different temperatures. The chilled and cold zones would also be designed with more substantial insulation materials for walls and the roof.

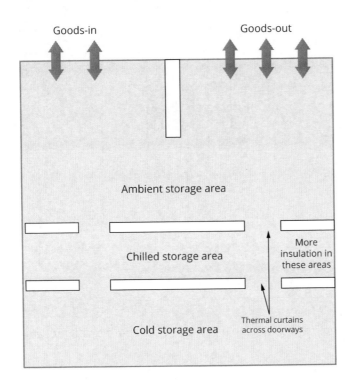

Figure 1.16 Temperature control zoning example from food supply chain

- Electronic components may need isolation from magnetic or electronic interference.
- Chemicals may have handling regulations and could be dangerous if spilled or mixed. Many have critical temperature ranges. Materials for clearing up spillages should be available near the items.
- Bottled gas requires special handling and storage, as it is flammable and capable of exploding. Gas is often kept outside the warehouse in secure cages, away from the building but also secure from potential attack.
- Liquid products can become more solid in colder weather. Some 'emulsions' may separate out in different temperatures.
- Fabric and garments often need protection from sunlight, damp conditions and pests.
- Packaging materials are vulnerable to rodent damage and damp conditions.
- Many metals are affected by a damp atmosphere and can corrode – making some unsuitable for stockyard storage.
- Food and food supply chain ingredients require avoidance of potential contamination and are likely to be subject to inspection by customers and authorities. Refined sugar is both highly absorbent and can absorb odours from other products.
- Many items may have special handling requirements. This could include gloves, goggles, face masks, respirators or full body suits. These items are often separated and require special training for staff.

The 'zoning' of warehouses, stockyards and stores is therefore of utmost importance (see figure 1.17).

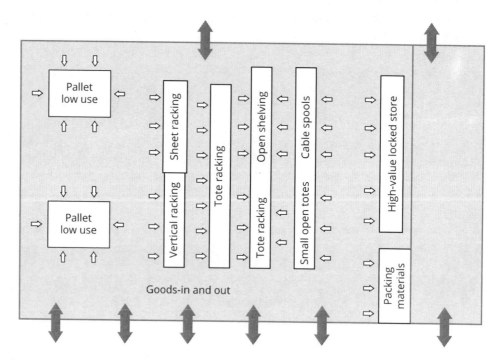

Figure 1.17 Example warehouse: different stock requires different storage and zoning

Check

Why might the zoning of a warehouse be an important requirement?

Give three examples of the types of zoning that may be required.

What type of equipment is required for stock handling?

Flow
The ability of stock to be moved around a facility in the quickest and safest way. A poor flow makes movements slower and reduces efficiency

Aisles
Clear areas between racking or pallet stacks

Having established that different types of stock and racking are likely, the type of equipment to be used will tend to dictate the amount of space around the storage and the access route taken by the equipment. Although it is tempting to suggest that costs could be saved by the avoidance of handling equipment, the objectives of safe working, efficiency and effectiveness dominate.

In figure 1.17, the palletised stock is in a clear area which will allow specialised pallet handling equipment to be used. Decisions on **flow** (covered later in this chapter) and sole or multiple operators will also affect the use of equipment and therefore the layout. Equipment to access higher levels in racking also needs easy access to the '**aisles**'. Notice that the arrows in figure 1.17 suggest single-side access in some cases and double-side access in other cases.

How much space is required for storage?

This may seem like an odd consideration, but it is important for several reasons. Some organisations have peaks in demand and therefore may also have peaks and low points in storage requirements. This could be linked to seasonal patterns and/or production changes. In some organisations there may be a balance of volumes for storage – when some items are in high stock, others are in low stock.

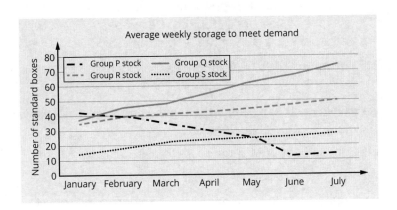

Figure 1.18 Example storage requirements for four groups of stock

In the case of figure 1.18, one item group (P) requires less storage space in July than in January but the other groups (Q, R and S) show increased storage requirements. The total storage requirement in this case for the groups featured could be set at the overall peak across the range PQR and S.

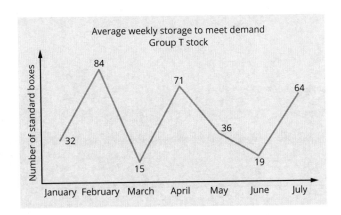

Figure 1.19 Irregular demand stock group example

In figure 1.19, the irregular demand probably results in a storage space allocation that in weeks of low demand looks excessive, but a high stock position is required simply to meet high demand weeks. Decisions need to be made as to storage allocation.

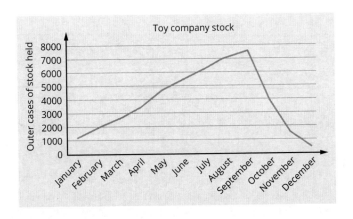

Figure 1.20 Example of stock build-up to meet very heavy seasonal demand

Figure 1.20 shows a problem often seen in product warehouses where there is a very heavy end-of-year demand. The diagram simulates the situation of one toy manufacturer – it has previously been revealed that over 80% of all retailer deliveries take place from October to December with a requirement to manufacture and store stock during the rest of the year.

Possible solutions to the high irregular or seasonal demand problems are listed below.

- Creating flexibility in the design of the building and layout to allow for seasonal additional storage
- Eliminating unused and unwanted stock to free up space
- Acquiring temporary additional storage
- Getting a supplier to hold additional stock for short-notice delivery
- Getting a supplier to deliver direct to customers or usage point
- Getting a specialist logistics company to support the additional demand

Additional space may be made available by introducing different racking or installing a 'mezzanine floor' if the ceiling height is high enough (see figure 1.21 and figure 1.22).

Mezzanine floor
A floor area typically inserted in a high-roofed building to create an elevated additional working or storage space

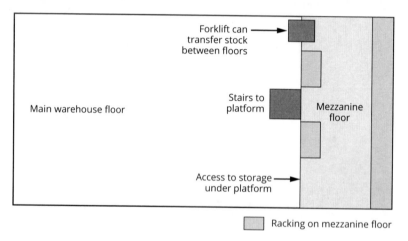

Figure 1.21 Plan view of an example mezzanine floor

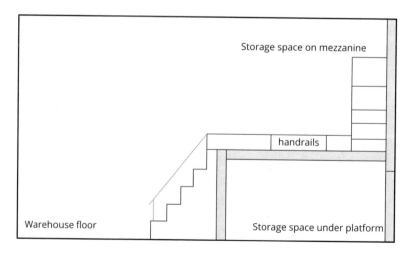

Figure 1.22 Side view of an example mezzanine floor

How much space is required for other operations?

There is a requirement for inbound and outbound goods areas within a storage facility – this could include goods for return to suppliers and packing facilities.

Space may also be needed for the temporary storage of items that require checking or testing (known as a quarantine area). This could include checking technical documentation or awaiting documentation.

There is a need for staffing areas to support warehouse operations, as well as a requirement for 'parking' stock handling equipment – this could include recharging or fuelling equipment.

Waste handling is a further consideration, as are additional stock handling tasks which might include the following.

- Unpacking bulk items and repackaging

- Adding additional labels

- Grouping products that must be sold together (for example, a desktop computer which also requires a display screen)

- Kitting – this typically involves the preparation of a range of items into a single unit for a specific use (for example, maintenance kits for industrial machinery that contain essential service lubricants, springs and seals; also some hospital stores prepare surgery packs for 'popular' treatments that include the most likely sutures, dressings and syringes required).

- Return (or reverse) logistics – handling items returned from customers or down the supply chain for exchange or refund.

All these additional requirements mean that the total space allocation is compromised. For example, space required for quarantine will depend on the checks to be undertaken. Detailed technical testing or microbiology reports could take days to complete, requiring more items to be stored in quarantine.

What are the future plans and how might they affect storage requirements?

Warehouses, stockyards and stores design should all consider future plans. If lower stock requirements are expected in the short-term (which could be because of more storage locations later or working with outsourced storage facilities) then limited investment might be expected.

If expansion of storage is expected, then some surplus space in the short-term will be needed to avoid a costly relocation (or a second warehouse requirement).

The impact of new packaging and technology may require different priorities, particularly if automation and significantly different stock handling equipment is installed.

What are the current advantages and disadvantages of stores, stockyard or warehouse layout and design?

Very few storage facilities will be 'right first time'. Many will have planned space and design features that appeared to suit a stated situation and plan. Over time, volumes and stock mix along with supplier lead times and demand are likely to mean a review is needed.

Quarantine area
Area set aside for items which are awaiting inspection or testing. There may also be faulty items or items awaiting return to the supplier. The idea is that these items must not enter storage or be made available until cleared for use

Kitting
Activity in a warehouse or store of assembling groups of items that are to be used together – a 'kit of items' is created for a specific task

Return (or reverse) logistics
The storage, handling and movement of materials or products in the reverse direction from original supply. This may involve faulty goods, surplus goods or claims under guarantee. Some organisations offer a return of spare parts for recycling or reuse; end-of-life recycling or scrappage is also possible

Check
How might future business plans affect decisions relating to warehouse layout?

Flow, space utilisation and flexibility

Flow

Bottleneck
A restriction inside a warehouse, store or stockyard that holds up or slows down activity. This may be caused by poor layout, access difficulties or simply the volume of picking or storage being handled

The principle of flow is quite easy – a store's facility or stockyard will receive goods, store them, retrieve them and make them available for internal or external customers. In following this pattern, a good flow will avoid delays and aid the efficiency of operations. Flow consideration means identifying the potential for delays caused by **bottlenecks**. An effective flow will avoid congestion and is often linked to a 'one way' system or simply clarity in the direction of movement.

Watching a large crowd entering or leaving a major event will reveal a natural flow. This can be encouraged by separating groups by introducing barriers, which could be along the line of travel or preventing crossing lines of travel. Visiting a large supermarket on a busy day will reveal a flow from entry to exit with most customers following a similar route and just a few crossing over and working in the opposite direction – this will cause inconvenience to the bulk of customers and slow down their progress.

Applied to a warehouse situation, the positioning or zoning already covered in this chapter will influence the natural flow. A faster flow is achieved by the pickers knowing where to store or retrieve the correct items, with reduction in the 'trying to find' time. A location map and signage is often a feature of a warehouse.

Warehouses, stockyards and stores may choose to label rows of stock. Others identify sections rather than rows. Each section within a row may have identification as well as each box, shelf or area. The stock management system (or simply an annotated stock list) will identify the location(s) of each item of stock held.

Identification can be achieved through letters, numbers, colours and symbols. Sometimes unique systems are devised, for example, cartoon characters for each aisle.

Inbound stock needs to be processed without interfering with picking or packing ready for outbound despatch. Picking operators should not have to constantly await other pickers finishing nor have to wait for equipment that has to be moved to another area or is needed for accessing stock.

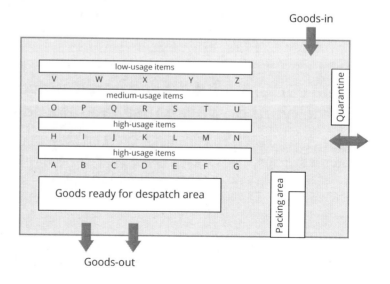

Figure 1.23 Typical warehouse with labelled picking areas

Figure 1.23 shows a warehouse with 'goods-in' and 'goods-out' areas separated – this is a good feature as it allows a natural flow from delivery to checking and to storage without directly affecting the goods-out operation or packing areas.

The situation is a little more complex when considering picking, packing and despatch. Consider an order requiring stock from many positions. An order requiring items from A J W R and G sections would involve a picker in a route of their choosing. Unless the order is reworked into the shortest distance, each order could be picked inefficiently. More importantly, the movements between sections could cause clashes with other pickers and equipment in aisles. Turning around some stock moving equipment within an aisle could be difficult.

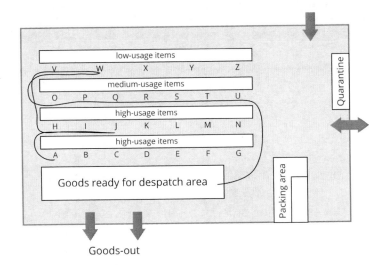

Figure 1.24 Potential journey of a picker

Figure 1.24 shows one potential journey pattern. There are 'returns' along the same aisles and there are several positions where other pickers with equipment could have difficulty passing each other.

A redesign could address many practical issues and improve flow.

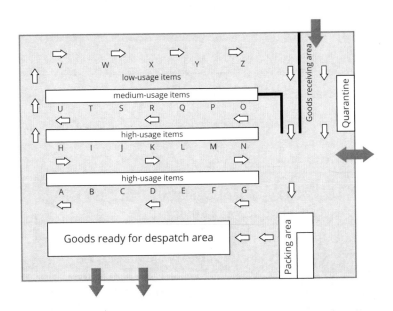

Figure 1.25 Improving flow with a 'one way' system and changed racking access

In figure 1.25, a 'one way' direction system has been put in place. One racking unit has changed position to ensure a flow is possible. Notice in figure 1.26 that the location letters on the plan have been reallocated – and the picking order is now rewritten to become A G J R W.

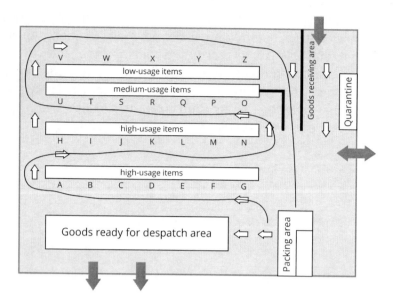

Figure 1.26 Picking route for AGJRW – no 'returns' or opposing traffic

It is important that the picking order is arranged to provide efficiency. Depending on the nature of orders and the size of the facility, flow may also be enhanced by processing several orders at the same time, so that a single journey around the system can pick several different orders. Some warehouse management systems can group orders requiring similar items, showing the order, item, location and position at the location (see table 1.1). Pickers can then place the required stock in different totes to match the orders.

Row	Section	Container	Product code	Pick number required	Picked ✓ ✗
17	3	Red 8	1624551	1	
18	9	Blue 2	2116684	5	
22	1	Blue 7	2154795	2 packs	
24	12	Blue 9	2189677	1 pack	

Table 1.1 Example picking list (arranged for flow and efficiency of picking)

Apply

For a storage facility that you have visited, what aspects of warehouse design and layout are featured?

If you have not been to any storage facility, then do try to visit one. If this is not possible, try applying the warehouse principles to a supermarket you have visited – although a supermarket is not a warehouse, flow and efficiency are just as important to customers. Are there any flow improvements that you can suggest?

Other efficient flow layouts

A 'through flow' layout is designed to work in straight lines (see figure 1.27). Significant design elements are separated into 'goods-in' and 'goods-out' docks. A 'one way' system is clear, which together with the other design features maximises the potential use of stock handling equipment.

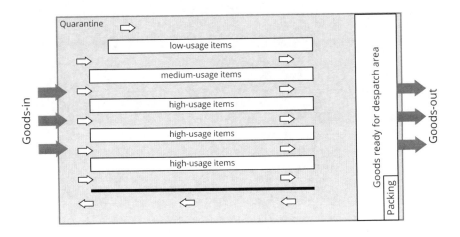

Figure 1.27 Typical layout using 'through flow' design principles

Picking-type separation can improve flow by separating items that require detailed picking by hand from those which can simply be lifted using equipment or handled onto equipment (see figure 1.28). With this type of design, the order can be split if stock is required from more than one area.

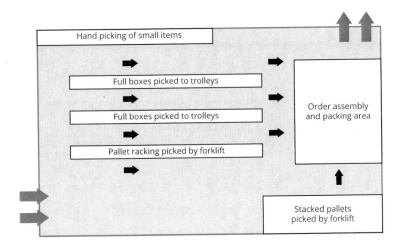

Figure 1.28 Picking split into three areas with flow to assembly and packing

A 'U-shape' layout is commonly seen – the main feature is that 'goods-in' and 'goods-out' are at the same end of the warehouse (see figure 1.29). This allows lifting equipment that has just been used for delivery to move a short distance to service despatch. Similarly, staff can supervise unloading and loading.

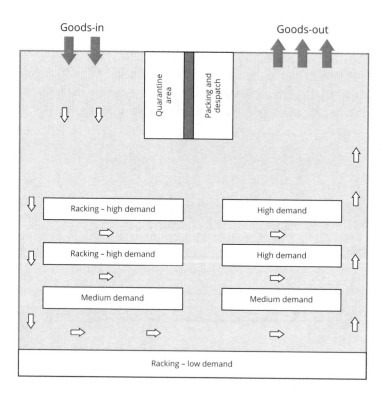

Figure 1.29 U-shape flow

There has been research undertaken that suggests that detailed analysis on typical storing and picking is required to establish the optimum layout. One example (Gue and Meller, 2009) dealt with pallet bulk storage and through a series of calculations determined that warehouses can have optimised layouts.[1] To deal with a specific ease of access and speed of return, two specific layouts were proposed as alternatives to 'straight rows' seen in most large-scale warehouses (see figure 1.30 and figure 1.31).

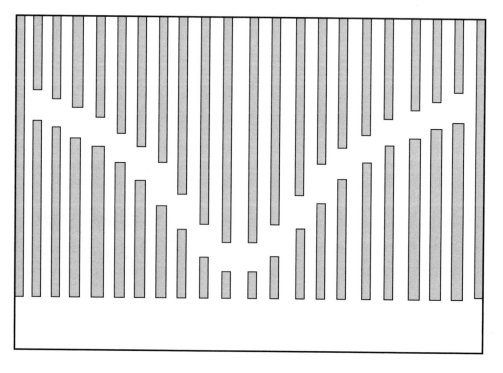

Figure 1.30 'Fan' shaped layout (Gue and Meller, 2009)

1.1 L01

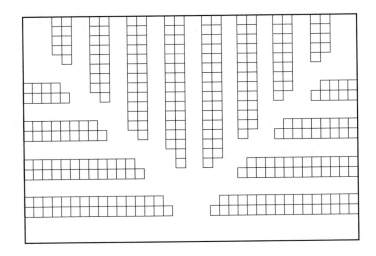

Figure 1.31 Herringbone-shaped layout (Gue and Meller, 2009)

Space utilisation

Whether owned or rented, premises are an expensive asset and organisations try to reduce the costs of storage by using an efficient and effective layout. There are many 'trade-offs' to be considered as wide spacing of stock that is easy to retrieve and wide aisles that give easy access cost more in terms of space available for the stock.

Narrow aisles and very narrow aisles

To increase the area available for storage, it may be possible to increase the number of racks by reducing the aisle space between racks. The aisle space required will depend on the type and size of stock stored, the size of the storage bins/pallets and the racking used. This chapter has also suggested that a 'one way' flow has advantages, and this also works well with narrower aisles.

- A typical warehouse with conventional racking has an aisle width that varies from 2.5m to 4.5m

- Narrow-aisle designs typically have aisle widths of 2m

- Very narrow-aisle designs typically have aisle widths of 1.4m

- For access to small items in small tote boxes that do not require equipment to access the stock, just 1m width might be required

(In each case, the plan layout, equipment and flow will determine the specific widths required.)

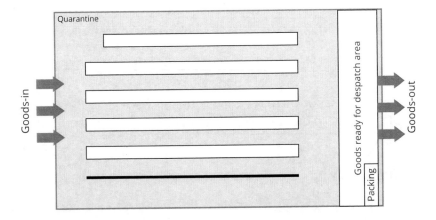

Figure 1.32 Narrow aisle width layout

Figure 1.33 Conventional aisle width layout

Figures 1.32 and 1.33 compare two different aisle widths, using the same racking and layout. The narrower aisles will restrict access and require different stock handling equipment. The narrow aisle could provide one full additional rack for storage.

Where forklift access is required, the aisle width will depend on the type of forklift, as a front-facing forklift would have to turn to position the stock in the racking whereas a specialist side-access forklift does not require as much width. Generally, the narrower the aisles are, the more specialist equipment is needed and the less flexible the storage becomes. As racking installations cannot be changed at short notice, this issue is important to research before commitment and installation.

This chapter has featured many plan-form layouts, but 'using the cube' is an important feature of space utilisation – we also need to think vertically.

It is possible to use racks that can take stock on shelving almost up to the available ceiling height – all that is needed is safe access equipment to store and retrieve. It is also possible to stack pallets on top of each other, although this will depend on the stability of the stack and potential damage to the stock. Specialist racks are available that would help support pallet stacks. From the examples in figures 1.32 and 1.33, an additional one metre of height could create significant additional storage on each racking fixture.

Installation of 'double deep' storage can increase the density of stock. This simply means that two sets of totes or pallets are stored in a position, one in front of the other. Again, specialist equipment would support this layout, in this case featuring 'double deep forks'. The advantage is that more storage space is available by eliminating one aisle, but this does mean that if access to the rearmost pallet is required, the front one will need to be moved first.

Carousel-type storage works on the principle of moving storage either vertically or horizontally so that the correct item can be picked. This type of storage (covered in section 1.3) saves space as a single access point is provided rather than access for each individual item.

Check

How can an organisation increase the volume of space available for storage without adding new buildings?

Space flexibility

Flexibility of layout and racking is beneficial if the stock requirement is either variable through the year or potentially changeable across the lifetime of the storage facility.

Basing the fixtures on standard-size pallets, tote boxes and having adjustable shelving should maximise flexibility.

1.1 **L01**

Many organisations establish fixed positions for stock items that are only reviewed periodically. This has the advantage that specific stock can be relied on to be in the same position time after time. But this also means that variances in stock volumes over time may result in some areas being over-filled and others with space available. The flexible alternative is to have random (or semi-random) positions. For random, any available suitable position can be used for stock – provided the location is correctly recorded. Semi-random positioning would take account of, for example, the frequency of access, keeping the high-frequency demand items easy to pick and close to the despatch area. In all cases the location of stock must be known – in the case of random and semi-random positions, there may be multiple locations that need to be known and regularly updated.

Warehousing decisions are inevitably based on estimates and the provision of permanent facilities often requires a long-term commitment – this could be seven years or more, depending on the facility and demand. As a result, capacity problems may be encountered.

Flexibility to meet additional or peak storage requirements can be met through the following.

- Temporary storage on site (for example, use of 40-foot trailers with containers)

- Temporary storage in other buildings, rented or owned

- Adopting **flexible warehousing** – this has two distinct approaches.

    ○ Use of warehousing also used by other organisations, with the idea that the area used by an organisation could be increased or decreased as others sharing the facility also change their requirements.

    ○ Very short-term warehousing is offered in the market where organisations may make their requirements for space open online to offers or bid for available space. This appears to be an emerging market (it has been in use since 2013) and service providers in the UK and USA typically quote a price per pallet per week with some also requiring a 'transaction fee' for movements of each pallet in and out.

- Suppliers holding stock with arrangements for short-notice deliveries or collections

- Use of third-party logistics company storage facilities

- 'Early' delivery of stock or supply on a 'consignment' basis by negotiation with customers (**consignment stocking** means that the customer does not pay until use or until a later date)

Flexible warehousing
Term used to describe any technique which allows the short-term ability to increase or decrease storage space

Consignment stocking
A facility offered by a supplier to a buyer to allow a delivery of stock to the buyer with payment only after it is used or sold to a customer

> *Remember*
> There are lots of different requirements for warehouses, stores and stockyards. These requirements are determined by the volume, size, type and weight of products as well as the equipment used for moving and storing them.

> *Apply*
> If you have access to a warehouse or large storage facility, take a look at the layouts, the ways things are arranged and the equipment in use.

1.2 Explain the use of product coding in inventory operations

Systems for product coding

It is very important for all organisations in a supply chain to use product codes so that the risk of ordering or delivering the wrong item is reduced. The choice of product coding is a decision for each organisation in a supply chain.

Own product code system

In many cases, an organisation will use its own product code system. This has the advantage that the organisation can construct a code that is effective and fits with its software and the variety of items covered.

Manufacturer's product code system

In some cases, an organisation will use a manufacturer's product code system. This has the advantage that the same code can be shared, and this can avoid potential errors. It should save time as there will be no need to interpret the manufacturer's code against the organisation's own code. The code system chosen by the manufacturer is likely to be effective as far as it is concerned but another organisation may find it has limitations and might not fit with its own software. Using a manufacturer's coding means that the item can be recognised by others in the supply chain. This may be an advantage as it adds traceability and customer acceptability, but it also reveals origins allowing customers to 'shop around'. A manufacturer's product code can be important when spare parts are being supplied.

Customer product code system

In some cases, an organisation will use a customer product code system. This has the advantage that the same code can be shared. It has the disadvantage that using the same code for other customers might be unacceptable to the customer who 'owns' the system. In some cases, a specific customer can be dominant in an industry and the product code system is adopted as an industry standard.

Industry standard code system

In some cases, an organisation may use an industry standard coding system. This has the advantage that the supply chain can standardise part numbering and the same system is used by different customers and suppliers. It may have the disadvantage that additional features of a product that could be added might not be permitted by the published structure and variants.

Multiple codes

Many organisations use multiple codes. It is possible for an organisation to have a product code given to customers for ordering, and additional codes that might signify, for example, the country of origin, year, month or date of production, use-by date, supplier, quantity in a pack, storage requirements, storage location or country of use. Later in this study guide, examples of codes and standard formats for the use of technology are described.

1.2 L01

Remember

Codes can be:

- **Numerical**: all numbers, no letters
- **Alphabetical**: all letters, no numbers
- **Alpha-numeric**: having a mix of numbers and letters
- **Random generated or created**: a random number generator is available from Microsoft Excel. Random numbers often help to avoid 'mis-keying error' as it is unlikely for consecutive numbers or patterns to be repeated. A random numbers and letters system can greatly reduce mis-keying but can make item sorting and immediate identification difficult.
- **Sequential**: this simply means that each new item added takes the 'next number' in a sequence, for example, 1000, 1001, 1002... A product code may have an element of sequential numbering, for example, 459/1001, 459/1002, 459/1003.
- **Structured**: where different parts of a product code have a significance, for example, for a home improvement retailer and trade supplier, 121769, which includes a code for 'own brand' paint (121) and an item number which is unique to the type of finish, colour and size (769). The same retailer uses a different code for other branded paints, using the same 'two part' codes so that the number for a very similar product would be very different (for example, 167040).

Apply

Match the codes in column A with the correct description in column B (the first code match has been completed as an example).

Column A

TRX18515, ZPB21518

12746, 17354

45124, 45125

ZWPCWQT

855/164

Column B

Numerical

Sequential

Alpha-numeric

Structured

Alphabetical

Stock keeping unit (SKU)
An identifiable item from stock. Organisations may assign individual SKU numbers of their own design or use industry or company standard numbers. Although an SKU relates to a single item, the item could be a box or pallet load rather than an individual item

The structure of product codes can be designed by suppliers or buyers. They can also be designed by industry agreement or adopting a standard that is already in operation.

Organisations often create their own **stock keeping unit (SKU)** numbering system, which may or may not have a meaningful structure. This may be used on its own or it may supplement the product code, for example the following.

Retailer product code 185747 (a cotton bed quilt)

Amazon Standard Identification Number (ASIN) B00A8RMZJY

The online catalogue lists both – the retailer product may help the customer to determine the match to the retailer's website, the Amazon code instantly identifies the unique reference used and is their SKU. Without the ASIN, Amazon could have several items with the same product code.

At random, an online search for SKU414676 reveals that this is used for many items, including the following.

- A UK wholesaler's six-pack of branded cola
- An Australian snack food
- UK flower seeds
- An Italian desk sold in Japan
- A Brazilian light fitting

This shows that for this type of product numbering, the same number could feature in both buyer product codes and supplier product codes but relate to different items. Multiple codes with some being specific to an organisation seem to be a good idea!

Structured codes can be designed to incorporate meaningful information if arranged in specific ways, for example, sizes, material types, colours, shapes, textures, country of origin or use, volumes and numbers of items in a pack. Here are some examples from real products.

0632803003 used by a Swedish fashion company.

- Style number 0632803, colour 003

4792/005 used by a Spanish retailer across multiple countries.

- 4792 is the product category (this one relates to quilted bedding), 005 relates to the specific style. For a specific size and colour, the code changes to 4792000530646 (the '/' is replaced by a zero)

VPK02BL used by a distributor of plastic boxes (totes) for use in stores and warehouses.

- VPK is the shortened product description (visual pick), 02 is the size, BL for colour blue

---

Apply

When you are in the supermarket, look at a variety of products – food products, stationery and garments. What are the different patterns that are used for each one?

Then visit an online retailer that sells lots of different items – do they follow patterns and are they grouped by type of product?

Remember

There are many different coding systems in operation – few are truly unique.

Check digits and validation

Many codes have integrated **check digits**. These are additional numbers or characters added to codes that a computer uses to verify the number is valid. The intention is to reduce the likelihood of mis-keying an item and hitting an alternative live item. Simple systems would, for example, only use a sequence with specific number ranges. More often, a system is devised which a computer can calculate using combinations of numbers. Given the number of variations possible, it is difficult to detect check digits in real examples unless basic codes are also provided.

Check digits
Numbers added to product codes which allow computer-based validation. These are usually created using specific number sequences and are designed to reduce the probability of errors

Case study

Product code designs in practice
The following are worked examples using different validation and check digit systems.

Example: adding up the digits
SKU455870 – when the digits are added up this results in 29, giving a code SKU45587029.

The next product number is SKU455871, which becomes SKU45587130.

Example: multiplying, then adding
There are many different systems that use this method – in the example below, each digit of a basic product code is multiplied by a different number (any numbers can be used; a sequence is not compulsory). The totals are added, and the final digit of the sum is added as a check digit.

digits of code	4	5	5	8	7	0		
multiply by	1	2	3	4	5	6		
result	4	10	15	32	35	0	addition	96
							final code	4558706

digits of code	4	5	5	8	7	1		
multiply by	1	2	3	4	5	6		
result	4	10	15	32	35	6	addition	102
							final code	4558712

digits of code	4	5	5	8	7	2		
multiply by	1	2	3	4	5	6		
result	4	10	15	32	35	12	addition	108
							final code	4558728

You will see that the last two digits of the final codes are now no longer sequential. The start of the code is still capable of errors, but this is 'solved' by the probability of hitting a correct number being low.

Example: 'modulus checking'
This is much more complicated and looks a bit like code breaking done by spies! The example below uses 11 as the modulus, but any number and any multipliers can

be used – these act as 'keys' to valid numbers – and the maths used means that it becomes much less likely that mis-keying will result in hitting a valid stock item.

digits of code	4	5	5	8	7	0		
multiply by	1	2	3	4	5	6		
result	4	10	15	32	35	0	addition	96
							divide by the modulus (11)	8 remainder 8
							Take remainder from modulus (11)	3
							Code becomes	4558703

digits of code	4	5	5	8	7	1		
multiply by	1	2	3	4	5	6		
result	4	10	15	32	35	6	addition	102
							divide by the modulus (11)	9 remainder 3
							Take remainder from modulus (11)	8
							Code becomes	4558718

digits of code	4	5	5	8	7	2		
multiply by	1	2	3	4	5	6		
result	4	10	15	32	35	12	addition	108
							divide by the modulus (11)	9 remainder 9
							Take remainder from modulus (11)	2
							Code becomes	4558722

When a computer deals with the stock number, it will either 'look up' the item (and not find it) or verify using a calculation such as the following.

4558703

digits of code	4	5	5	8	7	0	3	
multiply by	1	2	3	4	5	6	1	
								addition
result	4	10	15	32	35	0	3	99

The addition result is divisible by 11 with no remainder, making it 'valid'.

This technique has been used since the 1960s to issue and validate bank account numbers in the UK and has many industrial applications.

Check

Why is it important to use a method of validation when designing product code structures?

1.2 LO1

> *Remember*
> Unless there is an industry format, any user can create product codes in a format that is useful for itself and/or its customers.

Case study

Producing low-volume vehicles for special projects
An organisation had specific requirements for very low-volume vehicles that were adaptions from mainstream standard models.

The 'unique' special order additional parts needed to be easily identified for the project. This would help to support the provision of spare parts in the future, clearly identify a different specification and allow detailed cost accounting in concept/prototype, pre-production, production and post-production customer service. It was decided to use SKU codes which included the project/model number along with a vehicle number (where truly unique parts for a single vehicle were involved) or a vehicle series.

The coding system worked like this (the business did not use this exact detail).

Model number:	0127
Vehicle number	001, 010, 100, 200, 300 (for example, 001, 002 would be prototype models, 010, 011, 012 pre-production models, 100, 101, 102 production series)
Part family	100, 200, 300 (for example, body part, wiring and electrical, braking part, suspension part, engine part, interior part)
Part	1000–9999
Validation	one digit using its standard system

Example product: 0127 002 314 0006 8
In this simulation, the part would be for model 0127, vehicle 002, brake system (3) disc assembly (14), specification (6), check digit (8).

Example product: 0127 100 314 0009 6
In this simulation, the part would be for model 0127, vehicle series 100, brake system (3) disc assembly (14), specification (9), check digit (6).

Check

The significance of a check digit as part of a product code is to check the following.

a) the item has passed quality control

b) the design version that was used

c) that a product code has been correctly entered

d) the product's location row in the warehouse

Industry standard codes and code groups

The principle of having industry standard codes is long established. In some cases, these have origins with the original equipment manufacturer (OEM) or a supplier to an OEM. In other cases, an industry standard could have been created as part of quality, performance or conformance standards and documentation.

The following are some examples.

- **Car light bulbs**. Manufacturers use a standard numbering system and most suppliers use it for reference alongside SKUs. Most rear bulbs are either 380 or 382, and many suppliers integrate this in the part number (for example, ABD382) although some include it in the product description but maintain a separate unconnected SKU.

- **Batteries for small devices**. Batteries have multiple codes that can be used as the basis for product codes for many organisations. These have been developed by battery manufacturers but there are also standards organisations which can feature. There are small batteries commonly known as 'AA size.' International Electrotechnical Commission (IEC) standards have this as 'LR6' but 'MN1500' and 'HP7' are also used by manufacturers – it seems that different countries use different codes.

- **Military use**. The North Atlantic Treaty Organization (NATO) has a long-established coding system with the concept that a single product has a single description and fits a single specification. This principle makes sense if (as in the case of NATO), users from different countries may be operating in other countries alongside allies – a standard part could be supplied by any member country's staff to another country's staff. Parts of the 13-digit code are structured with product group classifications and (effectively) country of origin of the standards.

- **Health Service use**. Many health services across the world have some form of product numbering. In some cases, this comes from the 'authority to use' government documentation.

- **Books**. There is an International Standard Book Number system (ISBN). This is now 13 digits long, but earlier books may have shorter codes. The codes are structured, although different countries can allocate the country/region language, publisher and publication number codes in different ways. The important element is that the prefix allows computers to identify the code type. The result of the international standard is that it can be used wherever the standard has been adopted, whether or not the code exactly matches the country in which it is used. It can also be read in a form without the dashes. Figure 1.34 shows a UK ISBN pattern.

Figure 1.34 UK ISBN standard numbering example

- **Import and export**. Governments need to classify products into groups. This is to provide statistical analysis of movements, to prevent some products from entry and/or exit and to support import/export tax and quotas. The greater the use of a universal code, the less work in examining, testing and classifying at entry and/or departure is required.

> *Remember*
> The Harmonized Item Description and Coding System (abbreviated to HS for Harmonized System) is an international standard governed by the World Customs Organization (WCO). These are six-digit numbers, although countries may add either two or four digits to create further subdivisions. These are recognised by nearly all countries of the world, even if an alternative system is used as the prime system.
>
> The European Union member states incorporate the HS code into its own system – the additions being subdivisions and classifications used to determine any special duty payable, special arrangements or restrictions on entry.

- **Specific dangerous substances**. There are common substances (for example, liquids, solids, gases and suspensions) that should be identified to allow easy recognition and allow a wider range of those encountering the item to be aware of its content – and therefore any risks. The list is particularly important in transporting, handling and storing 'dangerous goods'. Although there are chemical symbols, these may be insufficient to cope with complex products. The United Nations has published 'Recommendations on the Transport of Dangerous Goods' which contains details of products with classifications and code numbers, which then indicate the expected care and safety requirements (see table 1.2).[2] Some organisations incorporate or add these to product codes. In most cases the UN code is separately labelled.

Classification	UN no.	Description
2.2	3163	Liquified gas
3	1993	Flammable liquid
4.3	3148	Water-reactive liquid
6.1	2902	Pesticide, liquid, toxic
8	1760	Corrosive liquid

Table 1.2 Sample of UN dangerous goods classification and numbers

> *Remember*
> There can be many different codes linked to a specific product. Each supplying or buying organisation may have product codes, SKUs and additional detail codes. Product codes are used to avoid errors, but a buyer must ensure the code chosen matches the dimensions, characteristics and quality required.

Use of product codes in practice

Reports suggest that there is a decline in the use of structured codes. This is linked to the much wider use of databases which can allocate different codes instantly and link these to specific orders but are transparent to the customer. This trend has been seen following the further development of online B2B and B2C transactions.

Some organisations input the product code to computers and/or mobile devices to open up database files or web pages. These can supply (for example, from a range of different organisations and industries) technical specifications, pricing, stock availability, demand statistics, delivery schedules, spare parts and servicing information, assembly instructions, bought-in price information and product quality information.

Each organisation in B2B supply chains are likely to use product codes – sometimes these are shared, but often each is designed to fit the specific business requirements and systems used.

Case study

Timber supplies product coding
A UK timber supplier offers a very wide range of sizes and types of timber to builders for use in construction. Without a product code, a purchase order or phone call would have to detail the item, like in the following example.

> *Prepared softwood timber planed on all sides, kiln dried, FSC certified, 50 × 150mm, 3m length.*

That is a lot of detailing and a lot of chances to miss out on something that could be important.

For one specific supplier A, the product code used is: 01PAR050150 (× 3.0m). This leaves little opportunity for errors as the main product code is unique to the product characteristics. The details of the product offered will be featured on the supplier website and/or in the supplier catalogue. The buyer specifying this product code will expect the product as detailed – and just the length is added. Both the supplier and the buyer can use the product code to identify the right product. The stores or warehouse can also use the product code for picking and checking the order. The delivery note and invoice will also show the product code, making checking faster.

Without the product code, time would be spent identifying the exact product required from a list or on a warehouse floor.

In the above example, the same style and measurement of timber is coded by three different suppliers as the following.

> Suppler C: 50150P (× 3m)
>
> Supplier S: 03100881 (this relates only to a 3m item)
>
> Supplier R: T8400049 (this relates only to a 3m item)

In this example of timber, there appears to be no 'industry standard' product code although the type and dimensions appear to be standard. Notice that supplier A and supplier C both incorporate the size within the code – this makes identification easier and avoids having to look up the product in a catalogue or online. Supplier A also incorporates 'PAR' which is an industry abbreviation for 'planed all round'. Supplier S seems to be using the first two numbers to show the length, but the remainder of the code appears to be insignificant. Supplier R prefixes all timber products with 'T' (bricks are 'B' and so on).

Each product code appears to be unique to one supplier. This has the advantage that it is identifiable as coming from a specific supplier, but a disadvantage is that multiple codes need to be used by buyers depending on the supplier chosen. Each supplier's product code is likely to be linked to a specific quality, so it is important to check that the product codes do relate to the same specification before ordering.

> *Apply*
>
> Identify some B2B products that your organisation routinely orders. Search on the Internet for the item (or a supplier catalogue). What clues are there regarding how product coding is designed and used? You may find sequential numerical codes, alpha-numeric codes or some form of easy-to-understand structured codes.

Linkage to product documentation

The product code is often the key to obtaining documentation relating to products. The following is the range of product documentation that could be available by entering a product code into a manufacturer (or retailer) website.

- Installation instructions
- Operational instructions
- Guarantee and warranty
- Technical specifications including temperature tolerances
- Safety instructions including safe disposal
- Electrical certification documents
- Packaging certification documentation
- Spare parts list, servicing requirements
- Product recall notices

Product codes and internal processes

Product codes are often used to link to internal processes. Some computerised inventory systems trigger alerts when specific items or volumes are ordered – this could be an out-of-stock warning or potential volume errors.

Product codes are used to generate 'picking lists' in the warehouse (see table 1.3). These are instructions to collect specific items from specific locations in the warehouse ready for despatch. More sophisticated systems will link the product code and quantity to the size and weight of the requirement and any special handling requirements. This allows the correct equipment to be used by the operators. Many systems will also plot a route for the operator to follow within the warehouse, which allows more efficient warehouse operations.

Order Number 10025698		Time: 14.02	Date: 01/01/2020
Product code	Bin location	Quantity required	Quantity picked (Picker to complete)
RT341	Row 13 Bin A4	1	
AR259-100	Row 14 Bin B1	1 pack	
CV189-100	Row 17 Bin A2	2 packs	
TT257-25	Row 17 Bin B7	3 packs	

Table 1.3 Typical picking list content

Product codes are also used to provide links to safety (for example, use of personal protective equipment), handling requirements (for example, type of equipment to be used), technical documentation (for example, chemical content, temperature controls) and despatch information (for example, type of packaging, labelling). Figure 1.35 shows a summary of these.

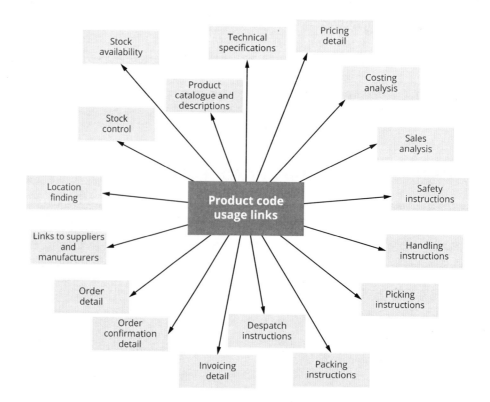

Figure 1.35 Summary of common usage of product codes

1.2 L01

Remember
Product codes are a means of identifying specific products – but they often support the use of internal and external systems which help efficiency and effectiveness in organisations.

Case study

Use of product codes in a supply chain for a consumer product sold online
This example shows the supply chain impact of an order from a customer/consumer back to a manufacturer. There are no additional warehousing or distribution links (such as import/export arrangements).

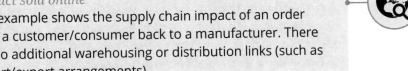

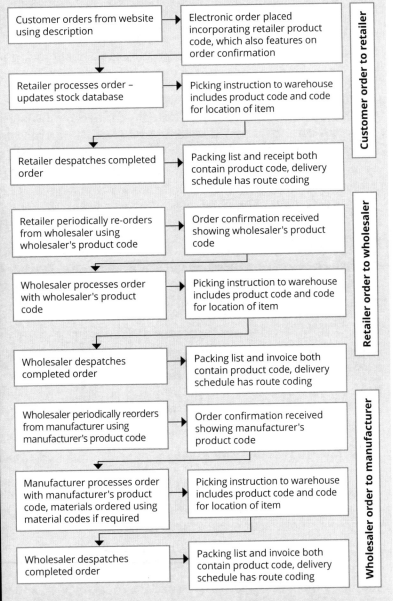

Figure 1.36 Supply chain impact of an order from consumer to manufacturer

Apply
Find some inbound deliveries – either to you personally or within your organisation. Check the packaging for order of numbers and bar codes and the packing list for product codes.

Bar coding

Bar coding is familiar to most people from labelling on consumer goods and scanning at shop tills. Using these systems, it is possible to provide itemised receipts and update pricing remotely as the price at the till uses a reference list. Many shops also use the data collected to update stock availability, analyse trends and trigger reordering.

The principle is that readable characters are converted into lines of different widths and gaps that can be read by scanning equipment. The equipment uses either laser or digital camera-type technology to 'read' the pattern and convert it back to characters. The character code is also provided next to the bar code lines, so that it can be manually entered if required.

There are multiple different types of bar code and it is possible to create one-off scanner-readable labels for lots of different business situations. Product bar codes that will be used by multiple organisations require the use of agreed standards. In cases of very widespread use, as in the case of fast-moving consumer goods, international formats are used, often with formal registration required.

The most common format in use is the 13-digit European Article Number (EAN-13). As this system is now incorporated into the formats for the International Article Number (IAN) and Global Trade Item Number (GTIN), it is most likely to have the widest appeal. The GTIN system is controlled by a 'not for profit' organisation known as GS1. GS1 specialises in standards for specific industries and membership is required to use the standards. EAN-13 is also compatible with Electronic Product Codes used in Radio Frequency Identification, covered later in this chapter.

The EAN standard also has a format for 8-digit versions (intended for small items, but research suggests most manufacturers just use smaller EAN-13 bar codes). Supplementary information bar codes are also covered in the standard which can be provided in addition to an EAN-13. Figure 1.37 shows a typical EAN-13 label: the design can vary but the line layout is standard.

Figure 1.37 Typical EAN-13 bar code

The number allocation varies according to the manufacturer and/or retailer. The content can contain numbers that relate to the GS1 member organisation registration, manufacturer code, product code and whether the product is 'store packaged'. This allows flexibility within a very wide range of options. Space allocation within the code allows interpretation of each group of numbers.

Specific numbers are allocated to specific product types – and two 'prefix numbers' (for example, 978 and 979 are reserved for published books so that the ISBN can be used; 979 is also used for an 'International Standard Music Number'). The final number is a check digit, which uses modulus 10 calculations.

The appeal of bar codes is enhanced by their flexibility and common usage. Organisations can code documentation as well as products; they can produce bar codes that are internally read and used or adopt industry, national or international standards. Multiple bar codes are commonly seen nowadays on products being delivered by couriers.

An alternative to conventional bar codes is the '2-D' bar code (see figure 1.38). This has many alternative names and several different standards in use. It can be substituted for bar codes, but it has the capability to hold a larger amount of data. Most scanners can 'read' this format. Early applications in consumer markets included labelling of vehicles and advertisements which, when scanned, opened websites in mobile devices.

Figure 1.38 2-D bar code

Bar codes can be used for many different supply chain operations.

- Identifying individual products

- Identifying groups of products (in outer packaging or pallets)

- Identifying the content of a purchase order or delivery

- Identifying the batch that items come from

- Identifying the original producer

- Identifying the routing of a delivery

- Identifying a production date, delivery date, use-by date

- Identifying a specific item being produced to a one-off specification

- Identifying the arrival and/or departure of a product at a location

- Allowing effective return and/or refund of products

Many of these elements allow the effective control of the stock and link to computer systems to update stock volumes, values and locations.

It is possible to add a bar code label to documentation to speed data entry – customer numbers, postcodes (zip codes), addressing detail, consignment numbers can all be converted to bar codes. Public libraries often use bar code systems for book issue – the stock is controlled by scanning in and out by use of the bar code.

Bar codes and fixed assets

Up to this point, it has been explored how bar codes can be used for inventory (stock) control. They can also be used to identify and locate **fixed assets**. It is good practice to maintain a register of all fixed assets in an organisation – in many cases this is a legal requirement which links to accounting and tax regulations. It is also an expected part of business insurance.

Bar codes can be used to label equipment used in an organisation. In many organisations, computer equipment is bar coded and when this requires maintenance or replacement, the specific items can be identified and tracked.

Labelling with bar codes clearly requires equipment and software to both create the labels and also to read them.

Bar codes can be printed on lots of different media but the creation of the bar code requires software that can meet the standard being used (without which the bar code might not be capable of being read as intended).

Fixed assets
An accounting term used to describe items acquired by an organisation which are not routinely sold but used within the organisation. Typical examples are land and buildings, fixtures and fittings, office and warehouse equipment. Fixed assets are also known as non-current assets

Bar code creation software is readily available at relatively low cost. The numbers themselves may well require membership of a standards group (for example, GS1) or it may be a case of meeting the requirements of a supplier or a customer.

The 'artwork' created can then be incorporated in packaging design or documentation sets. Alternatively (and particularly common in B2B), labels can be produced to attach to products or packaging. Labels can be printed individually to meet each need as it arises or in large batches in advance. Specialist label manufacturers can produce laminated versions and weatherproof versions if required.

Bar code readers can be 'static' and be in a fixed position, or portable. Many are configured so that they can also read typeface and collect additional information, such as names and addresses.

Fixed position readers require the item to be placed or passed over the reader. Some readers have the capability of reading at multiple angles – lasers are positioned so that they can read part using one laser and part using another laser.

Portable readers can be single-function or multi-function. A single-function reader would just collect bar codes, while a multi-function reader can input other information, for example, quantities. There are some specialist units that can be strapped to an operator's wrist. Many are 'wireless' and can link to other equipment or computers without requiring cables – these would require a wireless computer network. This type of device is sometimes seen in supermarkets by staff for checking stock, prices or next expected delivery.

Mobile devices with a camera, have free apps that use the camera to read bar codes. Many will also use the Internet to search for a match.

Check

Which of the following is true?

a) All bar codes must be registered with an industry regulator

b) There is only one format for bar codes

c) Bar codes are limited by the need to have fixed readers

d) Bar codes can be used for a wide range of data entry applications

Order tracking technologies

Order tracking has become an expectation of both business and consumer transactions. Prior to the development of tracking systems, customers were expected to contact suppliers for information – who would then try to locate the order and progress. Over time, software systems were introduced so that the progress of an order could be updated and the supplier could provide the customer with an update more efficiently.

Delivery companies and couriers required the ability to track the progress of a delivery – often via multiple locations – and needed to be able to confirm delivery completion and recipient detail. Some specialist companies recognised the value of this information and offered tracking services to customers, perhaps allowing the delivery messages to be forwarded by e-mail to the originator.

Nowadays, tracking is usually geared through Internet-based technology and can incorporate order processing updates, payment systems and delivery tracking. Organisations can invest in their own tracking systems but given the diversity of suppliers and supply chains it is unlikely this will be suitable for all purchases and sales. Organisations are more likely to use a combination of non-automated systems, their own system and those available via suppliers and third-party couriers and delivery businesses.

Most of these systems use bar code technology in combination with optical readers.

Case study

Typical business-to-consumer (B2C) online order process using tracking

The customer makes their order by completing a 'shopping basket' online with Retailer A. The Retailer A system confirms availability as the shopping basket is filled and allocates stock ready for the customer's order completion. Their basket contains a unique order number and product codes.

The order is completed by the customer, who gives their e-mail details and makes the payment online.

The order is confirmed on-screen and to the customer's e-mail, containing the unique order number and 'click here to track order progress' instruction (this opens the tracking web page). The purchase then enters the 'order being processed' list.

The company warehouse with the stock receives the order, converts it to a 'picking list' to extract the items using the order number and bar code. It then enters an 'awaiting picking' list.

The stock is picked – the picking list is completed and replaced by a packing list showing customer order number, bar code and address labels for despatch. The order enters the 'awaiting packing' list.

The order is packed and labelled with the bar code, ready for the delivery company. It enters the 'awaiting collection' list.

The delivery company collects and routes the parcel based on the bar code addressing detail, updating the location. The order enters the 'awaiting delivery' list, and the stock is recorded as no longer in the retailer warehouse.

The delivery company transfers the order via delivery hubs using the bar code to update. It enters the 'awaiting local delivery' list.

The delivery company delivers the order and obtains confirmation signature – a message is sent to the delivery company by scanning the bar code, and retailer A receives notification and records that the order is complete.

The customer opens the package which contains the packing list and returns label (both with bar codes) and instructions.

To enhance satisfaction, this retailer allows the consumer to track progress online by entering the order number and postcode – some require simply clicking a link. Some retailers prefer to use customer numbers alongside order numbers to generate data regarding the relationship and linking the orders.

At each stage, Retailer A can monitor individual orders and 'stage completion' or 'stage awaited'. Examples of checks are shown below.

- Number of orders more than one day delayed
- Number of orders awaiting picking
- Number of orders awaiting packing
- Number of orders awaiting collection
- Number of orders awaiting delivery
- Number of 'out of stock' positions reported at shopping basket stage

Order tracking: a typical courier/delivery business process

An order is placed online to a delivery company and the order number is logged. Size and weight are known, allowing the delivery company to charge an appropriate rate and plan the transaction. The customer is asked to print a label and attach it to the package – this is the addressing detail and has a bar code for the consignment. The request is scheduled using a software package and the customer receives a confirmation of the order and pick-up. The consignment number website tracking is live.

As the collection proceeds, some companies can issue notification updates of the estimated live pick-up time.

On pick-up, the system bar code is scanned, and this will update the status of the delivery. The bar code is scanned on arrival at a hub or transfer location and again when a vehicle starts the onward journey, with further updates.

On delivery, the signature of the recipient is taken on a handheld device; this reports delivery which can be seen by the customer and the recipient if they wish.

Consignments can be tracked and the cost of delivery against income calculated by the delivery company.

Collection and delivery times can be tracked and differences reported and investigated.

Case study

> *Apply*
> Look on the Internet for a local distribution company and postal service. What type of tracking is offered?

1.2 LO1

The use of RFID (Radio Frequency Identification)

Compared to bar codes, RFID technology is much more recent and uses some technology that is surprisingly complex for such small devices. The concept is that small devices can be embedded in labels or attached to tags which work with radio transmitters and/or receivers to identify themselves.

The two main types are 'passive' (it does nothing until asked, then can announce what it is and therefore can be tracked to where it is), and active (it periodically announces what it is and therefore can be tracked to where it is).

The RFID devices have a very small integrated circuit incorporating a small memory capability – many are smaller than 2mm square and 2mm thick. Despite its size, many can hold 2000 characters of data (about one full page of text). Many retailers simply use the tag as a thick label and print both sides with product information and perhaps a bar code – it is sometimes difficult to detect the device inside.

RFID (Radio Frequency Identification) Items which use radio technology for identifying itself and its location subject to having the appropriate hardware and software

Case study

Luxury products – using RFID for security
A luxury goods brand successfully introduced RFIDs in most of its products. High-priced garments were often pre-tagged at the point of manufacture, but the tag was hidden inside the lining or hems to avoid detection and possible removal. Other items were tagged at the import warehouse.

Tags were activated at store level on arrival. Staff received an initial alert as soon as tags were moved away from their display area and an alarm was activated should the items pass near the doors of the shop if the item had not been paid for.

The RFID device is more likely to vary in size according to the very thin integrated antenna – a small antenna has limited range, so a small antenna RFID would need to be close to the source of a signal, or base station. The operating range also depends on the radio frequency used, receiver capability and the environment. Some tags are only readable from under 1m, others can have a 100m range.

Larger RFID devices can fit into plastic enclosures, some of which have external batteries. Tags to suit special environmental situations are also available, including RFIDs to use on metal, RFIDs to use in damp or wet conditions and RFIDs that are corrosion resistant.

Tote box plastic seals have been adapted to include an RFID tag – this would make the tote box traceable inside a warehouse or confirm the departure or arrival of the box at different locations – the tag potentially also revealing the contents of the box.

Case study

Tyre manufacturers using RFID for 'whole life'

In the last few years it has been reported that many tyre manufacturers are using RFID tags embedded within tyres. Using external labels would allow use of the tag up to vehicle fitment for tyres supplied to car manufacturers or retail sale for the replacement tyre market. Using an embedded tag means that the RFID could be monitored through the whole life of the tyre.

This makes the identification of tyres that may be subject to quality recalls much easier. It is also possible that the RFID could give access to a log of repairs and usage.

Commercial vehicles are particularly suited to the technology as fleet managers may wish to track usage rates.

Many commercial vehicle tyres are re-treaded and those that are damaged in their first life could be identified.

RFID technology has been commercially available to the public for some time and there are devices available to track baggage at airports (the commercial version is also in use in some locations). Other applications include use in passports, library issue and security systems to secure access to computers and restricted areas.

RFID tags can be used to do the following.

- Track individual items
- Track boxes of products, cages of products and pallets
- Track containers with multiple loads
- Locate equipment within a building
- Trigger alarms should equipment or stock be removed without authorisation

Some organisations use one RFID in a single product in a consignment, rather than tracking all items. This reduces the volume of messages being transmitted and received and reduces tagging costs.

RFID tags require readers – there are many different types. Portable units can be handheld devices reading selected items. Similarly, there can be fixed units with the tagged item being positioned near the reader, or on a conveyor belt reading items as they pass. Many organisations with large volume movements use a 'gateway' – an arch equipped with the reading equipment often positioned across doorways or at the entry/exit of storage areas.

It is important to note that there are multiple standards in use for RFID – some of these are standardised for industries but there are also national standards in operation. These standards need to be investigated before investment as not all readers work with all tags.

Remember

Many order tracking technologies are now commonly in use in many industries. They help to create efficient and effective routines for processing and managing a wide variety of assets.

1.3 Contrast the impact of the use of different warehousing equipment

Materials handling equipment

There are many different situations that may require the use of materials handling equipment. For each situation there may be common requirements, but certain circumstances command unique requirements. This section will provide descriptions of a wide range of equipment and their uses.

Materials handling often involves lifting. Although different sources quote different 'safe loads' for manual lifting, it is possible to cause injury when lifting a 2kg load at full stretch, with picking up and putting down situations being more dangerous than holding. Staff holding heavy loads are also more vulnerable to being off-balance and may be more liable to trips, slips and falls. As a result, materials handling equipment is often beneficial to reduce or eliminate risks of manual lifting and moving stock.

Because of the potential hazards to operators and those in the vicinity of handling equipment, it is very important that operators and staff are trained in the safe operation of equipment. This is likely to include formal training sessions, and sometimes certification of training or licensing is needed before an operator can use the equipment. All equipment will have 'operating conditions' which will include maximum dimensions and weights. An organisation should make available the appropriate equipment required to handle whatever loads are expected at the location.

Dollies

These are sets of wheels that can be placed under stacks making it easier to move around. Multiple dollies could be used for a single load, but care should be taken with the height, weight and stability of the load.

Sack trucks

These have two wheels and feature a small base platform with a larger vertical structure – the base is positioned under the load and then tilted, so that the load is angled but supported by the vertical structure. It may be possible to move a stack of boxes using a sack truck, but it is not good practice as they are less stable than four-wheeled trucks and trolleys and require more care and effort when loading and unloading. In addition, boxes should not be stacked higher than the handle for safety reasons and to allow adequate vision.

Trolleys

There is a wide variety of wheeled trolleys available to support storage and picking operations. These can be simply moved around by operators or can be powered. Most will have corner protection against bumps and scuffs; all will have a maximum weight loading.

- Flatbed trolleys have a low load area that have no side supports. They have four or six wheels and offer extremely flexible transportation.

- Tote trolleys have fixed spaces for closed or open totes. These are effective for multiple-item storage journeys or multiple-order picking.

- Shelf trolleys have multiple shelves which allow boxes or loose stock to transfer to or from storage. These are also available with caged sides and backs.

Turntable trucks or articulating/narrow-aisle trucks

These are available in a range of sizes and weight loadings. They feature articulated front wheels that allow turning in a small space.

Roll cages

These are wheeled cages that are made up of a dolly-like platform with wire or steel mesh sides. Some have two mesh panels that are removable, and others have four. Some versions have two fixed sides with webbing straps to secure the other sides. Some versions can be dismantled completely, making storage and return from customers or to suppliers very convenient.

Order pickers

This is the name given to a variety of manual and powered devices – some with ride-on capability and some without. These allow for low-level, medium-level and high-level picking of various items. Many are equipped with forks to allow transfer capability of larger picked boxes.

Higher-level and narrow- or very narrow-aisle versions have the ability to elevate operators on the front platform to higher racking and pick items with full control on the elevated platform.

Pallet trucks

There is a range of equipment designed to move either euro pallets or bottom-boarded pallets. Pallet trucks have 'forks' which fit into the gaps at the bottom of pallets. When a lever is pulled, or a handle pulled downwards, the pallet is lifted just clear of the ground and can then be freely moved around the warehouse. When at the next position, the operator releases the lift mechanism and the pallet can be placed on the floor or pallet rack.

Pallet trucks are available in a range of sizes and weight loadings. In all cases, the maximum load needs to be considered.

Extra-long-forked versions can take a two-metre-long load, potentially allowing movement of two pallets. Narrow-forked versions are available that can work with different pallet standards and non-standard loads. Pallet trucks can be manual or powered but both types have hydraulic or pneumatic mechanisms to lift loads. Larger trucks have 'ride on' capability where the operator will stand or sit as the powered truck moves around.

Pallet stackers

These are designed to lift and stack pallets. They are fully mobile so can move around the warehouse. Height, reach and weight limitations in the storage facility will determine the appropriate model and features.

Grabs

Grabs are designed to hold stock either width-wise or from above. These are either specific devices designed for grabbing material or are available as an accessory for forklift trucks.

Drum lifters and loaders

These have shaped parts that allow operators to move large drums and stack them. There are some drum lifters and loaders that are produced for specific sizes and weights/volumes of drums. Drum lift attachments are also available for forklift trucks.

Counterbalance forklift trucks

The forklift is a highly versatile asset in most warehouses and stockyards. These are 'ride on' vehicles with high manoeuvrability. Forklifts may have simply a vehicle loading and unloading role, but in many cases, they are used for storing goods, maintenance of stock and retrieval of stock.

The weight of a load that can be transported and its lifting capability is partly determined by the height of the upright 'mast' nearest the operator, the load length and the counterbalance weight integrated within the truck. When lifted, most tip the load backwards slightly to balance on the upright mast assembly.

Reach trucks

Reach trucks are designed to work in a narrower aisle than a standard counterbalance forklift truck. Reach trucks are similar to forklifts, but the forks are moveable in order to reach the load and are then retracted back for transport. Reach trucks are more compact and can lift stock higher than the comparable counterbalance forklift. Some versions have 'side access forks' which allow their use in very confined spaces (for example, in narrow and very narrow aisles).

Vacuum lifters

This uses a vacuum pad which attaches itself to a product. The suction force allows the product to be lifted (and rotated and placed). Vacuum lifters are used for moving and positioning glass sheets, but are also seen lifting boxes, plastic sacks, sheets of building materials and pipework. Some models feature hydraulic arms which allow easy movement of the lifted load.

The lifting system will have a number of sucker pads and a vacuum capability which determines the maximum weight and largest items that can be lifted.

Roller systems

Fixed roller systems are typically used to transfer larger volumes of stock in box, tote or pallet form in larger warehouses. These can be 'gravity fed' (relying on a rise or fall in the position of the roller bed over the distance covered) or powered (which 'drives' one or more rollers in the set). Roller systems can be constructed to have 'turning points' to change direction and can be designed to turn corners. Roller systems can handle pallet loads. Some regular maintenance is required.

Although fixed roller systems lack flexibility and may have a high initial cost, a design layout can be created to maximise the benefits of this equipment. Fixed rollers can also support movements downwards between floors although powered rollers would be required for travel upwards.

There are also portable versions which can be used to unload vehicles (where the high end might be in a vehicle and the low end inside the dock) or inside a warehouse to move stock quickly from one location to another. One type can collapse into a small length when not in use and can bend along its length.

Apply

Research three or four of the different types of equipment described.

Consider
- What organisations would use them? How do they benefit the organisation?
- Who in the organisation would work on them – how much experience/training would they need?

Conveyor systems

These are a popular choice in some situations, particularly if transferring stock between floors by using a system of conveyor belts. Conveyor belts can be 'segmented' with lateral raised separators to keep items apart or be continuous belts. Belts can also be overlapped and shaped to allow them to change direction. Conveyor belts need power to drive them but can be equipped with sensors to slow down or stop when stock is static, or the belt is not in use. Fixed conveyor systems require careful planning and positioning. Maintenance is important and longer-term replacement cost of belt material needs to be considered.

Portable versions are available with wheels to allow vehicle loading and unloading or moving stock to higher levels in a racking system.

Cranes

Cranes can help to move bulky and/or heavy stock around a building. Overhead cranes are usually installed for very heavy loads. Gantry-type cranes are mounted in girder sections across the structure of the building. Some offer a single line of movement, but others can move in two directions and can therefore move heavy equipment and loads from one point to another within the structure.

Bridge cranes work on a similar high-level mounting but use smaller frames, covering a smaller area.

The load rating and positioning of overhead cranes is important as changes would be costly. Safety considerations are essential and when in operation there are often access restrictions, and audible and visual warnings in place to avoid accidents.

Carousels

Carousels are space-efficient, rotating devices which allow access to a large range of products from a single location. Designs are variable, with carousels rotating horizontally or vertically until the required item can be retrieved. The movement to reveal the required item can be achieved by manually moving the racks, using forward and back controls, by entering a shelf location on a keypad, entering the product code or by bar code, depending on the installation.

Stacker cranes

These are installed as part of the automation of warehousing and have fixed runs alongside racking, storing and retrieving pallets.

Access to higher levels

It is important to ensure safe working in storage facilities, and access to higher shelves or racking presents a challenge. Lifting at full reach becomes a problem at relatively low weight. There can also be danger for other workers who are around someone working at height, from the movement of equipment or dropping stock from a height. Conveyors and roller systems have already been covered in this section – both can be used to transfer stock between levels in a building.

Ladders can be used but these become unstable and even those with handrails are difficult to use when carrying stock.

Step sets are more often used for smaller heights – safer ones have large platforms at the top, wide steps, handrails and a wide base for stability. These are also available with lockable wheels, making them mobile. Specific 'docking platforms' are also available.

Platforms (or cages) are available in a variety of sizes and weight loadings – some suitable for lower heights and some for higher applications (the height that can be achieved depends on the design of the equipment used and the weight of the unit plus operator and stock load).

Some order pickers are specifically designed for storing stock and picking at multiple levels.

Scissor platforms are used in high-roof warehouses to gain access to lighting, high racking units and sections of wall and roof (some up to 13m). Alternatives are 'jib-type' platforms that have an extended reach capability; these are also known as 'cherry pickers'.

Some warehouses simply install higher-level access walkways for selected sections of racking, connecting to lifts for stock transfer and stairs for operator use.

Equipment for working at height is likely to feature equipment certified to a national or international standard. Local health and safety regulations may require organisation or operator certification, operating routines documentation and additional safety equipment. This is regarded as a high risk, and depending on the local legislation an organisation or individuals may be prosecuted for any breach of regulations.

> *Remember*
> There may be many options for moving and lifting stock – not all warehouses have a full range of equipment. It is important to use equipment which is designed for the load and activity which is required. All equipment requires attention to safety and some requires special training.

Waste storage and compression

Waste products from packaging, disposal of some stock and potentially spillages all require storage pending disposal. Different items probably require different processes and some may be of value, but some will have additional costs – so segregation is likely. Cardboard and paper volumes (if significant) benefit from folding flat and strapping. Some organisations use waste compression machines to use less space in storage and the disposal vehicles.

Weighing

Weighing is required in many situations in the warehouse.

- Inbound loads may need to be weighed to confirm delivery meets documentation provided.

- Weighing can establish the number of items in a box, tote or other package, provided the weight of the packaging is known or can be estimated.

- Weighing can establish that a load is appropriate to be moved by specific equipment or stored in a specific place (safe working).

- Weighing is used as part of periodic stocktaking for weight of stock or estimating quantities.

- Weight information is needed to establish packing weight limitations and to establish the cost of carriage and is needed to establish safe vehicle loading and that vehicle limits are not exceeded.

Common issues when considering weighing equipment can be the following.

- The size of the item

- The weight of the item (approximately) – scales tend to operate in ranges and will have a stated accuracy

- If the item is in packaging, a pallet or a tote box, the ability to use a 'tare' setting means that the item's weight only will be displayed (the scale deducts a preset amount or the result of previously weighing the non-product weight)

- The speed of accurate weighing – choice of equipment and its placement can make weighing activity quick or slow

- The ability to record, store, print and document the weight using links to computer networks or mobile phone-based software

There is a range of weighing equipment that is used in warehousing, stockyards and stores – in each case the nature of the product and the situation will vary the equipment used.

Weighbridges

Weighbridges establish a vehicle's weight either on a platform- or pad-equipped area near the dock or at the entrance to a facility. The concept is that the vehicle weight is taken before and after a delivery – the difference between the two weights represents the delivery made. This is suitable for loose material and liquids but can also be used as a check against other deliveries and despatches. Waste, scrap and recycling weight can be used as the basis of charging (or being given value for scrap). Weighbridges are also used to ensure that the total permitted vehicle weight is not exceeded.

Panels showing the weight of a vehicle can be positioned to be seen by the vehicle driver. Many systems print copy weight/date/time information, and some will create electronic records that can be used by computer software and/or transmitted to other locations.

Floor scales and platform scales

These are set into walkways, in packing areas or in dock areas. It is possible to weigh individual boxes or groups, pallets and stock cages. Weight labels can be printed and some organisations link this to the packing list and delivery information to show detail for transport billing and vehicle loading.

Conveyor belt scales

These can be installed to check that the contents of a box match the items expected. In modern **distribution centres**, a package label can be read, the consignment identified, and the actual weight compared to the expected weight, with items outside expectation held for checking. The conveyor may change the route of a package to match the handling requirements of lighter or heavier packages.

Forklift and pallet truck scales

Although a loaded forklift could be weighed using a platform scale, it is more convenient to use a device fitted to the standard forks of the forklift or pallet truck. This can be used to ensure the safe operating weight is not exceeded. Forklift truck scales can display the load being lifted and store the details of previous loads, making a total moved consignment weight possible.

Load cells

These can be fitted to silos, hoppers and tanks in a storage situation and provide a means of measuring the quantity of the contents on a continuous basis, making stock checks easy.

Suspended balance and crane scales

These measure the load from above – typically a strapped load or container with a top hook or eye is suspended and the weight is taken 'in the air'. Remote displays are often used to make reading the measurement easier. Stock like open-bagged aggregates have lifting handles or straps, making suspended balance or crane scales highly appropriate.

Counting scales

These are small scales with the ability to weigh items conventionally but can also count items by first providing a single item to weigh – after which it will show the number of items and the total weight. Some scales can be linked to printers to produce labels.

Distribution centre
A storage facility, usually smaller than the organisation's main warehouse, that is geographically sited to serve a specific area

> *Remember*
> The choice of weighing equipment will depend on the type of stock and the purpose of the weighing. Different products at different points in the warehouse may require weight checking, whether this is to accept goods, on arrival, for repackaging, for storage, to retrieve the correct amount or to prepare and account at despatch.

Case study

Use of weighbridge equipment in apple juice production

A large-scale processor of apples to make apple juice and similar products uses a single weighbridge to support the manufacturing plant in several ways including the following.

- Apple deliveries typically arrive in covered trucks, many with tipper mechanisms. On arrival at the single-entry checkpoint, vehicles stop to gain entry. The stopping point incorporates a weighbridge, allowing the vehicle weight to be taken.

- Apples are delivered to an open yard and emptied into a bay for inspection. Those in containers or pallets are also emptied and any packaging retained by the delivery vehicle. The initial inspection and acceptance are recorded. The vehicle is stopped again on exit, to allow the weight to be noted. The weights 'receipt' is provided, and this forms the basis of making an agreed payment per tonne to the supplier.

- Some other deliveries are also monitored by the weighbridge – notably the bulk sugar delivery.

- Waste removal is also monitored by weight, which allows a per tonne and per visit cost to be agreed, rather than a cost assumption of a full load.

The company states that it believes the weighing in and out of all vehicles helps to prevent theft as standard product weights can be used to establish an expected weight of any load leaving the site.

Checking dimensions and volume

'Dimensions weight scanning' equipment uses ultrasonic and infrared technology to measure items and incorporates a weighing table. Traditionally a checking or packing table might have edges or a back wall with marked measurements or long rulers. Alternatively, a range of standard pre-formed boxes can be made up with pre-printed dimensions and volumes.

Some technical measuring tools may be needed, particularly to check goods on arrival. These may include digital micrometers (generally for small measurements), digital calipers (for larger measurements) and laser measuring devices.

Containers of liquid could be weighed, and a look-up table consulted for checking the equivalent volume. Pre-prepared dipsticks can be used for checking the level of fluids, with markings equating to known volumes.

Racking and storage

Although storage on the warehouse or stockroom floor is not a good idea, it is possible to simply create a very low platform area for temporary storage. It is also possible to create an area for pallet storage that is not on shelves – although the height of stacking and stability would need to be considered.

Standard shelving in metal or with some wooden components can be installed for general storage – this can be very flexible, particularly if the shelves are vertically adjustable and shelf widths are wide.

Special racking is available to maximise the space usage for a wide range of items and the layout of the warehouse needs to allow for where they are intended for use.

- Pallet racking has the capability of supporting multiple pallets. There are many different types and one-off designs are also seen. The weight loading and type of pallet and the height of each pallet in each case needs to be considered and racking selected that is appropriate for the stock expected.

  - Standard pallet racking is formed of shelves so that each pallet can be independently stored and removed.

  - Adjustable pallet racking has a set standard width, enough to accommodate the width of a pallet plus a small margin on each side to aid easy positioning. The vertical spacing of shelving can be adjusted to allow taller or shorter pallet loads.

  - Pallet racking can be arranged in single-sided runs – a single depth of pallets is stored with access just on one side. This type of racking may be used on the perimeter of a warehouse, but it could be used where space is limited. Double-sided access is possible for some designs, again with a single depth of pallets. This maximises accessibility and is used in some 'one way' systems to aid flow. Double-sided runs can be built up from two single-sided runs 'back to back'.

  - Double-deep runs have pallet storage two pallets deep, which can be used to either store the same SKU in each position (front and back) or different SKUs. Where different items are stored in front from behind, it is necessary to move and position the front pallet to access the rear, then replace it.

  - Live storage pallet racking has multiple depths of pallets that are accessed from the front, but new stock loaded to the rear. This type of storage allows the pallet behind to move forward if the front one is removed.

  - Drive-in and drive-through runs have a different 'no shelves' design which allows equipment to enter the racks for storing and retrieval. The drive-in design has one access aisle and the drive-through can be accessed from both sides, so storage can be put in place on one side and retrieval the other side.

  - Post pallets look very different from the familiar timber or plastic pallets. These have a simple metal structure with four uprights and substantial 'feet' to take the load. These may be free-standing, but many are designed for the feet to interlock with the posts of another post pallet so that a stack can be created. These are also available in open-fronted cage versions or fully caged versions.

- Tote racking is spaced to allow easy access to boxes for picking or whole box storage retrieval. There are also 'open front' totes in a wide range of sizes that make individual item picking very easy. Live storage has tilted racking with access at the front and reloading from the rear – removal of the front tote brings the next tote into use.

- Bar, sheet and rod racks are all designed to allow safe storage, easy access and efficient space usage. Racks often separate sizes or types either vertically or horizontally (the choice depends on the length of item(s), weight and the degree of support required along its length to avoid bending).

- Cable spools are often mounted on dispensers allowing lengths to be cut. They can also be flat-stored on very narrow-set shelving.

- Stock cages are available in many sizes and can hold single items or groups of items. Cages with wheels offer flexibility as they can be moved around the warehouse without the need for other handling equipment.

Remember
The choice of storage equipment will depend on the type of stock, volume of stock and equipment being used. Storage equipment can save space and therefore costs. Storage equipment should make safe and efficient movement, storage and retrieval possible.

Palletisation and unit loads

Palletisation principles

The use of pallets has already been referred to several times in this chapter. There are many situations in which there is an expectation or a requirement that loads are palletised. There are many large polypropylene boxes that are designed with forklift 'gaps' at the base, simulating the pallet design. The widespread adoption of the pallet has resulted in many different pallet-based transportation and storage systems.

The widespread availability of forklift trucks and hand trucks equipped with appropriate forks encourages the use of palletised loads. There is a considerable saving in time to load and unload vehicles by palletisation compared to 'by hand' methods. Similar time savings are available by avoiding manual handling in the warehouse by using palletised loads. Bricks, blocks and paving slabs can be seen on display in many building supply yards. Bags of compost can often be seen displayed on the delivery pallet, avoiding the need for additional handling.

Unit load principles

Unit load
A term used to describe the grouping of different items into a convenient stack or stacks which make them easy to handle and store. Typically, this involves pallets and/or the plastic wrapping of a load

The concept of a **unit load** is to create a stable and secure, easy-to-move group of stock that is fast to load and unload from vehicles. Standardisation is an important theme of unit load system design. This is because the more items that are of similar size, weight and shape, more standard stock handling and racking can be used. This will offer greater density of storage and transportation. Although the pallet is most often connected with unit loads, the concept is flexible, and the use of skids and slips are also seen. A common theme is the use of wrapping and strapping to keep the load stable (and in some cases capable of stacking). Product trays and layer separators are also used.

In manufacturer terms, the preparation of a single product and delivery by the full unit load makes life very simple in the warehouses and for logistics. A full unit load is made up, wrapped and does not need splitting until later in the supply chain. No matter how many items or boxes are in a unit load, the count is 'one load'.

If the typical order does not work like this, then there is still the ability to stack many different products in boxes and wrap or enclose it in some way to create a mixed product unit load. This is less desirable as the mixed group does not lend itself to eventual storage in a product-ordered warehouse as it would need breaking apart.

Grocery retail
In grocery retail, it is common to see pallets used by manufacturers and delivered to supermarket distribution centres, with the majority stored on pallets. For the replenishment of stores, the bulk pallet stock is then split

Case study ≫

and the inner trays or boxes are then transferred to roll cages which becomes the new standard unit load. The supermarket store will then unload the roll cage to restock shelves, removing any remaining packaging after use and recycling or returning it to the distribution centre with empty roll cages.

In one supermarket group, fruit and vegetables are prepared in a packing warehouse and placed into standard reusable and collapsible plastic rigid trays supplied by the supermarket. These trays can be stacked and are transferred to distribution centres using roll cages. The stock is then split to meet supply requirements and the mixed load of rigid trays is stacked in a roll cage. On arrival in store, stock replenishment takes place and empty trays are collapsed for the return journey to the distribution centre.

The use of a tote box as a unit load is very common in semi-automated and automated warehouses.

Some supply chains and situations dominated by the requirement for logistics have written standards for unit loads, specifying sizing, weights, strapping, wrapping and labelling. There are international standards for testing stability, compression and the impact of vibration. Some retail supply chains specify how a pallet must be loaded which may include the following.

- 'Face up' stacking, (which could be, for example, to show a bar code, and use-by or production dates)

- Maximum height and weight of unit load

- Edge, top and bottom protection

Pallets

The pallet itself is the key requirement to any palletised system. The basic design has a slatted top, a block layer with gaps for fork access and a bottom slatted layer to create a stable platform.

European pallets are only manufactured under licence from the European Pallet Association and must conform to standard UCI435-2 specifications; they measure 800mm × 1200mm. Standard UK bottom board pallets measure 1200mm × 1000mm. Other European and international sizes tend to be proportional to the standard pallet size. There is a wide range of different standard sizes and these can be driven by conventions (and availability) in different countries and different industries. The largest common size is 1200mm square (48"×48"). The size of pallets is important as this may determine the width and depth of racking and the fit to the load bay of vans, lorries and trailers.

Pallets are available in timber (the most common type), plastic/resin, cardboard, composite materials and even steel. All have maximum weight loading ratings. There are one-way pallets that have fork access spaces from the front or the back and two-way pallets that can be access from all four sides. It is an expected part of pallet use that they are reused or recycled.

To aid logistics, even an oversized single item could be secured to a pallet to make transportation and storage easier. Large-scale users of pallets need storage space for pallets not in use. There should also be a system of recovery of pallets from end users. Some organisations charge for a pallet with a delivery, with the cost refunded on return. Some organisations rent pallets rather than buy them, so the recovery of pallets from customers becomes important.

Skids

These are generally described as single-deck pallets and do not have a bottom-slatted layer. This makes them less bulky and cheaper than conventional pallets but also less universal in their use.

Slip sheets

This is a system of unit loads that does not use a pallet base. The concept is that a thin sheet of suitable material the same size as the load is placed under the load. The slip sheet can be made of plastic or a form of boarding. It has one or more 'lips' which allow lifting equipment to slide under the sheet rather than on top of the sheet and under the load. The lip of the sheet is grabbed by the lifting equipment and pulled back to the forklift platform. Unloading works in reverse with the load and slip sheet being pushed off the forks and the slip sheet released.

Using slip sheets means that no pallets are required, which makes a size and weight difference to all transport and storage. Slip sheets are reusable, light and take up very little space.

Slip sheets require special 'push and pull' forklift accessories and usually use 'thin and wide' forks.

> *Check*
> Which of the following may be used as part of a 'unit load' stock movement and storage system? (Select any that are appropriate.)
> **a)** Pallets
> **b)** Roll cages
> **c)** Tote boxes
> **d)** Shrink-wrapping
> **e)** Slip sheets

Packing and packaging

Different products require different packaging that will depend primarily on the nature of the product, its size, weight and relative fragility. Objectives of packing and packaging include the following.

- Protect the product from damage in transit through to the final user
- Protect other products being damaged by the product itself
- Protect the handlers of the product from harm
- Comply with transport and/or legal requirements
- Meet an organisation's image and marketing objectives
- Meet an organisation's environmental commitment
- Meet a cost target in order to maintain profitability

Cardboard boxes (cartons)

1.3 LO1

These are used in very large quantities in supply chains. Most box suppliers offer a range of sizes and specifications.

- Single wall boxes have a single layer of corrugated cardboard.

- Double wall boxes have two corrugated cardboard layers and are stronger.

- There are specific boxes that are 'food safe'.

- Each box type will have a maximum weight loading and may have weaker or stronger 'walls' and different construction which might make them less suitable for some situations. Joins inside boxes can be glued or glued and stapled.

- Some boxes have multiple 'score lines' across the sides – this allows the box to be made up in different sizes, which could make distribution costs lower if based on size or volume. These boxes can also reduce the amount of void fill used.

- Some industries have established standard carton sizes to aid use of standard stock handling, racking, transport and shipping. In many cases the sizing is related to pallet load dimensions.

	Length mm	Width mm	Height mm
BDCM1	595	289	390
BDCM2	394	292	394
BDCM3	597	292	394
BDCM4	400	300	200
	Length inches	Width inches	Height inches
BDC1	24	11	14
BDC2	16	11	14
BDC3	16	11	7

Table 1.4 Bulk Distribution Carton Metric (BDCM) and Bulk Distribution Carton (BDC) standard box sizes

Table 1.4 shows examples of standard box sizes that have been used in the retail trade and are used for transfers of stock of garments and in mail order and online warehousing. In many cases these will be stacked onto pallets and wrapped to create unit loads suitable for transport and standardised transport.

Postal services and delivery service businesses will base fees on the sizes and/or volumes of parcels in addition to weight restrictions and weight-based fees. Businesses select a packaging method and size that works to maximise value and minimise waste.

Although capable of recycling and reuse, any product has energy consumption when produced and environmental impact through to the end-of-life. Some supply chains have a reuse policy with used cartons being returned to the supplier for future use rather than disposal or recycling.

The strength of a box or carton is also dependent on the final closing and taping – there is a significant difference in the strength of a filled box if it is sealed using a heavy wrap and strapping than a simple paper strip.

The outer carton can be used as a means of additional marketing and brand awareness, but additional printing also adds to the packaging cost. Other organisations prefer not to identify the type of goods or supplier in this way to avoid potential theft.

> *Check*
> What are the advantages of using 'industry standard size' cardboard boxes in a supply chain?

Cardboard pick trays and boxes

To avoid picking into a tote and then transferring the contents to packaging, there are cardboard carton products that can be used for picking but then become the basis of the packaging. The top of the box is either already joined to the base or a top is added after void fill or wrapping the contents. These are particularly helpful where a conventional cardboard box may be too large.

Plastic bags and poly bags come in a very wide range of sizes and strengths. The range allows them to be used as instructions and documentation enclosures, product wrapping, bagging of groups of products, wrapping of boxes (often using a shrink-wrap technique). Many designs come as 'self-seal' with adhesive strips ready to secure the ends.

Labelling and handling instructions

In many cases, the dimensions and weight of a consignment should be noted on documentation and on the consignment itself.

Typical labelling (or by means of a pre-printed box).

- Gross weight (the total, with packaging)

- Net weight (the consignment without packaging)

- The dimensions (length, width and height)

- The 'cube' (cubic space, whether in m^3 or ft^3)

Handling instructions are often in large, clear font, but there are standard symbols used which include 'this way up', 'fragile', 'protect from rain or damp conditions', 'protect from sunlight', 'handle with care', 'sensitive to temperature', 'do not use lifting hooks', 'recyclable' and 'store no higher than x high'. There are other symbols for 'hazardous chemicals' and 'heavy load' is usually shown as an exclamation mark with 'Heavy Load' printed on the outer packaging. See figure 1.39 for examples of these.

Specific hazardous goods labelling, together with UN codes for transportation of hazardous goods are also a requirement. Goods for import and export may need specific wrapping and packaging and outer boxes or pallets will need to be labelled for customs clearance and/or documentation by showing the Harmonized Item Description and Coding System (abbreviated to HS for Harmonized System).

Figure 1.39 Standard symbol set seen on outer packaging (Source: Shutterstock.com/ Anton Prohorov)

Void filling

This is the general term given to the challenge of filling the space left in a box after the products have been packed. This means that the products inside can move around and could be damaged.

Many different materials are available, and each has advantages and disadvantages.

- Polystyrene chips and beads have good protection potential but do not have a good environmental profile.

- Chips of maize-based starch products are bio-degradable and can be created in a variety of forms.

- Vermiculite is a mineral based, light and absorbent material that is usually in very small pieces. It also has fire resistant characteristics.

- Shredded paper or a shredded wood-based material 'wood wool' is a lightweight solution. Use of non-confidential office paper is sometimes used, but the shreds are so narrow it is unreadable.

- Cardboard chips and shredded cardboard also avoid the environmental issues of plastic-based fillers and can be recycled or even reused.

- Paper and cardboard rolls come in large sizes and can be furled around a product in a box or made into loose balls of void fill.

- Bubble wrap is a polyethylene product with air pockets. This is available in sheet form, but it is most often seen in large rolls, which are cut to size.

- Air-filled cushions are larger plastic pockets which come in flat sleeve-roll form. A machine fills the pockets with air and seals the pockets using a heat source, creating a stream of joined pouches. If not reused, the pouches are pierced after first use and this makes the volume very small compared to the inflated pouch.

- Self-expanding foam can be used – this expands to fill a void when activated.

Important considerations for void fill are primarily whether the fill prevents damage in transit. Other factors are the total cost of the materials and machinery, the labour requirement, time taken and environmental impact. In the spirit of supply chain awareness, the potential for reuse and disposal issues for the recipient should also be considered.

Edge and corner protection packing

Outer cardboard boxes will provide some protection to products, but an impact to the box on an edge or corner may defeat the ability of void fill or inner packaging to protect the product. Edge strips of cardboard or polystyrene can be added inside the box – these can also be attached to the outside (polystyrene additions can be wrapped onto the carton or pallet).

Product trays

These may be flexible inserts for boxes to accept many different types and shapes of products or custom made to fit the product shape. Those made to fit standard-size packages are cheaper and more flexible. Custom-made trays avoid additional void-fill material. This is seen in packaging for consumer electronics, where many thousands of units may be used each week, making the cost per unit low (there is no additional packing) and protection high.

Layer pads and layer trays

These are dividers between layers placed in a cardboard box, tote box, roll cage or pallet. The objective is to maintain stability of the packaging and make it easy to remove items. The pads can be as simple as a layer of paper or corrugated cardboard. Some layer trays have been designed to fit the shape of items precisely. In retail grocery situations, suppliers often provide layer trays designed to become on-shelf containers which both continues to protect the product and present the product to the customers.

Protective sleeving

This can be made of a variety of materials. Extruded plastic and elasticated cardboard products are available, as well as inflatable products featuring air pockets.

Packaging and wrapping tape

A range of self-adhesive or gummed tapes are available in different widths, colours, materials and strengths. Basic self-adhesive tape is suitable for securing wrapping or smaller parcels. Stronger tapes, and ones with reinforcing fibres, can help to make a package more secure. There are tapes available that are designed for outdoor use and others that are suitable for cold or damp environments.

Some tapes can be pre-printed with a company name, which makes opening and resealing obvious. Tapes can be printed with storage or handling warnings (for example, 'fragile' or 'caution, heavy box' or symbols used in transport handling). Some tapes are colour coded which could indicate the type of contents.

Heat-shrink wrap

Individual boxes or items might benefit from a protective heat-shrink wrap which can seal the product in place.

Pallet wrapping

Pallet wrapping is simply the use of a stretch film (like domestic-use cling film) to completely encase the load to the base of the pallet. The film is overlapped to add strength. The film used can be transparent or coloured (to mask the content or to colour code loads) and comes in a range of different thicknesses and strengths.

Pallet wrapping is often seen as a way of the following.

- Securing the load
- Reducing the impact of a leakage from the wrapped pallet or other pallets
- Reducing the damage from scuffs and bumps
- Giving the pallet load protection against tampering
- Weather protecting the pallet load

Although pallet wrapping can be done manually, there are manual application devices that make wrapping quicker and more effective. There are also semi-automatic and fully automatic platforms with wrapping 'arms' for heavy-use situations.

Strapping

Strapping is often seen in warehouse and store situations. In an office setting it is most often seen securing boxes of printer paper. Polypropylene or polyester are the materials most often used. The wider the strap, the stronger it will be. Using more than one strap and straps for length and width will create a strong brace for the stock. Strapping material comes in a roll and the material is tensioned before being cut and 'welded' to create a tight band. This type of strapping is not reusable.

Metal straps are also available. These often use a 'buckle' or crimped sleeve for securing the strap. Many metal straps are not reusable.

Webbing straps are also available which work like ordinary belts. These can be useful for securing a load.

The straps should not be used to lift the loads as this could cause damage to the stock – strap marks can sometimes be seen on the stock (this problem has also been reported and solved by a furniture importer with additional internal packaging).

Manual strapping devices are available but for regular pallet, box, tote and roll cage strapping either semi-automatic or automatic machines are more effective and faster.

Remember
Packaging should be adequate to protect the contents from damage and to prevent the contents from damaging or harming other products, handlers and the environment.

Apply
If you have access to a 'goods-in' area, take a look at the deliveries there. How are they packaged? What inner packaging has been provided?

Environmental standards for packaging

In principle, use of any materials involves an environmental cost. Some packaging materials use a lot of natural resources and energy to produce. The journey taken by packaging from raw material to manufacturing and then to the initial user also incurs a 'carbon footprint'. The weight of packaging contributes to the fuel usage of vehicles while the volume used can add up to additional journeys or the use of larger vehicles. Finally, the reuse, return, disposal or recycling will also involve addition to the environmental cost.

It is therefore not surprising that there are environmental standards which relate directly to packaging and packaging materials.

Regulations on packaging

These vary widely from country to country. In some countries, specific local problems result in regulations. Examples are easily found relating to food packaging, timber pallets and dangerous goods. Many regulations relate mainly to the safety of the public and some relate much more to disposal implications. Some regulations use taxes to discourage use, but some countries do not invest in reuse or recycling schemes or encourage more use of less 'harmful' packaging.

The diversity of guidelines, regulations and standards means that tracking a product and its packaging through a supply chain becomes an important part of considering the packaging to be used.

In the European Union, the EU Packaging and Packaging Waste Directive requires each member state to enact laws. It is up to member states to comply with or enhance measures to follow the principles, provided these do not restrict trade or freedom of movement of goods. The result should be a uniform approach which improves environmental packaging performance. To create uniformity, the EU has provided packaging regulations which follow a series of definitions and principles.

In the USA, a 'market led' approach dominates, with different federal regulations in place in different states – there are even city-based differences, particularly based around consumer packaging.

Supply chain initiatives

Some supply chains have packaging standards in place. These supply chains are often driven by end-user market situations or environmental expectations and sometimes by taxation or regulation. These initiatives may meet the local requirements of one country but exceed the requirements in another country. It is more likely that a supply chain can meet more requirements if the standard adopted meets 'trading block' or 'regional standards', or even an international standard that is adopted by countries.

International environmental packaging standards

There have been some international packaging standards for many years relating to air, sea, road and rail cargo. These contribute to the safe handling of loads and therefore the avoidance of risk caused by split or spilt loads.

The International Organization for Standardization (ISO) is well known for standards documentation, many of which become adopted by organisations and industries. Some specification-based standards are also adopted in whole or in part by countries and trading blocks. ISO has previously provided test descriptions for the assessment of packaging performance.

ISO published standards relating to environmental packaging standards in 2013, and the latest review (2018) confirmed the standards for another five years.

Some countries appear to be actively promoting the standard on government or government agency websites. Elements of the standards have appeared in local standards for specific products.

ISO objectives were to provide a set of procedures which aim to do the following.[3]

- Reduce environmental impact
- Support innovation in products, packaging and the supply chain
- Avoid undue restrictions on the use of packaging
- Prevent barriers and restrictions to trade

For our purposes, the most relevant here are the following.

- **ISO 18601: General requirements for the use of ISO standards in the field of packaging and the environment**[4]

    This standard specifies requirements and procedures for using the suite of standards. They are applicable to 'a supplier responsible for placing packaging or packaged goods on the market'.

    This concept of supplier responsibility encourages a supply chain approach rather than a 'not my problem' approach.

    This standard introduces the themes of selecting a system of packaging that considers a whole life approach – so 'poor' assessments for reuse, recycling, material recycling, energy recovery and organic recycling may result in a changed packaging system.

- **ISO 18602: Packaging and the environment – Optimization of the packaging system**[5]

  This standard covers the concept that there is an optimum packaging system. In ISO18602 terms, the packaging system covers the following three areas.

  - Primary packaging (the packaging in immediate contact with the product)

  - Secondary or group packaging (the packaging designed to contain one or more primary packaging together with any protective materials)

  - Tertiary, distribution or transport packaging (the packaging of items specifically for distribution or transport)

  The optimum balance in this standard weighs the environmental impact of losses that may happen with no packaging or inadequate packaging against the environmental impact from excess packaging.

  This means that the result of an assessment could be the following.

  - Adding packaging weight or volume

  - Reducing packaging weight or volume

  The standard does not consider the type of packaging as a part of optimisation, only the efficient use of material.

  The standard also includes '... determining the amount and minimization of substances or mixtures hazardous to the environment and determining the amount of four heavy metals (lead, cadmium, mercury, hexavalent chromium) in packaging.'

- **ISO 18603: Packaging and the environment – Reuse**[6]

  This standard 'specifies the requirements for a packaging to be classified as reusable and sets out procedures for assessment of meeting the requirements, including the associated systems'.

  Themes of closed-loop reuse (where the packaging returns to origin or is used between members of an organised group of users) and open-loop reuse (where the packaging is used again between different organisations) are included. Ultimately reuse items will come to their end-of-life, which is covered by the remaining standards.

- **ISO 18604: Packaging and the environment – Material recycling**[7]

  This standard 'specifies the requirements [and assessment procedures] for packaging to be classified as recoverable in the form of material recycling while accommodating the continuing development of both packaging and recovery technologies...'

  The standard uses definitions which clarify expectations of packaging recycling. This includes a broader definition of the recycling process, which excludes energy recovery and fuel use.

- **ISO 18605: Packaging and the environment – Energy recovery**[8]

  This standard 'specifies the requirements [and assessment procedures] for packaging to be classified as recoverable in the form of energy recovery'.

  The standard reflects the interest and practice of burning 'waste' to create hot water, steam or electricity.

- **ISO 18606: Packaging and the environment – Organic recycling**[9]

  This standard uses technical definitions of the processes and expectations of organic recycling. This involves 'biological waste treatment processes applied to used packaging to produce compost (in industrial composting plants) or compost and biogas (in anaerobic digestors).'

  The standard reflects the interest and practice of commercial operators and this is not related to landfill-type operations.

> *Remember*
> Packaging is essential, but adds costs to the supply chain and the choices available can also have a significantly different environmental impact.

The use of automation in warehousing

Automation in warehousing is not new but has a low overall use. As technology changes and becomes more affordable, part or full automation of some warehouse tasks becomes justifiable. Technology can change quickly, but this section will give examples of technology and activities that can be automated, and the methods used rather than the detailed technology used.

Table 1.5 presents a summary of automation technology.

Technology	Description
Warehouse Management System (WMS) software	This is the umbrella phrase used for a wide range of systems available. They form the basis for reporting, alerting, calculating, communicating, decision-making and giving directions to hardware – particularly supplying warehouse automation equipment with locations, load information and timings.
RFID tags (Radio Frequency Identification)	This technology uses radio waves and is described in section 1.2. Since introduction, RFID technology has spread from stand-alone equipment to be integrated with the WMS and other internal and external software.
Bar codes	This technology was outlined in section 1.2. Bar code usage has developed significantly, and it is still used to identify individual items, packages and loads, with more up-to-date applications for warehouse location matching, vehicles, origins, destination and routing instructions.
Handheld devices	A range of handheld devices have been developed – some using mobile phone-type devices and others based around a rugged tablet. Many have either integrated bar code scanners and/or RFID scanners. There are also wireless accessories available, so sensors and hands-free devices are becoming common. Voice activation, audio instructions and even 'gesture commands' are now in use. Most devices are constantly updating and being updated by the WMS.

1.3 L01

Technology	Description
Smart glasses or interacting goggles	These can provide directions to locate or position stock. Being 'line of sight' they can also give instructions by displaying messages.
Automated guided vehicles (AGVs)	These are platforms that follow a route to storage. There are different systems available, some using location tracking to direct the AGVs and some with fixed routes. There are also some equipped with RFID systems which confirm which products are on board and where the stock has been left.
Automatic operation vacuum lifters	It is possible for a vacuum lifter to be programmed for repetitive tasks (for example, loading boxes to and removing boxes from a conveyor). It is also possible for them to have instructions to sort loads.
Automated storage system with stock to picker	Traditional picking is undertaken by the picker finding the stock and picking it. These systems collect the stock, pallet, tote or box and bring them to the operator to select from, before returning the remainder to storage.
Computer-controlled conveyor systems	Computer-controlled conveyors can determine routing for any individual item and move it to the correct area. These use bar code or RFID technology.
Automatic packaging machines	These detect size, weight and type of product, determine the type of packaging, and wrap it. Areas equipped with a high level of automation may have automatic or semi-automatic void fill and box assembly to minimise the box size. Any semi-automated or automated equipment requires specific health and safety procedures and safeguards. Systems are often geared to stop operating following a stop instruction – this can be triggered should an unexpected object (including a person) be detected. It is possible for staff to wear tags which automatically shut off equipment when they are near. Zoning with 'no go' areas is also in use – in some cases access doors are locked and walkways checked before equipment operation.

Table 1.5 Automation technology

The following case studies give more detail on the application of automation and semi-automation.

≪ Case study

Semi-automated process for goods received
In this case, the organisation's objective was to enhance the processes for receipt of goods.

On delivery to the warehouse, goods need to be checked to ensure they are not damaged and are verified

GRN (goods received note)
A document or electronic entry recording that goods have been received by an organisation. This is usually prepared after a visual inspection, although in some organisations formal acceptance testing may be required before the GRN is created

against the packing list supplied. The boxes received are opened in turn on a table with both RFID and bar code scan capabilities. The supplier is selected by the operator from the integrated Warehouse Management Software system.

A **goods received note (GRN)** is created from the operator product scanning and the system compares it to any purchase order on file from the supplier. Any missing items are identified and the GRN is issued electronically back to the supplier. A supplier payment is made or diarised for a later date in accordance with the contract held. Both the order placer and the originator receive text or e-mail messages to confirm goods have been received.

If customers are awaiting deliveries, internal instructions from the system are triggered for order fulfilment.

Apply

This case study features some processes that are 'fully automated' and some that require human activity or intervention.

Complete the following table to check your understanding of the case study and the principles.

Activity	Human activity	Automated activity
Product checking		
Packing list checking		
Missing items notification		
Payment to supplier		
Notification to order placer		

Semi-automated goods storage and retrieval
In this case, the organisation operates a system in a large business-to-business warehouse with up to fifty daily inbound deliveries and thousands of outbound deliveries to customers each week. Deliveries made are either palletised, in boxes, in company reusable boxes or are oversized single items.

- Palletised loads that are single products are moved by hand truck to a pre-storage platform and checked. The electronic GRN is produced and items are added to the WMS. Bar code pallet identifier labels are added to the pallet – these will be readable, so they can be read by scanners in the warehouse. The weight and size are registered by the platform and the system identifies suitable space and racking availability. The pallet is rewrapped for storage. The system takes over and the conveyors will take the pallet to the very high pallet racking. Automated pallet stackers move the pallet to the required position without any human intervention. The pallet can be recalled by entering a request on the system.

- Stock in mixed boxes and pallets are opened and checked. The electronic GRN is produced and items added to the WMS. The items are either placed into empty tote boxes (mostly single items, but mixed item totes are also used) or loaded to pallets and wrapped. The tote boxes already have bar code identifiers – the correct box codes are entered in the WMS to match the inbound products. The tote boxes then enter the tote box automated storage area – the system identifies the eventual location and, if other stock is already held, it will ensure that a different aisle is used, and that earlier stock will be drawn first. Boxes can be recalled by entering a request on the system.

- Company reusable boxes are checked, then moved to totes to enter the tote storage system.

- Oversized items are checked, GRNs created, and placed in open shelving with the aid of access platforms by staff.

For stock issues, a 'stock to picker' concept is used. The system identifies an operator and supplies a purchase order from a customer together with a packing list, packaging labels and copy invoice if appropriate. The system delivers, via conveyor, an empty delivery tote box to the operator. The system directs recovery of a series of stock-filled tote boxes which appear at the picker's workstation.

The instructions to pick the correct volumes are supplied on-screen. The operator picks and confirms the items, closes the box and the box returns to automated storage. At the end of picking the order, the operator closes the delivery tote, confirms completion and the delivery tote moves along the conveyor to packaging. (The conveyor system can track tote identification and computer direction and routing takes place along the conveyor system.) Any pallet-based items or oversized stock is collected to form the full order with the delivery tote box.

Apply

In the above case study, what aspect of the storage system allows mixed boxes and pallets to be placed in storage as this is usually avoided in conventional warehouses?

Picking system guidance and 'smart glasses'

Most WMS systems either have manual entry for operators to identify where stock has been stored or the operator has been directed where to place it by the system. For picking, the system can direct the operator to the correct storage bay. In some cases, this may be simply a route with references to row and shelf. There are systems which indicate directions by arrows on a handheld device or truck-mounted screen – these are a bit like satellite navigation in cars, and if the operator goes the wrong way the system will continue to adjust the route.

Other systems work with 'smart glasses' which 'illuminate' the pathway and indicate the shelf or location required. When stored in the identified place, an operator can confirm storage is complete, or with some other systems, the shelf location 'reports' arrival through RFID or stock movement equipment location sensors.

Ocado: use of AGVs for storage and retrieval of stock

This case study features an online grocery order fulfilment centre and an unusual concept for storage that is very different from a conventional warehouse. This is a 'stock to picker' system with a difference. If you have access to the Internet, you can find descriptions or a video by searching for 'Ocado automated picking'.

The inbound goods are transferred to standard multi-purpose containers and their contents detailed on the system. The stock containers are then picked up by AGVs on a grid from above. The AGVs can move in four directions and have small guides that keep them precisely on the grid. The units have internal power sources that can run at variable speeds which means they can avoid each other using wireless technology and complicated control systems.

The AGVs then move to a vacant stock location (it just needs to be empty as there is little or no zoning apparent) and the box is dropped into the space below. There are multiple vertical slots for boxes beneath the 'surface' of the grid.

The AGVs take the boxes to operator positions – but these are also equipped with robot arms to lift the products, read the bar codes and place the items in delivery boxes.

Case study

> *Apply*
>
> Research automated storage and retrieval systems. If you have access to the Internet, look up 'warehouse automated storage and retrieval system'. As technology progresses, this is a good way to find the latest applications. There are likely to be many videos, which are better than descriptions to capture what these systems can do. Look at three different sources and answer the following.
>
> - What type of activity is shown?
> - What benefits does this automated storage and retrieval system offer to organisations?

Stock maintenance

The integrated WMS can identify stock volumes and values which may be outside expectations. It can prepare outside expectations inspection lists, identifying locations. Routine stock checking can also be managed by the system, with operators directed to count and report in stock numbers – the system can then report differences for investigation.

The system can continuously report changes in demand (in the case of web-based sales, it can also refer to product enquiries and items in 'shopping baskets'). It can predict potential stockouts and overstocks, with perishable goods being flagged if expected demand is less than the 'expiry' date stock held.

If a product is connected to a customer's stock management system (as is the case with many supermarkets and some general retailers) the system may provide recommendations for replacement stock volumes and automated reorders with suppliers.

Packing

Automation and part automation have been successfully introduced to packing, as shown by these different uses of automation.

1. The packer receives the picked order, selects the order number on a panel and is provided with a packing list and a recommendation for packing boxes or packaging. The packer either checks the order using a bar code reader or checks a screen for RFID matching. The packer can go ahead and pack, getting printed labels and moving the parcel(s) on for delivery.

2. It is also possible that the packer can just release the order to an automated packing system which will pack, wrap and label as required.

3. Following packing, an automated system could sort packages by customer (for collection or for aggregation), location, routing or prioritisation. The system can prepare routing instructions against allocated transport or carriers – it can give a transport company the volumes, weights and distances ahead of a collection (this is sometimes referred to as a distribution planning system). A system that also allocates vehicles is part of a distribution resource planning system.

Fixed asset (equipment) control

It is possible to monitor movement and location using RFID technology and for warnings to be given if it moves outside the expected zones.

Making automation choices and decisions

The range of ideas and applications for part and full automation seems to be increasing. The examples show high commitments to efficiency and effectiveness in warehouse operations. Despite this, there are some important considerations prior to investment.

Much depends on the mix of volume and frequency of movement in and out of a warehouse. The nature of the products and the size of the warehouse also affect the scale and type of automation possible.

The following are some typical questions that are raised.

*   What are the volumes of movements of stock seen or expected in a warehouse?
*   What are the costs of these movements in terms of staff costs and equipment costs?
*   What are the alternative automated system costs, in terms of installation, energy use and maintenance?
*   What are the likely gains in terms of efficiency and effectiveness of automating an activity?
*   What are the risks of automation and can these be eliminated or reduced?

Ultimately, it is the 'return on investment' that is often the essential calculation – do the quantifiable savings exceed the cost of investment?

The practical view is that there are often some warehouse activities that could be automated with efficiency and effectiveness gains.

Apply

Many years ago, a household electrical equipment manufacturer wished to make the preparation of retailer deliveries much faster – the picking process was labour intensive but extraction of the items from the racking was quite quick. Creating loads on pallets was time consuming.

It was decided to provide automated stacking of boxes on pallets and automated plastic wrapping. The optical devices installed allowed precise placement and the wrapping system was estimated as at least four times as fast as the previous part-manual equivalent.

*   What were the benefits of this automation?
*   Why do you think the company did not invest in a fully automated picking and order preparation system?

Remember

Automation and semi-automation is designed to enhance efficiency and effectiveness, but each different location and requirements are likely to produce different specific cost and time savings.

Chapter Summary

This chapter has provided much detail regarding both the principles of storage and the decisions that are made to support efficient and effective management of stock.

Organisations will take a different view on locations, size and type of storage facilities depending on their requirements and stocking decisions. This chapter has suggested there are many factors that contribute to these decisions.

The use of product codes and the technologies used reveal a diversity of options and the benefits of working to standards, whether these are industry based, or manufacturer or customer supported. The use of bar codes and RFID devices can significantly improve efficiency and effectiveness.

There is a very wide range of stock handling equipment to choose from – the chapter has outlined the need for safe working. Automation and semi-automation are trends that have improved stock management performance in many organisations.

Recommended reading

CIPS Knowledge Sources: These are CIPS prepared quick guides to themes and are available to members on the CIPS website – there is also a search facility.

- Warehouse Management Systems: www.cips.org/en-gb/knowledge/ procurement-topics-and-skills/operations-management/warehousing1/ warehouse-management-systems-wms/

- Warehousing: www.cips.org/en-gb/knowledge/procurement-topics-and-skills/operations-management/warehousing1/

Other sources:

Logistics Manager Magazine: News and report information regarding different aspects of logistics is available by e-mail; the website is www.logisticsmanager. com/. UK produced but with many international stories carried.

Warehousing Magazine: UK Warehouse Association – UK-based trade association with access to online magazine: www.ukwa.org.uk/category/publications/

Warehouse and Logistics News: Regular news publication with UK-dominated examples: warehousenews.co.uk/

Lysons, K. and Farrington, B. (2016), *Procurement and Supply Chain Management* (9th ed), Harlow: Pearson. Comprehensive compendium of theory and practice featured across many of the CIPS levels.

Richards, G. (2018), *Warehouse Management: A Complete Guide to Improving Efficiency and Minimizing Costs in the Modern Warehouse* (3rd ed), London: Kogan Page. Dedicated overview of warehouse operations including technology updates.

End of Chapter Assessment

IDENTIFY

1 Which of the following best summarises the operations of a warehouse?

a) To maintain high stock volumes at all times and to ensure stock is always available when required by customers

b) To ensure stock held is accurately recorded and correct any errors found

c) To safely and securely maintain a storage facility in alignment with an organisation's objectives

d) To maintain a minimum stock level in the cheapest location in order to reduce the costs of operation

IDENTIFY

2 An organisation may choose a 'local warehouse structure'. Which of the following situations does this fit?

a) Where the organisation needs immediate stock availability close to customers

b) Where the organisation requires a solution with the lowest total volume of stock

c) Where the organisation would benefit from automation

d) Where the organisation wishes to reduce 'out of stock' situations from additional demand

IDENTIFY

3 Which of the following summarises the main methods used to base decisions about storage facilities and locations?

a) Cost per square metre, size of premises, locations of customers and suppliers

b) A qualitative and quantitative analysis of requirements and option comparisons

c) Competitor analysis, detailing locations and costs with the objective of matching

d) A systematic review of all stock held and cost per order trend calculations

IDENTIFY

4 Which of the following statements relating to warehouses is true?

a) Multiple floor structures allow more flexible layouts compared to single floor structures

b) It is important to maximise the amount of daylight entering a warehouse

c) It is important to ensure that all stock is arranged by product code to improve efficiency

d) Single floor structures allow for greater use of stock handling equipment

5 Which of the following explains the role of 'docks' in a warehouse layout?   IDENTIFY

  a) They provide an area for staff which is safe from forklift operations

  b) They provide space for items that are awaiting checking and entering stock

  c) They provide easy access to load and unload vehicles

  d) They provide room for packing and unpacking goods

6 Which of the following statements relating to warehouses is true?   IDENTIFY

  a) Kitting is the preparation of a range of products into sets ready for use

  b) Mezzanine floors should only be used for forklift operations

  c) Picking lists are always arranged in product order number

  d) A U-shaped layout offers the most efficient storage and retrieval of stock

7 Which of the following statements is true?   IDENTIFY

  a) More warehouses reduce the total cost of storage

  b) Fewer warehouses reduce the transport time to customers

  c) The total cost of storage includes the total warehouse costs and the total transport costs

  d) The highest total cost of storage occurs when only one warehouse is used

8 Which of the following statements relating to product coding is true?   IDENTIFY

  a) Product codes are unique and comply with international standards

  b) Check digits are used to validate product codes

  c) RFID tags can only be read when in range of a gateway or reader

  d) Bar codes should only be used on items for sale in retail shops

9 Which of the following defines the 'optimisation of the packaging system' according to ISO18602?   IDENTIFY

  a) The efficient use of material to avoid product damage and excess packaging

  b) Maximum use of recycled cardboard in outer cases and void filling

  c) Labelling of all parts that may be recycled with the correct international symbols

  d) The process of tracking the environmental impact of all packaging materials

10 Which of the following is the term used on packaging for the weight of a consignment without the packaging?   IDENTIFY

  a) Gross weight   c) Base weight

  b) Tare weight   d) Net weight

IDENTIFY

11 Which of the following statements relating to materials handling equipment is correct?

a) Reach trucks are designed to operate in narrower aisles than counterbalanced forklifts

b) Conveyor belts can only operate in straight lines

c) Dollies are parts of a forklift that support the forks when lifted

d) Roll cages are used for inverting drums to help unloading

References

1 Gue, K. R. and Meller, R. D. (2009), "Aisle configurations for unit-load warehouses", *IIE transactions*, Volume 41, pp. 171–82

2 United Nations (2015), *Recommendations on the transport of dangerous goods* [online]. Retrieved from: www.unece.org/fileadmin/DAM/trans/danger/publi/unrec/rev19/Rev19e_Vol_I.pdf [Accessed on: 7 March 2019]

3 ISO (2013), *Packaging and the environment – General requirements for the use of ISO standards in the field of packaging and the environment* [online]. Retrieved from: www.iso.org/obp/ui/#iso:std:iso:18601:ed-1:v1:en [Accessed: January 2019]

4 Ibid.

5 ISO (2013), *Packaging and the environment – Optimization of the packaging system* [online]. Retrieved from: www.iso.org/obp/ui/#iso:std:iso:18602:ed-1:v1:en [Accessed on: 8 March 2019]

6 ISO (2013), *Packaging and the environment – Reuse* [online]. Retrieved from: www.iso.org/obp/ui/#iso:std:iso:18603:ed-1:v1:en [Accessed on: 8 March 2019]

7 ISO (2013), *Packaging and the environment – Material recycling* [online]. Retrieved from: www.iso.org/obp/ui/#iso:std:iso:18604:ed-1:v1:en [Accessed on: 8 March 2019]

8 ISO (2013), *Packaging and the environment – Energy recovery* [online]. Retrieved from: www.iso.org/obp/ui/#iso:std:iso:18605:ed-1:v1:en [Accessed on: 8 March 2019]

9 ISO (2013), *Packaging and the environment – Organic recycling* [online]. Retrieved from: www.iso.org/obp/ui/#iso:std:iso:18606:ed-1:v1:en [Accessed on: 8 March 2019]

CHAPTER 2
Understand the key elements of effective inventory control

Learning outcome

By the end of this chapter you will understand the key elements of effective inventory control.

Chapter overview

2.1 Differentiate between the different classifications of inventory

You will understand:

- Opening stock, work in progress, safety stock and finished goods
- Obsolescent and redundant stock
- Direct and indirect supplies
- ABC classifications of stock that may apply
- Dependent demand and independent demand items of stock

2.2 Identify the direct and indirect costs of holding inventory

You will understand:

- Acquisition costs
- Holding costs
- Cost of stockouts
- Options to reduce costs while mitigating any negative impact on service levels

2.3 Identify techniques associated with inventory control

You will understand:

- Subjective and objective forecasting
- Reorder quantities and levels
- MRP and MRPII
- ERP
- Just in time
- Lean
- Inventory performance measures – lead times, service levels, rate of stock turn, stockouts in a given period, stock cover

Introduction

In this chapter you will learn about how inventory is controlled. The terms 'inventory' and 'stock' are used interchangeably. As seen in chapter 1, both terms refer to the goods and materials that are held by a business with the ultimate purpose of being sold, incorporated into goods or services to be sold, or used in the general operation of the business.

In the first section, the different ways of classifying inventory will be looked at. Then both the financial and service-delivery implications of holding stock and why stock levels need to be managed will be considered. Finally, having understood what stock is and why it needs to be managed, in the third section various methods of doing so and how performance is measured will be looked at.

2.1 Differentiate between the different classifications of inventory

There are a number of ways that the stock held by a business can be categorised or classified. The key distinctions usually made are the following.

- Opening stock, work in progress, safety stock and finished goods
- Obsolescent and redundant stock
- Direct and indirect supplies
- ABC classifications of stock that may apply
- Dependent demand and independent demand items of stock

Opening stock

Opening stock is the starting amount of inventory that a business has at a fixed moment in time. This could be the start of a financial year, another reporting period or ad hoc **stocktake**. The concept of opening stock must not be confused with raw materials.

Opening stock could be raw materials at the start of the manufacturing process, but equally could be items in a store which are completed and ready for despatch – **finished goods** – or it could be somewhere between the two – known as **work in progress (WIP)**.

The concepts of 'opening stock' and 'closing stock' are, essentially, accounting definitions. They are used to assess how much inventory is being held either as physical stock or in value terms. Finished goods obviously have a higher value than raw materials.

Closing stock is the inventory held at the end of the period under consideration. Thus, the closing stock of one period is automatically the opening stock for the next. There is no gap between stock accounting periods. It is much like a bank balance. The closing balance on one statement is the opening balance on the next.

Determining how much inventory is held, or the value of it, is known as stocktaking. Traditionally a stocktake would occur at the start/end of the

Opening stock
The inventory held at the start of an accounting period

Stocktake
An audit check of the stock physically held; this may be by amount or value, or both

Finished goods
Products ready for sale and/or use

Work in progress (WIP)
In inventory management the expression relates to stock part-way through a manufacturing process; in the services sectors the term is also used for anything between order and delivery

Closing stock
The inventory held at the end of an accounting period; becomes the opening stock for the next period

accounting period, whether that was the financial year or every quarter. A stocktake could be implemented for other purposes, for example, on a random basis as a means of checking for suspected fraud or theft, or for a valuation of the company prior to the transfer of ownership.

With modern inventory control techniques (see section 2.3), stocktaking occurs on an almost continual basis. Nevertheless, the concepts of opening and closing stock are still valid; the electronic monitoring of stock simply means that it is far easier to ascertain what those are. Physical stocktakes may still be used where theft or fraud is suspected or where there are indications of errors in the electronic data processing.

> *Remember*
> Opening stock and closing stock are accounting terms. They relate to the amount or value of inventory at a point in time.

Raw materials, work in progress (WIP) and finished goods

Another way of classifying stock is to look at what is physically held and where it sits in the production process. The normal breakdown in a manufacturing situation would be raw materials, components, work in progress and finished goods.

Raw materials (or primary materials) are the basic materials from which a product is made. They have generally had very little, if any, processing from their naturally occurring state. They include things like timber, metals, minerals etc.

Secondary **components** are processed or part-assembled pieces which go into making the finished product. For example, an exhaust system is a component of a motor vehicle. From an inventory perspective, a component is something which is bought in a part-assembled state specifically in order for it to be incorporated into the larger finished article.

Work in progress (WIP) is stock that is being processed – converted from raw material/component to finished article – and has not yet had the final manufacturing process completed. WIP can be at various stages in the manufacturing process, depending on how many processing operations are required. Managing the flow of WIP is very important as if mistakes are made in processing or the sequence of operations is not followed fewer finished goods will be produced for a given amount of input.

Finished goods are, as the name suggests, products which have been converted from raw materials and (sometimes) components, through the manufacturing operations (WIP) into a finished item. These can be sold directly to the end customer or be held in stock ready to be used.

The value of stock increases as it goes through this process, with finished goods being the most expensive. This is known as the value chain as shown in figure 2.1.

Raw materials
The basic inputs to manufacturing a product, usually unprocessed or having had very little pre-processing, for example: metals, minerals, timber, fibres

Components
Manufactured items bought in to include in a larger final product, for example, exhaust systems for vehicles

Figure 2.1 Types of stock in relation to production process

Considerations at each stage of the production process

Why do we need to think about the production process when considering inventory management? Does it matter how much stock is held at each point in the production process?

The detail of the costs of inventory will be looked at in detail in section 2.2 and methods for managing inventory in section 2.3. In the most simple terms: how much of each type of stock (raw materials, components, WIP and finished goods) is held has to be balanced. The factory or processing plant has limited space for holding inventory, as its main activities are manufacturing and processing. Space therefore has to be allocated across the various types of stockholding.

How much stock needs to be held at each stage depends on many factors, which will be examined in later sections. The basic points in summary here, however, are the following.

- There must be sufficient raw materials and components stock to ensure that the production can be kept running at its optimal efficiency level without disruptions or downtime.

- Work in progress should be literally 'in progress' – that is it should not be sitting waiting for orders or waiting for blockages in the later processes to be cleared. An efficient production process will, by definition, reduce WIP to optimal levels.

- Finished goods inventory is the most valuable and needs to be the most protected in terms of storage conditions and insurance. It needs to be sufficient to meet normal order volumes in order to maintain customer service.

Depending on the nature of the goods, there may be a need to plan for unexpected influences, such as unseasonable weather or shortages from other suppliers which might increase demand. At the same time, holding stock for too long also has its risks.

- Redundancy and obsolescence (see below)
- Overstocking can cause backlogs in the production process making for inefficient use of factory space and equipment

Safety stock

Finally, when looking at inventory in relation to the production process we need to think about safety stock (also known as buffer stock). This is stock in excess of what is expected to be needed.

One purpose is to prevent disruptions to work in progress affecting the amount of finished goods inventory on hand. A buffer of WIP stock can be installed at any stage of the processing, allowing for production to continue by using the safety or buffer stock until the problem is resolved. Safety/buffer stock in finished goods allows for unpredicted or unscheduled demand.

Holding safety stock reduces the risks of stockouts, when the organisation is unable to meet an order or continue production due to lack of finished goods or input materials. The level of safety stock to be held is calculated allowing for restocking times, unseasonal demands or disruptions in the supply chain.

There are disadvantages in holding too much safety stock (see 'holding costs' in section 2.2 and 'just in time' and 'Lean' in section 2.3). The costs of holding the

Redundancy
The state of being no longer needed or surplus to requirements

Obsolescence
The process of becoming outdated

Safety stock (buffer stock)
Stock held as a contingency or insurance against disruption or unexpected demand

Stockout
Having no or insufficient materials to continue production or the finished goods to meet an order

stock must be taken into account, as does the possibility of having too much working capital tied up in high-value stock.

In thinking about the costs of stockholding, however, it is useful to firstly grasp the 'value' of the stock being held. This naturally varies depending on the type of the stock. When making stock-management decisions it will be necessary to consider both absolute values (in monetary terms) but also relative values (between different inventory types – which is the more valuable to be held?).

Table 2.1 summarises types of stock and gives an overview of how the relative value might be assessed.

Type of stock	Description	Value
Opening stock	The amount of stock at the beginning of an accounting period	Depends on physical nature of the stock held – raw material, components, WIP or finished goods
Raw materials	Basic input materials – only limited prior processing or none	Acquisition cost, lowest value of stock held
Secondary components	Products that are combined with others to produce the finished goods, acquired in the processed state	Higher than raw materials, but still at acquisition cost
Work in progress	Stock part-way through manufacture that has not been finished	Not completed – so not full value – but costs of processing already carried out makes it more valuable than materials and components
Finished goods	Goods which are completed and ready to be used or sold	Finished goods are the most expensive and need to be stored in good conditions
Safety or buffer stock	Stock, WIP or finished stock that is kept as a buffer to smooth out any disruptions or unexpected demand	Depends on where in the process the buffer is held. If safety stock does not act as a buffer it could affect the production throughput and the sales of finished goods
Stockout	Running out of inventory	Lost sale and equipment downtime

Table 2.1 Types of stock in relation to production process

Remember
Safety stock is a kind of insurance; it is stock held to manage unexpected situations either in relation to disrupted production or unexpected demand. There may be various batches of buffer/safety stock at different stages of the production process.

Check
What is the difference between opening stock and raw materials?

Apply
Work-in-progress stock items are relatively easy to identify in a manufacturing business but more difficult in a service provider organisation. Think about a training provider – what might they be holding that could be considered work-in-progress? How does it compare with a manufacturing situation?

Hint: think about stock levels, ability to rework and potential for writing off the costs.

Obsolescent and redundant stock

Most stock is useful and valuable. However, there are two types of stockholdings which are to be avoided as much as possible. These are obsolescent and redundant stockholdings.

Definitions

The words 'obsolete' and 'redundant' are often misused in ways which can lead people to think they mean the same thing. In fact they are very different. It is useful therefore to start with some dictionary definitions.

The *Oxford English Dictionary* states that 'obsolete' means 'no longer used or practised; outmoded, out of date' and 'obsolescence' is 'the process or fact of becoming obsolete or outdated, or of falling into disuse'. 'Redundant', on the other hand, means 'superfluous, excessive; surplus; unnecessary'.[1]

Relating the definitions to stock

Obsolescent stock therefore is stock, usually finished goods, which is in good condition and satisfactory working order but for which demand is irreversibly falling towards zero. Once this demand reaches zero the stock can be considered 'obsolete'. It cannot be used or sold in its current state. Food ingredients which are out of date are another example.

It is essentially worthless in monetary terms unless it can be reworked or converted into another saleable product. An example might be upgrading an outdated smartphone to another one with additional capacity, or dismantling the product to reclaim the raw materials, for example, extracting the copper and gold from electronic equipment. Whether either option (reworking or reclamation) is viable will depend on the complexity and cost of the process involved. In other words, would the net gain be worth the effort?

2.1 **LO2**

An important point to remember about obsolescent and obsolete stock is that it is, to all practical purposes, a permanent condition. It is extremely rare for something which has become obsolete to find a new lease of life. It *can* happen through fashions in the marketplace. Vinyl records have for a long time been considered near-obsolete but recently there is a resurgence of interest. In general though, for obsolete goods to become valuable again, it would take a significant technological or cultural shift which made their replacement no longer viable. The timescales for these kinds of changes are very long – too long for any business to simply hold on to the stock and 'wait it out'.

As has been hinted under the definitions, redundant stock is not the same as obsolescent stock. Not only is it in good condition and satisfactory working order, but it is also still being used somewhere by someone.

Redundant stock can be used; there is a potential demand for it, just not from the current or intended user. It can be redirected to other users in its current form. It can be thought of as 'over-supply' in its current location.

Case study

Obsolescent or redundant?
An example of obsolescent stock is black-and-white televisions (or indeed cathode ray tube televisions). They may work perfectly well as designed, but the specification in the market has changed. There simply is no demand for the product. The lack of demand is so unlikely to reverse that it can be considered permanent.

An example of redundant stock is the supply of polystyrene package fillers, when the organisation has opted to change to paper fillers, for either environmental or cost reasons. The polystyrene nuggets can still be used by another business. It does not need to be reworked for a different customer or supply chain channel.

Remember
Obsolescent stock is heading towards a position where there will be no demand for it at all. Redundant stock is still marketable, but is not needed by the company that currently owns it.

Impacts and costs of obsolescent and redundant stock

Organisations need to avoid holding redundant or obsolescent stock. The most obvious reason for this is that storage space should not be used to hold things with limited, diminishing, or negative value.

Holding stock costs money: warehouse space, insurance and security all have a revenue cost (an ongoing financial outlay) attached to them.

There is also the stock-auditing cost of repeatedly counting the same goods.

Working capital
A company's current assets minus its current liabilities; a measure of a company's ability to cover its short-term debts

Written off / to write-off
In relation to costs: accepting that they cannot be recouped (for example, through sale of the asset purchased); in relation to debts: accepting that they will not be paid; taking a potential 'asset' and marking its value down to zero in the accounts

Obsolete stock will cost money and resource to be removed, whether by turning it into something else or recycling whatever can be reclaimed in the way of raw materials or even simple scrappage to landfill (transport, fees, taxes). If none of this can be recouped through rework or raw material reclamation, the stock has a negative value.

There is also the 'opportunity cost' of the wasted factory capacity, raw material and processing time, that is the value that could have been derived from those things had they been better deployed.

How does this feed through to the company balance sheet? What are the real financial impacts of holding obsolescent or redundant stock? **Working capital** is the lifeline of any business. It is never good practice to have too much cash tied up in stock. If that stock is in demand and turned over quickly, there is less of a sound rationale for the investment – sales and revenue keep flowing – but if stock is not moving and is unlikely to move then the monetary value has to be reconsidered.

For redundant stock, the value may need to be discounted to allow for the additional storage costs prior to disposal – or for a literal discounting of the sales value to enable a quick disposal. For obsolescent or obsolete stock, the likelihood is that its value will need to be **written off** (i.e. accounted for as zero) in the balance sheet.

This does not just reduce the asset value and working capital available for the business to use, but naturally also undermines any *projections* on profits which can have knock-on effects on inward investment and/or share price.

> *Remember*
> Both obsolescent and redundant stock cost the organisation money each day they are held. There are direct revenue costs and the capital value is also diminishing.

Causes of obsolescence and redundancy and how to avoid them

Section 2.3 considers techniques for managing inventory, including ways of reducing unwanted stock. The following is an overview of the causes of obsolescence and how to avoid them.

Causes of obsolescence

Obsolescence is a function of market development. The obsolescence itself is largely beyond the control of individual organisations. The main causes are the following.

- **Technological change:** new products offering more or better functionality, for example, in computing, medicine or in everyday objects, such as televisions, or private vehicles.

- **Cultural change:** previously normal practice becoming unacceptable, for example, in energy generation or minerals or fossil fuels extraction where the negative environmental impacts become more important, or cigarettes where the product itself becomes increasingly frowned upon.

- **Legislation:** it is important enough for certain products to be banned for being dangerous. Creating smokeless zones in urban areas which banned the use of coal, or banning dangerous pesticides from being used in the agriculture sector.

2.1 L02

Causes of redundancy

Redundancy is a function of organisational change and/or weaknesses in organisational management. It is largely within the control of the individual business. The main causes are the following.

- Poor forecasting of demand
- Weak customer relationships leading to cancelled orders. Orders may also be cancelled for other reasons well outside the supplier's control
- Overstocking/poor stock control
- Change in internal policy, for example, moving to more eco-friendly products or packaging, or deciding to discontinue a given product, in a rapid and uncontrolled manner

Ways to avoid redundant or obsolete stock

Despite the difference between them, the means of avoiding having obsolescent or redundant stock are essentially the same and include the following.

- Good market knowledge and accurate forecasting
- Good stock-control techniques, including regular stock audits to identify slower-moving stock
- Good inter-departmental communication so that the impacts of policy changes can be identified in good time and accommodated by running down stocks prior to changes being made or allowing for a phasing in of the change
- Just in time supply chains
- Reduced batch sizes in production
- Good sales and operating planning (S&OP)

The first three of these go towards identifying the specific issues as early as possible and planning accordingly. The remaining three assist in reducing stock levels overall and so also the levels of redundant or obsolescent stock.

How to deal with redundant or obsolescent stock

If the planning and mitigation measures fail and redundant or obsolete stock is identified, as such, it needs to be removed from the current inventory location as quickly as possible.

Redundant stock could be sold on to another client (or depending on the nature of the stock another producer). This might be at less than book value but would still recover some of the potential losses.

Where obsolescence is identified early, discounting prices can help sales. Again this will yield lower than expected returns, but the viability of taking this approach should also factor in the gains from freeing up warehouse space and the even higher costs if the stock is still held at the point at which it becomes truly obsolete.

It may be possible to rework some obsolescent/obsolete stock in-house to produce saleable items or some value could be gained by selling the finished goods off for scrap if the raw materials can be extracted and recycled. In both cases this will depend on the technical ease and therefore costs of being able to do so. Some products, such as PVC, are difficult to recycle and it may not be cost efficient to try to do so. These are unlikely to have even scrap value. The worst-case scenario is disposal to landfill, which is inadvisable if it can be avoided, both from the environmental point of view and the financial costs of such disposal.

Just in time
A production methodology pioneered by Toyota where stock is acquired literally 'just in time' to be incorporated into the production process. It is a means of reducing stockholdings and reducing waste in production systems

Book value
The notional value of stock as set down in a company's accounts; it is an estimate of value which may or may not be achieved or may indeed be exceeded

Remember
Remember obsolescence is a process and it takes time.

Summary

The key features of obsolescent and redundant stock are summarised in table 2.2.

Type of stock	Causes	Options when identified
Obsolescent: still in good order, but demand is diminishing and will fall to zero	Technological, legislative and cultural change	Discount for quick sale; rework; sell for scrap; dispose to landfill
Redundant: still in good order, no demand internally or from identified customer but still demand in the marketplace	Poor forecasting; cancelled orders; poor stock management; changes in internal policies	Sell, potentially at discounted price
Summary of costs associated with both obsolescent and redundant stock		

- The loss of manufacturing capacity
- The stockholding costs – warehouse space, insurance, security, auditing
- Loss of profit on unsold products
- Wasted inputs (raw materials)
- The loss of working capital
- Disposal costs, especially if to landfill

Table 2.2 Summary of key features of obsolescent and redundant stock

Remember
Good market knowledge and detailed planning is the key to avoiding obsolescent and redundant stock.

Check
What is the difference between obsolescent stock, obsolete stock and redundant stock?

Apply
Think about your own organisation (or another organisation with which you are familiar). Can you identify any stock being held that is either redundant or obsolescent? If so, try to find out whether the organisation has a plan for dealing with it.

Direct and indirect supplies

A further way of categorising supplies (whether held as stock or being used immediately) is by their function.

Direct supplies are those which are directly incorporated into the finished product. They could be raw materials or components, but they are processed into the goods for sale. Note that these products/goods may themselves be components which are sold to a manufacturer of a more complex product; they are not necessarily completed consumer goods going directly to the end user.

Indirect supplies are different in that they are not incorporated into a product that will be sold to a customer. These are the supplies required to keep the business functioning and the factory operating. They are the products used or consumed in turning the direct supplies into finished stock.

Indirect supplies can be anything from machinery spares, tools, oils and lubricants to protective clothing to sanitary consumables to back-office equipment and supplies, such as ICT or stationery.

It easy to understand back-office stock and supplies as being indirect, but it can be less clear when thinking about a manufacturer's production floor. A potential point of confusion is that what might be a 'direct supply' for one manufacturer becomes indirect for another.

For example, think of a car assembly plant. The engine and its components are direct supplies: they form part of the finished product. The tooling and assembly robots used to assemble the car are indirect supplies; they are not a saleable product, from the perspective of the car factory. Note that these classifications are from the point of view of the business concerned. Naturally for the supplier the robots are a finished product, so from *their* perspective anything that goes to make the robot is a direct supply, but for the car assembly plant anything relating to the robots is indirect.

The supply chains for direct and indirect supplies can be different and the inventory strategy needs to reflect this.

Generally, compared to indirect supplies, direct supplies have the following.

- A higher overall value, as a greater quantity is used

- Less variety of parts compared with **MRO inventory**

- Quicker turnover (sometimes expressed as '**higher stock turn**')

> *Remember*
> Direct supplies are those items which are 'directly' incorporated into the finished product which will be sold on (even if that product then becomes 'indirect' for the firm that purchases it). Indirect supplies are those which are not incorporated into finished products but are needed to keep the business running.

ABC classifications of stock

ABC classifications are applied to stock and its management is based loosely on the **Pareto principle**, better known as the **80/20 rule**.

Direct supplies
Supplies that are integrated into the finished product

Indirect supplies
Supplies not incorporated in the finished product but which keep the business and factory operating

Inventory strategy
The overall approach to how stock is managed, including order points, quantities and values, physical placement of stock etc.

MRO inventory
Maintenance, repair and operations inventory; includes, for example, items such as cleaning equipment or office supplies

Stock turn/stock turnover (high or low)
How many times stock or inventory is being used/sold and purchased/replenished over a given time period

Pareto principle (the 80/20 rule)
The theory that 80% of outcomes result from 20% of inputs, for example, 80% of sales are to the top 20% of customers; 80% of spend on inventory is accounted for by the top 20% of stock items

Pareto was a nineteenth-century Italian economist who noted that 80% of the land in Italy was owned by 20% of the population. The concept was expanded by management consultant Joseph M. Juran who found that roughly 80% of quality problems result from 20% of potential causes. The concept continues to be expanded. For example, it is now a generally accepted belief within sales and marketing – though not necessarily proven – that 80% of sales come from 20% of clients.

In the realm of inventory management, the Pareto principle implies that 80% of stock value will be held in 20% of the items commonly held as stock items.

Establishing an ABC classification in practice

In a manufacturing plant – whether it is producing cars, or telephones, or fridges, or pre-fabricated buildings – the same principles apply.

Car assembly plants are usually used as examples because most people are familiar with what goes into a car and because the automotive industry has led the field in applying the relevant principles for decades.

The Pareto analysis then works as follows.

1. Give each stock item a code or 'part' number.

2. Identify the frequency of use for each 'part' during a given period (such as a month, or a quarter).

3. Identify the value of each 'part' – at the simplest level the value of a part is the cost of having acquired it, but for work-in-progress parts the input costs of the part-processing need to be accounted for.

4. Multiply the frequency of use during your given period by the value of each part to give a 'cumulative value per period' figure (for example, $ per month).

5. Plot each part number on a graph in descending order of the cumulative value on the X-axis and the total cumulative value of all parts per period on the Y-axis. This will produce a Pareto-curve, which mapping the X- and Y-axis meeting points will likely show that 80% of the stock value is tied up in 20% of the stock parts (as measured by part numbers). This is Category A stock.

Remember
Remember that this is about types of stock not volumes. The point of the analysis is to determine sensible volumes of each type.

Tail spend
Spend that is not actively managed; it is a small proportion of total spend (10–20% under each spend category) but has a large number of suppliers accounting for it

It will likely also show that the next 30% of part numbers account for 15% of part stock value – Category B – with the remaining 50% – Category C – covering only 5% of value (commonly known as **tail spend**.)

These outcomes are summarised in table 2.3 and figure 2.2.

Inventory type by part numbers and value		
Inventory type	**Percentage of part numbers**	**Percentage of total costs**
A	20%	80%
B	30%	15%
C	50%	5%

Table 2.3 The 80/20 rule applied to stock part numbers

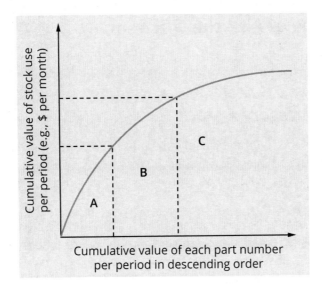

Figure 2.2 Graphical representation of the Pareto principle in ABC categorisation of stock (Source: adapted from www.simmssoftware.com/wordpress/?p=2295)

The values and usages need to be determined over a typical cycle period, which could be a year or more, to allow for any seasonal demands to be smoothed.

Case study

Seasonal demand
Many products have variation during a year: clothing has weather-related peaks; confectionery has highs at Christmas and Easter; domestic vehicles in the UK have peaks around the dates of the new registration numbers coming into effect. Other products might have more infrequent peaks: for example, ribbon and rosette manufacturers in the UK and the USA have peaks associated with election campaigns; similar effects are associated with major sporting events, such as the Olympics and the FIFA World Cup.

If stock movements are linear then three months of data could be sufficient.

It should be remembered that the figures quoted in this section are 'typical' or 'averages'. They will vary from industry to industry and organisation, but the principles remain the same.

Part of the role of the inventory manager and the procurement professionals working with them is to understand the exact boundaries between Categories A, B and C. For example, the 80/20 and 15/30 (A to B split) might turn out to be 75/20 and 20/30 for a particular organisation. The better the data, the better the implications of categorisation can be managed. The beauty of adapting the Pareto principle is that it can be used as starting point in the absence of fully forensic data analysis of all stock items. It can be assumed that the top 20% are where the initial focus needs to be.

Check
What is the Pareto principle (or 80/20) rule? How does it apply to defining ABC categories of stock?

Implications of ABC classification

The purpose of classifying stock in this way is to differentiate on how these parts are managed.

Managing Category A stock

Category A items are the most closely managed and controlled (with daily actions). They constitute the smallest in number of stock items (20%) but the largest in value (80%). Using the example of a family car, a Category A part number might be the engine.

Having a small number of parts classified as A allows for greater visibility of stock turnover. It is easier to focus on a smaller number of items so these high-value parts can be more closely managed. We will look at exactly how this is done using the scheduling techniques described later in the chapter.

Stockouts of any part, large or small, high or low value, can stop a whole production line. However, with high-value, high-cost parts a very fine balance is needed between having too much buffer stock tying up valuable working capital, and ensuring production keeps running. This has been the driving force behind Lean manufacturing pioneered and perfected in the automotive industry over many decades. It has also been behind the development of widely used enterprise resource planning (ERP) tools. Lean and ERP will both be examined in detail in section 2.3. Both approaches are designed to balance the equation of no stockouts with little or no excessive inventory.

When looking to optimise the stock value and turnover time of Category A parts, remember that they represent 80% of the value: four times as much as the rest of Categories B and C combined.

Having good stock control, adjusting demand for any seasonal variations, having responsive and agile suppliers all are necessary to keep production facilities working while ensuring that capital is not tied up in warehouses full of Category A stock.

Managing Category B stock

Category B items require less attention with weekly or monthly checks.

These are the medium-value items accounting for 15% of the total value and on average about 30% of the total number of parts. Compare this with Category A: one and half times as many stock items (30% against 20%), but with less than a quarter of the value (15% against 80%).

Consider the family car example again. Category B parts might include the body panels. These are still a valuable stock item with a large number to manage. Tight control and tracking is still important, but balancing the risk of stockout against using buffer stock here is less of a financial challenge, as the stock value of type B products are less than a quarter of type A.

Holding buffer stock is easier to justify since it ties up less working capital.

It is important to remember that while the stock value may not be high, the size and delicate handling required of some stock items needs to be factored in to stock profiling.

Stock profile
The description of stock items in terms of value, rate of turnover, storage characteristics etc.

The car body panels and glass windscreens are both large in size, taking up a lot of storage space and can be easily damaged or broken. They may need special dedicated storage racks, which suggests reducing the level of buffer stock held even if the simple ABC categorisation suggests it can be increased.

This is a clear illustration as to why none of the stock categorisation or stock profiling methods should be used in isolation. Inventory management is a specialism in itself. Setting specialist storage requirements aside, however, Category B parts need less tight controls than Category A items, due to the lower value.

2.1 LO2

Managing Category C stock

Category C items are usually ordered as required, with frequent orders and often large batch sizes. These are low-value items making up 5% of the total value, but 50% of the total part number count.

Use the family car example again. Category C parts include the bolts, nuts and other fasteners holding the car together. All of these parts are necessary for the functioning of the car and – just as with Category A and Category B parts – not having any one of them would stop a production line.

The difference here is the complexity of the number of parts to be managed, compared with types A and B and their significantly lower value. This lower value means less working capital will be tied up in stock if larger quantities are held as 'safety' or 'buffer' stock. It is therefore more acceptable to hold such stocks.

Monitoring and controlling such a large amount of part numbers of low value, needs a different approach. Having a simple stock reordering system, using a minimum stock level with a larger ordering quantity, is one of the most appropriate ones to use.

Alternatively this 'tail end spend' could be outsourced to one supplier to manage and co-ordinate on your behalf.

> *Remember*
> Category A stock has the lowest number of items, but the highest value – it needs the greatest input of stock-management resource.
>
> Category B stock is medium number and middle value – it needs direct focus but far less resource input than Category A.
>
> Category C stock will have a large number of items, but account for little capital investment. This is 'tail end spend'. In proportionate terms it is low value and requires limited stock control. It should not be ignored however as the figures may still be significant. Outsourcing management of this spend can be cost effective.

Dependent demand and independent demand items of stock

This section discusses dependent and independent demand items of stock, the differences between them, how to manage the stock and the approach needed.

Yet one more way of classifying stock is based on how frequently it will be needed. This feeds into stock turnover rates (or 'stock turn'), that is the frequency with which old stock needs to be replaced with new stock to ensure that the supply continues to flow out to customers (in the case of finished goods) or to production (in the case of WIP stock or indirect stock).

Clearly if stock is not replenished at the appropriate rates production will be halted and/or orders will not be delivered on time. Later sections will investigate

Dependent demand
The requirement for a stock item which is directly related to and therefore dependent upon the rate of production (examples are: raw materials, components, energy)

Independent demand
The requirement for a stock item which is not directly related to, and is therefore independent of, the rate of production (examples are: machinery spares, office equipment and consumables)

methods for managing stock turnover more fully. The following introduces the concepts of **dependent demand** and **independent demand** as they relate to stock items.

The number of products required is determined by estimated customer demand. That demand will normally be a combination of firm orders and estimates based on past performance. It will be affected by seasonal factors, sales initiatives and market competition. In a sense the demand for the final product is 'independent' to the extent that it is outside of the production process.

The stock of finished goods needs to be held at a level which will meet estimated order level, but it is clearly a demand level which is only partially within the control of the organisation to predict.

Imagine any factory production line: at every point along it, something is added, from the very first raw materials to sub-assemblies and completed components until the finished article is completed.

If the demand for the completed article (whether it is a computer, a motor car or a handbag) is determined by how many customers have either ordered the item or are estimated to be likely to do so within a relatively short timeframe, then logically the demand for the inputs to production – that is the stock of raw materials and components – is also directly dependent on that same variable: the number of real plus estimated orders.

By contrast 'independent demand' stock items are those for which the turnover rate is not directly correlated with the production rate, or the order rate. After reading the previous sections it should be clear that most indirect supplies will fall into this category. The number of hard hats or overalls an organisation will require has no direct relationship to the rate of production. Clearly if more staff need to be employed to accommodate extra turnover (or conversely if staff are laid off during lean times) there will be a related shift – but within normal operational parameters customer demand does not have an impact.

Likewise, the call on spare parts for equipment may increase with the degree to which they are being used, but it is an unpredictable relationship and not one that can be directly correlated with output demand. Some machines will function better at higher output rates than others.

Therefore, most indirect supplies are independently demanded. The further away from the manufacturing 'shop floor' the supplies are deployed, the less dependent they become on customer demand. Governance will still require the same reports – and use up the same amount of computing power and stationery in producing them – irrespective of production rates. Resources (and therefore supplies) deployed in recruiting and training staff are similarly separated from fluctuations in output rates.

These examples should make it clear that talking about 'independent demand' does not suggest that there is no linkage back to dependent demand. Clearly budgets for back-office activity are highly dependent on sales and income in the medium to long-term. The point is that the link is not a direct one.

Dependent demand in the automotive industry
Dependent demand is the internal demand for the parts and sub-assemblies used in manufacturing the finished product. A fixed quantity of parts is required for each finished product. The number of finished products is dependent on sales.

Case study

In manufacturing the list of parts used to produce the finished item, in this case an all-terrain vehicle, the components that go into each sub-assembly is determined by the **bill of materials**. Figure 2.3 shows the headings for the bill of materials.

2.1 L02

Bill of materials
List of all the components, including the quantities required, to produce the required number of units of the end product[2]

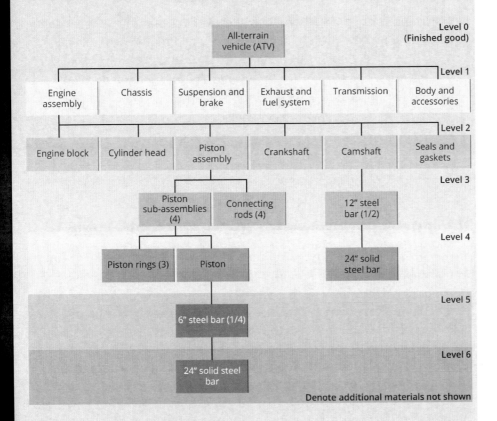

Figure 2.3 A structured level bill of materials (Source: Wisner/Tan/Leong. Principles of Supply Chain Management, 5E. © 2019 South-Western, a part of Cengage, Inc. Reproduced by permission. www.cengage.com/permissions)

The final level (Level 0) is an independent demand product in this case: the all-terrain vehicle. Customer demand for the vehicles is ultimately outside of the control of the manufacturer. Because everything below that level is dependent upon the demand for the product itself and therefore the rate of production within the factory, predicting the customer demand is key to scheduling the manufacturing capacity needed, making the sub-assemblies, ordering products from the supply chain and the raw materials needed at the very start of production.

This illustration of a bill of materials for a motor vehicle shows the complexity involved and will involve all the different types of stock from raw materials through WIP to finished products.

Sales and operations planning (known as S&OP) should determine how many vehicles the motor manufacturer intends to sell in a given period, for example, 10,000 vehicles per quarter, and the manufacturing capacity and scheduling will be generated to make that number.

While there may be flexible capacity within a production line, most complex products are usually made to regular demand. Matching with 100% accuracy the production output to sales demand is usually very difficult to achieve. Buffer stocks can help alleviate, or decouple sales from manufacturing output.

A good example is the registration of new motor vehicles in the UK. In September and March the registration starts with a new number showing it is a new vehicle; this drives demands to a peak, and more vehicles are registered during these two months.

This could cause production difficulties within the car factories. Having surplus capacity to switch on as needed would require £10 million of extra tooling. Add to this that car factories and their supply chain partners usually take a break in the summer for maintenance work.

Managing this independent (in this case 'customer') demand to ensure delivery to time and customer satisfaction can only be achieved by having strategically timed safety or buffer stock to minimise stockouts at all of the dependent demand stock levels.

Variances in dependent demand stock levels

Techniques for managing stock levels will be discussed in later sections, but it is important when grasping the principles to understand that the levels of stock held during a year *may* vary to deal with seasonal variations in demand in a way that enables production to continue at a steady rate. This is not an absolute rule. It depends upon the ease with which production rates can be adjusted in combination with the costs of storing the product concerned. If the storage costs are relatively low and production capacity is not very flexible, then it makes sense to keep production steady during the year and adjust stock levels. Conversely, if production can be varied (for example, if it can be switched between different product lines) then it makes more sense to keep stock levels low and vary production on a season basis. An example is car factories: demand in the UK always peaks at the twice yearly new vehicle registration time of March and September. This causes seasonal variants in demand which needs to be smoothed by levelling production.

Variances in independent demand stock levels

Independent demand stock levels will be determined by aspects of the business other than sales and production rates. For example, the age of the production equipment might affect maintenance stock requirements (newer equipment needing fewer repairs than older machinery). Strategic initiatives such as rebranding might require increases or changes in stock levels of back-office supplies, such as stationery, uniforms and marketing collateral.

Apply

For your own organisation or one with which you are familiar, identify what items are held in stock. Which of them are dependent-demand items and which are independent-demand?

2.2 Identify the direct and indirect costs of holding inventory

In this section direct and indirect costs of holding inventory will be looked at, namely the following.

- Acquisition costs

- Holding costs

- Costs of stockouts, and options to reduce costs while mitigating against any negative impacts on service levels

Generally accepted accounting practice (GAAP) values the inventory itself (the actual physical stock) as an asset. However, valuable working capital is tied up in stock, which can affect the **liquidity** of the business. Liquidity is a key requirement of ensuring the business is solvent, i.e. has available cash resources to pay its liabilities when they fall due.

While the physical stock can be counted and valued, there are extra costs associated with purchasing, holding and issuing stock.

If stock is not present when it is needed, stockouts occur, which have costly knock-on effects. Whether it is a lost sale or increased machine downtime, it all needs to be considered when determining how to ensure the right amount of stock is in the right place at the right time.

Acquisition costs

Acquisition costs naturally include the price of the stock being purchased but there are also costs incurred in placing the order to the supplier for the goods required. While the cost of the stock itself depends on the amount purchased, the time and costs involved in placing an order is theoretically the same for any quantity: they are fixed. For example, a purchase order for 1 tonne or 1000 tonne of steel costs the same to raise.

In practice there may be small variations in the costs of ordering since higher-value orders may need to be authorised by a more senior person in the organisation. While the time taken to physically authorise a requisition is the same for an Executive Director as it is for a Purchasing Manager, the cost of that time will be higher for the Director. The increase however will not be proportionate to the increased value of the order.

Ordering or acquisition costs include some or all of the following.

- Preparing the requisition

- Supplier selection and approvals

- The time and costs of the procurement process

- The IT ordering platform

- Other **EDI** links to suppliers

- Preparing the purchase order

- The cost of the **ERP** system time

- Printed stationery

- Progressing or chasing the order

Liquidity
The ease with which assets can be converted into cash. A firm with a high-value asset base but low liquidity may struggle to meet its debts on time

EDI (electronic data interchange)
A computer-to-computer exchange of business documents in a standard format between different organisations

ERP (enterprise resource planning)
Business process management software that uses a system of integrated applications to manage the business and automate many back-office functions

- Receiving and receipting the goods
- The cost of the materials or goods
- Handling
- Inspection or part approval and management of sub-standard goods
- Dealing with mismatched receipts and wrong invoices
- Approval and payment of invoices

These can be summarised into the following three main groups.

1. **Preliminary costs**: costs associated with actions before raising the purchase order.

2. **Placement costs**: the cost of raising the purchase order and ensuring the supplier receives it.

3. **Post-placement costs**: the costs after the purchase order has been raised, necessary to get the goods to the requestor and payment to the supplier.

Measuring these costs can be difficult. Having more purchase orders raised by a given purchasing team could reduce the cost per order, which might be seen as a saving in staffing costs. In reality, having more lower-value orders raised rather than fewer higher-value ones is an indication of inefficiency.

Ways to reduce these costs are discussed later in the section, but having **purchasing cards** for Type C inventory is one example.

Acquisition costs follow the typical procure-to-pay (P2P) model. Figure 2.4 shows the main elements of the process. Each stage of it, preliminary, placement and post-placement, has a cost associated with it.

Purchasing card (procurement card)
Essentially a credit card owned by the company that enables an officer to make low-value purchases without the need for formal requisitions and purchase orders

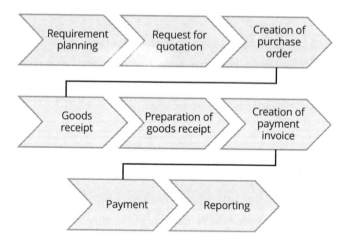

Figure 2.4 Procure-to-pay workflow

> *Remember*
> Every stage of the P2P process incurs a cost. These add up to the total cost of acquisition.

Holding costs/ carrying costs
Costs associated with the storage and handling of physical stock

Holding costs

Once the purchase orders have been raised and the goods or products have been delivered, these need to be stored. Costs associated with storage and handling of the inventory are known as **holding costs** or **carrying costs**.

There are two different types of holding costs.

- Costs related to the value of the goods
- Costs related to the physical characteristics of this inventory

Costs related to the value of the inventory include the following.

- Financial costs, for example, the interest on the working capital tied up in inventory, which may be the bank borrowing rate or the company's target for return on capital
- Cost of insurance – the higher the value of the products, usually the higher the insurance premium
- Losses due to product deterioration
- Losses due to obsolescence and redundancy of inventory (see section 2.1)
- Losses due to theft, accidental damage etc.

Costs related to the physical characteristics of the inventory include the following.

- Storage space: the rent, rates, the storage racking, IT systems and maintenance and repair costs of the building
- Power, heat and lighting of the store
- Movement equipment – forklift, scissor lifts, pallet trucks etc.
- Labour costs – to run, handle, inspect, audit and issue the inventory stored at the facility
- Administration costs – maintaining the stores records including any documentation required, ICT and other equipment and consumables

While the physical goods values are known to be exact, as they are defined on the purchase order and matched invoice, the holding costs can be less easy to calculate.

These costs should never be underestimated. Running warehouse or stores are expensive and often the costs are not very visible as they are hidden in general overheads. Clearly identifying the holding costs is a first step towards better utilisation of storage space and inventory management to lower the costs per unit stored.

> *Remember*
> The costs of holding stock are not merely those associated with the building/space in which it is stored. There are costs relating to the value of the stock and others relating to its physical characteristics.

Costs of stockouts

A stockout is simply a situation where an inventory item is not available when required. It is 'out of stock'. The stores failed in its requirement to satisfy demand. This inevitably has knock-on effects either for production or sales or both, which in turn incur costs.

The costs associated with a stockout include the following.

- Loss of production output – there will be no production until the stockout is resolved (new stock is acquired). For factories operating 24/7 with no spare capacity, this lost output will not be able to be recovered.

- Costs of machine downtime and of overheads spread over a reduced level of output.

- Costs of any action required to deal with the stockout, which may include the following.

  ○ Buying from another more expensive supplier.

  ○ Paying more for urgent delivery of replacement items, either because the transportation is actually more expensive (for example, air freighted rather than the slower and cheaper transportation by sea) or simply because the supplier charges a premium for express delivery.

  ○ Switching to another form of production.

  ○ Using alternative parts or materials which may incur extra costs due to a need to quality check, sample and approve them.

Even when the stockout has been remedied there may still be the following.

- Loss of customer goodwill through inability to supply or late delivery

- Loss of sales or new orders

- Loss of market creditability

Where stockouts are frequent and affect for example, workers' ability to meet bonus targets, there will also be costs associated with declining morale which is known to reduce productivity. In the worst cases it will affect the ability to recruit and retain staff.

Like holding costs, the costs of stockout are often not visible and likely to be hidden in stores overhead and general production costs. Nevertheless the cost of stockouts must be estimated and made as transparent as possible in order to emphasise the importance of good inventory management which in turn will help to ensure that it is properly resourced.

Estimated stockout costs should be expressed in annual values, ensuring their compatibility with acquisition and holding costs.

Check
What is a stockout and what additional costs does the business incur as a result of such an event?

Options to reduce costs while mitigating any negative impact on service levels

Having discussed the costs of acquiring and holding stock and the cost of not having the stock to satisfy demand (stockout costs), now options will be looked at that are available to reduce these impacts without compromising on service levels.

The options include the following.

- Using lead times and costs of holding as part of a price evaluation

- Strategically placed safety stock

- Vendor-owned stock (at point of use)

- Increased overall inventory levels

- Understanding demands and seasonal/ad hoc fluctuations leading to more accurate forecasting

- Sourcing decisions based on supplier performance, not just purchased prices

- Using KPIs to improve supply performance and eliminate the bottlenecks

- Robust **supplier relationship management (SRM)** using agreed KPIs to drive continuous supply chain improvements.

Using lead times and costs of holding as part of a price evaluation

Taking order lead times and the costs of holding inventory can influence the contract award decision. The total costs of acquisition can be reduced if these are taken into account when choosing the source of supply. A useful worked example is provided by Cavinato et al. (in *The Supply Management Handbook*) in their introduction to balancing the cost of inventory and lead times against stockout.[3]

2.2 L02

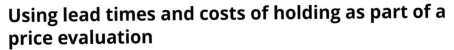

Supplier relationship management (SRM)
The strategic managing of all interactions with a designated supplier organisation

Case study

Cavinato's use of supplier lead times in supplier selection

The Acme Drill Company carries one week of inventory per one week of supplier lead time for steel. They have three steel suppliers and calculate inventory holding costs at 75% of the inventory cost.

Steel usage is 5000 pounds per year and Acme's standard cost (that is their average price paid) is $12.50/pound. Three quotes have been requested for a new high-speed steel rod and are received as set out below.

Supplier	Price	Lead time (weeks)
Able Corp	$12.25	10
Baker Co	$12.65	7
Charlie Inc	$13.10	2

If the purchase price variance (PPV) – the actual price minus the standard price – is a heavily weighted selection criterion, the procurement team may be inclined to buy from Able Corp. This would keep them below the standard costs and create a favourable positive variance even though increased inventory will be a result. The amount of inventory held for Able Corp would need to be ten weeks' worth, whereas it is seven for Baker Co, and only two for Charlie Inc.

If the price is adjusted for the cost of inventory, the results change.

$$\text{Carrying cost per week} = \frac{75\% \text{ per year cost to carry}}{50 \text{ weeks per year}}$$
$$= 1.5\% \text{ per week}$$

Therefore:

Time factor = Quoted Price × 1.5% per week cost to carry × weeks of lead times

This results in a different set of costs.

Supplier	Price × Time factor	Adjusted price
Able Corp	$12.25 + $12.25 (0.015 × 10)	$14.09
Baker Co	$12.65 + $12.65 (0.015 × 7)	$13.98
Charlie Inc	$13.10 + $13.10 (0.015 × 2)	$13.49

When the total costs, including inventory, are used to make the decision, suppliers must compete on lead times as well as on price.

Able Corp. have the lowest purchased price, but Charlie Inc. have the best overall costs.

This example shows that using lead times as part of the cost calculation can encourage the supply chain to become more responsive enabling stock and inventory to be replenished at a faster rate reducing both the holding costs and minimising the risks of stockouts.

(Source: adapted from www.industryweek.com/software-amp-systems/ hidden-costs-offshore-sourcing, quoting from "Calculating the Impact of Increased Leadtimes of Foreign Purchases", presentation by Michael Harding, Institute for Supply Management, Las Vegas)

Strategically placed safety stock

The need for safety or buffer stock was discussed in detail in section 2.1. To recap, safety stock can be finished products or raw materials or components either held centrally or strategically placed at the relevant locations in relation to the production process. The point is that this is stock in excess of what is expected to be required. It provides a safety margin against more being needed than anticipated.

This could be due to unexpected demand (particularly in the case of independent demand items – a particular machine developing an intermittent fault, for example, or a particularly dry summer resulting in unanticipated demand for CO_2 as beer sales increase).

Alternatively, it could be due to quality control issues not discovered at the point of delivery with a particular batch of input-stock having a high failure/defect rate.

Holding extra stock will always improve customer service levels, or at least reduce the risk of them falling. This implies that the higher the service level target the greater the requirement for larger amounts of safety stock.

From the commercial perspective this means that the organisation must factor in the extra costs associated with holding safety (buffer) stock when it sets its customer satisfaction targets and when bidding for business. Are the gains (reduced losses) sufficient to outweigh the extra cost?

There is no simple answer. It will depend upon the absolute costs involved and the impact of customer satisfaction on demand (which in turn may depend upon the competitiveness of the relevant market).

2.2 L02

Therefore, determining the optimum amount of safety stock to be held firstly requires a statistical analysis of orders and lead time data to establish averages and the range of normal deviation from the average. This can then be used to determine probability of stockout for any individual stock unit.

Then there needs to be a cost–benefit analysis for each type of stock.

- What is the probability of a stockout occurring?

- What are the cost impacts if it does?

- What are the costs of holding safety stock at different levels, in different locations (which will have speedier access if required to be used)?

This is very similar to any other risk management approach.

1. Assess the risk, which is the combination of likelihood and severity of impact.

2. Assess the cost of mitigating the risk (in this case, of holding safety stock).

3. The difference between the expected demand inventory levels and the point at which the likely and potential cost of stockout falls below the cost of holding additional inventory defines the safety stock.

The point at which the inventory matches the safety stock level is the reorder point.

Having determined the levels of safety stock to be held, the next stage in designing the mitigation of the risk is to decide *where* the stock should be held.

Naturally the characteristics of the stock itself will have a role to play in the decision-making process. If it needs to be kept in sterile conditions this causes limitations which do not apply if it is a standard nuts-and-bolts part that can happily sit in a bin beside an assembly line.

Nevertheless, the safety stock needs to be rapidly accessible. Ideally there will be a through flow, with stock to be used next as close to the point of use as practical, standard inventory held possibly slightly further away and safety stock coming in as new stock in the central store (see figure 2.5).

Figure 2.5 The stock journey – a reminder that buffer or safety stock is simply a proportion of that held, not a designated batch of physical stock

Where production capacity is limited or expensive to increase (a bottleneck operation) it may be necessary to have safety stock placed within the sequence of production operations to minimise any effects of this bottleneck process breaking down.

To be able to do this good knowledge of the production capabilities and capacities of each process is needed to identify the bottlenecks. Likewise, the ABC categorisation of stock can assist in determining sensible holding levels: a Type C item is cheaper and more easily justified than the more expensive Type A.

Check
How does an organisation determine what levels of stock should be held as buffer or safety stock?

Vendor-owned stock

Particularly in the case of maintenance, repair and operating (MRO) inventory items, wherever there is a large number of unique stock keeping units (SKUs) coupled with independent demand there is an increased risk of stockouts if insufficient inventory is held, but at the same time in many cases there may be potential for low stock turn. The latter increases the risk of obsolescence or redundancy.

One option to manage these contradictory risks is to source MRO products from one supplier (vendor) who maintains a stock of these MRO parts ready to be used at the point of customer consumption.

The supplier owns the stock until it is used by the purchaser; only then is the purchaser invoiced for it.

The supplier does frequent stock checks: weekly or twice weekly was the norm but with the increase in technology, stock levels can be checked in real time on an ongoing basis. Restocking levels are agreed and automatic.

Where stock turn is low and there are potential risks of redundancy or obsolescence the stock levels can be reduced by the supplier (vendor) recovering the goods and selling through other purchasers. This avoids any loss to the first purchaser and reduces the risks of over-production by the supplier.

Effectively this approach shares the costs of stockholding between the supplier and the purchaser. The purchaser still needs to provide the physical storage space with its associated costs of rental, heat, power etc., but saves the opportunity cost of having working capital tied up in the actual goods. The supplier is carrying the risk of the goods not being needed and therefore potential loss while in storage, together with any additional costs if the goods are reclaimed for use elsewhere, but does save the costs of physical storage thus reducing their own warehousing requirements.

Insurance costs could sit with either party depending on the contract agreed between them, although the insurance risk of the building is likely to sit with the buying company.

Although originally and primarily used for MRO stock, the approach is equally applicable to direct materials where the physical characteristics make them suitable. Electronic components is one example of a product group which suits the vendor-owned stock model.

Clearly for the vendor-owned-at-the-point-of-use model to work, a high degree of trust between the supplier and purchaser is necessary, particularly with regard to the handling of the products on-site. Electronic tracking systems and automation in warehouses and distribution networks reduce the human interface and, provided the systems themselves are demonstrated to be reliable, reduces risks of mishandling, theft and fraud.

Increased overall inventory levels

Perhaps the most obvious method of reducing risks to service delivery is simply to increase the inventory level overall: simply hold more stock.

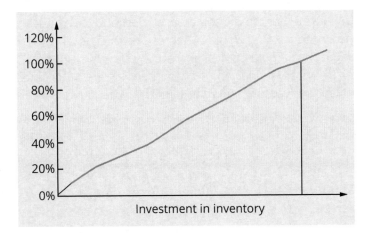

Figure 2.6 Direct correlation between service levels and inventory (Source: Lysons, K. and Farrington, B. (2012) Purchasing and Supply Chain Management (8th ed) Pearson Financial Times, p.319)

Figure 2.6, reproduced from Lysons and Farrington research (*Purchasing and Supply Chain Management*), shows a direct correlation between service levels and inventory investment.[4]

Despite fluctuations it is a relatively straight line relationship between investment in inventory and service delivery. Service levels will never reach 100% perfection due to the number of other variables in play, but there is a point at which inventory holding reaches a maximum, that is holding more (or indeed managing what is held more efficiently) will not have any further impact on service delivery.

The implications of this for deciding upon the degree to which overall inventory *should* be increased are not simple. While the line in figure 2.6 shows roughly a one-to-one correlation, that will only be true in some sectors. For other types of industry the line may be steeper or shallower: in other words the gain in service delivery achieved by a given increase in inventory investment will be greater or lesser. Naturally, this feeds into the decision-making as to whether that investment is warranted.

Remember
Options for improving service delivery include holding more safety stock or alternatively increasing overall stock levels. However, both approaches can significantly increase costs and are only viable if those increases are less than the likely costs of stockouts.

Understanding demand levels and seasonal fluctuations leading to more accurate forecasting

Understanding the user/customer demand for the stock items under consideration and whether that demand has any seasonal variations is critical to maintaining service levels.

Past data needs to be combined with any new or changing influences in order to predict the future demands and manage the variations.

The degree of fluctuation influences how much extra supply chain capacity and/or inventory safety stock needs to be available so it can be accessed at need.

Having additional suppliers to meet increased demand can reduce the need to carry as much buffer stock as would otherwise be the case, provided that all suppliers work to the same technical and quality standards. When this works accurately, the inventory curve can be smoothed in spite of the excess demand resulting in no extra inventory and maintained service levels.

As always, there is a cost attached. Data analysis, forecasting and scenario modelling require investment in personnel, ICT hardware and software and interpretation skills. Justifying this expenditure may itself be dependent upon the degree of fluctuation. Where seasonal variation is highly predictable, such costs may not be warranted. If the influences are less clear or more complex, the investment can be more easily justified.

The widespread adoption of just in time (JIT) techniques particularly in the automotive industry has greatly reduced costs with increased service levels as well as the additional benefit of increased problem visibility. These systems are entirely reliant on the ability to model and predict future demand.

Sourcing decisions based on supplier performance, not just purchased prices

Total cost of ownership (TCO)
The total cost of an asset including its purchase price and operation costs over its whole life cycle

As seen in the Cavinato case study, making purchasing decisions purely on the basis of the unit price can be more expensive than decisions made with an understanding of the **total cost of ownership (TCO)**. The case study only looked at the acquisition and holding costs, whereas TCO covers the whole life cycle of the product. Even so, simply factoring inventory costs into sourcing decisions in itself delivers real cash savings, while at the same time reducing the risks of service failure.

Consistently applying this approach to sourcing helps motivate the supply chain to become more agile with shorter lead times and the ability to increase delivery capability at short notice.

Using KPIs to improve supply performance and eliminate the bottlenecks

Driving continuous improvement with suppliers has been long proven to increase performance and drive out costs by eliminating waste, and eliminating constraints in the supply chain. Having good-quality KPIs agreed with suppliers can drive improvements in their delivery performance, highlighting areas for improvement with actions following to solve these issues permanently. Supplier relationship management (SRM) is invaluable at driving long-term value for two parties and improving performance. Creating framework agreements for long-term deliveries without managing the framework and the individual call-off contracts via data generated from good-quality KPIs should never be the case.

Remember
Having the right KPIs is important to measure improvements.

Apply
Think of three important KPIs to measure inventory in a car assembly factory.

2.3 Identify techniques associated with inventory control

The final section of this chapter deals with the different techniques associated with controlling inventory. At the end of this section you will understand the following points.

- Subjective and objective forecasting
- Reorder quantities and levels
- MRP and MRPII
- ERP
- Just in time
- Lean
- Inventory performance measures – lead times, service levels, rate of stock turn, stockouts in a given period, stock cover

Subjective and objective forecasting

Before the different types of forecasting are discussed, it is useful to understand what **forecasting** is, namely: a decision-making tool used by many businesses to help in budgeting, planning, and estimating future growth. In the simplest terms, forecasting is the attempt to predict future outcomes based on past events and management insight.[5] In everyday life predicting the weather is called the weather forecast.

Lysons and Farrington state that forecasting should involve asking six basic questions.[6]

1. What is the purpose of the forecast?
2. What is the time horizon?
3. What techniques are most appropriate?
4. On what data must the forecast be based and how shall it be analysed?
5. In what form shall the completed forecast be presented?
6. How accurate is the forecast?

Forecasting techniques can be either subjective (qualitative) or objective (quantitative).

Subjective forecasting

Subjective forecasting uses qualitative information, that is information based on human opinion and insights that are not shown by hard data.

It uses expert opinion, market research, surveys and structured questioning methods such as the **Delphi method** (see below).

None of these are precise techniques and do not use hard data. Sometimes such data is not available for the subject. Take, for example, the launch of new products: there are no sales figures or failure rates to examine.

Forecasting
Decision-making tool used by businesses to help in budgeting, planning and estimating future growth

Delphi method
A structured forecasting technique using a panel of experts and a number of rounds of questioning. Responses are shared after each round and the experts encouraged to reconsider their own responses. It is intended to achieve a consensus view

In this scenario there may also be very limited subjective data. Henry Ford was famously quoted as having said, 'If I had asked my customers what they wanted they would have said a better horse.' He gave them the Ford Model T motor car. In that case not only was there no hard data on mass produced vehicles – they simply did not exist – but also even the subjective data (opinion and perception) would have been restricted.

Similarly, in a more recent example, in 1984 when Apple introduced the iPod, it created a whole new way of listening to music.

This illustrates why expert opinion may be required in addition to, or instead of, general market surveys. Mass market cars and music downloads were, at the time of their launch, concepts that most people simply would not be familiar with. Not only would there be no data, there would also be no experience either.

Only once in production could data on sales be gathered.

Subjective approaches

The commonest subjective techniques include the following.

- **Market surveys**: interviews or questionnaires completed by a selected group of people can be used to understand likely future sales and in particular what might influence such sales (either positively or negatively); it can help determine what current customers like and dislike about current products, and also why non-customers do not buy. This information can feed into sales projections (forecasts) which in turn will influence production rates and stock-need levels.

- **Employee surveys**: in terms of inventory control useful information can also be gathered from employee surveys. Those people actually working on production lines or in warehouses may have insights into how and when stockouts are likely to occur, or the reasons for fluctuations in stock deterioration, that either support or counter the information from the figures.

- **Expert knowledge**: gathering experiences from subject matter experts helps form opinions. Examples of such experts whose opinions could be drawn from include the following.

  o Executives, especially sales and technical

  o External consultants

  o Professionally qualified engineers, lawyers, medical personnel and other technical experts

These all have first-hand knowledge of what is needed to satisfy market demand and understand market/product trends which can be transferred into forecast predictions. The strength and depth of their knowledge determines the value of their opinions. Each expert will have their own views and these may conflict with the views of other equally qualified experts. As with predicting the stock market or forward commodities purchases, experts are often wrong.

> **The Delphi method**
>
> One approach that tries to refine expert opinion is the Delphi method. This involves several rounds of questionnaires being put to a panel of experts. After each round, the responses are aggregated and then shared anonymously with the whole panel who are invited to reconsider their own response in the light of others. The theory is that the range of responses will decrease through this process and converge on a consensus, in other words: a subjective prediction based on collective rather than individual knowledge and experience.

2.3 L02

> Again, from the inventory perspective, these opinions can be used to predict sales levels which lead to production rates and stock-need levels.
>
> They can also be used to predict likely technical developments, which could inform judgments (predictions, forecasts) about future redundancy or obsolescence of stock already held, or likely to be acquired in the short to medium term. Such forecasts might imply that stock levels should start to be reduced – or if components will continue to be needed that might be phased out by their producers, that stock levels need to be increased.

- **Test marketing**: this is often used to assess the market reactions to new products especially the more innovative ones. Products are assessed for their appeal with a sample group to test the market reaction prior to significant capital investment. One example here is the launching of prototype new cars to assess whether it is worth investing the hundreds of millions of dollars in new production lines.

Objective forecasting

Objective forecasting uses quantitative techniques. These are based on hard data – facts and figures – that remove the human element of the subjective approach.

The techniques are based on a set of observations measured at successive equally spaced points in time which produces a **time-series** data set. To assist in interpretation the series is usually depicted in graph form.

The principle is that the information on what has happened in the past can be used to predict what will happen in the future. The following five elements are used to do this.

1. The average, mean or median point of the observations.

2. Trends – an increase or decrease in the average over time.

3. Short-term cyclical movements – which could be indicative of seasonal influences. Examples would be summer/winter clothing or spares for central heating boilers.

4. Long-term cycles – these may be unpredictable or unexplained.

5. Random errors – variations which cannot be explained, usually erratic or inconsistent movements. (Note: these may be indicative of a cyclical effect which the time-series is too short to pick up.)

Two main statistical techniques used in inventory forecasts are the following.

- **Moving average**: a calculation to analyse data by creating series of averages of different subsets of the full data set. It is commonly used with time-series data to smooth out short-term fluctuations and highlight longer-term trends or cycles.[7]

- **Weighted average**: a calculation which attaches more importance to some elements of the data than others.

The most widely used method in inventory forecasts is a combination of the two known as the **exponentially weighted moving average (EWMA)**. This applies a series of calculations to each moving average so that the weighted value of the older subsets of data reduces exponentially (that is the weighting itself changes the further back it goes).

The theory is that more recent data is likely to be a better predictor of future behaviour than older data, on the basis that future conditions are more likely to be similar to current conditions than to those which existed ten or five years ago.

Time-series
A series of data points indexed (or listed or graphed) in time order

Exponentially weighted average method (EWAM)
A statistical methodology which can be used give more importance to the most recent data

In terms of inventory management this would be true because of changes in automation levels in both the inventory management itself and the production and/or distribution processes it supports.

Although objective forecasts are more accurate than subjective ones they can only ever be as good as the data upon which they rely. If the data itself is not accurate, the forecast will also be very unreliable.

Even with accurate data, demand can be distorted by activity within the supply chain, which might show as spikes or troughs on the data graphs. Any such apparent anomalies should be investigated to be properly understood. Statistical averaging will smooth out such occurrences, so if forecasting is done purely on that basis, the next time such a distorting event occurs the result could be a stockout or inventory overload, causing storage capacity issues.

Examples of things which can distort demand include the following.

- Unplanned sales promotions
- Sales team incentive
- Over-ordering by customer – due to historical poor delivery performance
- Cancelling of these over-orders
- Changes in bulk freight volumes, masking the true demand

Bullwhip effect
Distorted demand increasing up the supply chain

It can clearly be seen how this would affect the individual firm. The effect of demand distortion is amplified as you move up the supply chain from the source of the distortion. This is known as the **bullwhip effect**. It is named from the way the movement of a whip increases down its length. A small movement at the wrist of the person holding the whip translates into a series of increasingly large movements towards its end. The longer the whip, the greater the effect.

The effect is also known as the Forrester effect after Jay Forrester who first described it in *Industrial Dynamics*, having observed that the further you travel up the supply chain the greater the observed distortion appears and the level of safety stock held increases accordingly.[8]

> *Remember*
> Subjective forecasting uses qualitative methods (surveys, opinions) which relay on perception and opinion. Objective forecasting uses quantitative methods (facts and figures). Both methods have to make assumptions about how closely (or not) the future will resemble the present and the past. Forecasting is never exact.

Reorder quantities and levels

This section discusses reorder quantities and levels. It will focus on independent demand stock.

There are three widely expected reorder ways used for independent demand.

- Fixed quantities
- Economic order quantities
- Time or periodic review

For dependent demand, MRP, MRPII and JIT are used, each of which will be looked at in more detail below.

Fixed-quantity orders

Fixed-quantity orders are those with a predetermined quantity every time. The same amount is requested on each order. The order level (the amount ordered) is the quantity to be used during the order lead time plus a safety margin.

> The simple formula used to determine this is:
>
> maximum usage × maximum lead time

The reorder level may be indicated by having a two-bin system. Two bins of stock are present, once one has been consumed and is empty, it is the signal to reorder.

In more technology-based systems, an IT system tracks inventory usage and triggers the fixed order to be placed once stock falls below a certain point.

Economic order quantity (EOQ)[9]

The single most expensive part of the acquisition cost is the cost of the goods or products being purchased. The idea of an ideal or optimum order quantity has been discussed for many years. The most commonly used formula dates back to 1913, when Ford W. Harris wrote an article called 'How Many Parts to Make at Once.' This optimum amount is referred to as the economic order quantity (EOQ).

The EOQ is a decision tool used in cost accounting. It is a formula that allows you to calculate the ideal quantity of inventory to order for a given product. The calculation is designed to minimise ordering and holding costs.

The EOQ formula makes a number of assumptions. The following is assumed.

- The same quantity is ordered at each **reorder point**.
- Customer/user demand for the stock item is known.
- The relevant ordering and holding costs are certain.
- The **purchase order lead time** is known.
- The cost per unit is fixed (that is it does not change with the amount ordered; there are no quantity discounts).
- Inventory levels and customer/user demand are monitored carefully enough and sufficient inventory is held to ensure no stockouts occur.
- There are no quality costs (all quality-related effects are ignored).

Assuming these factors to be true, the EOQ formula then uses the following three variables.

1. **Demand**: the number of units of a stock item required for a specific period of time.

2. **Ordering cost**: cost per order of raising and issuing the purchase order, receipting, and making payment.

3. **Holding cost**: the costs of physically storing one unit of the stock for the same period of time used in determining demand.

Reorder point
The point either in time or in a process when the next order should be placed

Purchase order lead time
The time period from placing an order to delivery of the goods

Note that the ordering cost is calculated *per order*. The holding costs are calculated *per unit*.

According to Harris' formula the economic order quantity is equal to the square root of [(2 × demand × ordering costs) ÷ carrying costs]

It's easier to visualise as a regular formula:

$$Q = \sqrt{\frac{2DS}{H}}$$

Where:

Q is the economic order quantity (units)

D is demand (units, often annual)

S is ordering cost (per purchase order)

H is carrying cost per unit

Example: Harris's economic order quantity

An outdoors equipment shop sells a line of men's hiking boots. One particular model costs $45 per pair. The shop sells 100 pairs of hiking boots a month (that is 1200 per year).

The shop adds up the total time spent by everyone who is involved in the ordering process and payment process, and determines that the combined time to process each order is one hour. Based on average salary and benefit costs, it calculates a cost per order of $50. The shop also calculates that the holding cost is $3 per unit. That rate covers the occupancy costs (rent, business rates, light, power etc.) of the physical space where the goods are stored, insurance of the goods and the opportunity cost of holding the inventory.

The EOQ is then calculated as follows.

Economic order quantity = square root of [(2 × demand × ordering costs) ÷ carrying costs]

⇨ EOQ = square root of [(2 × 1200 × ($50)) ÷ $3]

= square root of [$120,000 ÷ $3]

= square root of 40,000

= 200

Thus, the ideal order level is 200 units. At that level, the shop minimises ordering and holding costs.

*An often quoted cost to raise one purchase order, going through one cycle of the procure-to-pay process, is $50 to $100 per order. This varies hugely between organisations depending on salary rates, the degree of automation and generally how efficient the process is.

Case study

EOQ works best for repeat purchasing and MRO items. Having inaccurate data can exaggerate holding costs, causing the models to be modified to accommodate changes in usages, demands and products.

2.3 LO2

Apply
Consider the EOQ formula and evaluate how useful it is in a practical situation (for example, in determining reordering quantities for stores items), giving particular consideration to the assumptions it makes.

Periodic review systems

Period review systems use time-based stock replenishment triggers rather than specified-quantity signals. The relative importance of the stock item determines the frequency of checks. Once stock levels are checked a variable quantity will be ordered to bring stock back to a particular level, 'topping up' the stock.

Table 2.4 shows a suggested checking frequency based on the earlier described ABC classification.

Stock type	Suggested checking frequencies
A	Daily
B	Weekly
C	Monthly

Table 2.4 Suggested frequencies for inventory checking by ABC stock classification

Type A are expensive individual stock items, so the cost is minimised by holding less stockholding, but frequent checks are needed to avoid stockouts, whereas Type C products have lower individual value, more can be held and they can therefore be checked less frequently.

The review establishes current stock levels. A variable amount will then be ordered to replenish stock held. In order to work out that variable amount there needs to be a defined 'maximum' amount of stock to be held.

Lysons and Farrington suggest the following mathematical formula to determine the maximum stock level.[10]

$$M = W(T + L) + S$$

Where:

M = maximum stock level

W = average rate of stock usage

T = review period

L = stock item order lead time

S = safety stock

Choice of method

Fixed-quantity orders work well if the stock item is used at an inconsistent rate, but they require a reliable trigger system and consistent lead times. If the lead time is variable the reorder trigger may be too late to avoid a stockout.

Periodic- (time-) based review systems are most appropriate where orders and suppliers have regular delivery intervals, especially if that supplier delivers more than one item in that delivery.

Economic order quantities are highly technical to work out, and rely on too many assumptions which mostly do not hold true in the real world. The more practical methods are generally preferred.

> *Check*
> What are the three main methods of determining stock order levels for independent demand items?

MRP and MRP II

For dependent demand stock the recommended approach is what is known as material requirements planning (MRP) and the wider developed version manufacturing resource planning: MRP II. These are computerised systems for inventory flows and inventory management.

> Material requirements planning (the original MRP) is defined as 'a method of provisioning which depends upon a master manufacturing schedule as distinct from statistical predictions. The 'schedule' defines when finished batches and items are needed for production. It is then broken down into components and sub-assemblies and each of these broken back to provision (purchase or supply) raw materials or parts.'[11]
>
> MRP was developed in the 1960s specifically for dependent demand in assembly operations. Its clear aim is to ensure either purchased or in-house manufacturing assemblies are available just before the required next stage or operation of the production cycle. It tracks the work in progress (WIP) throughout the end-to-end manufacturing processes, assisting the supply chain team to deliver the right supplies at the right time.
>
> The system answers the following questions.
>
> * What items (stock) are required?
>
> * How many of them?
>
> * When?

MRP process overview

The MRP process is as follows.

1. Using known customer orders and forecast demand, a master production schedule (MPS) can be created. This should allow for seasonal fluctuations. This sets out the scale and rate of production needed to meet the demand at the right time. This tells us how much needs to be produced and how fast.

2. The next stage is to look at what is needed to produce each of those numbers at that rate, how much of that stock is available and how much needs to be created (in-house production) or bought (purchase orders).

    The bill of materials (BOM) sets out all of the materials, sub-assemblies etc., needed to produce each item. This is simply scaled up for the relevant production numbers. Refer back to figure 2.3 for an example of a BOM.

Inventory records show how much stock of each of the BOM items is currently held. They should also show average usage rates, failure/loss rates, lead times (which can be worked from order points and delivery receipts) etc.

3. The MRP software then combines the MPS, the BOM and the inventory information to work out the net requirements of what to purchase or produce and when.

    These net requirements are worked out using the following equation.

    Net requirements = Total requirements – Available inventory

    Where:

    Total requirements = Gross requirements

    Available inventory = Inventory on hand + Units on order

Crucially it also calculates when each of the stock items will be required. It can then do the following.

*   Place (or trigger the placing of) orders with suppliers

*   Reschedule (or trigger the rescheduling of) instructions:

    o   to postpone and/or cancel open orders

    o   adjust inventory coverage (change items in stock either by type or quantity)

*   Expedite overdue orders or trigger mitigation activity to avoid a stockout

The process is summarised in figure 2.7.

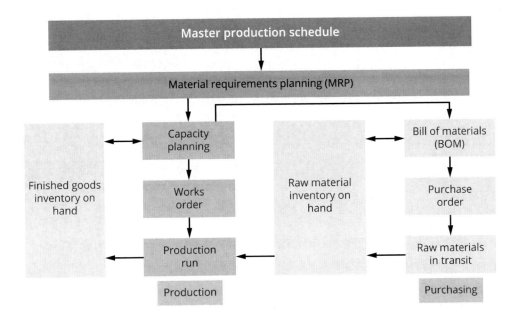

Figure 2.7 Illustration of MRP

A powerful benefit of MRP systems is the capacity to produce exception reports, which show deviations from normal planning and performance. These enable anomalies to be investigated with a view to improving future forecasting.

In summary, material requirements planning is an electronic system for combining the following.

*   Known demand

*   Forecast demand

- Bill of materials for the final product

- Inventory records

This will determine what inventory is required and when and to trigger orders or in-house production to ensure that it is available when needed.

It is most suitable for the following.

- Dependent demand items

- Non-uniform or lumpy demand, that is where demand is not continuous

- Job, batch or flow production or where all are used together, because of its flexibility

> *Remember*
> MRP is used in manufacturing to determine which materials will be required at each point in the process. The inputs are orders, forecast demand, the bill of materials and the inventory records.

MRP II

As explored, MRP only looks at the 'materials' that go into the production process. This was subsequently developed to look at all of the resources required.

Compton and Jessop[12] define it as:

> ❝ *a development from 'materials requirement planning' [which] encompasses the planning and scheduling activities associated with production resources to match output needed and supplies available.* ❞

In MRP II the production process is still driven by the master production schedule (MPS) but there are now additional inputs from the following.

- Production control

- The supply chain

- Engineering and technical teams

- Finance teams

- HR

- Facilities in terms of buildings and energy and other utilities requirements

This extension to the original MRP is only possible because of the expansion of computing capability.

MRP II: process overview and contrasts with MRP

MRP II co-ordinates data from wider sources including engineering, procurement, marketing, sales, production, inventory, human resources, finance and so on to incorporate the wider business plan and strategy, rather than output purely based on demand.

'What if' analysis
Analysis-based scenarios exploring whether something will happen or not

MRP II software packages have the ability to run scenarios and **'what if' analysis**. This enables any of the relevant variables to be changed to see what impact that would have overall. For example, if sales forecasts were exceeded by a given percentage does the organisation have the production capacity to match them?

If not and it has to outsource some of the production what are the financial implications? Which part of the production is most easily or most cost effectively outsourced? The costs of acquisition and holding costs of inventory clearly need to be fed into all of these scenarios.

Unlike MRP, MRP II also covers planning for plant and equipment, wider financial implications and human resources as well as stock and materials inputs. Better financial controls and more detailed budget impacts result from the wider data sets used.

The need to have all of the inputs to ensure the system works drives greater co-ordination between the different teams ensuring information flows better and the negative impacts of **silo-working** where information is kept at departmental level are reduced.

Silo-working
Restricting information to the department that produced it

> *Remember*
> MRP II moves beyond purely the materials required in the manufacturing process to include other inputs such as plant, equipment, personnel and finance.

Despite the wider coverage, MRP II does still only cover the requirements of the 'manufacturing' element of the business. It does not look at the business as a whole. For example, HR data being input into the system has been discussed, but this is only the human resources required for the manufacturing process. It may also cover the personnel required to directly manage inventory (processors and store personnel), but it does not consider wider impacts on, for example, back-office services such as payroll staff or procurement teams.

The next development in planning techniques, therefore, goes beyond MRP to consider the whole business. The next stage then is enterprise resource planning (ERP).

Enterprise Resource Planning (ERP)

Enterprise resource planning (ERP) is the latest development of MRP and MRP II. Compton and Jessop define ERP as:

> 66 *A system for the coordination of planning and execution of business on a wide basis, between links in the supply chain involving more than coordination.*[13] 99

To extend this, ERP can further be described as the planning of organisation-wide resource requirements by using technology to capture and assist in analysing real-time data from all functional areas across the organisation.

It was first developed by the Gartner Group (an IT applications company) in the 1990s, driven by increased computer technology and the necessity for certain processes to be implemented. MRP, MRP II and ERP could all, in theory, be possible with purely paper-based data systems and manual calculations. However, it is the speed of computers that means the calculations can be done quickly and cheaply and accurately enough for them to be worth the time involved.

Figure 2.8 shows the key business links for an ERP system.

Figure 2.8 ERP links

As systems across businesses become increasingly integrated (for example, the inventory control system linking directly to the purchase order system and being capable of auto-generating orders within certain parameters), the potential benefits of ERP become easier to access.

Table 2.5 illustrates the capabilities of an ERP system.

Business function	ERP capabilities
Human resources	Recruitment, planning, training, skills matrices, labour utilisation
Procurement and supply chain management	The whole procure-to-pay cycle, from requisition to paid supplier invoices; supplier performance measures such as timeliness of deliveries, order lead times, defects rates etc.
Logistics and inventory management	Warehouse locations, delivery tracking plus all of MRP II outputs
Finance	Accounts payable and accounts receivable, cost management, financial reporting, payroll, budgeting
Manufacturing	Tracks and reports all orders through the end-to-end production process; plus all MRP and MRP II outputs

Business function	ERP capabilities
Project management	Project planning, resource planning, project costing, time and expense, performance units, activity management
Engineering	All drawings, change requests, material specifications stored in one database allowing access from all

Table 2.5 ERP links

ERP systems facilitate information flow across and between all functions, creating a more coherent focus on the performance of the enterprise (that is, the business organisation) rather than individual departments or teams.

> *Remember*
> ERP systems look at the resources required across the organisation as a whole.

ERP is not the end-state development however. Gartner has continued its work and incorporated developments in the Internet and the high-speed processing that permits data to be captured and shared in real time across the whole supply chain and with any relevant external stakeholders. This led to ERP II being launched by Gartner in 2000.

The main improvements from ERP to ERP II are the following.

- The capability for collaboration across whole supply chains.

- The widening of the basic concepts so that they are not just applicable to manufacturing but can be used across all business and sectors, including services sectors, public, private and third sector operations.

- Functionality has become more user-focused – a common development in all business applications is the assumption that reports will be accessed. directly by practitioners in the relevant field (be that inventory management, procurement or HR) rather than by business analysts.

- A move towards open protocol systems that permit integration with other proprietary software so that the benefits can be accessed without having to completely replace all existing business software systems.

The advantages of ERP over MRP II include the following.

- Improved customer service levels

- Reduced inventory levels

- Better inventory accuracy

- Improved cash flow and revenue collection

- Increased factory efficiencies – achieved by better resource location and capacity planning

- Rework and scrap in the manufacturing processes are reduced

Implementing a full ERP system is not an easy option. They are complex systems and the disadvantages include the following.

- ERP is perceived as difficult and expensive to implement.

- There is a tendency towards customisation of standard ICT modules and packages which should be avoided as it adds to the cost and complexity of both implementation and the final system-in-use.

- The hidden costs can be high. Implementation is time-consuming and needs skilled input from the implementing organisation, which either requires recruitment of specialists for the duration of the project or takes key implementation team members away from their day job.

- As with any new software there are training requirements for users, but also an ERP system implementation may require a culture change within the organisation – a greater readiness to share data across departments and beyond the organisation, for example.

- ERP systems, due to the multiple tasks being performed, can make decisions take hours. This encourages the use of separate supply chain management (SCM) and distribution requirements planning (DRP) systems, which can make smaller decisions more quickly, in minutes – allowing instant feedback.

However, the ERP does provide greater visibility of information providing opportunities for lower cost and greater efficiencies across the whole enterprise. If properly implemented it allows for agile and global business relationships.

> *Apply*
> The most widely used ERP systems are SAP, Oracle, and Microsoft Dynamics NAV. Read online more about the functionality that each provides and consider the pros and cons of one system over another. Then consider an organisation you are familiar with. Which system best suits the organisation's procurement needs and why?

Just in time

Just in time (JIT) is a production control and inventory management concept pioneered by Toyota and first embraced by Western companies in the early 1980s. It began in the motor industry and is still most relevant in manufacturing situations.

Womack and Jones describe 'just in time' as:

> *A system for producing and developing the right items at the right time in the right amounts. Just in time approaches just on time when the upstream activities occur minutes or seconds before downstream activities, so single piece flow is possible. The key elements of just in time are flow, pull, standard work (with standard in-process inventories) and take time – the available production time divided by the rate of customer demand, setting the heartbeat of the Lean system).*[14]

The *Official Dictionary of Purchasing and Supply* puts it more simply:

> *a production philosophy whereby what is needed is made when it is needed, and not before.*[15]

The technique was envisioned by Toyota's Taiichi Ohno as a method for facilitating the smooth flow through the production cycle, but JIT can only work effectively if machine changeovers – changing from making one product to another – are dramatically reduced. Each machine needs to be capable of producing a variety of outputs with no or very limited re-tooling or re-calibration thus allowing for very flexible manufacturing responding to changing customer demands.

This allows upstream manufacturing operations to produce tiny amounts of each part (single-piece flow) and then produce another tiny amount as soon as the amount already produced is summoned by the next process downstream.

Even so, for JIT to work effectively the downstream production process has to be levelled. **Schedule levelling** (or **heijunka** in Japanese) is a practice of smoothing production in a way that results in producing a given number of items a day, despite the demand for those items fluctuating.

This can only be done with good data on both maximum levels of demand and average levels of demand, and with the ability to hold sufficient inventory to meet maximum demand where it occurs out of sync with the production rate.

Heijunka (schedule levelling)
Smoothing out production rates

> **Case study**
>
> *Levelled production rate*
> If demand per week for a product varies between 700 and 1500 units, the organisation will be faced with the potential of having to produce 700 units one week and more than double the next; the figure could be completely different in week three. It is more efficient if production can proceed at a steady rate than enable the maximum demand of 1500 to be met, while at the same time holding no more 'in hand' stock than is necessary. The levelled production rate will always need to be above 700 per week, to ensure a contribution to inventory (stock in hold) sufficient to ensure that when maximum demand occurs it can be met without totally depleting the amount held.

The better the ability to predict future demand, the easier it is to level production schedules. When production levelling fails, there are two impacts.

- **Downstream**: (either internally or externally) reputational and potential financial cost resulting from failure to deliver

- **Upstream**: (either internally or externally) to avoid a repeat situation safety stock (holding of spare inventory) will be increased

Although the 1950s Vice President of Toyota, Taiichi Ohno, is generally credited with pioneering JIT, along with the related disciplines of **Lean** manufacturing and **total quality management (TQM)**, it should be noted that the concept is older than that. Henry Ford used many of these principles of minimal inventory in the making of the Model T. In 1924 the supply lead time from processing the raw material to the final product was just four days.

Lean
Manufacturing system based on the minimisation of waste

Total quality management (TQM)
Organisation-wide efforts to improve outputs through continuous improvement in internal practices

> **Remember**
> Just in time aims to reduce or eliminate inventory by producing goods or components immediately before they are required.

Why adopt JIT?

JIT clearly has benefits for inventory management. If materials or components are produced or acquired immediately before they are needed, then they are not being held in store and all of the costs associated with stockholding are eliminated.

In practice JIT is not quite 'immediate' but even so, the stockholding costs are significantly reduced. This, however, is just one of the motivators for JIT.

All of the Toyota principles were formulated around the concept of eliminating waste in the production and distribution system. The JIT objectives of eliminating waste can be summarised in the 'five zeros'. It aimed to achieve the following.

- **Zero defects**: using the total quality management teaching of Deming, JIT aims to have all products meet or exceed the customer quality requirements.

- **Zero set-up times**: no or reduced set-up times for production lines and machinery so that there is less (ideally no) downtime where machines or lines are not producing anything, which in turn means shorter production times, and therefore shorter lead times achieved while holding lower inventories. Techniques used to support set-up time reduction include single minute exchange of dies (SMED) and the teachings of Shigeo Shingo.

- **Zero inventories**: JIT aims to reduce batch sizes to a quantity of one, a single-piece flow. In practice this is unlikely to be achieved, but as batch sizes are reduced, all of the typical types of inventories, raw materials, WIP and finished stock are reduced. No safety or buffer stocks are needed.

- **Zero handling**: process mapping tools identify where operations are duplicated; systems are then redesigned to reduce or eliminate handling operations.

- **Zero lead times**: this is the ultimate aim of JIT. While it is difficult to achieve, adopting small batch sizes coupled with increased flexibility does lead to shorter lead times.

Kanban

At the heart of the just in time system is the scheduling signal to the next operation to deliver the next batch.

Kanban is another Japanese term. It means 'signboard' or 'billboard'. In effect the Kanban process in JIT and other Lean manufacturing operations simply refers to anything which enables the triggers for inventory management (or any other part of a process) to be literally visible.

The two-bin stock management process referred to earlier predates the Japanese development of the system. It was introduced in the UK in the Spitfire manufacturing plants during World War 2, but Toyota (particularly under the leadership of Taiichi Ohno) fully developed the system.

At its simplest it is very clear that when one of the bins is empty, a call for delivery of more stock must be made – whether this is a request from production to stores, or stores to place an order to the supplier, the principle is the same.

Some commentators describe the situation involving an outside supplier as a three-bin system: one bin is at the production line, the second bin is in the on-site store, the third bin is at the supplier. Again, the principle remains the same.

Single-piece flow
Situation in which products proceed, one complete product at a time, through various operations in design, order-taking and production, without interruptions, backflows or scrap (Womack and Jones, 2013)[16]

Kanban
The signal to move to the next process

It creates a 'pull' which cascades backwards to the beginning of the manufacturing cycle, thus saving on inventory costs in each step of the chain.

2.3 LO2

> *Remember*
>
> In the Toyota system there are six rules which must be implemented for the Kanban system to function effectively[17]:
>
> 1. Each process issues requests (Kanban) to its suppliers as it consumes its supplies.
>
> 2. Each process produces according to the quantity and sequence of incoming requests (triggered by downstream Kanban).
>
> 3. No items are made or transported without a request.
>
> 4. The request associated with an item is always attached to it.
>
> 5. Processes must not send out defective items.
>
> 6. Limiting the number of pending requests makes the process more sensitive and reveals inefficiencies.

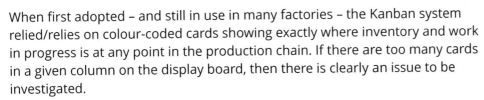

When first adopted – and still in use in many factories – the Kanban system relied/relies on colour-coded cards showing exactly where inventory and work in progress is at any point in the production chain. If there are too many cards in a given column on the display board, then there is clearly an issue to be investigated.

Developments in technology mean that Kanban has been developed into an electronic tool – which in turn is now being integrated with ERP systems. It is no longer the production workers who need to know when the bin is empty, it is the automated reordering system.

> *Check*
> What is Kanban and how does it relate to just in time?

As with all systems, JIT is not suitable in all circumstances. Table 2.6 sets out the advantages of JIT and the situations when it might not be suitable.

Advantages of JIT – why use it?	Disadvantages of JIT
• Lower inventory holding costs • Reduced scrap costs • 'Right first time' product quality • Design – fast response to engineering changes • Back-office costs – fewer suppliers, reduced or eliminated expediting, simplified communications • Productivity – reduced rework, no inspections, lower set-up times	• Inability of suppliers to move quickly to demand changes – suppliers need to be flexible and agile • Where having no safety stocks makes the company highly vulnerable to supply failures • Type C stock items where holding inventory is less of an issue • Where savings from buying in bulk are greatest

Advantages of JIT – why use it?	Disadvantages of JIT
• Finance – reduced inventories of purchased parts, work in progress and finished goods	• For products which have short life cycles or have rapid design changes
	• For jobbing or small batch production
	• Culture co-operation between all disciplines falls short
	• Closeness of suppliers to their customer – longer travel means more sources of disruptions

Table 2.6 Advantages of JIT production and stock management contrasted with situations when it might not be suitable

Two things are essential from the supply chain for JIT to work effectively.

- All parts must arrive where and when they are needed, in the right quantities. The final part of this section describes the relevant KPI for this: 100% OTIF (on time, in full).

- All parts must be usable. There can be no allowance for scrap or defects or buying extras to cover general losses in the production cycle.

If this cannot be achieved rather than the stock arriving just in time, it comes just too late.

Achieving these essentials is not easy. The procurement function needs to have strong links and long-term relationships with suppliers. These must be based on trust, co-operation and mutual benefit. Suppliers need to invest in quality team training and achieving quality certification. They also need to work on reducing waste in their own supply chains.

Finally, supplier production and sales teams also need to work closely with other in-house teams, especially engineering and product development to bring innovation to designs and suggest specification changes.

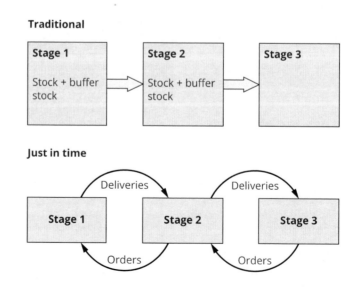

Figure 2.9 Comparison of traditional flow with JIT (Source: adapted from www.presentationeze.com/just-time-lean-manufacturing/)

The simple reordering signals used in JIT are shown in figure 2.9.

JIT is more than just a production control and inventory management system, it is a never-ending improvement culture. It is not suitable for every environment but the approach to eliminating waste can be used in most applications and will improve the flow of production and reduce inventory costs. While single-piece flow is the ideal inventory level, having this small amount of Type C class inventory would not be practical; a Kanban signal can still be used, but with a greater inventory than one.

JIT II

As with MRP and ERP, JIT has also evolved into JIT II. Registered by the Bose Corporation in 1991, JIT II is a customer – supplier partnership. In a JIT II relationship, a supplier representative – referred to as in-plant – is paid by the supplier but functions as a member of the customer's procurement team. They raise the customer purchase orders for that supplier and are involved in product design, production planning and value analysis.

For the supplier to dedicate staff to this and trust the customer in sharing their costs and internal processes, and also for the customer to trust the integrity of that employee managing orders, a long-term relationship must exist, usually via an **evergreen contract**.

Evergreen contract
A contract that is renewed automatically from year to year until cancelled by either party

Lean

'Lean' – originally called 'Lean manufacturing' the term is generally shortened as it is now deployed across other sectors, including service sectors[18]. It works hand-in-hand with JIT and its cultural principles.

Compton and Jessop define Lean supply as:

> *the approach to supply employed where Lean Production takes place. The use or consumption of materials or parts brings new material into existence, thereby avoiding stocks or unnecessary work. Suppliers are expected to provide defect free materials at the right time to meet customer requirements and employ Lean supply ideas themselves.*[19]

Lean thinking is aimed at driving value and eliminating the effects of waste in a production line, and in service-industry flows. **Waste** in a production system takes a number of forms. The pioneer of these approaches, Taiichi Ohno of Toyota, identified seven key types of waste (see table 2.7).

Waste
Anything that does not add value to the product

Types of waste	Description
Defects	Faults or mistakes that need correcting
Inventory	Holding too much stock can lead to increased storage costs
Movement	The activity and movement of people that does not contribute to the production of the product or service
Waiting	Machinery and/or people that are idle while waiting for parts to be delivered or upstream processes to be completed
Over-production	Producing more than is needed

Types of waste	Description
Over-processing	Unnecessary processes of production
Transportation	Any unnecessary movement of machinery, parts or vehicles

Table 2.7 The Seven Wastes

Six Sigma
Statistical technique for measuring variations within production processes, with the aim of eliminating them. The Six Sigma premise is that variations create defects and other forms of waste

Used in conjunction with Six Sigma approaches to reducing defects, Lean thinking is the powerful antidote to these seven wastes.

It requires the ability to specify value, line up value-creating actions in the best order, conduct these activities without interruption whenever someone requests them and perform them more and more effectively. In short, Lean thinking is 'Lean' because it provides a way to do more and more with less and less – less human effort, less equipment, less time and less space – while coming closer and closer to providing customers with exactly what they want when they want it.

These ideas were defined by Womack and Jones as the five principles of Lean.[20]

1. Specify value
2. Identify the value stream
3. Flow
4. Pull
5. Perfection

The starting point for Lean is **value**, which can only be defined by the ultimate customer. It meets the customer's needs at a specific price at a specific time.

The **value stream** is a set of all the specific actions required to bring a specific product or service (or combination of both) to the customer. This requires the following three critical management tasks.[21]

- **Problem-solving task:** running from concept through detailed design and engineering to production launch
- **Information management task:** running from order-taking through detailed scheduling to delivery
- **Physical transformation task:** proceeding from raw materials to a finished product in the hands of the customer

Once value has been specified and the value stream for a specific product mapped by the Lean enterprise and the wasteful steps eliminated, the next step is to make the remaining, value-creating steps **flow**.

The first visible effects of converting from departments and batches to product team and flow is that the time required to go from concept to launch, sale to delivery and raw material to the customer falls dramatically. When flow is introduced product designs are completed in months, not years, and inventory reduced by 75%. The customer **pulls** the product from supplier as needed rather than the supplier pushing products into inventory waiting for demand.

Organisations are beginning to identify entire value streams and accurately specify value. This allows them to continually add value to a product, and in turn allows customers to receive value from the organisation. With this value-oriented mindset, organisations are increasingly generating ideas to reduce waste and thereby reduce time, effort, cost, inventory and error while continuing to offer a product almost perfectly aligned to the customer's needs. The initial four

2.3 L02

principles of Lean thinking are a continuous loop. Targeted efforts to increase value identify hidden waste in the value stream, hindrances are revealed and can therefore be removed, direct communication between product teams and customers enables value to be specified more accurately, and value flow and receipt can be enhanced.

Table 2.8 summarises the advantages and disadvantages of Lean.

Advantages	Disadvantages
• Reduced waste – lower costs • Removes inventory – especially safety or buffer stock • Product lead times to market are shortened • Customer satisfaction increased, along with sales • Increased productivity • Morale increased, as more involved and engaged	• Cannot deal with turbulence • Needs a stable business • Difficult to accommodate external changes to the processes • Need to halt production processing to implement the Lean changes

Table 2.8 Advantages and disadvantages of Lean (Source: adapted from Lysons, K. and Farrington, B. (2012), Purchasing and Supply Chain Management (8th ed) Pearson Financial Times)

> *Check*
> What is a value stream and how does it relate to Lean supply?

Value stream mapping tools

Finding the value and identifying the value stream need tools to define them. Hines and Rich identified seven value stream mapping tools. These are set out in table 2.9.[22]

Mapping tool	Purpose and application
Process activity mapping	Reducing waste by eliminating unnecessary activities, simplifying or changing sequences
Supply chain response matrix	Reducing lead times and inventory levels
Production variety funnel	Targeting inventory reduction and changes in the processing of products with varying activity patterns
Quality filter mapping	Identifying, for improvements, the location of product and service defects, internal scrap, and other inefficiencies

Mapping tool	Purpose and application
Demand amplification mapping	Identifying demand changes along the supply chain within varying time buckets to manage or reduce fluctuations in regular, exceptional and promotional demand
Decision point analysis	Involves identifying the point at which products or services stop being made in accordance with actual demand and start to be made against forecasts alone. Indicates whether pull or push processes are used
Physical structure	Overviewing a particular supply chain from an industry perspective. This information may result in a redesign along the lines indicated for process activity mapping

Table 2.9 Hines and Rich's value mapping tools. (Source: adapted from Hines, P. and Rich, N. (1997) 'The seven value stream mapping tools', International Journal of Operations & Production Management, Vol. 17 Issue: 1, pp.46–64)

Inventory performance measures

To monitor inventory performance and track improvements – as with all aspects of the business – key performance indicators (KPIs) are required. The general rules of setting KPIs apply: they must focus on what matters most and they must be associated with targets; there is little value in reviewing the indicators if the information they provide about performance is not acted upon. Targets, as always, must be SMART: specific, measurable, achievable, relevant and time bound.

As always the number of KPIs used should be limited and focused. Capturing data and reviewing them takes time and costs money. This is only worthwhile if the actions which follow can drive real improvement in the business.

A number of key performance indicators have been devised to measure the extent to which an undertaking has the right quantity of inventory in the right place at the right time. The most useful are set out in table 2.10.

Time bucket
The period of time specified

KPI	What it measures
Delivery performance – OTIF (on time in full)	What quantity was delivered on time (within the given time bucket) against what quantity was required in that time bucket. Targets should aim to increase OTIF deliveries.
Lead times	The length of time taken to obtain stock from the time a need is ascertained to time the need is satisfied. Targets should aim to reduce lead times.

KPI	What it measures
Service level	Measures the actual service level attained in a given time bucket; the calculation being: $$\frac{\text{Number of times the items are provided on demand}}{\text{Number of times the item has been demanded}}$$ Targets should aim to improve the ratio.
Rate of stock turn	Indicates the number of times a stock item has been sold or consumed and then replaced in a given time period, using the formula: $$\frac{\text{Sales or issues}}{\text{Average inventory}}$$ Appropriate stock turn rates vary. The stock turn for food is greater than for car sales.
Stockouts	Measures stock not being available to meet the demand. There are a number of measures that could be used. Examples include the following. • Volume or material unable to be supplied as a percentage of sales • Volume or material unable to be supplied as a percentage of orders • Number of product lines on stockout as percentage of total product lines • Number or volume of product on back order (that is orders received which cannot be fulfilled) Targets should aim to reduce the percentage or number whichever measure is used.
Stock cover	This is the opposite of stock turn; it indicates the number of days the current inventory will last if sales/usage continues at the predicted rate. The simple way of expressing this is: $$\text{Days of stock coverage} = \frac{\text{Current quantity in stock}}{\text{Anticipated daily rate of usage}}$$ This ratio can be used to evaluate the effects of longer lead times or danger of imminent stockouts. The optimal length of stock cover will vary depending on stock profile, lead times etc.
Costs	Targets should aim to drive down the costs of acquisition and holding, not merely to remain within budgets.

Table 2.10 Inventory KPIs

Chapter Summary

Stock can be categorised in the following different ways.

- Opening and closing stock
- Work in progress, safety stock and finished goods
- Obsolescent and redundant stock
- Direct and indirect supplies
- ABC classification
- Dependent-demand items and independent-demand items

There are costs associated with holding inventory in terms of acquisition and holding costs, and also with stock not being available (stockouts); there are various options available to reduce these.

Key techniques used in managing inventory include the following.

- Forecasting
- Setting reorder quantities and deciding when to reorder
- MRP and MRP II
- ERP and ERP II
- Just in time and JIT II
- Lean

A range of KPIs can be used to monitor inventory management and the purpose of the targets to be associated with them.

Recommended reading

Lysons, K. and Farrington, B. (2016), *Procurement and Supply Chain Management.* Harlow: Pearson

Chopra, S. (2014), *Supply Chain Management.* Harlow: Pearson

Womack, J. P. and Jones, D. T. (2013), *Lean Thinking.* New York: Simon & Schuster

Cavinato, J. L., Flynn, A. E. and Kauffman, R. G. (2010), *The Supply Management Handbook.* New York: McGraw-Hill Education

---

End of Chapter Assessment

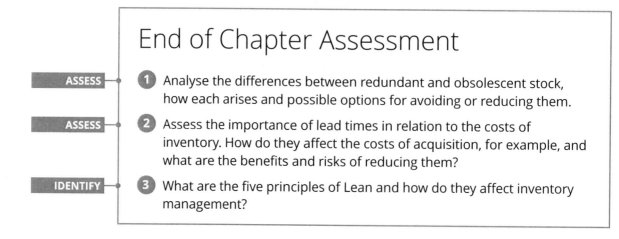

ASSESS — ❶ Analyse the differences between redundant and obsolescent stock, how each arises and possible options for avoiding or reducing them.

ASSESS — ❷ Assess the importance of lead times in relation to the costs of inventory. How do they affect the costs of acquisition, for example, and what are the benefits and risks of reducing them?

IDENTIFY — ❸ What are the five principles of Lean and how do they affect inventory management?

4 Discuss the differences between 'push' and 'pull', and give examples of where you could use both. — DISCUSS

5 Investigate and discuss the 'waste' in your organisations? What steps could you take to minimise this? — IDENTIFY

6 Explain the differences between objective and subjective forecasting? — EXPLAIN

7 Use the economic order quantity formula to calculate a reordering quantity for one of the stocked items of an organisation with which you are familiar. — EVALUATE

8 List the differences between JIT and JIT II. Which could be applied to an organisation with which you are familiar? — LIST

References

1 Oxford English Dictionary (n.d.). Oxford: Oxford University Press.

2 Compton, H. K. and Jessop, D. A. (2012), *The Official Dictionary of Purchasing and Supply*. Cambridge: Cambridge Academic

3 Cavinato, J. L. (2006), *The Supply Management Handbook*. New York: McGraw-Hill Education

4 Lysons, K. and Farrington, B. (2012), *Purchasing and Supply Chain Management*. Harlow: Pearson

5 Ahmed, D., Elkettani, Y. and Kasem, A. (2016), "Application of statistical methods of time-series for estimate and predict of the food gap in Yemen", *International Journal of Innovation and Applied Studies*, Volume 16, Issue 1, pp. 94–101

6 Lysons, K. and Farrington, B. (2012), *Purchasing and Supply Chain Management*. Harlow: Pearson

7 MoneyVan (2015), *RW's simple MA ride* [online]. Retrieved from: moneyvan.ca/rws-simple-ma-ride [Accessed on: 8 March 2019]

8 Forrester, J. (1961), *Industrial Dynamics*. Cambridge: MIT Press

9 Boyd, K. (n.d.), *Cost Accounting: The Economic Order Quantity Formula* [online]. Retrieved from: www.dummies.com/business/accounting/cost-accounting-the-economic-order-quantity-formula/ [Accessed on: 1 March 2019]

10 Lysons, K. and Farrington, B. (2012), *Purchasing and Supply Chain Management*. Harlow: Pearson

11 Compton, H. K. and Jessop, D. A. (2012), *The Official Dictionary of Purchasing and Supply*. Cambridge: Cambridge Academic

12 Ibid.

13 Ibid.

14 Womack, J. P. and Jones, D. T. (2013), *Lean Thinking*. New York: Simon & Schuster

15 Compton, H. K. and Jessop, D. A. (2012), *The Official Dictionary of Purchasing and Supply*. Cambridge: Cambridge Academic

16 Womack, J. P. and Jones, D. T. (2013), *Lean Thinking*. New York: Simon & Schuster

17 Ohno, T. (1988), *Toyota Production System: Beyond Large-Scale Production*. Portland: Productivity Press

18 Compton, H. K. and Jessop, D. A. (2012), *The Official Dictionary of Purchasing and Supply*. Cambridge: Cambridge Academic

19 Ibid.

20 Womack, J. P. and Jones, D. T. (2013), *Lean Thinking*. New York: Simon & Schuster

21 Ibid.

22 Hines, P. and Rich, N. (1997), "The seven value stream mapping tools", *International Journal of Operations & Production Management*, Volume 17, Issue 1, pp. 46–64

CHAPTER 3
Understand the concept of through life cost

Learning outcome

By the end of this chapter, you will understand the concept of through life cost.

Chapter overview

3.1 Analyse the contributing factors when establishing total cost of ownership

You will understand:
- Purchase price
- Hire or lease
- Acquisition costs
- Usage costs
- Maintenance costs
- Operation
- Utilities
- Training
- Disposal and end-of-life costs

3.2 Compare the factors to consider when building a total cost of ownership model

You will understand:
- Include all costs
- Use best estimates of values available
- Hidden costs – global sourcing, risks associated with extended supply chain
- Only develop for larger purchases
- Ensure senior management support
- Cross-functional support – ensure access to data
- Teamworking – reduce data collection time

3.3 Identify the contributing elements to end-of-life costs
- Decommissioning
- Removal or disposal processes
- Legal aspects – waste management
- Environmental factors
- Triple bottom line – people, planet, profit

Introduction

This chapter will consider a very wide range of issues which contribute to 'through life cost'. Many of the themes will be familiar from experience as a consumer when buying products for everyday home use. Other elements may be familiar from higher-priced items purchased or advertised.

Organisations are involved in the purchase, lease and hire of a wide range of items – some with a short lifespan and some much longer. Organisations also purchase (or procure) many different materials, products, services and equipment. Many of these purchases share through life cost elements and assessment techniques.

The principles covered in this chapter are practical and logical. Buying low-cost disposable items may seem like a simple decision that has a low impact on business finances – but there may still be cheaper alternatives or ones that are less environmentally damaging both in terms of production and at end-of-life. For example, a specific boiler (furnace) may have a low purchase price but high running costs and a short lifespan before replacement, but another may have low running costs and an excellent environmental rating but a high purchase price.

This chapter will consider the work of a buyer, and challenge the concept of short-term, financial-only considerations. Quantitative, financial assessments, alongside estimates and assumptions that form part of qualitative, opinion-based assessments that may be difficult to quantify will also be looked at.

Fixed assets
Accounting term used to describe items which are in possession but not intended for routine sale. Typically, these include vehicles, fixtures and fittings, land, buildings and machinery. Most accounting standards have detailed rules on fixed asset requirements and descriptions

Current assets
Accounting term used to describe stock items in an organisation which are routinely bought and sold. Accounting conventions also include cash and money the business is owed (debtors/receivables) as part of current assets

 3.1 Analyse the contributing factors when establishing total cost of ownership

Purchase price

At first glance the purchase price may appear to be an easy issue to consider – but specific products or services may have different characteristics, specifications and performance. They may also have different capabilities in terms of longevity (how long can it work before it has to be replaced?) and reliability (how often will it break down?).

This first section will consider a range of different price-related aspects, some of which may apply to both **fixed assets** (typically equipment and machinery used in the business) and **current assets** (the stock which is used or bought and sold). In some cases, the comments can be seen to relate more to one type of asset than the other.

In many retailer-to-consumer markets, the price payable is the price shown on the product or on a website; buyers can check competitor prices and may make use of a 'price comparison site'. Unfortunately, the business-to-business market is not as clear. In many cases, manufacturer-to-wholesaler and wholesaler-to-retailer price lists are only available to organisations applying to be customers. Registered customers may be sent price lists or given passwords to access online information. Supplier price lists often have 'valid from' dates and 'valid to' dates – but many also have the warning that specific item prices could be changed without notice. Many countries have legislation or court practice that a published price list is only an illustration until a quotation is provided or an order confirmation is received.

A price list may be rigidly followed by some businesses, but for others it is a starting point for a range of variations that could be offered or negotiated. These may be based on, for example, the type of organisation, the size of the order and historic spending patterns.

Fixed price, market price and adjustable price

In most cases, buyers expect a fixed price from a supplier following the issue of a **request for quotation** or supplier response to a **tender** for a purchase, rather than one that might change. It is important to establish whether the quotation is a fixed price or whether it is subject to change for any reason up to the point of order and between order placement and order completion.

Fixed price

This gives the buyer an assurance that the cost is known and will not change (subject to the timescale or quote detail). There is also the benefit that quote comparisons are based on the same basis at that time and that constant updates prior to commitment are not needed.

Unfortunately, prices do change – they are vulnerable to demand and supply and competition – and in some cases government regulation or taxation. Organisations that can get a fixed-price agreement with a supplier for a period of time have an assurance that the price will not increase. This will allow forward planning and (if appropriate) the ability to provide confirmed prices to customers themselves.

To quote competitive prices, suppliers need to ask 'how many do you want?' and 'over what timescale?' Organisations can place fixed-quantity orders over a period (a 'standing order'; for example, 250 items per month for six months). They can also commit to a volume over a period of time and then ask for deliveries in the volumes required from time to time (a 'call off order'; for example, a commitment to buy 2000 items could be completed by a first order of 300, followed by 800, then 200, then a final 700).

Organisations in countries which have high inflation rates may find it impossible to establish fixed prices. It is also possible that the price is significantly inflated to allow for inflation over the period requested.

It looks like supplier fixed prices are the 'right answer', but it is possible that prices could reduce over a period of time, leaving the buyer paying a higher price than the current 'market price'.

> *Remember*
> The terminology used in the quote is important, and if it is unclear then the buyer should clarify this with the seller.

Market price

The market price is the amount payable to acquire a specific item at a specific time. This could be the stated price available from a single supplier or range of

Request for quotation
A standard document or electronic request from a buyer to a supplier detailing a requirement and requesting a quotation. Some also request other information which may include stock availability and technical detail

Tender
A formal process of requesting a response to a detailed requirement from a buyer. The tender principle is designed to allow competitive bids with an evaluation of a number of supplier responses

Commodity markets
Raw material or part-processed product markets with established standards and trading allowing published prices reflecting demand and supply

Hedge
A technique of taking a position either in current stock or future stock to offset potential losses should the price move. A hedge will have a cost of trading and may involve the use of technical financial contracts

suppliers. A different price is obtained using different variations of the definition that might be used by suppliers.

- 'The price applicable is the current list price on the day of order placement'.

- 'The price payable will be the lowest of the list price of the top three suppliers in the week prior to order placement'.

- 'The price payable will be the average of published prices for the top three suppliers in the month prior to purchase'.

- 'The price payable will be the lower of our published price and competitor X as published on the date of receipt of the order'.

All these leave some uncertainty relating to the price paid and the discretion of suppliers to price. For some items purchased, there may be a regulated market where prices may be fixed.

There are also organised **commodity markets** trading standard materials and agricultural products. These have constantly adjusted prices reflecting supply and demand. The markets allow for 'spot' buying (immediate trading), forward buying, forward selling and 'options' to buy and sell. These can be used to **hedge** the risk or secure a price that will support a quote, bid or purchase decision. The historic prices for commodities allow buyers (and sellers) to consider the price trends and price volatility (the extent and frequency of changes).

Adjustable prices

Some purchase contracts operate over a long period of time or the buyer may require a price for a project that has a long time to run before materials or labour is required. Both buyer and seller will wish to limit or avoid a risk of overpricing and underpricing.

In these cases, either a part-fixed/part-adjustable price or a wholly adjustable price is possible. These may be only 'upward' adjustments although many agreements can also have 'downward' adjustments or both upward and downward adjustments.

Agreements for adjustable prices will have specific wording.

- 'The quoted price may be increased by up to 2% to reflect increased costs, subject to a 30-day notice period or by mutual agreement'.

- 'The quoted material price for stages 4 and 5 of the project will be reviewed in year 3 and adjustments agreed between the buyer and seller to reflect market prices at that time'.

- 'The materials cost quoted is based on a current exchange rate of xxx, the quoted price may be increased or decreased should the exchange rate change more than 3%'.

There are also situations where there are more difficult 'unknowns' to deal with. Some organisations establish the basis of a price with a supplier which can then be applied to the contract or series of purchases. Here are some example solutions that can be used.

- 'The price payable for items ordered will be the list price (as amended in January and June) less 5% discount' (this is simply a continuing discount on list price).

- 'For a minimum volume of x and a maximum of y per delivery, the price payable is $z'.

- 'This price is based on 46 hours of technical programme development according to the specification. Additional hours for installation and support will be $x.'

- 'The architect will prepare and submit plans for approval based on the requirements for a fixed price of $x. Subsequent amendments and attendance at meetings will be subject to a separate quote based on $y per day.'

Use of 'reference indices'

These work on establishing a price basis at an initial fixed date (which could be a date of quote or date of contract). A specific published price index could be used which relates to the item, material or category of spend – this could be government-based or a trade association. Alternatively, a mixed formula could be agreed with constructed indices.

As the index moves up, the percentage change from the initial fixed date to the cost calculation date can be calculated. The percentage change can then be applied to the original cost basis and the revised cost claimed.

> *Apply*
> Think about your own organisation or one you are familiar with. Are there circumstances where adjustable prices have been used? How were these established?

Discounted price

Most buyers would like the idea that they have a price that is less than the published or list price. Many suppliers are prepared to offer lower prices, provided it has some justification. Some industries expect to offer sliding-scale, discount-off list prices subject to the value of an order, the value of the new account or even the opportunity to offload some stock. For longer-term customers, a standard % off list price could also be documented. Some sales management software has preloaded profitability information regarding different products and scales of discount permissible. 'You don't get if you don't ask' is a traditional view of the need for buyers to be prepared to negotiate.

Promotional price

A promotional price may be offered by suppliers to stimulate interest and orders – sometimes this is intended to encourage larger volume orders from existing customers. In other cases, it may be to attract new customers or be a wholesaler offer because of a manufacturer's promotion. It is possible suppliers will promote to clear excess stocks or in anticipation of excess stocks.

Other variations include the following.

- **Linked promotions**: a price reduction for one item if ordered with another item
- **Order value promotions**: reductions for ordering more than a certain value of products
- **Free issue promotions**: order a number of items and additional item(s) are free

Payment arrangements and payment in advance

The cost of goods or services can be affected by payment terms. 'Trade credit' is often available for B2B transactions although this can vary across industries and 14, 30, 60 or 90 days after delivery are common.

- **Payment in advance or on delivery**: this may allow a buyer to negotiate a discount if the normal supplier terms are trade credit.

Consignment stocking
A technique of acquiring stock from a supplier and only paying when sold or used rather than paying following a trade credit period

- **Delayed payment**: an additional negotiated credit period may benefit the buyer as this can prevent finance costs of earlier payment or the opportunity to gain interest on funds.

- **Consignment stocking**: buyer costs can be reduced by a supplier agreeing to provide stock which is only invoiced when used (or when sold). A variation is 'sale or return' where stock is available to the buyer but can be returned if no longer required or at a fixed time after supply. Again, this can prevent finance costs of earlier payment or the opportunity to gain interest on funds.

Volume-based pricing

A volume pricing basis could be proposed by buyer or seller. The concept is that there will be different prices for different volumes purchased. Sometimes the lower rate applies to all volumes purchased and sometimes only the volumes above a certain figure. Table 3.1 shows a typical volume price structure.

Product	Price per pallet 1–3 pallets	Price per pallet 4–9 pallets	Price per pallet 10+ pallets
ABCX	$450.50	$420.35	$400.50

Table 3.1 Typical volume price structure

Although volume-based pricing normally works on the basis that larger volumes are lower priced on a per unit basis, there are situations where the supplier may require a higher cost per item for larger volumes. This could happen when additional transport and equipment is needed for larger volumes – or even requiring a 'contract out' to another supplier, affecting its cost structure.

Multi-part pricing

A multi-part pricing basis could be proposed by buyer or seller. The concept is that there will be two or more elements that are charged as part of an overall price package.

In some markets the two elements that make up the overall price package are the following.

- A fixed sum payable for service availability through a 'standing charge' (which is commonly paid monthly or quarterly)

- A 'usage fee' based on metered usage

For example, a business may have a low energy usage, but a high overall bill owing to the fixed sum element. Proportionately, the fixed sum element for a high-usage business is less relevant. Neither pricing element should be ignored.

Printed consumer product packaging
For an organisation purchasing printed product packaging, a typical pricing structure may have the following.

- Design and artwork preparation fee

- Tooling costs for production

- Production cost based on number of units

- Delivery cost to packing warehouse location

Depending on the item, the additional costs may add significantly to the cost per item.

Number required	Design fee (one-off, not volume dependent)	Tooling (one-off, not volume dependent)	Single-drop delivery	Production cost	Total cost	Cost per item ($)
100,000	$2500	$8500	$150	$15,000	$26,150	0.261
200,000	$2500	$8500	$150	$30,000	$41,150	0.206
300,000	$2500	$8500	$150	$45,000	$56,150	0.187

In this example, the impact of the fixed costs can be seen on the cost per item. The example also assumes no discount for larger orders. The design fee is a one-off that would only be paid again for a redesign.

Should this business wish to change supplier, provided the business owns the design rights, it can give the design to other suppliers to produce and not incur the cost again. The tooling cost, however, may need to be repeated for a new supplier unless the type of production equipment is the same and the business' ownership of tooling was agreed. Generally, production like this becomes cheaper with large volumes ordered, produced and delivered in a single batch.

Apply
Using the information in the table above, calculate the cost per item for 500,000 items, assuming the production cost increases in the same way as it has for other volumes.

Remember
Although volume-based pricing works on the basis that larger volumes are priced lower on a per unit basis, sometimes a supplier requires a higher cost per item for larger volumes (for example, additional transport and equipment is needed, or the supplier may need to 'contract out' to another supplier) – this will affect its cost structure.

Delivery costs

A supplier price may 'include free delivery', but in reality, this is a cost that must have been considered as part of pricing. This is particularly important for remote locations or international purchases, where the additional cost could be considerable. Some suppliers will absorb any additional costs and have incorporated a typical transport cost in their price. In other cases, a separate charge may appear on an invoice or even a separate invoice sent to the buyer. Transport costs are also covered as part of acquisition costs later in this chapter.

It is also likely that larger volumes or weights of load are higher costs. Here are some different examples based on recent wholesale price lists.

Example: wholesale flowers
Minimum: 50 flowers, no maximum

Example item 200 flowers, $1 each, one delivery per week

Delivery option	Cost of flowers	Delivery cost	Total cost	Cost per item
Standard weekday delivery	$200	$22.90	$222.90	$1.11
Saturday delivery	$200	$35.66	$235.66	$1.18
Delivery before 9am weekdays	$200	$32.90	$232.90	$1.16
Delivery before 9am Saturday	$200	$52.50	$252.50	$1.26

Wholesale Flowers: Minimum 50 flowers, no maximum.

Example item 200 flowers, $1 each, 100 per delivery, two deliveries per week

2 × Standard weekday delivery	$200	$45.80	$245.80	$1.23
1 × Standard, 1 × Saturday delivery	$200	$58.56	$258.56	$1.29
1 × Delivery before 9am weekdays 1 × Delivery before 9am Saturday	$200	$85.40	$285.40	$1.43

In this example, if a retailer requires flowers twice weekly, there is a significant difference on a per-stem basis. Ignoring the impact of the delivery charges would leave the retailer expecting higher profits than is possible. A single weekly delivery results in a lower per-stem cost but may result in wastage as flowers have a limited freshness.

Case study

Check
Why might a purchaser be reluctant to agree a 'standard delivery charge' for regular small orders from a supplier?

Retrospective volume discounts

This type of arrangement could be offered by the buyer or the seller as a solution to the problem of an uncertain volume required over a period of time. It allows a review of volumes or values of orders with a resulting discount allowed by the supplier in alignment with the agreement made. The discount is sometimes placed on the internal account of the buying organisation to offset current invoicing, paid to the buying organisation's bank account or 'free issue' goods allowed to the value achieved.

Case study

Discounts in operation

A multi-national supplier deals with a large national retail organisation which buys a snack food product to sell at a high retail price.

The list price shows that a lower price per case is available based on the number of full pallet loads bought each month. The retail organisation orders volumes on a continuous basis to maintain stocks with some variability across the year, resulting occasionally in lower or higher discounts.

The price per case negotiated is almost a 10% discount off the manufacturers' pallet load list prices.

The buyer is also offered an annual retrospective discount event with a difference – a three-month target figure is set by the seller that is higher than historic monthly sales seen by the retail organisation. The retail buyer accepts the challenge. Towards the end of the three-month period it is clear that the target will be met (the organisation had set a retail price that is slightly lower, and this has helped to increase demand).

The 'reward' is a 'buy one get one free' period for the retail organisation. This allows the retail organisation to offer the public a high level of discount on the product.

Hire
A legal commitment with terms and conditions allowing the owner of an asset to charge fees to a renter. The period of rental is usually fixed, although some rentals can be 'open' until the return of the asset

Check
Explain three ways in which a purchase price can be varied.

Remember
Whether it is a stock item or a 'fixed asset' purchase, there are many factors that contribute to the purchase price to consider.

Hire or lease

All organisations have occasional requirements for equipment to meet specific needs. The work of a buyer should consider whether the need is best met by a purchase, as there are alternative options available.

- A purchase requires an ability to finance the sum required
- A purchase suggests the equipment will have enough use to make ownership beneficial
- A purchase suggests the organisation has storage space for the item

Both **hire** and **lease** offer alternatives to outright purchase.

Lease
A legal commitment with terms and conditions allowing the lessor (who owns the asset) to charge 'rental' fees to a lessee (who will be able to use the asset). The terms and conditions will detail the responsibilities for maintenance, insurance and end-of-contract rights and responsibilities

Hire

Car hire may be thought of as an appropriate example of hire. However, although many personal car hire contracts can be relatively low cost and for just a few days, the concept of hire can be much more flexible and cost beneficial than purchasing the asset.

The range of items available for hire is dependent on the location and demand – but the following are some examples from specific business sectors.

- **Location**: office buildings, warehouses (rental agreements for fixed periods)
- **Event planning**: tables, chairs, carpets, marquees (large temporary structures) floor panels, costumes, flowers, lighting, audio-visual equipment, air conditioning, heating
- **Catering**: fridges, cookers, ice makers, plates and glassware, cleaning equipment
- **Construction**: surveying equipment, test equipment, excavators, diggers, dump trucks, pile drivers, cranes, scaffold towers, tarmac layers, formwork, cement mixers, pumps, specialist cutting equipment, hoists, access platforms, temporary buildings for site use
- **Logistics**: temporary additional storage buildings, space in other warehouses, shipping containers, tractor units, trailer units, stock moving equipment including forklifts

Hiring does have some characteristics that may be considered as part of the decision before going ahead.

- Hiring means that the asset is not owned, and the organisation requiring the asset cannot control the cost of hire or its condition on arrival
- The organisation requiring the asset must agree to the terms and conditions of hire
- The cost may appear inexpensive in the short-term, but as the asset may remain un-hired for some time in its life, the hire fees will need to also cover the non-hire time
- There may be times when the asset is already on hire and an alternative cannot be found – this may affect operations of the organisation requiring the item

Some advantages of hiring are obvious, but others are less obvious.

- Hiring reduces the need to borrow money for purchase or commit funds to being 'locked up' in asset ownership. This is also known as the opportunity cost – the funds can be used for other projects that could create profits or avoid losses.
- Hiring specialised equipment for low-use situations makes sense – if purchased, the asset will remain unused for some of its life.
- The company owning the asset will store it when not in use; ownership implies there is somewhere for its safe storage.
- Most maintenance of the asset is the responsibility of the owner – the hirer may be liable for replacement of some working parts or damage.
- Hiring does not 'lock in' an organisation to a specific type or technology. A small machine is sometimes beneficial, a large machine can be more efficient – a purchase may have to compromise.
- Buying an asset with, for example, a five-year life would be an expensive mistake if technology was changing and making the equipment obsolete.

Opportunity cost
A term from economics used to consider that funds used for one purpose could have been used for a different purpose with a better financial outcome

It is possible to hire an 'operator' as well as the equipment – this means there is no need to have staff trained to use all equipment and that the hired operator should be able to be effective and efficient from start-up. Some equipment requires a licensed operator.

It is possible for the hired equipment to be transported to the location for use. This could save a lot of time and money, and for heavy oversize plant it could avoid the need for oversize load transport ownership.

At the asset's end-of-life, disposal and recycling are the responsibility and cost of the owner.

The decision to rent rather than purchase starts with a simple 'payback' calculation – for this, a comparative purchase price is needed, along with the rental cost and the number of occasions the asset is likely to be needed in a foreseeable period. More complex calculations are needed with higher cost of purchase assets. If finance is not available to an organisation, rental may be the only choice. For hire, a range of supplier quotes should be undertaken in a similar way to a purchase as different fees, equipment and contract terms may be offered.

Case study

Hire of equipment: 'simple comparison' payback calculation

Example: Professional audio-visual equipment

A major IT hardware company with a series of product launches across a large geographic area and needs the use of a very high-quality projector suitable for large-scale events. It has found a projector for large-sized images with excellent detail and capable of 3D projection. It is typically used in main-stage exhibitions and show venues. Purchase and hire prices are as follows.

- Day rental $1250

- Weekly rental $3750

- Purchase price $32,000

Using these figures:

	If the requirements are...	Then the rental cost is...
Week 1	1 event, 5 days total	$3750 (week rate)
Week 2	2 events, 2 days each	$3750 (week rate)
Week 3/4	5 events, 2 days each, 14-day period	$7500 (week rate ×2)
	Total days required = 23 days, 4 weeks	Total cost $15,000

For comparison, the purchase price is $32,000

Using the weekly rate, $32,000/$3750 = 8.5 weeks (9 weeks) usage is required to justify purchase.

The item is not bulky, so storage should not be a problem. Although bulbs may need replacement ($400), the equipment should have at least a three-year life.

In this example, even if all the planned events take place, the cost of purchase exceeds the rental cost and rental is preferred. The opposite view may be taken if this pattern was seen annually, as the purchase price is nearly met in the second year ($30,000 rental cost, $32,000 purchase cost), Buying becomes a clear decision should the same pattern be seen in year three ($45,000 rental cost, $32,000 purchase cost).

Apply
Read the case study above. What other factors should the IT company consider when considering renting?

Lease

An alternative to purchase or rent is a lease. This is a contract to take possession (but not ownership) of an asset for an agreed period with payments on a regular basis. Leases on buildings follow these principles but will be subject to 'land law' regulations which can vary from country to country. Although a lease can be created between any two (or more) parties, the most likely scenarios are the following.

- The current owner leasing to a commercial user

- A manufacturer or distributor leasing to a commercial user

- A specialist leasing company buying an asset and leasing to a commercial user

- A specialist leasing company liaising between a buyer and a seller and financing the lease

Before making a commitment, the leasing business owning the asset (the lessor) will need to assess the risks of the organisation agreeing to lease (the lessee). The lessor will typically calculate the payments required to cover all costs, including financial costs, and include a profit. At the start of the contract the lessor may also anticipate the value of the asset at the end of the contract and allow some allowance or even reduced rental payments to reflect this. Detailed terms and conditions will be included in the contract – these may include responsibilities for insurance, repairs and maintenance.

The lease detailing is dependent on the requirements of the lessor and lessee. The timescale for a lease is highly variable, with some being less than 12 months and others being many years. Confusingly, the payments made from lessee to lessor are referred to as rentals – the use of the word reflecting that this is not just a loan, the lessee does not own the asset.

Some leases require an initial 'deposit' payment (for example, equivalent to three months' rentals), and if payments are missed then the lessor may reclaim the asset and claim any compensation for breaking the contract.

At the end of the lease term, most lease agreements require the asset to be returned to the lessor – the contract is at an end with the final payment. With some leases, the lessor may negotiate a separate sale of the asset to the lessee. In other leases there is an option at a stated price at the end of the term.

Equipment leases are often constructed around local or national tax allowances available – sometimes these are specific to particular types of asset.

3.1 L03

Lease arrangements can be made with insurance provided and charged by the lessor or without (in which case, the lessee requires insurance). They can also be with or without maintenance, repair and replacement parts or equipment included. These cost responsibilities need to be detailed in the agreement.

Leasing contracts have the following advantages.

* The initial purchase cost of an asset is avoided

* The rental payments can be met from everyday trading income – as the asset is used it contributes to rentals

* The cost for the lease period is known (and probably fixed)

* The asset is normally stored or in use at the lessee's premises

* The comparative interest charge included in the rental is often at a better interest rate than an equivalent loan

* A lease with full risk of insurance, maintenance, servicing and spare parts with the lessor makes financial planning and risk management easier

Leasing contracts also have the following disadvantages.

* The contract is expected to run for the whole term stated. Breaking the contract may incur additional fees.

* The requirement that the asset was leased for may change (smaller or larger volume may be required, less frequent use or just no longer needed).

* Newer or better technology may become available, but the organisation is locked into the contract.

* The lessor's estimates of residual value of the asset may be underestimated – so in retrospect the cost was higher than it should be.

* The contract agreed must be followed – if payments are missed the asset may be recovered and additional charges levied. If the asset is damaged at the end of the contract, additional fees for repairs may be charged.

<< Case study

The Frank Hotel
A four-star traditional hotel has encountered some problems with using a laundry service provider. In the past the business had collections of used laundry three times a week with deliveries at the same time. Occasional late deliveries created problems, and the quality of some cleaning was not to the expected standard.

The owners investigated creating its own laundry unit in a building previously used to store furniture no longer in use. The business owners wanted large-scale washers, dryers and sheet presses and the total investment was looking very high – the owners also had an ongoing project for air conditioning and room upgrades.

The owners obtained price comparisons and used a specialist commercial laundry equipment supplier to assemble options. The final package featured two washers, two dryers and a sheet press. The lease periods were different for each machine, reflecting different life expectancy of machines and the potential need to upgrade.

Outright purchase may have been possible for part of the equipment, but this would have left a borrowing requirement for the remainder or a postponement of the room refurbishment. The hotel was later able to reduce its linen stock as a one-day laundry turnaround was possible.

Remember
There are more options possible than just purchase when an organisation needs a fixed asset.

Acquisition costs

Most organisations focus on the purchase price of an item, but acquisition costs can add significantly to the purchase price – these may be 'hidden' or less readily identifiable. (Acquisition costs were covered in chapter 2.) Acquisition costs are incurred every time a purchase is made, whether it is a large-scale purchase or a small-scale purchase. The costs of shopping for someone include the following.

- The cost of travelling to and from the shops
- The time taken (including planning the shop and putting away the shopping), calculated as a cost per hour
- When shopping online, the time taken to research, choose and place an order

This means that shopping costs more than just the cost of the items brought home or delivered. If someone goes shopping (or 'browses online') but does not buy anything, then a cost is still incurred. Generally, the higher the cost of the item, the more likely it is that it will need to be researched in advance and the more time will be spent on making a decision. There are also situations where the cost may be high and there are many alternatives that need to be considered before a purchase can take place. These complex purchases could take many weeks to research and review.

Apply
Think about your last personal complex purchase.

- What research did you undertake and how long did it take?
- How long did it take to identify suppliers and get quotes or details?
- Were other people involved, and if so, how much time did this take?

In organisations, the acquisition costs are a little more involved, but the principles are the same. Every purchase involves a series of activities and there are probably good reasons for each activity. In many cases these activities are control features to reduce or eliminate risk. In some cases, the involvement of other staff and managers are there for the prevention of fraud or to avoid expensive mistakes. In other cases, it may just be a situation of organisational structure and process choice.

Very few organisations calculate a cost of acquisition by adding up the involvement of each person against a specific purchase. It is easy to track the number of hours or days taken from identification of need to fulfilment, but awkward and time-consuming to track the minutes for each transaction. Some project management software encourages the tracking of the hours spent on each activity against a budgeted time.

Some organisations take the total view of the cost of purchasing staff plus an allowance for other costs and divide it by the numbers of orders placed each year.

Staff costs	$150,000
Other costs	$45,000
Total cost	$195,000

Purchase orders for year 925

Cost per order $195,000/925 = $211 per order.

This looks like a reasonable approach – but the averaging which results masks the possibility that some purchases are very quick and have low acquisition cost and others could take a long time, have lots of changes and require a lot of intervention.

Some organisations try to get buyers to consider the time taken on a purchase in terms of efficiency. Efficiency relates to the effective use of resources (time, people, money and equipment). Buyers may have a personal cost per hour in mind as they are considering time taken on an activity.

The cost per hour is often estimated, or a standard expectation provided. Some work on annual salaries, plus employment taxes and expenses, divided by working days (with deductions for training) and effective hours per day: for example, ($62,500/220 days working)/7 hour day = $40.58 per hour. Some organisations extend this to allow for management supervision, so in this case $50 per hour may be used.

Effectiveness is how well the work is done (error or fault free). This is much less easy to assess as some errors are immediately apparent, but some may take some time to discover and could have multiple causes.

Efficiency and effectiveness are affected by the systems and procedures to be followed and the availability of staff or managers at each stage of the process.

Many buyers can recall very long and involved acquisition processes. Quicker, lower acquisition cost transactions tend to be the following.

- Repeat purchases with an established supplier

- Standard 'catalogue' low-cost purchases

- Familiar products

Slower, higher acquisition cost transactions tend to be higher-risk contracts, including the following.

- New products and sectors

- Requirements that are not finalised, with continuous changes

- High-cost, long-term contracts

- High-cost **capital expenditure** items

- Use of formal tenders rather than supplier selection and purchases

- Service contracts with multiple variations and options

- Projects involving interaction of many suppliers

- Acquisition regulated by government or complex corporate governance

Capital expenditure
Money spent on acquiring and maintaining fixed assets bought by an organisation which are used within the organisation rather than bought for resale. (Typically, these assets are land, buildings and equipment)

Check
Why should an organisation monitor acquisition costs for purchases?

Consumables
Items which are typically required as part of a process, but which do not form part of a finished product. A machine may require cleaning products to maintain performance – the liquids and industrial wipes would be consumables

Site preparation

Site preparation may well be required for larger fixed asset purchases.

Most equipment has requirements to gain access to replace components and **consumables**. Changes may be needed in the layout of the installation area to allow for loading, unloading and access door clearances. The requirements are often outlined in installation and operating manuals, which will also detail the appropriate operating conditions (usually high and low temperature and humidity measurements) along with any ventilation and power supply specifications. It is also possible that the floor area may need to be checked for weight loading requirements, which would need to include the weight of any lifting or moving equipment. The result of this work could mean requirements for floor strengthening, additional cabling or electrical installations.

The journey of the equipment from point of arrival at the premises to the final installation point will also need to be checked for dimensions and weight loading. Requirements will need to be detailed, possibly with the help of specialist installation contractors or delivery contractors.

Installation

Installation requirements will vary according to the type of equipment and operational requirements. The responsibilities of the site owner, operator (if different from the site owner), contractors and suppliers should be detailed. For larger or more complex equipment, it is usual for the supplier (or a nominated/agreed contractor) to install and for the customer not to attempt to use it until the installation has been completed and 'handed over'.

Acceptance testing

Equipment should have been tested by the manufacturer prior to shipment. The more complex the equipment, the more likely it is that a formalised 'Factory Acceptance Testing' (FAT) is undertaken. Although this is normally undertaken by the supplier at the supplier's premises, it may be advisable to have the buying organisation's staff also involved in this testing. FAT should be conducted with a document set to show what has been tested and how. Any technical details, such as specific settings, resulting tolerances and noise or vibration should be documented so these can be used for comparison during customer installation. It should also incorporate any compliance statements and certification (for example, electrical safety certification). Any installation or operating instructions or guides should also be tested at this point.

On installation in the customer's premises it is advisable to have a similar approach for the supplier to test that the installed equipment is correctly installed and operating as expected. The supplier (or a specialist installer) will probably need to work with the customer to ensure safe installation – any electrical supply may need to be isolated to avoid affecting everyday operations in the event of failure. After confirmation of safety and effective operation, the customer should test the machinery under supplier supervision. 'Customer acceptance testing' (CAT) should be pre-planned and this should reflect the type and range of activities commonly used in practice by the customer, rather than a supplier demonstration pattern. Some equipment requires much more rigorous testing, as shown in table 3.2.

Acceptance test activity	Rationale/comment
Testing of operating manuals and directions	Ensures theory matches practice, an opportunity to refine and develop operating procedures
Health and safety, for example: Electrical testing Ensuring that any 'kill' emergency switches or automatic shutdowns work Ensuring machines cannot be used if machine guards are not in place Personal protective equipment, for example, for noise, heat/cold handling, eye protection	Allows new health and safety routines, notices and documentation to be provided, ensures designed-in safety is in operation
Load testing (adding weights progressively up to the designed maximum)	Ensures design and/or specification limits are met without failing or apparent loss of performance
Dry running (where the machinery is run but nothing is made)	This can reveal, for example, overheating, leaking lubricants, or vibration problems
Stress testing (running at a maximum load or volume)	Ensures design and/or specification limits are met without failing or apparent loss of performance
Soak testing (most often connected with IT systems, where the cycle of usage is multiplied up to ensure systems continue to perform)	Ensures design and/or specification limits are met without failing or apparent loss of performance
Compatibility testing (how the new equipment works with other equipment and particularly the IT infrastructure and software)	Ensures performance of new and existing equipment, to make sure it operates appropriately when run together with other equipment
Use of the full range of production materials and/or sizes	Ensures performance works with the range of materials as used by the customer, rather than supplier test materials
Use by a variety of operating staff	This supports the training requirement and identifies variables that may not be recognised by those unfamiliar with customer operations
Trial replacement of consumables and replacement parts	Ensures replacement routines are known and that accessibility is assured

Table 3.2 Acceptance test activities

All functions of the equipment should be tested, as a faulty machine (or one that does not conform to expected specification) may present a problem in 'proving' a fault after acceptance and payment.

From an IT point of view, compatibility with the full range of software and interactions with other equipment and programmes need to be tested. Working on a stand-alone basis is simply not enough as priorities and ways of communicating can create conflicts when used together.

Check

Why is it important for organisations to establish acquisition and installation costs for fixed assets before making a commitment to go ahead?

Site preparation and installation of automated teller machines (ATMs)

Case study ≫

Banks and independent operators install ATMs in bank locations, supermarkets and workplaces. Each site will vary with regard to ease of access, ease of installation and cost.

General pre-installation principles that are often used are the following.

- **Technical infrastructure**: meeting the online requirements at the ATM site and the data processing centre

- **Installation location**: assessing likely usage, physical changes to premises, electrical and IT cabling, property owner permission, planning permission

- **Delivery arrangements**: access to external or internal location, parking or suspension of traffic, prevention of damage to paving and/or internal surfaces

- **Security**: site security, safety of customers and additional CCTV or alarming

In the case of one bank, the decisions for installation were made based on an ATM development and replacement plan which was developed and then reviewed annually. Although the Head Office set the overall strategy, the regional management made decisions and approved the budgets.

Installation planning and installation was a multi-discipline effort, with local, regional and Head Office staff involved. Architects managed the installation design and drawings in conjunction with technical staff. Local installation contractors worked in conjunction with a Head Office department which co-ordinated the technical infrastructure, training, liaising with the delivery company and working with the manufacturer (which had to supply, test and commission the ATM before staff training and approval for 'live' operation).

The bank itself organised delivery of the machine from a specialist delivery service as this provided a warehouse for new and old machines with the opportunity for refurbishment and recycling of the parts. (The manufacturer would have contracted some of this work to a specialist itself.)

This bank operated four different styles of machine and the replacement programme meant that it could order ATMs by the hundred, securing a production run at the ATM factory which produced a significant saving per machine. A panel of regional contractors were used that were familiar with bank requirements and the manufacturer's installation requirements.

> *Remember*
> A supplier may offer a packaged cost (which may be convenient) but there are likely to be additional costs and looking at alternative suppliers and specialists may have cost advantages and/or other benefits.

Reducing acquisition costs

There are many methods available to reduce acquisition costs. Many of these require a change of approach by organisations. Organisations will wish to maintain some aspect of control, but if they wish to maximise value, control elements are arguably best put in place for higher-risk purchases and projects.

The following is a range of typical techniques used to reduce the acquisition cost.

Buyer discretionary spend

Many buyers have a value and/or type of purchase they are empowered to order without reference to colleagues or managers. This is quite often set at a low value (there have been examples of 'zero discretion' in some organisations, with every transaction being seen and signed off by managers). There could also be different spend limits for inexperienced and experienced staff and for routine purchases compared to one-off contracts. In each case, orders above a personal spend discretion are signed off by the appropriate staff level, managers or the board of directors. Table 3.3 shows examples of tiered responsibility and levels of discretionary spend.

Role	Repeat purchase orders	New purchase orders	New contracts
Buying assistant, up to one year in post	Up to $1000	Up to $250	$0
Buying assistant, after year one	Up to $2500	Up to $1000	$0
Buyer, up to one year in post	Up to $5000	Up to $2000	$0

Role	Repeat purchase orders	New purchase orders	New contracts
Buyer, after year one	Up to $7500	Up to $5000	Up to $2500
Senior category buyer	Up to $15,000	Up to $10,000	Up to $5000
Supply chain director	Up to $30,000	Up to $30,000	Up to $30,000

Table 3.3 Tiered responsibility and levels of discretionary spend

'User buying'

Some items that are established standard specification could be left for users to undertake ordering themselves, rather than involving a buyer. Control is maintained by training and limiting the users to specific suppliers, items and total spend. For example, this is often routinely in place for low-value hospitality and travel costs.

Vendor managed inventory (VMI)

This is the generic term given to a range of techniques which involve suppliers in supporting the purchasing process by doing more than just reacting to an enquiry or purchase order. This can include any or all the following.

- Physical checking of stock at customer warehouse or retail outlet
- Reporting on volumes sold and seasonal expected trends
- Recommending order volumes
- Reverse logistics – reporting on returns and recommending actions
- Monitoring the condition of assets (and maintenance for capital expenditure equipment)
- Maintaining stocks in warehouse units, whether customer owned, supplier owned or third party
- Where the work has contributions from supplier and buyer, the common phrase used is 'co-managed inventory'

Case study »

Vendor managed inventory (VMI)
Organisations like the idea that staff time is maximised doing work which adds value.

Vendor managed inventory has many applications and versions.

Supermarket stocking: Herbs and spices (direct store delivery and stock management)
These items come in a large variety but collectively represent a relatively small spend for supermarkets. Stock control and reordering would be proportionately more expensive than some other categories in-store. The supplier offers visiting representatives with stock. The representative checks stock on the shelves

(typically weekly) and records remaining stock. This is compared to the previous visit and the store can check sales and stock against the records available if necessary.

The supplier's representative then refills the shelves to the previously agreed volumes, completes a 'delivered order' form on paper or electronically which is confirmed at store level. The supermarket is then invoiced for payment.

The supermarket extends this scheme and the supplier stock check is the point at which the sales for the previous period are recorded and an invoice raised – in this way the supermarket benefits from 'consignment stocking'.

Industrial manufacturing: small fixings (direct delivery and stock management)

The supplier visits the customer site and checks stock remaining across the range of products supplied and locations. Records of usage are compared, and stock is replenished at that time. The delivery is signed for and the supplier places stock at the point of use or in storage.

Supermarket: Large volume sales (vendor stock monitoring and distribution centre delivery)

In this example the supermarket allows the vendor to monitor retail store sales activity by allowing access to specific product 'live' sales. The vendor can prepare orders to 'top up' stock to an agreed level. These are delivered to supermarket distribution centres which add them to standard supermarket delivery visits.

The easiest gains from VMI are from suppliers that already have established systems and procedures. Where VMI is part of a new contract requirement, many suppliers may incur additional unwelcome costs and time is needed to establish routines, procedures, systems and responsibilities.

Two-bin Kanban

Although this is linked to **just in time (JIT)** processes, the principle of Kanban can reduce acquisition costs. (Kanban and JIT are discussed in detail in chapter 2.) Typically, two tote boxes are in operation for a product. When the first is empty the second one is used and it is the signal for a reorder which could be done, for example, by the following.

- An operator taking the stock card from the box and leaving it in the designated place for a reorder

- Using a bar code reader to alert the buyer or direct communication to the supplier

- A supplier on a VMI delivery visit taking the box away and bringing back a full one on the next visit

Just in time (JIT)
A range of techniques which are dedicated to the systematic elimination of waste, including the elimination of delays and streamlining of processes

By using a Kanban process, the routine process of involving a buyer is avoided – this 'standard reorder' process is set up by a buyer but does not routinely require a buyer's involvement. The replenishment is faster and more efficient.

Product catalogue

Items are listed and sources predetermined. The objective is the standardisation of items used, eliminating the search and quote time for a user or a buyer. There is a requirement for catalogue management or updating. The simplest catalogue system is to select single suppliers for specific categories and allow Internet user access with password use. This also maximises the benefits of placing a larger spend with a smaller number of suppliers.

More complex catalogues, with selected items from multiple suppliers, can be assembled by an organisation using suitable software.

e-Procurement techniques

IT systems which support procurement using integrated software can significantly reduce time taken in the procurement cycle. Costs are reduced in terms of less paper required and each order being completed much faster, and with the elimination of a lot of filing.

An extension of the product catalogue could provide users with pre-authorised items to place orders direct with suppliers.

The requisitioning process can also be speeded up by entering details into on-screen forms and internally transferring these to a buyer. Using integrated software, a buyer can 'lift' the detail and transfer it to a potential supplier for a quote or select a supplier and transfer a purchase order electronically. Management approval can also be done electronically.

If a supplier has similar software, then order confirmations can be received electronically, followed by copy despatch notifications and packing lists. Invoicing can also be advised electronically, with direct bank payment to the supplier on the due date.

Procurement cards

These are corporate payment cards which may run from a specific bank account, charge card or credit card operator. The idea is to allow the cardholder to buy products and services direct, rather than following a multi-stage traditional requisition form involving a buyer. Travel arrangements and hotel bookings are very common uses for cards held by non-buyers. They can also be used by buyers to make immediate payments (typically for lower-value purchases and buying on the Internet). Some organisations have a simplified authorisation system for these transactions and most have some restrictions on their use.

Check
List three ways in which acquisition costs may be reduced in organisations.

Usage costs

This section will focus on the most often seen situation of usage costs connected with capital expenditure equipment.

A usage cost may be part of a multi-part pricing agreement. This is sometimes used where equipment on rental or lease has replacement parts which have a limited life and a high cost. An example is a photocopy machine lease that specifies a cost per month (or 'rental charge') plus a cost per copy which increases if more than a number of copies is exceeded in a month. This is to reflect the expectation that heavier use will result in more maintenance visits and replacement parts – it is therefore important to assess the likely usage as the 'allowance' part might be under-used or over-used. Some photocopier contracts may include provision of preventative maintenance and some spare parts.

It can also be part of a vehicle rent or lease agreement – where mileage more than a certain figure is charged an additional amount per mile or kilometre. This reflects the reduced value of the vehicle at the end of the lease should the mileage be higher than expected.

Energy usage is also a usage cost. Although two comparative machines do the same job, there can be significant differences in the energy cost of running the equipment. For example, there are differences in the cost of fuel (gas, electric, petrol, diesel) for forklift trucks and the time or distance for which the trucks can be used.

Any annual cost can be converted into a usage cost. Management accounting principles can be used to identify costs that can be directly attributed to a project or as the basis of costing work to arrive at a price (see figure 3.1). Organisations often use averaged usage and average costs per hour as the basis for price bids.

Annual Cost			$426
Days in the year		365	
Less weekends	104		
Less holidays	12		
Working days		249	
COST PER WORKING DAY	Annual cost/working days		$1.71
COST PER HOUR, 8 hour day	Cost per working day/hours per day		$0.21
Average job using equipment each day		4	
COST PER JOB	Cost per working day/average jobs per day		$0.43
Job A: Three hours using equipment			
Based on cost per hour	3 x 0.21		$0.64
Based on day rate - no other jobs	1 x 1.71		$1.71
Based on average cost per job			$0.43
Job B: Two days using equipment			
Based on cost per hour	16 x 0.21		$3.42
Based on day rate	2 x 1.71		$3.42
Based on average cost per job			$0.43

Figure 3.1 Worksheet for calculating per day, per hour and per job costs

In figure 3.1, using different bases of calculation arrives at different costs. Notice that Job A and Job B have the same cost allocation using the average cost per job; when using a day rate or cost per hour there are different costs.

Usage rates for continuous-use machines can also be calculated, as in figure 3.2.

Equipment Cost			$36,000
Annual cost 3-year life	Annual cost/number of years' life		$12,000
Annual production expected low estimate	12,000	cost/production	$1.00
Annual production expected high estimate	18,000	cost/production	$0.67

Figure 3.2 Example usage rates: impact of volumes

Figure 3.2 shows that the cost of the machine on a per item basis will decrease as volumes increase. This can also form the basis of 'whole life costing' calculations, which are looked at later in this chapter.

Maintenance costs

Maintenance costs can vary widely from equipment to equipment and are likely to be driven mostly by the amount of usage. Maintenance includes periodic servicing, repair and/or replacement parts. Some equipment can be designed for 'zero maintenance'. This could be because the equipment has sealed units, or the construction of the item does not provide for replacement parts – so the equipment runs until failure or eventual replacement. Alternatively, the cost of maintenance could exceed the replacement cost of the item (for example, an item costing $3000 requiring parts replacement of $1500 and a labour cost of $2000) – this is 'uneconomic repair'.

Organisations may have a range of options when considering maintenance, although rental and leasing may have contractual requirements included. There may also be conditions of guarantees and warranties requiring maintenance to be undertaken – if not followed these could limit or prevent claims.

Corrective maintenance

Corrective maintenance (also known as reactive maintenance) is the term used to describe maintenance only undertaken when parts or the equipment fail. This may be a perfectly sensible option if parts are held in stock and are easy to fit and/or technical staff can attend quickly – so that the loss of production time is minimal. In other cases, the savings made from not servicing may be much lower than the costs of a breakdown.

Scheduled (routine) servicing

Scheduled (routine) servicing (also known as preventative maintenance) works on a plan, determining the recommended service requirements of equipment or periodic intervention at predetermined intervals. The scheduling can happen following the equipment completing a number of 'cycles' or uses. This is often set by taking the 'mean time between failures' statistics into account. For example, a photocopier could have a 'technical clean' by a specialist every six months or 10,000 copies and a monthly clean of rollers and trays by staff.

Routine servicing is intended to take appropriate action rather than awaiting a breakdown. Although the servicing will take the machine out of operation, this can be planned, and this should be more efficient than a breakdown incurring unexpected delays. Some equipment has sensors to give early notification that a service is required, and some equipment can even 'report' a service requirement using connections to Internet monitoring software.

In some cases, the absence of routine maintenance can result in more significant damage and failure. For example, oil filters in cars could be left unchanged until the engine stops. Unfortunately, the oil filter condition could block oil supply to the engine, causing significant engine damage, so routine replacement along with new oil is sensible.

Different manufacturers may recommend different maintenance patterns. There are examples of some high-performance cars that need servicing two or three times more often than some other models.

Bought-in and self-maintained options

Equipment varies hugely in terms of maintenance. The following are some examples of cases.

- There is no owner/user maintenance possible – this may be because of the technical knowledge, tools and skills required, but this could also be to deter customers from potentially damaging the equipment.

- The terms and conditions of guarantees and/or warranties may state that only the manufacturer or supplier may undertake repairs.

- Health and safety regulations may require authorised or registered persons to conduct maintenance, test and periodically certify safety.

- Training and continuous experience may be required to diagnose and efficiently solve maintenance problems.

- Replacement parts are easy to source, and instruction manuals clearly show diagnostic and replacement instructions.

Organisations considering self-maintenance of equipment should start by assessing the technical training and skills required. The employment of one person for maintenance of all types of equipment may leave the organisation vulnerable in the event of multiple machine failures (or staff absence).

Organisations considering bought-in servicing should be assured of the capability of maintenance staff and their availability. These arrangements need detailed contracts with agreed **service level agreements (SLAs)**.

In some cases where complex equipment is involved, the maintenance may be provided by a manufacturer's technician present at the installation site. An example of this is typically the conveyor systems used in airports and postal sorting. This helps in improving service and potentially reducing call-out costs and delays.

Organisations should also ensure that the bought-in service organisation has experience of the specific equipment and (where applicable) is 'manufacturer authorised'. Costs of both parts and bought-in labour can also vary widely.

Service level agreement (SLA)
This is a term used to describe a performance requirement. These are most typically expressed as contractual requirements. SLAs focus on measurable activities

Replacement and spare parts

In some cases organisations await a requirement before ordering replacement parts. In cases where the equipment is vital for operations, any delay may be undesirable. It may be possible for the organisation to keep stocks of spare parts. For other organisations, this is done as part of a spares contract with an assurance of maintenance of spare parts and a service level agreement (SLA).

In the absence of a contractual agreement, there may be no commitment for permanent stocking of spares from agents, distributors or even the manufacturers. The spare part problem may become even more difficult should the equipment be a 'one-off' or it is some time since the original manufacturing had ended. In some cases, alternative compatible parts may be recommended, although some may require changes to the equipment.

There are some cases of manufacturer- or dealer-supplied replacement parts being of identical specification to non-manufacturer parts – but the non-manufacturer parts may be significantly cheaper. In some other cases, non-authorised parts can be a much lower specification and lifespan.

Service-included and maintenance-included packages

Some equipment suppliers will offer initial servicing 'free' (it is included in a purchase price or other agreement). Some will also offer packages with a single payment or periodic payments to cover a number of years. These packages often provide comfort and confidence as a fixed price has been agreed and many suppliers offer impressive service standards and effectiveness. Unfortunately, these packages do not always represent good value for money – sometimes the 'risk transfer' results in servicing limited to a bare minimum or a reluctance to undertake preventative work.

More common issues are that the supplier will need to estimate the number of repairs alongside maintenance. As a result, the supplier may need to price high, in case the buyer requires higher support. Some equipment may need minimal maintenance in year one, as it is 'under manufacturer warranty' – so the cost is only for subsequent years.

These packages should be capable of easy comparison between different suppliers to check value for money. It is sometimes possible to check on the frequency of replacement and costs of standard parts as well as the cost of labour or 'call out' charges.

Guarantees, warranties and extended guarantees and warranties

Many suppliers will provide an initial period of guarantee or warranty to cover breakdowns or failures. In many cases, these are manufacturer-type commitments and the details may vary between suppliers. In some cases, only repairs are included but others may provide for replacement or provision of temporary replacement of equipment under repair. These may also have limitations on use or circumstances that make the guarantee or warranty void (for example, unauthorised servicing or parts).

Extended guarantees and warranties may be offered as part of a package price or they may be offered for an additional cost. Buyers may like the idea of a further period of 'known cost' maintenance but the supplier or insurer will need to set a price that covers the most likely volume and cost of repairs. Larger volume purchases of capital equipment tend to offer packages for 'total care' including replacements.

Guarantee
A commitment from the seller (or original equipment manufacturer) that should a product not meet a stated quality in a specified period then it will be repaired, replaced or refunded. There are likely to be terms and conditions. The guarantee is usually written

Warranty
A commitment that the product will perform as stated for the specified period. The detailing of the warranty will determine the rights of the owner and responsibilities of the seller. A warranty for a period longer than the guarantee (or with enhanced rights) may be offered for an additional cost

Case study

Desk-top computers: a snapshot view of B2B extended warranty offers
An organisation wants to purchase a mid-range computer. It chooses a specification 'base unit' and undertakes research to compare warranty offers available.

The first retailer-based research showed some difficulty in obtaining more than a three-year agreement (one-year manufacturer plus two years extension). Many businesses have a three-year replacement cycle in place and this does coincide with proportionately higher computer failures.

One quote is for unlimited repairs or replacement, but the other quote suggests that three repairs would be undertaken before replacement. Typical quotes are $160 for a computer costing $650. Given the first year is effectively 'free', this equates to $80 per year of additional cover.

The proportion of cover cost to purchase price is 25% in this case. For many businesses this would be regarded as a high additional cost, particularly if all computers were covered in this way.

Dealing direct with the manufacturer's website shows more options than the retailers. One offers an on-site customer visit with potential repair for three years at $65 (10% of the computer purchase price).

There are also much higher quotes for 'one off' one-year higher-level support ($1800 for 24-hour, seven-day attendance with a four-hour maximum delay).

Some manufacturers also offer additional services for tracking equipment performance and data security. Many manufacturers suggest a 'whole business' approach with maintenance contracts to suit the business need.

This example shows that there is high variability in service available and that the price of extending a warranty is worth investigating with multiple quotes.

Apply

Which of the following do you think are the most important factors for a business buying a desktop computer extended warranty?

- Speed of service response
- Lowest cost of extended warranty
- Comprehensive cover for faults and repairs
- Replacement desktop during repair
- Five-year cover
- 24-hour service calls

Many guarantees and warranties are funded by the organisation selling the item or the original manufacturer. This is often taken as a financial risk although some guarantees and warranties are underwritten by insurance. While this provides a third-party assurance, it leaves both the supplier and the insurance company with a need to generate a profit.

Although some social media sites and technical forums may reveal common maintenance issues, there are few clues to establish the likely breakdown or failure rates across the range of manufacturing and commercial equipment available.

Calculation of 'value for money' of extended warranties is far from clear, particularly as estimates are not likely to be based on verifiable data – and older equipment may not use the same technology.

Manufacturers often monitor failures via guarantee and warranty claims or service reports. Traditionally these take the form of graphs of failures over time. These graphs are used to predict future expected failures, with the hope of overall improvement. Although the percentage of failures is likely to be very low, they traditionally follow the following pattern.

- Failures at or just after initial use – this equipment may have passed initial factory quality control, but early use causes the equipment to fail – possibly because of component failure under load.

- Failures in 'normal useful life' – this is likely to represent occasional failures of components which could be increased by operator misuse or very heavy use.

- Failures towards the end of designed or expected life – this is the stage in which failures are likely to be more common. Moving components may become out of their expected tolerances or major parts that are not designed for replacement are wearing out.

Figures 3.3 and 3.4 show two different capital asset failure rate 'bathtubs'. Unfortunately, organisations buying capital assets will not know whether 'their' equipment will be an early failure, a late failure or fault free throughout its life.

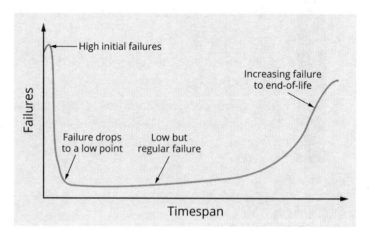

Figure 3.3 Failure 'bathtub' example for a capital asset

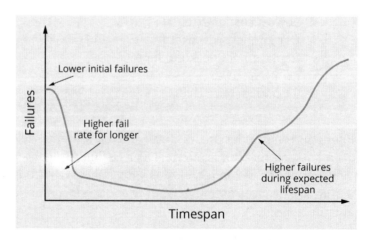

Figure 3.4 Different failure profile for a different capital asset

Because of failure uncertainty, extended warranties may be preferable.

> *Remember*
> Factors to consider for extended warranties are the following.
>
> - Cost of cover compared to replacement cost
> - Cost of a failure or breakdown, along with the time to recover
> - Expected number of maintenance events in the period to be covered
> - Relative ease of replacing equipment, including installation

Total productive maintenance concept (TPM)

This is a concept with origins in Japanese manufacturing techniques that has been developed and interpreted over time. The overall objective is to maximise overall equipment effectiveness. Although designed for manufacturing, the concept can be in-part applied to other equipment.

Overall equipment effectiveness is assessed on availability, performance and quality: therefore, these have a direct link to maintenance and the impact of poor work and breakdowns.

Among the TPM principles are the following proactive and preventative techniques.

- Training and education of operators to ensure effective use and knowledge of the equipment

- Health and safety awareness and operation

- Responsibility for everyday machine care is with the operators

- Planned maintenance to reduce probability of stoppages and slow working

- Quality maintenance to ensure quality defects are detected and corrected

> *Check*
> Give three aspects of maintenance which should be considered before purchase and monitored during ownership.

> *Remember*
> Maintenance issues are highly variable and some asset maintenance could contribute to a large increase in costs whether the asset is rented, leased or purchased.

Operation costs

Costs of operating equipment and premises can vary widely. Previous sections have considered maintenance costs and later sections consider utilities.

Cost of operating capital assets

Operation costs can include the setting-up time prior to operation. This can vary from machine to machine – time spent setting up and not in use is hidden wasted time. Requirements for cleaning equipment can also vary – 'self-cleaning' design elements can mean a longer time in operation and less probability of a stoppage. Some machines require a high level of technical training, while others require simple demonstrations. Some machines require constant monitoring, but other machines may have automatic stopping and signals so that one operator can monitor many machines. These examples show that an understanding of the operating requirements is needed prior to acquisition.

Car and lorry fleets need regular management to ensure that servicing and repairs are undertaken. Additionally, local vehicle taxes and periodic official tests may be required. Although these tasks are often managed by an organisation's own staff, outsourced fleet management is available. In this case, the internal costs and requirements for maintaining technical knowledge are replaced by the outsourced service provider, often with access to better vehicle acquisition deals and maintenance costs.

Cost of facilities management

This is the term given to a wide range of operational tasks that are required to maintain an organisation's premises. In some cases, organisations look to use specialists to provide some on-site services and maintain control of others. In some cases, the 'outsourcing' of many premises-based services extends to potentially the whole provision of premises and, for example, the security, catering, desking and warehousing.

The objective of internal or outsourced facilities management is to provide an appropriate level or service and expertise which represents good value for money. Using outsourced services allows an organisation to buy into the expertise (and potentially the buying power) of the provider. It also means that the everyday responsibility for the contracted services passes to the provider, allowing the organisation to focus on other tasks.

Options available for facilities management are the following.

- Wholly internal facilities management
- Single-service: selecting specific task(s) to be done by one or more contractors
- Bundled-service: grouping similar services together to be done by one contractor
- Total facilities management: a single comprehensive contract with a contractor

Cost of heating, cooling, air conditioning and lighting

These are all environmental operation requirements in different situations. The nature of the premises and technical specifications of these fixtures and fittings will contribute to costs. Different equipment will have different energy requirements and efficiency.

Cost of consumables

This cost is made up of the items that are required to support the use of equipment. Typically, these are items like specialised cleaning products, lubricants and fluids that are needed. These can add to the cost of ownership, particularly if the items can only be acquired from the original equipment manufacturer or agents.

Case study

A case of consumables: counter operations in a retail bank

Many years ago, a bank researched the purchase of counter-based computers. After proving the overall concept, the detailed **cost benefit** of the machines was estimated, based on the cost per machine.

The detailed contract discussions and price negotiation were then scheduled – and the development team calculated the use of 'consumables' based on some trial locations.

The machines were configured to meet the bank's requirements and had a small integrated printer to provide document prints and an immediate record of every transaction in print form. The two consumables that dominated were the ink-impregnated audit paper rolls and the ribbon unit for the printer.

Based on the usage of the audit roll, a replacement would be needed every two days for each active machine. Although the cost for one machine over a year was modest, a projection to the requirement over an initial 1000 machines with another 4000 to follow meant that the consumables cost would be a significant addition to the machine purchase price of $1500 over the six-year expected life. Adding an allowance for consumable cost increases made the six-year projections look difficult to justify.

The team challenged the 'manufacturer only' ribbon unit and secured a small reduction on list price, but design rights and low production meant this could not be sourced from another manufacturer. These were expensive at around $15 but were only needed once every three months on high-use machines.

The audit roll was challenged on many fronts – the quoted cost price of $1.20 was reduced by the manufacturer to $0.80 based on the volumes. Although the printer warranty was subject to 'use of authentic manufacturer supplies', the manufacturer admitted that the paper used was a standard industry specification. As a result, the team sourced a variety of alternatives and selected a roll supplier that had supermarket contracts in place. The roll chosen was more than twice the length of the original (so less time was spent changing rolls) and a trial proved no operational problems. The supplier price agreed was $0.85 per roll. The team also changed the standard line spacing to reduce roll use on each transaction. The result provided a significant change to the cost–benefit analysis and the investment went ahead.

The machines were still in use in many locations ten years after the original calculations.

Cost benefit
A calculation that considers the benefits resulting from a specific cost or process. Some benefits may not have monetary values

Check
List three examples of operating costs which may be used by a buyer as part of a fixed asset purchase decision.

Cost of utilities

These are the services consumed by organisations that are used by both organisations and individuals. Typically, these include electricity, gas, mains water, telephone, broadband and media.

Different countries may have different approaches to utilities.

- A traditional monopoly market with a single dominant provider, often state owned or state controlled

- An oligopoly market, with a few dominant providers, often state regulated

- An 'open market' with few limitations for providers which may or may not be the subject of state or industry self-regulation

All utilities are sensitive to demand and supply. The infrastructure of utilities means that they are built for a demand level. Economics principles suggest that, unless there is state intervention, utility costs will rise if demand rises. It also suggests that cost increases must be passed on to the user.

There are different cost structures that can be used for utilities as per the following.

- Costs based on usage with fixed per unit costs for a period

- Costs based on usage with variable, market costs per unit

- Costs with a low rate for low usage and a higher rate for higher usage

- Costs with low (off-peak) time elements and high (peak) time elements

- Two-part costs with a fixed-cost element and a rate per unit

- Costs quoted against a variable wholesale commercial market price

- Costs based on type of user (some industries may be charged differently)

- Energy costs based on 'origin' of energy sources

- Water costs may have two elements – one for provision of water, the other for waste water

Although telephone, broadband and media utilities share the 'fixed infrastructure' issues with energy and water, there is more packaging and variability to meet customer requirements. Broadband suppliers will quote different prices for different speed of transfer and volume of traffic.

Some markets have developed 'brokers' that will aggregate customer demand and negotiate packages for the buying group. Some industrial customers have their own generators that can feed electricity to the grid in exchange for payment.

Remember
Utilities may be difficult to allocate to different activities, yet can create a significant additional cost if high-usage machinery is operated or cost control is not undertaken.

Training

Training for the use of equipment is important as incorrect use could do the following.

- Affect the quality of a product
- Cause damage to the equipment
- Reduce the operating life of the equipment
- Cause death or injury

Many equipment suppliers provide initial training to operators on-site as part of an installation package. In other cases, off-site training or computer-based training may be offered.

Some machinery requires certification of training, sometimes by an independent assessor. This may also be a licence-type requirement in order to meet legal requirements.

It is a good idea to ensure that training records are maintained. Staff should not be asked to operate equipment unless they have received training and they have recent experience. Refresher sessions for those returning to the equipment would be sensible.

Case study

Aircraft operational training
Given the high standards required to operate aircraft, training in different aspects of aircraft operation is rigorous.

- To release an aircraft into service after maintenance, a licensed and certified technician is required to sign a confirmation of airworthiness. To have this capability, technicians undertake a course that is aircraft model-specific which takes about one month.
- Airline pilots require flying hours experience in general but also require 'type training' specific to a model. This usually involves a blend of flight experience and significant simulator work using type-specific procedures.
- Cabin crew require specific training and certification in order to have assigned tasks working on board commercial flights.

Forklift truck training
Different types of forklift and other heavy moving equipment requires training for safe use. In most countries there will be regulations requiring operators to be certified and/or there will be regulations making an employer responsible for not having trained operators.

For one country researched, each different style of truck required documented training; moving to a different design required a training course of one to five days and certification.

Non-operators also need training on sites where forklift-type vehicles operate – they will need to know the zones of operation, and procedures, and wear high-visibility clothing.

Training manuals and operating manuals

It is a good idea to have these available for all staff near to the equipment. Some of the best examples have photographs showing key parts of the equipment taken on-site with illustrated step-by-step guides.

Disposal and end-of-life costs

Disposal and end-of-life involves a range of different situations requiring different processes. The processes are similar for 'current asset' stock (for example, goods for resale, materials for manufacturing, bought-in components) and fixed assets (capital assets, for example, manufacturing equipment, computers, office furniture), where these are not items being produced or routinely sold.

- **Obsolete stock**. This is stock which has been assessed as having been replaced by other stock or outdated, perhaps by a change of user requirements or technology. Sales or usage is likely to be zero or very low and the market has just 'moved on'. The costs of maintaining storage of this stock may exceed the sales or benefit of maintaining the item(s).

- **Redundant stock**. This is stock which an organisation has no foreseeable requirement to use or is no longer marketing. It is possible that the stock may have users and a demand, but this will not be in the normal business experience of the organisation.

- **Surplus stock**. This is stock which is 'overstocked' – which could be a case of over-ordering by misreading trends, an order cancelled by a customer, an unexpected downturn in the market or a mistake. For fixed asset stock, it could be a case that fewer machines are required to meet a production or task. The stock is likely to be 'current' but there is just too much of it for current requirements. In some situations, (for example, fashion garments or computer components), organisations need to act on surplus stock identified before it becomes obsolete.

- **Scrap stock**. This is stock that is considered as having no conventional market for the items' original intention. Rather than considering alternative sales or uses, the item(s) will be sold for scrap or alternatively disposal may be a cost to the organisation. This may be the consequence of faulty or damaged goods, equipment that cannot be repaired or material 'off cuts' that are too small or cannot be matched to other materials. It may also be required for returned or replaced items and perishable goods that have date-expiry or are no longer fit for transport or use. There is a strong belief that potential scrap should be viewed firstly for reuse and recycling. Scrappage is likely to be the ultimate destiny of obsolete, redundant or surplus stock that cannot find an alternative use or market.

Accounting implications

Disposal of both fixed assets and stock may have implications in the accounts of organisations. The value of fixed assets as shown in the accounts may have been adjusted over time to reflect changing values. The disposal event may result in a final change of value that may require a cost of disposal, write-down, write-off or profit on disposal.

'Current asset' stock that is disposed of rather than used or conventionally sold may also require special treatment in the accounts in order to identify the difference between ordinary trading and disposals.

Legal obligations

There may be situations where an organisation has legal obligations when considering disposal.

- A purchase contract may contain clauses preventing resale of item(s) without express permission of the supplier (or an intellectual property owner). This is designed to prevent actions taken by the buyer affecting the market. There may also be clauses preventing export (which may apply to military equipment and some technology).

- There may be local legal requirements for any scrap to be documented and the disposal method and/or organisations to be licensed (this may be the case with chemicals and other hazardous materials).

- There may be local or national taxes to pay for disposal, which could be imposed on the owner of the waste or the disposal contractor.

- Specific regulations may apply to some types of waste. For example, in the European Union countries, there are typically regulations relating to batteries, electrical waste, packaging, asbestos, refrigerants, laser products and vehicles at end-of-life. Plastics are also often subject to specific regulations.

> *Check*
> Explain three of the general descriptions used for the disposal of stock.

Costs

The cost of disposal in terms of monetary value will vary widely according to the circumstances and whether any residual value can be achieved. Some heavy machinery may require specialist removal equipment (and some may require removal of walls or ceilings). Machinery may need decommissioning which could involve drainage of coolant and/or lubricants, and dismantling.

Disposal for waste may incur transport costs and processing cost and taxation charges. Transport and processing costs are generally based on volume and weight.

The cost of disposal in terms of environmental impact may be much more difficult to quantify. Established waste contractors may be able to supply information relating to the ongoing environmental impact and risk following removal of scrap or waste from an organisation's premises. For many organisations, the whole life implications will potentially result in an impact within their environmental annual reports.

The cost of disposal is also increased by staff time involvement in whichever process for disposal is followed. There will be a trade-off between the staff cost of exploring disposal options against the potential financial benefits and environmental impact of the disposal.

Compare the factors to consider when building a total cost of ownership model

A total cost of ownership (TCO) model can apply to any stock item. In practice, the short-term nature of 'current asset stock' means that the detailing required and the number of tasks to track make using the model expensive in terms of time taken to record and document costs accurately. Parts of the model can, however, be usefully used to highlight differences and help to make current asset stock decisions. (TCO was also discussed in chapter 2.)

The concept of TCO has been developed by many different authors and adopted by government departments, agencies, and commercial and voluntary organisations. There is no single definitive document set that applies to all purchases – the detailing will change according to the complexity of the purchase and timescale. Additionally, some organisations commit to documenting the environmental impact – this could be 'whole life' environmental impact or concentrating on one or more elements (for example, CO_2, energy, waste volume or weight).

A TCO model is most often associated with fixed asset stock, such as equipment, machinery and vehicles. Although 'ownership' is in the title, the same type of systematic cost model can be used for lease decisions and comparisons between purchase and lease.

> *Remember*
> If you are searching for information about TCO, you will find that the letters are also used by an organisation which certifies sustainability of IT products. Whist sustainability is often included in the total cost of ownership model, IT sustainability certification does not include the full range of costs.

TCO models are most often used at the following times.

- Prior to an investment decision, in order to allow comparisons between options

- During the lifetime of an asset, where additional costs have been encountered or new asset investment opportunities are considered

If a TCO is prepared prior to investment, it is reasonable to follow this through and track actual costs against original forecast costs. This way of using TCO adds a learning element to the activity, with the possibility of better forecasting in the future and therefore better budgeting. Figure 3.5 shows an overview of the total cost of the ownership cycle.

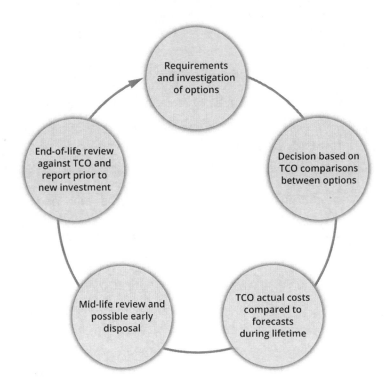

Figure 3.5 Overview of total cost of ownership cycle

Include all costs

In this study guide, there have been sections devoted to purchase price, acquisition costs, usage costs, maintenance costs, operating costs (including energy and water), training costs and disposal costs. All of these are required for the TCO model although the detailing and relative importance of each element will vary between projects.

Decisions are required regarding the extent of detailing – some organisations allocate standard fixed sums or percentages of spend for some elements rather than creating detailed predictions. Some organisations require an associated additional section of a TCO devoted to the 'cost of change' – this is particularly valid as some change options may require minor changes and some may require major changes and retraining.

There are likely to be quite a lot of assumptions made as only contractually confirmed costs will be fixed and other costs will be subject to change. One of the most difficult assumptions would be the effective lifetime of use of equipment in a business.

- For a vehicle on a fixed-term lease, the period is a definite (unless the organisation cancels the contract early or the vehicle does not perform as promised). If the maintenance and spare parts are also included, the confidence of being able to predict TCO accurately would be high.

- For a purchased production machine, the supplier may indicate a designed life, but this is not likely to be guaranteed. The life of the equipment will be dependent on the environmental conditions, how long it is run each day and the cleaning and maintenance. It is also possible that the machine may become redundant before its expected life is complete – this could be because of a change of production method, product design or that improved quality or faster processing could be achieved with a new machine.

- For a purchased boiler (furnace), there may be a life expectancy, but there is a greater likelihood of parts requiring replacement rather than a boiler replacement which extends the lifetime. While this is a good feature, the ultimate lifetime is difficult to project as parts availability may not be guaranteed and more fuel-efficient boilers may offer cheaper operating costs after a while.

- For a forklift truck, the effective lifetime may be different for different energy sources – electric truck batteries will have a life dependent on the typical load and cycle of charge and discharge. A diesel or LPG/petrol truck will have a lifetime linked to the performance of the engine and maintenance regime. All types are likely to have a reduced lifetime if used outdoors rather than indoors.

Finance costs

An organisation may have funds, borrow from a lender, obtain extended credit from a supplier or take a lease in order to finance a fixed asset. In each case there will either be a cost of finance (or a loss of interest income if the organisation uses its own funds).

Interest costs will vary between sources, which means that the options need to be evaluated. Interest rates may be quoted, but the basis of interest also can vary. Because of this, the total cost of finance should be compared. Figure 3.6 shows three options.

Option A: Bank borrowing		Option B: Supplier finance	Option C: Lease
Deposit requirement	40,000	25,000	(advance payments) 4401
Sum borrowed:	40,000	55,000	lease only
Term in years	5	5	5
Monthly repayment (including interest)	788	1108	1267
Total cost five years	47,280	66,480	76,020
Cost of finance	7280	11,480	8020
Loss of interest on deposit	4163	2602	416
Total cost of income	11,443	14,082	8436

Figure 3.6 Three finance options (simulated for $80,000 value equipment requirement)

These options require different amounts of initial capital, shown as 'deposit requirement'. Estimates based on the potential loss of interest by placing the deposits have been calculated (in this case at 2%, compounded over five years). Notice that the lowest initial deposit in this example is leasing (option C) – it also has the lowest cost of capital.

The table does not show the whole financial picture, as there is a projected end-of-life or residual value of $20,000, but this is only available with options A and B, (with this lease, the equipment ownership is retained by the leasing company). The leasing company will have assessed the 'residual value' to reduce the total cost as part of the overall contract. Some leases require additional payments from the customer at the end of the contract should the asset be unusable or in a poor condition. This type of comparison table does support the decision-making process. This type of table is likely to be one of the features included in a 'fixed asset acquisition proposal report' which are often required in organisations.

Check
Why is it important to think about the financial options when considering higher-cost fixed asset acquisition?

Detailing costs, budgeting and investment appraisal

Before the acquisition of fixed assets, many organisations have an approvals procedure which usually requires a series of financial and risk assessments, along with detailed implementation plans – some will have an 'initial proposal' and later 'detailed proposals for approval' stages.

Organisations tend to adopt or adapt techniques coming from management accounting in order to provide clear detailing of costs. As there are no fixed rules for this type of work, organisations determine the content, layout and either specify assumptions or ask for these to be explained. There are often template reports used, so that the same type of information appears in the same sections. By using the same techniques for each option available, it is possible for direct comparisons of the lifetime costs, including the cost of finance and the impact of inflation.

		One-off costs	Annual costs
Pre-project costs:	Preliminary research	✓	
Acquisition costs:			
	Staff time	✓	x
	Premises preparation	✓	x
	Utility preparation	✓	x
	Transport/delivery	✓	x
	Installation	✓	x
	Staff training	✓	(?)
	Acceptance testing	✓	v
Purchase costs:			
	Quoted price	✓	x
	Spares	✓	x
	Maintenance contract	✓	x
	Other additional costs	(?)	(?)
International purchases:			
	Import taxes and duty	✓	(?)
	Translation costs	✓	(?)
	Compliance testing and documentation	✓	(?)
	Banking costs	✓	(?)
	Currency risk cost	✓	(?)
	Other additional costs	✓	(?)
Usage costs:			
	Insurance	✓	x
	Energy costs	✓	x
	Consumables	✓	x
	Routine waste	✓	x
	Software updating	(?)	(?)
	Other additional costs	(?)	(?)
End-of-life costs:			
	Investigation	✓	x
	Legal compliance	✓	x
	Decommissioning	✓	x
	Removal costs	✓	x
	Scrap recovery income	✓	x
	Scrap/disposal cost	✓	x

(✓ – expected or possible cost, x – not applicable, ? – dependent on situation)

Figure 3.7 Typical cost detailing for a fixed asset purchase

Figure 3.7 shows that there may be significant annual costs and end-of-life costs connected with fixed asset acquisition. The detailed cost breakdown needs to allow for the impact of time – some costs may decrease, but in most cases both labour costs and material costs would be expected to increase over the projected life of the asset.

Allowing for cost increases in the detailing of costs could be done in a variety of ways, by the following for example.

• Looking at historic general cost increases and extending the trend for the lifetime of the asset for each of the non-fixed costs

• Taking the best current estimates for future costs from industry or national statistics and applying these to the non-fixed costs

• Making individual assessments on each cost element

This could result in each cost element being increased by a flat percentage (for example, 5%) each year from a firm 'current cost'. Similarly, some costs could increase by one percentage and others by another percentage. It is important that the basis for the cost estimates is stated.

Remember
The assumptions and predictions made for non-fixed costs are very unlikely to be 100% correct. Estimates are usually made with reasonable confidence when projecting forward for the first year or two. Having confidence for the costs after year five of the projections can be difficult, but some investment projects require accurate estimates in excess of 25 years.

Apply
1. Think of your own personal expenditure. If you were asked to predict your expenditure for next week, could you detail your prediction accurately? What about a prediction for a week in six months' time? What would your confidence be about predicting your expenses for a week three years from now?

2. Fuel costs can change over a period of time, sometimes up and sometimes down (it depends on the start point chosen). Could you accurately predict your usage and the price of fuel three years from now?

The document set for the fixed asset acquisition proposal needs to have summaries of the various costs arranged in various ways. One of these is the overview of the costs along with the timing over the anticipated lifetime of the asset. Figure 3.8 provides an example of the 'cash flow' for one simulated project.

					Cost and Disposal Estimate Summary			
Year	Purchase cost	Acquisition cost	Annual fixed costs	Annual other costs	Disposal value less disposal costs	Total costs	Cash flow	Cumulative cash flow
0	80,000	1840				81,840	−81,840	−81,840
1			600	200		800	−1450	−83,290
2			600	300		900	−1550	−84,840
3			600	500		1100	−1750	−86,590
4			600	350		950	−1600	−88,190
5			600	350	18,500	950	17,550	−70,640

Figure 3.8 Example cash flow showing total cost of ownership

In figure 3.8, the columns appear to be logical and follow the pattern of this chapter. 'Year 0' is a convenient label for the start of ownership, although some expenses may have been incurred before purchase. The remaining years summarise the costs and show both the single year position cash flow and the 'cumulative' position for the project. Some fixed costs are shown, with some costs that are variable estimates. At the end of year 5, it is assumed that disposal will take place, and in this example, (even after some costs are incurred,) there is an anticipated income.

The TCO is $70,640, but over the expected life of the asset, this figure could be either of the following.

- Lower (if variable costs are lower or income from disposal is higher)

- Higher (if variable costs are higher or income from disposal is lower)

It is also possible that the asset will not continue for the anticipated five years – it could be subject to early disposal or it could continue in service for longer.

There has been a strong emphasis on costs so far (the title of this section suggests a 'total cost of ownership'), but to evaluate the financial commitment, more than just costs is required.

In order to assess the impact of a fixed asset purchase, it is important for the document set to indicate the benefit, income or savings that the investment will bring to the organisation. This element is sometimes called the 'cost–benefit analysis' and calls for estimates of, for example, volumes of items produced, or hours of work saved. Using the same simulated example as in figure 3.8, another table has been produced as figure 3.9.

			Project total cost of ownership and savings estimate summary				
Year	Purchase cost	Total costs for year	Disposal value less disposal costs	Total costs	Cost savings predicted	Cash flow	Cumulative cash flow
0	80,000	1840		81,840	0	–81,840	–81,840
1		800		800	16,250	15,450	–66,390
2		900		900	17,063	16,163	–50,228
3		1100		1100	17,916	16,816	–33,412
4		950		950	18,811	17,861	–15,550
5		950	18,500	950	19,752	37,302	21,752

Figure 3.9 Total cost of ownership with cost savings example

Figure 3.9 now shows a summary of costs on the left, with the savings expected clearly indicated. In this example, the scenario is that expensive components are bought in from a supplier, but the proposed asset will enable manufacture with the savings indicated. These are estimates based on volumes and the projection suggests the external supplier would continue to increase prices over the five-year timescale.

The cash flow now looks very different, with a significant net benefit contributing to a rapidly increasing cumulative cash flow. The predicted result at the end of year 5 is a surplus which is heavily dependent on the disposal value. This is most encouraging but remember that it is based on assumptions.

The same table can be used to illustrate another management accounting technique – this asset has a 'payback' of five years (the cash flow shows a positive figure at the end of year 5). The earlier a project achieves payback, the less vulnerable the project is to minor inaccuracies in estimates.

Check

List four examples of information which may be contained in a 'project total cost of ownership and savings' analysis.

Apply

Which project is 'better'?

Look at two similar projects (Project S and Project T), compare the tables and follow the statements.

Project S total cost of ownership and savings estimate summary							
Year	Purchase cost	Total costs for year	Disposal value less disposal costs	Total costs	Cost savings predicted	Cash flow	Cumulative cash flow
0	25,000	950		25,950	0	−25,950	−25,950
1		1200		1200	9,750	8550	−17,400
2		1200		1200	10,238	9083	−8363
3		1200		1200	10,749	9549	1187
4		1200		1200	11,287	10,087	11,274
5		1200	3500	1200	11,851	14,151	25,425

Project T total cost of ownership and savings estimate summary							
Year	Purchase cost	Total costs for Year	Disposal value less disposal costs	Total costs	Cost savings predicted	Cash flow	Cumulative cash flow
0	32,500	2550		35,050	0	−34,050	−34,050
1		400		400	11,500	11,100	−22,950
2		400		400	12,075	11,675	−11,275
3		400		400	12,679	12,279	1004
4		400		400	13,313	12,913	13,916
5		400	8500	400	13,978	22,078	35,995

Both Project S and Project T have the same projected usage lifetime.

Project S has a lower initial investment requirement.

Project T has very high 'total costs for year 0' compared to project S but much lower annual costs.

Project T has a higher 'disposal value less disposal costs' at the end of year 5.

Project T has a greater annual savings prediction in each year.

Project S has a marginally better payback than project T (both are positive before the end of year 3).

Project T has a significantly better end-of-project cumulative cash flow ($35,995 compared to $25,425).

So which project would you choose to support and why?

There is another problem with the timescale of a project, which is the 'time value of money'. In the examples above, significant benefits are projected across five years. Leaving aside the accuracy of the figures, there is still the question of whether the values shown as positive cash flow are 'worth' the same amount as they would be today.

Management accounting can provide indications of today's value of future benefits (the **net present value or NPV**). These require calculations to adjust each year's figures – but this requires an interest rate to 'discount' the figures.

3.2 L03

Year	Purchase cost	Total costs for year	Disposal value less disposal costs	Total costs	Cost savings predicted	Cash flow	Cumulative cash flow
0	32,500	2550		35,050	0	–34,050	–34,050
1		400		400	11,500	11,100	–22,950
2		400		400	12,075	11,675	–11,275
3		400		400	12,679	12,279	1004
4		400		400	13,313	12,913	13,916
5		400	8500	400	13,978	22,078	35,995

Project T total cost of ownership and savings estimate summary with net present value

2% discount rate applied   NPV = $31,551

Net present value (NPV)
An accounting term for an amount in the future, adjusted to 'today's' value by a calculation. This allows a comparison between different projects on the same basis

Figure 3.10 Net present value (NPV) calculation

Figure 3.10 has a 2% annual discount rate applied to the net cash flow for each year, with a cumulative effect across the years. The result is that the value of the project in today's terms has reduced to $31,551. For this project, this difference is not significant. It is possible to have a project with a positive cumulative cash flow but a negative NPV, which would suggest that in today's values the project is not cost beneficial.

These management accounting techniques are also used as part of budgeting and tracking costs after purchase, typically with cost codes identifying different costs.

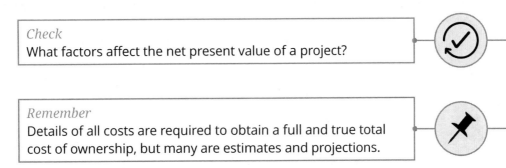

Check
What factors affect the net present value of a project?

Remember
Details of all costs are required to obtain a full and true total cost of ownership, but many are estimates and projections.

Use best estimates of values available

Many of the figures used in a TCO model are future estimates based on factual evidence. These estimates may be based on a buying organisation's previous experience (which may or may not reflect new performance), supplier estimates (which may be based on historic performance, a designed performance level or their hopes) or 'standard costs' that are used when estimating costs of similar items.

The objective is that all known costs are established, confirmed or estimated using the best possible sources.

- Past projects should be checked for spend and overspend with evidence of unexpected additional costs.

- Suppliers should be asked for any installation or implementation checklists or example invoicing detail that can confirm the costs already indicated.

- Suppliers may be able to provide examples of trade-in values for equipment previously sold.

- Suppliers with a significant interest in environmental issues (or where a government has placed a requirement on manufacturers) may be able to supply details of materials that may be recycled. Some may have established dismantling facilities and/or have contractors ready to process parts or machinery – this helps to estimate some of the end-of-life costs.

- It may be possible for the supplier to provide 'reference sites' where recent installations have been completed. It is possible that a direct competitor would be unhappy with providing information nor allow a supplier to provide detail. There have, however, been many cases of collaborative work within industries and across industries.

- Any 'standard costs' included should be tested to ensure that the latest project is likely to follow previous time and cost allowances.

Brainstorming across different internal functions could produce previously unconsidered additional costs. This could be run as a 'blind' activity with all contributing items – some may well already have been detailed, but a new emphasis or more detail might be provided.

Brainstorming
A series of techniques used as part of creating a range of options to solve a problem or series of problems. The idea is to promote open and diverse ideas

Hidden costs – global sourcing, risks associated with extended supply chain

As there have been many identified requirements for estimates and projections, it is expected that there are likely to be some 'hidden costs'. Although this chapter has covered the need for all costs to be included, some specific costs and risks relate to global sourcing and the extended supply chain. As before, the focus will be on fixed asset 'capital equipment', although many aspects are shared with current asset stock purchases.

Country risk

Working with suppliers in other countries (or where a supplier is working with suppliers in other countries) leaves the buying organisation with a series of country-based risks. In extreme cases, an organisation's image and reputation may be adversely affected by association with specific countries or with an industry or area.

Many factors may affect the supplier and the supplier's ability to perform the contract. These may include the following.

- Actions by governments to restrict or refuse export/import

- Imposition of higher taxes

- Restrictions or prohibition on the use of certain materials, substances or processes

- Restrictions on borrowing and investment

- Revaluation of a currency or actions causing currency values to wildly fluctuate

- Restrictions on the availability of funds from other countries

- Restrictions on making payments to other countries

- Industrial relations problems and civil unrest

- Human rights issues and social justice problems

- New or revised laws, increasing costs for the supplier

- Energy or infrastructure failures
- 'Natural' disasters (some countries are more vulnerable than others)

Research should be undertaken to assess the probability of these risks. There are often government reports available outlining the overall standing of countries. There are also specialist reports from international accountancy and consultancy practices outlining relative risk. Credit reference agencies also classify country risk and can undertake individual organisation credit risk analysis.

> *Remember*
> Organisations are vulnerable with extended supply chains – it is important for 'critical' supplies to have documented supply chains and effective risk assessment.

Logistics and transport issues

There may be a need to decide on a method of transport against time taken for delivery and cost. The arrangement, risk and cost of transport could be the buyer's, the seller's or a defined split of responsibility. Risks associated with transport tend to increase with the number of methods of transport used, the distance and the time taken.

Typical transport costs can be quoted by a variety of carriers and transport specialists. The supplier could be asked for an **ex-works** cost, with the buyer arranging collection by a specialist carrier. Alternatively, a fully delivered cost could be requested by the buyer. Preparing for international transport is likely to involve special packing and documentation. Each different combination of responsibility and risk usually has different costs.

Each supply chain may involve many other links which would only be identified by questioning the potential supplier(s). This could involve other countries, adding to the costs and risks.

Ex-works
The term given to a price for collection from the supplier's location rather than delivered to the buyer's site

Export and import and taxes/non-tax barriers

Global sourcing involves export from one country and import to another – this may be transparent from the supplier discussions, but it could be (wrongly) assumed that permission is not specifically required for import and export from one country to another. All international transactions require documentation sets with clear origins of products or materials. Creation of the document sets could represent added costs to the supplier or buyer.

Export and import between two countries may require licensing and/or payment of taxes or duty payments. Licensing may require specific payment and could also involve a government approval process. The rates of tax or duty may be varied over time – so there may be an increase from the time of ordering to the time of delivery, or spare parts may be affected. The difference in rates of tax and duty may create a difference in delivered cost between the supply of similar products from two different countries.

Local regulations relating to specific products may mean that testing on arrival in a country is required in order to ensure compliance has taken place. In some cases, this may be done by the testing of the product(s) in advance (at a cost). Other non-tax barriers to entry may include detailed translated contents and instructions, environmental controls, specific design requirements and chemical or active ingredient restrictions (which may apply to consumables).

Responsibility and costs relating to documentation, compliance and testing could be agreed between the buyer and seller.

Contractual issues

International sourcing adds some special issues relating to contracts. Clearly the risks described so far need to be considered for detailing in the contract.

The contract itself also needs some attention – the contract needs to specify which country of legal framework and the location of any court which applies in the event of an action or interpretation. Even if these aspects are detailed, there is still a higher risk of dispute resolution taking longer and the remedies being less certain than if both parties are in the same country.

As it is expected that equipment will be in use for its projected lifetime, the contract could include a spares availability clause, stating that stock will be available for the period required.

Currency issues

If the purchase is to take place in the buyer's currency, then the buyer will not need to cover for the possibility of a change in the value of the contract. The supplier will (or should) take actions to prevent the contract value from adversely affecting its business. As a result, if the supplier accepts the additional risk and costs of currency movement, it may recover these by charging additional costs or raising the price.

As some machinery is only 'built to order' or 'built to specification', there is a chance that the cost expressed in another currency may change during the build and before final payment is due.

Some currencies can vary by a large margin during a year, but others can have a limited variation or 'volatility'. A snapshot of a 52-week period of exchange rates reveals some stable and some volatile currencies.

Currency	USD1 52-week high	USD1 52-week low	% variance	Currency	USD1 52-week high	USD1 52-week low	% variance
Australia	1.42	1.24	14.64	New Zealand	1.55	1.35	15.20
Botswana	10.56	9.43	11.98	Nigeria	363.00	358.00	1.40
Brazil	3.88	3.15	23.15	Poland	3.84	3.31	15.81
Canada	1.33	1.23	8.71	Russia	70.36	55.78	26.14
China	6.97	6.26	11.31	Saudi Arabia	3.75	3.75	0.07
Czech	23.05	20.19	14.16	Singapore	1.39	1.30	6.32
Euro	0.89	0.80	11.14	South Africa	15.44	11.58	33.32
Ghana	5.00	4.40	13.64	South Korea	1143.63	1055.20	8.38
Hong Kong	7.85	7.80	0.63	Switzerland	1.01	0.92	9.22
India	74.34	63.39	17.27	Taiwan	31.02	29.03	6.86
Japan	114.12	104.84	8.85	Tanzania	2300.00	2233.00	3.00
Kenya	103.55	99.55	4.02	Thailand	33.47	31.12	7.55
Malawi	727.00	614.00	8.40	Turkey	6.91	3.73	85.02
Malaysia	4.20	3.86	8.59	Uganda	3730.00	3605.00	3.47
Namibia	13.98	11.55	21.04	UK	0.79	0.70	13.10

Figure 3.11 Selected currency 52-week values against US$

Case study

Currency values

Look at figure 3.11. Notice that some currencies are volatile (they move by a large percentage in the period reviewed, while some only change by a small percentage). For example, the Malawi currency has a variance of 18.4% – it is not known whether this may be repeated in the following year, nor whether the current exchange rate is 'high' or 'low' compared to rates in three months' time. It may be that the extreme rate variance only happened for a short period – so this is well worth investigating.

Consider the following worked example. If an organisation in Uganda ordered equipment for USD50000 when the exchange rate was USD1 = 3605, then it would expect to pay USD50000 × 3605 = 180 250 000 in local currency. If the exchange rate when payment is due was USD1 = 3730 it would have to pay USD50000 × 3730 = 186 500 000 in local currency.

Alternatively, the percentage change will give roughly the same figure – 180 250 000 + 3.47% = 186 504 375 (the minor difference being as a result of 'rounding' of exchange rates and percentages).

Clearly these rates would have represented the extreme view and the actual calculation rates may not represent these extremes – it was possible to 'gain' and pay a lower sum in local currency than the original expectation, but it is not possible for the Ugandan organisation to wait for the exchange rate to change if a contract has been agreed!

Apply

Undertake calculations using your own currency for the same transaction. What would be the likely reaction of management for the 'hidden' additional cost? (If your home currency is not in the table, you can find a source (which could be a financial newspaper or a currency conversion website) to see what the extreme variances would have produced last year.)

Remember

A currency risk can be assessed using previous rates, but there is no certainty that these rates or trends will continue.

There may be other 'hidden' situations that involve a currency risk. In the example supply chain in figure 3.12, an organisation (Customer E) may have initially bought equipment in its own country (from Distributor D) and paid in its own currency.

The supply chain for the equipment might reveal potential lifetime concerns.

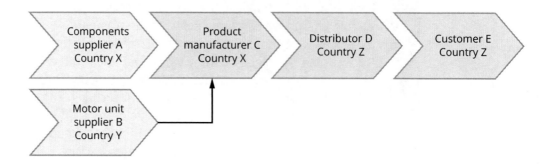

Figure 3.12 Supply chain showing major parts sourcing detail

Figure 3.12 provides more detail and reveals the following.

- Product manufacturer C has two major suppliers in different countries – and is selling to Distributor D in yet another country

- Customer E may be aware of the origins of the manufacture but may not be aware of a significant other country involvement

Now, the currency risks are the following.

- Purchases by manufacturer C are affected by the value of the currencies of country X and Y

- Purchases by Distributor D are affected by the value of the currencies of countries X, Y and Z

- Purchases by Customer E are therefore also affected by the value of the currencies of countries X, Y and Z

These will all have a potential for 'hidden losses' for the purchase of replacement parts over the lifetime of the asset.

The different contracts in place in the supply chain may dictate the winners and losers. It is possible that Customer E may have agreed a fixed price in local currency from Distributor D, but that just means that Distributor D is taking the risk of currency fluctuations. Customer E may have achieved a long-term cost advantage.

The point here is that the risk to Distributor D may eventually result in an inability to pay the manufacturer C, which could result in this supply chain failing – either the manufacturer stops production or it may make losses.

Alternatively, if Customer E fixed a local currency price, it may mean that it pays more than if it followed the currency values over a period of time – it risks losing business to more competitive businesses.

> *Remember*
> Without an understanding of the supply chain and linkages, the 'hidden' risks and costs could affect the whole life cost accuracy.

Ethical issues

Countries have variable performance and reputation for the variety of issues covered under the heading of ethics. It would be wrong to stereotype specific countries (or industries) as there is good practice and bad practice to be found anywhere. There are close connections to the 'triple bottom line' covered later in this chapter.

Ethical issues may be connected to legal requirements in some countries. Unfortunately, this is highly variable and as a result there is a wide variation of what may be regarded as unethical. In many cases, there is likely to be consideration of 'it may be legal, but is it ethical'?

Key issues for organisations are likely to be the following.

- **Dual standards**: issues that would not be acceptable in a buyer's organisation but are accepted as a supplier's business practice

- **Supply chain mapping and auditing**: the immediate supplier may have been audited and has the 'right policies', but does the audit and policies principle also apply to the extended supply chain?

High-profile difficulties are often reported with the following.

- The difference between a minimum legal wage and a living wage

- The difference between employment legislation and employment best practice

- The differences between audit requirements and expectations when working across sectors (for example, dealing with equipment manufacturers rather than food producers)

- The differences in attitudes to environmental impact of operations, including materials and waste (different countries may have different regulations and commitment)

In the context of this section, organisations will expect the same or similar commitment to ethical values and practices from suppliers as they would internally. A fixed asset purchase is affected by the initial purchase and any subsequent consumables and replacement parts originating from the same supplier or an alternative supplier.

The 'hidden additional cost' from the extended supply chain comes from the increasing need to ensure that an ethical supply chain is in place. It is a choice between the following.

- Visits and auditing the supply business itself

- Using a third-party auditor to visit and audit

- Relying on a certification to a national, international or industry standard (for example, SA8000, ISO20400, ISO26000)

Doing this in a 'home country' with a local supplier should be easy – the business environment is understood, there should be no major cultural differences and no translation issues. Difficulty comes with international sourcing and the extended supply chain. This will involve additional cost and is more likely to involve third-party auditing, alongside the follow-up reading of reports and likely encouragement to improve performance. The buyer may become effectively 'locked-in' to the supplier for spare parts (and potentially servicing) – this makes a post-purchase poor performance in ethics very difficult to manage as there may be little leverage at this point.

Professional ethics should also be documented, and standards upheld. These are easier to manage if a professional association or trade body has standards in place, particularly if these are a condition of membership or certification. The following are examples.

- Chartered Institute of Procurement and Supply

- International Ethics Standards for the global property market

- International Ethics Standards Board of Accountants

- Chartered Insurance Institute
- CIPD (Human Resources Professionals)

Organisation-developed ethical codes addressing the specific values and expectations of staff are more likely to be seen in the context of capital expenditure purchases. These should cover multiple disciplines. These can echo the type of content of the professional bodies and the expectations of stakeholders. Those for government and government agencies are likely to be much more detailed.

> *Remember*
> Organisational ethical codes linked to disciplinary procedures (if not followed) are more likely to be effective than voluntary codes of practice.

Translation costs

Translation of contractual documentation, instructions and important documentation for supplier assessment is likely to be required where different languages are involved. This may well require specialist translators familiar with the terminology and business practice.

Face-to-face negotiation may require a different approach, with indications of how something is said, rather than just what is said. Some organisations request 'translations back' (from original language to translation and back to original language) to ensure that the meaning and phrasing has not changed.

Significant costs could be incurred that would be additional to any single-language contract being considered.

International payment costs

Each payment to another country will incur additional bank transaction fees. If specific mechanisms are involved (for example, a 'letter of credit'), then additional costs of application and documentation will be needed.

> *Check*
> Identify five different aspects of purchasing internationally which may add additional costs.

Only develop for larger purchases

As may be seen by the content in this section, the development of a full TCO model with multiple assumption statements, estimates and variations are only likely to be cost effective for larger purchases. Unfortunately, this leaves the variability of 'what is a larger purchase'?

Organisations often set internal standard operating procedures and those for TCO are often driven by senior management and enacted by the finance and purchasing functions.

A larger purchase could be determined by the following.

- **Lifetime**: one which has an estimated life in excess of, for example, three years

- **Spend (annual)**: one which has a connected annual spend above, for example, $5000

- **Spend (initial cost)**: one which has an initial spend in excess of, for example, $25,000

- **Spend (percentage of capital expenditure)**: one that exceeds, for example, 25% of annual capital expenditure

- **Importance**: one which is essential for production or service performance

- **Risk**: one which, if it fails, would have a significant immediate risk to the business

The objective of TCO is to include all costs, but the acquisition cost element itself could be severely affected by an extended TCO. The TCO itself requires assumptions and estimates. Major purchases are likely to require project management and 'change management' to oversee the purchase, installation and implementation.

The hope with TCO models is that they achieve added value by a dedicated focus on risk and cost – so that the benefits are greater than the cost involved.

Many organisations choose to undertake the full TCO model for some purchase decisions and selected elements where the risk is lower and/or the benefit of a full TCO is not clear.

Ensure senior management support

It is expected that important and high-risk/high-spend decision-making are driven from the senior management (board level or equivalent). This is also sensible as this high level is often likely to have the ultimate approval on this type of spend.

Decisions on high-value projects are often part of an established annual strategy, planning and budgeting cycle. As a result, most organisations will have a series of senior management meetings throughout the year which can both review progress on plans and review projects being undertaken. It is important that a representative of the procurement staff is present at these meetings to contribute and ensure early professional support. Individual members of the senior management team are often nominated to 'champion' a particular project to the executive team, rather than having a detached approach based on documentation.

> *Remember*
> Senior management may wish to establish policies for higher-risk/higher-spend items, perhaps with a tiered approach that may require more detail and discussion for these items.

It may be possible for organisations to adopt industry or international standards as part of policies (for example, ISO15686 deals specifically with assessing the 'service life of buildings'; many suppliers in specific industries suggest a TCO format or offer templates).

Standard document templates and supporting notes are often provided in organisations. Organisations with templates tend to have greater reliability and fewer 'missing' cost assessments. Those with spreadsheet analysis templates for option comparisons benefit from familiarity and standardisation. Some organisations have created online archives ('knowledge libraries'), so that examples are readily available and end-of-life reviews can take place.

> *Remember*
> Senior management are often required to authorise significant spend, so it follows that early involvement and awareness will provide better awareness and more effective decision-making.

Cross-functional support – ensure access to data

This chapter contains a very wide range of costs that need to be identified, analysed and collated. Although it is expected that there will be a responsible person for organising and preparing a TCO report, it is expected that internal departments and functions support this work. Some staff and functions may initially be reluctant to share detailed operational detail and costs. In some organisations, there may be a fear that wider access to documentation containing sensitive information could be dangerous – even if this is only for internal use.

It is helpful if high-risk/high-spend decisions are driven from the senior management (board level or equivalent). The basis of investigations should be known to the various functions within the organisation which may be providing operational detail, costs or estimates.

It is often beneficial to appoint an internal 'project manager' for specific TCO projects – this could be from the part of the organisation that has most direct interest in the equipment being investigated. Where possible, this should be a higher-level manager in order to ensure their requests are respected and responses are received.

Although involvement will vary according to the project and organisation, table 3.4 shows an overview of the functions and contributions typically seen for a TCO project.

Function (internal department)	Potential contribution examples
Purchasing/supply chain	Liaison with potential suppliers and existing suppliers. Contract detail, supplier evaluation and ratings
	Tracking spend trends, quality and lead times for spares and consumables
	Liaison with internal customers and departments
Engineering/design	Technical requirements, processes, integration and future requirements
Accounting/finance	Historic cost code analysis
	Details of financing options and cash flow
	Use of investment appraisal techniques to compare project options including discounted cash flow

3.2 L03

Function (internal department)	Potential contribution examples
Operations/manufacturing	Details of current usage rates, time to process, wastage, accuracy, start-up and close-down times, breakdowns and maintenance. Efficiency and effectiveness KPIs.
Legal/compliance	Regulations and standards to be met, contract terms and clauses
Health and safety	Past experiences, current requirements and future risk/impact and safeguards including personal protective equipment
Marketing	Market research, market segmentation and planned targeting for future products and business, impact of price points and competition

Table 3.4 Typical contributions to a TCO project

Remember

Cross-functional support means it is more likely that better information is provided to senior management who will then be less likely to require further departmental confirmations.

Teamworking – reduce data collection time

Although 'ownership' of the creation and monitoring of a total life-cycle cost model is beneficial, establishing a team approach helps in many ways, including the following.

- It adds to the development of a total-organisation commitment to decision-making and the future. Teamworking on data collection may encourage participation in evaluation and implementation work.

- The collaborative work on a TCO project helps to break down departmental and management/staff barriers. This encourages more collaboration on everyday work and other long-term projects.

- The originator of the information is the one best placed to add an additional context to any data. There may be a story behind sudden high costs or equipment availability.

The internal team can also be aided and supported by external participants. The potential suppliers should be able to offer their own research findings and (at least) comparisons of the performance of their own equipment, the cost of maintenance and spare parts and the anticipated lifetime of the equipment.

The internal team members could be asked to liaise directly with external suppliers and specialists to discuss available data and receive reports direct from externals, in each case working to agreed confidentiality safeguards.

With similar confidentiality safeguards, the internal team should be able to exchange data internally with colleagues on the TCO team and seek views and opinions for clarification.

Remember

There are a lot of processes and specialist input required for a TCO. Using staff and managers that understand their specialisms can save a lot of time and gain collective support.

Check

Why is an organisation more likely to undertake a full TCO activity for major projects?

Which elements of a TCO might be applied to smaller-scale purchases?

3.3 Identify the contributing elements to end-of-life costs

There are many elements that make up end-of-life costs. The precise make-up will depend on the nature of the item(s) and whether disposal by sale, scrappage or eventual reuse is expected. Some end-of-life items will not feature all the aspects covered in this section.

The starting point for an end-of-life decision can be traced back to the acquisition decision and the assumptions made.

A new acquisition will have an anticipated life. Details of the asset will be normally recorded in an asset register. Historically these have been paper ledgers, but computerised accounts often have provision for an asset register, which makes tracking easier.

Reference to a **fixed asset register** should reveal the age of the fixed assets and their planned life. This means that it should be possible to periodically review the fixed assets and plan for their replacement. Planned replacements make budgeting easier and should allow for enough research rather than rushing decisions for disposal and replacements.

Although this chapter concentrates on costs, many organisations require investigation of potential for offsetting costs by generating income for the asset(s). Before any decision for end-of-life is made, it is important to check the policies and procedures of the organisation. Of special importance are the following.

- Fixed asset disposal policy (if there is one)

- Environmental policy (which may direct disposal decisions and detailing)

- Health and safety policy (which may direct hazard identification, risk assessment and the use of specialist contractors)

- Purchasing policies and processes (as contractors may need to be identified, assessed and selected)

- Finance and budgeting procedures (which may state who is able to authorise disposal and the accounting entries required)

Fixed asset register
A document which typically details the fixed assets in the possession of an organisation, their date of acquisition, age, original cost and current cost. Some organisations also annotate maintenance costs and likely cost of disposal or current sale value

3.3 L03

Case study

Fixed asset disposal policies and procedures: a snapshot view

A review of ten UK-based commercial organisations covering retail, manufacturing and service industries was undertaken by the author. This revealed that all had specific procedures for fixed asset accounting, (most commented that this was provided as part of integrated enterprise resource planning software), but most commented that any disposals would be dependent on the asset and the situation.

All these organisations feature IT asset disposal policies in order to comply with the legal requirement for waste electronic equipment. The IT asset documentation is probably also linked to the high risk of data or systems knowledge being compromised. Organisations also commented on general waste disposal procedures ensuring authorised contractors are used.

Public sector and university documentation for disposal policies and forms are available on the Internet as the sector is expected to have transparent policies available for public inspection. A common theme was the dominance of accounting procedures and sign-off requirements. There were few references made to a process for extracting value from disposals. There were few cross-references to environmental policies and procedures – most had separate general guidance for environmental commitment rather than explicit asset disposal.

Summary: Although it can be argued that this is a very limited snapshot and those responsible for disposal in organisations may have specific instructions and guidance, there is evidence to suggest that more practical guidance for disposal of fixed assets is needed in many organisations.

Apply

Consider the organisation you work for, or one you are familiar with. Research whether there are specific policies and procedures for the disposal of fixed assets.

Following approval for disposal, it is important to start planning – it is beneficial to check the current status of the equipment and situation.

- Is it working? (If it is not, and it is still needed, then the cost of getting it working needs to be balanced against the time needed to replace the equipment and the cost of any loss of business or additional cost of contracting-out the work.)

- What is the maintenance and servicing situation? (Maintenance contracts with end dates may cease to operate after expiry, leaving the organisation with no service cover. Alternatively, a significant increase in cost may be charged by the contractor. Some equipment (for example, lift equipment) may require a current safety certificate for it to legally operate.)

- For leased fixed assets, when does the lease end? (At the end of the lease term, many contracts have a requirement to return the asset to the leasing organisation. Additional fees may be payable, or the rental payments may significantly increase.)

- What spares are in stock? (These could be returned to the supplier for credit or sold either with the equipment or on the open market.)

- What should be the last day of operation? (This needs to be planned for as staff and production planning will be affected and a schedule of activities will be needed.)

Check
1. Why is it important to have policies and procedures for end-of-life assets?
2. Why is it important to make plans for fixed asset disposal?

Decommissioning

Decommissioning will typically be required for machinery where a commissioning process was followed during installation. Decommissioning may involve many stages, and depends on the type of equipment and the reason for decommissioning.

- Whether the asset is being sold on or scrapped, the manufacturer's recommended procedure should be carefully followed. This may require experienced contractors and decommissioning activities should be documented.

- When being decommissioned, it may be recommended that access is restricted around the location of machinery for health and safety reasons.

- The item may need specialist removal of, for example, chemical residue, hazardous material, laser equipment, high voltage power supply cables and IT cabling.

- Cleaning of the machinery is often required as part of decommissioning. Cleaning may use more potentially harmful chemicals than have been previously used and these may require extra attention to personal protective equipment and ventilation.

- Any coolants and/or lubricants will need to be drained and disposed of in an appropriate manner – this will probably be the same as any maintenance routine, but some sealed units may contain liquids that are not normally managed.

- If the item is to be sold on, parts will need to be packaged and documented. Some surfaces may need to be cleaned and then prepared with preservative.

An unexpected decommissioning and removal
Many years ago, a commercial property leaseholder scheduled a $2 million refurbishment of a building with an agreed extension to the lease term. Detailed plans had been completed by professional architects and the

Case study

main contractors selected. Approvals had been received and planning permissions granted.

When an electrician checked the basement for potential new cable routes, lighting cables were found leading to a locked room labelled 'no staff access'. The room contained a redundant oil tank for a boiler installation that had been removed long before. The basement was not part of the refurbishment plan. The contractor reported minor leakage around the pipe joints with the tank. It was clear that the previous occupant had failed to decommission the tank.

A specialist contractor was required, and this revealed there was still oil in the base of the tank and pipes. The oil needed to be removed and pipes cleared. The tank needed to be removed and this could only be done by cutting it up, as it had been installed before the concrete walls and floors had been constructed. It was explained that this was regarded as a high-risk operation and all other work was suspended for three days while this was done. As a precaution, the fire service was on standby and special equipment and trained technicians were required.

The leaseholder incurred additional specialist costs and a small delay to the works. The leaseholder was relieved that this was not discovered later, as the removal was complicated and the access route to exit the building required a lot of cleaning up.

> *Remember*
> Decommissioning may require specialist input. The buyer will have to identify, evaluate and select an appropriate supplier, adding costs to the end-of-life budget.

Removal or disposal processes

Removal or disposal processes will vary as regards content and complexity and are typically dependent on the following.

- Type of equipment and the incorporated components and materials
- Type of installation
- Location of the equipment and accessibility
- Handling and processing requirements for the disposal method

Smaller equipment which has low risk and can be easily moved as a complete item will not require a complex removal or disposal process. Simple research procedures, recommendations for disposal and sign off will still be required – and there should be a checklist which covers common issues, risks, documentation and accounting requirements.

In complex removal or disposal situations, a project-based approach is likely to be required with a detailed full costing and risk analysis in advance. It is quite possible that there will be many options to be considered, with the potential for many contractors and specialists for evaluation and selection. Depending on organisation policies and procedures, disposal may need senior management approval. Internally, there will be costs incurred and the asset value will need to be dealt with by a series of accounting entries.

This next section provides some examples of processes which are often provided as a starting point for staff and managers to adapt and reflect the specific requirements for asset removal or disposal.

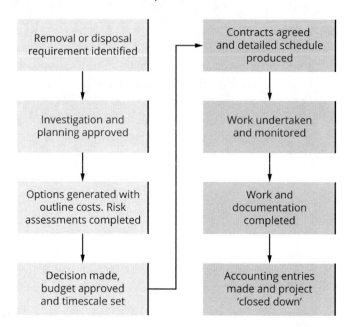

Figure 3.13 Example overview of a process for fixed asset disposals

Figure 3.13 shows a process with the major stages using a project-based approach. This process has the advantage of being easy to adopt as the basis for most disposals and each stage can be adapted to reflect the specific requirements for each asset. Each stage could be linked to operational guidance notes and template forms.

The timescale to follow a process like this can be very short for simple disposals but quite long where, for example, significant research, tendering or premises changes are required.

Remember
To support staff who are planning for a removal or a disposal, it is important to provide clear processes and standard routines.

Risk assessments process

The principle of risk assessment is that each stage of an activity is subjected to a 'what could happen?' question. General risk assessments are often in place for multiple purposes and these may even extend to strategic-level risk assessments. The risk elements are then usually converted into a 'risk register' which may be supplemented by a report.

Identification of risks are usually followed by an assessment of probability of the risk becoming reality. There is also an assessment of the impact of the risk becoming reality (the consequences). Probability and impact are often given scores against a descriptive table to supplement the description (this allows a focus on higher-risk and/or higher-consequence entries). Alternatively, each risk probability and impact could be classified as 'high', 'medium' or 'low'. In order to reduce or eliminate the risk, some 'mitigation' measures are considered, and additional safeguards considered.

Responsibilities for monitoring and managing risks, or categories of risk, are often allocated to specific staff or managers. In many cases, contractors may have contributed to the risk assessments and could be named as responsible (for example, where an area has been signed over to them for work). Contractors may provide their own document set to cover the works undertaken.

For routine activities, a combined risk register is often maintained. For more complex work, separate environmental and health and safety risk registers are beneficial as these can be more detailed to meet specific subject area requirements.

> *Remember*
> Risk assessments form an important way of managing processes – thinking ahead and making plans is better than the shock of an undiscovered risk becoming reality.

Environmental risk assessment process

Given the risks involved with some fixed assets and the importance of environmental impact, a formal process is a good idea, and this may already be included in an organisation's environmental policy.

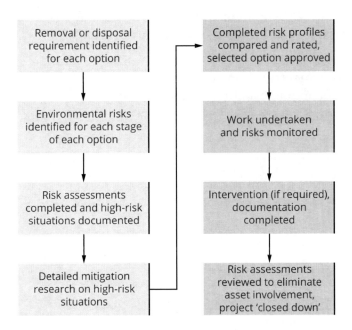

Figure 3.14 Example of an environmental risk assessment process

Figure 3.14 shows a process with the main stages of managing environmental risk. This process has the advantage of being easy to adapt as the basis for most disposals. Each stage could be linked to operational guidance notes and template forms. Organisations that have ISO14001 certification (or similar) are likely to have a more complex and detailed approach in each stage.

Environmental risk assessments should be prepared specifically for each significant disposal. This is because many of the activities will be non-routine and may require special safeguards. As contractors may be involved, they should contribute to the preparation and detailing of the document.

> *Remember*
> Organisations that have made a commitment to 'whole life' environmental concerns are also likely to follow through the environmental risk. These organisations will consider later waste processing and any residual product environmental risk, even though they may have no legal responsibility.

Some disposals (for example, contaminated waste, products containing radioactive agents and asbestos) and any processes involving known higher environmental risk may already have prescribed routines and procedures for risk assessment and management. Construction businesses often provide a full and specialised risk register for works planned and may be involved in an 'environmental impact study'. This may include the impact of a building on the transport infrastructure, local services and natural environment. Although this primarily applies to new build situations, any demolition or soil movement could require a specific assessment in a planning application.

Examples of environmental impact study issues typically include major risk issues, noise, vibration, nuisance, transport impact and impact on the public.

Further environmental risk factors are covered later in this chapter.

Health and safety risk assessment process

A health and safety risk assessment follows a similar pattern to a general risk register. Each stage will question the activities being undertaken and the risks involved. Many different layouts are used.

Some risk assessments focus on the activity first, but other styles include the creation of generic health and safety risks in the style of a checklist, with the objective of provoking a yes/no response. Table 3.5 shows one example with typical content.

A: Activities prior to removal							
Specification category	Specific activities	Source of risk	Probability of risk & score	Potential impact and score	Total score	Mitigation and control measures	Link to regulations
Chemical and/or hazardous material	Cleaning products during decommission	Spillages, interaction with other chemicals. Chlorine and acetone fumes. Inhaling and ingestion	Low risk if mitigation measures followed 2	Personal injury risk, pollution risk, damage to stock 4	8	Chemical safety data sheet is followed and personal protective equipment is used. Eye wash and clean-up packs required. Area restricted to contractors only	Yes – legal requirements apply

Table 3.5 Example health and safety risk assessment register entry

The register layout in table 3.5 is arranged in stage order – this table is for 'stage A: prior to removal'. The 'specific category' shows the general nature of the risk and fits with a checklist style, with specific activities being more descriptive and directly linked to the project. Scores in probability and impact in this example are scaled 1–5 with 5 being a high risk. The total score is the result of multiplying the two individual scores.

Other items on a health and safety risk 'checklist' would include the following.

- Methods of lifting and lifting equipment risks
- Sharp objects, use of tools and powered equipment
- Processes using welding, grinding and gas-type cutting
- Working at height and/or in confined spaces
- Dust and other airborne particles and contaminants
- Loads falling from a height or tipping over
- Floor/platform weight loadings
- Floor surfaces and suitability
- Physical waste handling and disposal

Check
Why is it important to consider a full range of risk assessments when disposal of fixed assets is being considered?

Selection of specialist suppliers

Organisations should have an established selection procedure for suppliers. When considering removal or disposal, the assessment needs to include project-relevant additional considerations. These may include the following.

- Specific experience in the type of project being planned
- 'Reference sites' – the ability of a buyer to check work and standards with the supplier's previous customers
- Certificates, registrations and licences to operate (or evidence these have been acquired in the past in situations where these are site-specific)
- Contract detailing, with specific interest in accountability and responsibilities both on the buyer's site and after the disposal has taken place
- Insurance cover detail
- Commitment to providing risk registers or contributions to the organisation's risk registers
- Details of the proposed disposal 'supply chain' and evidence that environmental, ethical and health and safety principles are in place

Processes relating to sale of assets

Sale of assets involves buying staff in using their commercial awareness and skills in a different way. The methods used in a typical sale are again presented as a project.

Under an organisation's standard procedures, senior management involvement and decision-making may be required, although in some cases the nature and value of the asset may result in delegation to a suitable manager.

The project starts with an objective, which may be different according to the situation. Working to an approximate date or deadline, the objective may be to do the following.

- Maximise the income from the sale

- Recover the value of the asset shown in the accounts

- Recover the value in the accounts after paying the costs of sale

- Cover the costs of disposal from the proceeds of the sale

- Remove and dispose of the asset before significant additional costs are incurred (this is unusual)

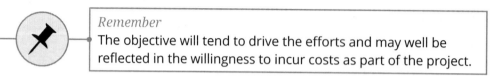

Remember
The objective will tend to drive the efforts and may well be reflected in the willingness to incur costs as part of the project.

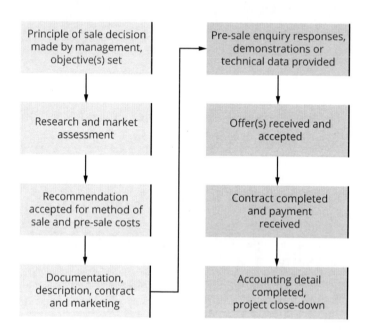

Figure 3.15 Example process for fixed asset sale

Figure 3.15 presents a general-purpose process which can be expanded with additional detail as required by the nature of the sale project.

The research and market assessment may well involve part-exchange opportunities, resale to the original supplier, research for customers within the same industry and in alternative industries. Extending sale research to other countries is possible although this would require additional potential costs in terms of translation, shipping and certification. Technical and trade journals or their websites may give indications of past sales (particularly where advertisements have been placed).

Many commercial auctions publish price information following an auction and these may contain condition information, age, technical detail, reserve prices and prices achieved.

Pre-sale costs may involve up-to-date servicing or replacement parts. It may be beneficial to have a technical report prepared by a professional expert or the original manufacturer. Some buyers may require a demonstration of the equipment in use before making an offer, while others may make a demonstration a condition of sale. Samples of produced items may be beneficial, particularly if these show work to fine tolerances. Agents may require 'sign-on' commissions in advance of the sale as sometimes items fail to find a buyer and the agent may have contacts and expenses which may otherwise be uncovered.

> *Remember*
> Any advertisements will need to have a budget. Descriptions and any claims made must be accurate and (where possible) verifiable rather than opinions. In legal terms, false claims made either in writing or in person may leave the selling organisation liable – these are usually called 'misrepresentations'.

A contract for the sale needs to be prepared – the more complex the sale, the more detailed the contract. The general principles are common across most local legal frameworks across the world. This syllabus does not expect technical knowledge on contracts, but for general information, the contract probably includes the following.

- The item sold needs to be described

- The sale price, payment amount(s), payment method and payment date(s)

- The right to transfer ownership is usually stated and the point of transfer of responsibility (it could be when the item is delivered or at a specific time and day)

- The responsibilities of each party are described (for example, who is appointing contractors, who is organising delivery)

- Any guarantees or warranty period and what is covered

- The country of the legal framework which applies to the contract and the court jurisdiction which would apply in the event of a dispute

- Fixed asset sale projects also require detailed scheduling of activities and liaison with various specialist contractors

> *Remember*
> The sale of a fixed asset involves more than an advert and accepting a payment.

Accounting for the disposal of fixed assets

When an organisation disposes of a fixed asset, it is likely that some accounting entries will be needed. Organisations may have 'enterprise'-type accounting software that has easy-entry information screens which can then undertake the accounting entries. The routines are likely to be well known in organisations with an accounting department.

The technical entries may vary according to the accounting standards used, but the usual requirements are the 'derecognition' or removal of the asset from the balance sheet of the organisation. This may be a simple subtraction of the net amount from the total of fixed assets, but there may be a requirement to provide more detail about the disposal and a statement in the notes to the accounts is often needed.

Things that often need to be detailed in the accounts are the following.

- Recording the asset's original cost and accumulated depreciation expense up to its sale or disposal date, ready for annotating the annual accounts and notes

- Removal of the fixed asset's cost in the accounts

- Removal of the fixed asset's accumulated depreciation (the value written off over the period of ownership)

- Recording any income from the disposal and detailing any costs incurred in the disposal

- Recording any difference between a value for the asset previously reported in the accounts and the amount received as a gain or a loss

If the organisation has received a gain on the asset's disposal, taxes may need to be paid. Similarly, any losses may be allowable as a tax-deductible event. Much will depend on the accounting conventions in place and the taxation regulations – but these principles are in alignment with international accounting conventions.

Legal aspects – waste management

Legal aspects relating to waste management will vary widely in different countries. In some cases, there may be little legislation, but waste management may be self-regulated or simply licensed. It is common to have documentation requirements to track activities and volumes or weight of waste. In many cases, there will be specific legislation relating to high-risk products and substances.

Examples include the following.

Toxic chemicals and gases

These might be in the form of residue, tanks, liquid reservoirs or even in pipes supplying or draining the equipment.

The legislation may require specific health and safety and general handling requirements, including the following.

- Planning the activity

- The use of personal protective equipment

- The use of specialist contractors

- The documentation of the type and volume of chemicals and how these must be packaged, labelled and transported

- The disposal method may be prescribed by the regulations or terms of a licence

Electronic equipment and batteries

Electronic equipment is likely to contain recyclable metals and potentially harmful metals, like mercury. Batteries can vary by type but may contain contaminants and harmful metals. This makes them unsuitable for landfill as any harmful substances may leak out and cause pollution.

The site owner usually has legal responsibility for any damage, injury or pollution caused by waste. Any contractor chosen by a site owner must comply with any local regulations (for example, certification or registration). The situation of a contractor working on-site to remove waste may not change this general principle – the contractor may have a liability, but the site owner remains responsible until there is a formal transfer of responsibility. In countries where these principles are not in place, there may be some uncertainty regarding responsibility – this could be overcome by having a contract with clear clauses.

In many cases, there will be requirements to separate waste and recycle materials where possible.

Remember

Governments sometimes charge taxes on specific types of materials at their end-of-life in order to reflect environmental issues. Sometimes these are on ultimate disposal (for example, landfill charges) and in other cases by the volume or weight of specific materials handled by organisations, whether the 'originator' or the 'processor' of waste.

Case study

e-Waste: a continuing problem

e-Waste is the term given to the very large range of electrical devices that have come to their end-of-life. These include televisions, computer monitors, computers, mobile telephones, refrigerators and air conditioners – although a very large number of other home and industrial products also contain electronics. Over the last ten years or so, the global problem of e-waste has provided some surprising news stories.

There have been many indications that much of this waste is not really waste, because not enough has been done to extract the materials that can be recycled and reprocess or reuse some potentially harmful and some scarce materials. Some reports indicate that 'easy' extraction is sometimes done, with the remainder openly burned, with toxic chemicals being released.

There have been reported cases of e-waste being exported to developing countries as a solution to avoid high costs of processing in developed countries. At first glance this appears logical as cheaper labour makes the processing more economic. Unfortunately, there have been multiple examples of export resulting in just dumping of unprocessed e-waste in countries that probably cannot afford to clean up the dumps to avoid environmental damage. In some cases, the legitimate waste processor had a supplier contract for e-waste but inadequate management by the supplier allowed the export to sites that were dumps rather than reprocessing facilities.

Following this publicity, some manufacturers have 'banned' the export of e-waste. There has been a waste electrical and electronic equipment directive (WEEE) that affects every EU state for a number of years – this effectively bans the export of e-waste from member states.

The United Nations Environment Programme's Basel Convention has ongoing work on improving the environmental performance of e-waste in developing countries and promoting the general concept that the export of waste is not appropriate, but export of reuse equipment is appropriate.

Environmental factors

Specific environmental factors will vary widely given the potential range of items and materials for disposal.

Disposal issues start with the original specification of purchases, whether these are fixed assets or stock. Specifications can be extended to include issues relating to end-of-life environmental factors, such as the following.

- The materials used (and whether these can be reused or reprocessed)

- The design of the items – whether the parts can be easily disassembled

- Labelling of parts to indicate recycling or processing to be used

- The designed life of the items and the real-world usage lifetime

- Provision for potential refurbishment of parts rather than waste processing

- Specifying chemicals, coolants and lubricants that are easier to process at end-of-life with less impact on the environment

- The provision of product-specific end-of-life dismantling and processing centres

- Documentation relating to decommissioning and end-of-life disposal provided as part of the specification to allow assessment by the buying organisation

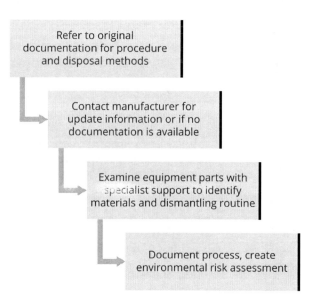

Figure 3.16 A suggested starting point for environmental risk assessment

Figure 3.16 suggests a logical process – this includes contacting the original manufacturer as there may be up-to-date views on decommissioning and disposal.

If the disposal investigation results in a range of potential options, each of the options should be compared for their environmental risks and total environmental impact.

- The specific environmental risks of each of the processes involved

- The material(s) and substance(s) involved

- The processes available for the specific materials and substances

- The resource consumption of the processes

- Any by-products of the processes, including residual waste

- Potential pollution risks

- Transport movements (CO_2 emissions) and risks-in-transit (for example, spillages within a vehicle, the impact of combustion)

- Where reuse or recycling is involved, the residual end-of-life requirements and consequences

A risk register is commonly used to summarise the risks – it can take some time to document the risks and quantifying some of these issues can be very difficult as information is not always available. As a result, many organisations use summaries featuring general classifications of low, medium and high risks and estimates based on available information.

Environmental risk assessment theme	Disposal option A	Disposal option B	Disposal option C
Decommissioning risk	LOW	LOW	LOW
Dismantling risk	LOW	LOW	LOW
Transport risk	LOW	LOW	MEDIUM
Reprocessing energy use	HIGH	LOW	MEDIUM
Reprocessing risk	MEDIUM	MEDIUM	LOW
CO_2 assessment	HIGH	MEDIUM	HIGH
% reuse	82%	76%	74%

Table 3.6 Comparative table example using selected criteria and estimates

Table 3.6 is an example of a comparison table. The selected criteria are appropriate although the broad categories confirm that comparisons may be difficult. In the examples provided, would option B's lower percentage reuse be justified by the lower level of CO_2 and energy use?

> *Remember*
> There may be some situations where a high environmental risk with extensive consequences may eliminate one or more options.

It is important in these situations that the risks have been documented, mitigating actions designed and decisions made with appropriate and documented reasons.

Organisations committed to environmental issues may already have sophisticated modelling tools for this type of assessment – some specialist contractors and original manufacturers may be able to supply useful data.

Triple bottom line (TBL)
The principle that organisations should not solely operate for a profit but also operate for a bottom line of people and planet. People and planet do not have an absolute financial or numeric result, but the care taken to optimise the end results still apply

Case study

Dismantling vehicles

As part of a European Union directive, the dismantling of end-of-life vehicles became an essential part of waste processing in member countries.

Manufacturers now supply dismantling contractors with information sheets for each model within six months of launch. These are computerised, free of charge and indicate the various parts that can be recovered – some are identified for reuse (refurbishment or remanufactured options are mentioned). Different materials are identified so that some are removed to avoid later pollution, some may be recycled using specific processes and metals separated for reprocessing. Separation of metals is sometimes undertaken by shredding the prepared remaining bodyshell.

The objective is a recycling achievement of 85% and a recovery target of 95% or better. 'Type approval' for new cars in the EU is not granted unless the new car can produce this result.

Some car manufacturers have set up their own dismantling and reuse centres. One manufacturer reports that this enables a greater understanding of wear characteristics and designed-life components.

Remember
A reduction in use of new resources and incorporation of reused or recycled materials should produce a much more sustainable supply chain.

Check
List four examples of disposal which may involve an environmental risk.

Triple bottom line – people, planet, profit

This concept is at the heart of the principles of sustainability – the **triple bottom line (TBL)**.

Ecological footprint
A technical term used to express the impact of activity in terms of the area of land and water usage required to support the activity and waste assimilation

- People relates to socially responsible corporate awareness and behaviour, both internally and in the wider community.

- Planet relates to environmental awareness and behaviour, minimising its **ecological footprint**.

- Profit relates to the need to maintain an economic, financial position that is sustainable, most often related to continued operations.

The concept suggests the three elements need to be balanced. In simple terms this means the following.

- An organisation ignoring 'people' internally may decide to impose new working conditions or not to undertake training and development.

Ignoring the employment conditions within the supply chain may result in accidents or the forced closure of a supplier. In these situations, an organisation's business performance may suffer, and this is likely to affect its financial performance ('profit').

- An organisation ignoring 'planet' issues may decide to continue using materials that use scarce or environmentally damaging origins. Ultimately, the materials are likely to become more expensive or simply not available, putting the organisation in an unsustainable position. In the meantime, it is likely to find adverse public relations affecting sales and a cost of the extra efforts in defending its position.

- An organisation that is not sustainable economically ('profit'), may well become less 'people' and 'planet' sensitive, creating a downward spiral.

In the context of disposal, there are some specific themes which link directly to these principles of sustainability.

Socially responsible disposal

An organisation arranging disposal would be expected to ensure that any supplier is using a disposal supply chain which is socially responsible – this is likely to include the following.

- Ensuring that all staff and the public are safeguarded from the short-term and long-term effects of disposal: this will be more than just the use of personal protective equipment.

- Ensuring employment practices of the disposal supply chain matches or improves on the policies and practices of the organisation arranging for disposal.

- Consideration of disposal methods which minimise the potential risk and impact to people.

Environmentally responsible disposal

In principle, there is no disposal which could be viewed as 'environmental' as any use of resources and subsequent disposal has an impact on the environment. As disposal may include unnecessary waste, it follows that a reduction of materials and processes to an overall minimum is desirable. Avoidance of disposal as waste in favour of reuse or repurpose of materials and items may be a more environmentally responsible solution. This fits with another connected concept: the circular economy.

The circular economy concept suggests that organisations should view resources as valuable and keep them in use for as long as economically viable, extracting the maximum benefit and value from them and then attempting to recover materials and value, possibly regenerating products and materials at the end of each cycle. The cycle can be the following.

- **Closed loop:** involving the same type of use (for example, the materials from waste batteries being used to create new batteries or recycling used cardboard to create new cardboard)

- **Open loop:** involving a different type of use (for example, the materials from used wooden railway sleepers being reused as garden raised beds)

- **Mixed loop:** involving some materials being reused for the same type of product and other materials being used differently (for example, tyres can be remoulded, but if they are unsuitable then they can be shredded, metals separated and the 'rubber crumb' used for road construction)

Circular economy
A principle of maximising reuse and value extraction of materials and products rather than disposal without consideration of outcome

Some trade-offs may be required as a disposal process may require long transport distances (CO_2 emissions and energy use being higher than local disposal) and the process may involve high energy use (energy and CO_2 use may be higher than local processes) but the result may be less environmental damage and greater reuse of the resulting material.

Economic disposal

It would be desirable for any organisation to consider the most economic disposal at end-of-life. With greater commitment to environmental concerns and the increased costs of 'disposal as waste', there are now specialist businesses that have integrated other people's waste into their own processing. There are also waste infrastructures established or being developed to take advantage of potentially profitable material recovery.

Investigation is needed for disposal of significant volumes or where value is expected.

Obsolete stock and equipment

This should be assessed for possible alternative uses and markets. The original suppliers could be contacted as there may still be a demand unknown to the buying organisation. Previous customers for the stock could be contacted in case they still have a need and/or may be sourcing from another supplier. Specialist dealers may buy the stock or equipment, with the intention of using their own contacts or extracting scrap value. There may be an active market in another country which may allow the organisation to sell-on the stock or equipment. The objective is to move the stock or equipment and obtain the best value possible or limit the losses incurred.

Redundant stock and equipment

This should be assessed for any opportunity to find a buyer and recover as much value as possible. Original supplier(s) should be contacted as they may offer some value or credit against goods still in use (or a part exchange for equipment). Previous customers may still have a use for the stock item(s) even though no orders have been received from them. Specialist dealers may find it easy to use their contacts and find buyers as the stock or equipment is still current in the marketplace.

Surplus stock and equipment

Stock could simply be held until it is used up through normal trading. It is more likely that some action is needed for stock – this probably starts as promotional efforts through established customers and attempts to interest new customers. There is a danger that heavy promotional stock sales and bulk stock sales to specialist dealers may result in the 'flooding' of products on the market. Any over-supply will affect follow-on sales and price discounting will affect the market's view of the price of the items after the surplus is cleared. Surplus materials could be offered back to material suppliers; surplus bought-in products offered back to the original product suppliers.

Surplus industry-specific machinery could be sold to specialist dealers or advertised in appropriate trade magazines. There may be industrial surplus agents that could find a potential buyer for a commission. It is possible that other organisations in the sector could be contacted owing to the industry linkage.

Remember
The objective is to maximise value recovery without affecting the reputation of the organisation.

Scrap and waste

Scrap material may have a market and value that is not immediately apparent. Some materials have known scrap values and yet organisations may currently pay for removal. Scrap values work best if the material has an established market and is separated from other scrap and waste. As a result, it may be economically beneficial to incur some costs to separate waste types.

Many organisations will pay for scrap to be removed, but in some cases, there is a significant remaining value that could be partly recovered. Examples are the separation of scrap into identifiable groups; timber use in new material and multiple uses for organic matter.

Waste (whether routine or from the stripping out of equipment) benefits from competitive quotes. Some waste contractors have different capabilities and 'solutions' to waste processing. In some cases, the contractors in an area or for a specific type of waste all use a single processor – so it may be a case of finding out more about their industry.

Waste liquids should not be mixed as the processes used to manage this waste are expensive and unnecessarily risky to manage.

Economic disposal extends to return schemes, which may have been commonplace in the past for local B2B transactions (for example, deposit-and-return schemes for fruit and vegetable wooden cases, drink barrels and bottles, and sacks).

Check
Give an example where a disposal may satisfy the 'triple bottom line' principle.

Remember
The waste solution is not sustainable. There is likely to be increased pressure on organisations to justify the type and volume of waste produced as environmental interest, government action and economic costs of waste have their effect.

Chapter Summary

This chapter has explained the multitude of different aspects linked to the concept of through life cost.

All aspects of acquiring stock and fixed assets have been questioned in some way – this has a natural focus in terms of the various costs involved, but also the linkage to the environmental, social and people impact of the decisions being made in organisations.

Many procurement activities benefit from policies, procedures and processes – this chapter has presented a mix of common 'best practice' and some concepts which are not always documented in organisations.

Successful procurement often relies on good research and the elimination of hidden costs and potential consequences of decisions.

Recommended reading

CIPS Knowledge Sources: These are available to CIPS members via the CIPS website and provide an overview of theory and application.

- Whole Life Costing: www.cips.org/Documents/Knowledge/Procurement-Topics-and-Skills/5-Strategy-and-Policy/Whole-Life-Costing/1/Whole_Life_Costing-Knowledge_Works.pdf

- Sustainability and People/Planet/Profits: www.cips.org/Documents/Knowledge/Procurement-Topics-and-Skills/4-Sustainability-CSR-Ethics/Sustainable-and-Ethical-Procurement/1/Triple_Bottom_Line_TBL.pdf

- How to Develop a Waste Management and Disposal Strategy: www.cips.org/Documents/About%20CIPS/Develop%20Waste%20v3%20-%2020.11.07.pdf

- Risk Assessment and Templates: www.cips.org/en/knowledge/tools-and-templates-revised/risk-analysis--management1/?&accordion=4

Other sources:

Lysons, K. and Farrington, B. (2016), *Procurement and Supply Chain Management*, Harlow: Pearson. Comprehensive compendium of theory and practice featured across many of the CIPS levels

Commodities: World Bank pubdocs.worldbank.org/en/283421538517311854/CMO-Pink-Sheet-October-2018.pdf. Provides an overview of price trends from an independent source

GS1 Vendor Managed Inventory for ECR: shop.gs1.ch/en/A~29250/2~10101~5/Supply-Chain-Management/Dokument/Best-Practice-in-Implementing-Vendor-Managed-Inventory-%28VMI%29. Detailed planning/implementation guide from the standard setting organisation for bar codes

International Organization for Standardization (ISO): www.iso.org/home.html. Home page of ISO standards descriptions and requirements

UN Sustainable Development: www.un.org/sustainabledevelopment/development-agenda/. Source for sustainability development objectives which are widely used and referenced

UNEP E-waste: www.basel.int/Implementation/Ewaste/Overview/tabid/4063/Default.aspx. Source for electronic waste standards adopted by many countries

Ghana e-waste: www.theguardian.com/environment/2011/may/16/uk-ewaste-dumped-ghana. UK newspaper report of e-waste disposal problem

End of Chapter Assessment

1 Which of the following describes 'consignment stock'?　　IDENTIFY

   a)　Stock ready for despatch awaiting packing or collection

   b)　Stock that is awaiting delivery because the order cannot be fully completed

   c)　Stock that is held by the customer and only paid for when used

   d)　Stock that has been supplied in replacement of faulty goods

2 A buyer has requested a price for an estimated very large amount of packing materials with monthly orders, over a twelve-month period. The supplier is willing to offer a significant discount for the volume estimated but is concerned that the buyer might only order a small volume.　　IDENTIFY

Which of the following offers an appropriate solution that meets both the buyer and supplier positions?

   a)　A retrospective discount payable after the volumes ordered meet the original total requirement

   b)　Payment in advance from the buyer based on the estimated order volume

   c)　A variable market price with an additional payment if the estimated volumes are not reached

   d)　Multi-part pricing with variable delivery costs based on volumes delivered

3 Which of the following explains the term 'opportunity cost'?　　IDENTIFY

   a)　The loss of hire income when an asset is not being used by a customer

   b)　The difference in cost between the current market price and a discounted price

   c)　The concept that funds committed to a purchase could have been used for other, more profitable activities

   d)　The cost of assessment of different potential ways of acquiring fixed assets, including whole life cost calculations

4 Which of the following is a disadvantage of leasing a fixed asset?　　IDENTIFY

   a)　The total cost of the lease is usually unknown at the outset as the contract period is not set

   b)　The rental payments are subject to increases during the lease term

   c)　Leases are expected to run for the contracted term with additional costs if cancelled

   d)　Leases require asset insurance which is not required if the item was purchased

IDENTIFY

5 Which of the following is likely to have a low acquisition cost?

a) Purchases requiring tenders

b) Purchases involving long-term fixed assets

c) New low-cost purchases with new suppliers

d) Repeat purchases with existing suppliers

IDENTIFY

6 Choose one answer to complete this sentence: Purchasing cards are primarily used in order to:

a) avoid research on pricing and quality

b) reduce the acquisition cost of products and services

c) improve an organisation's cash flow

d) provide details to suppliers of buyers and their spend limits

IDENTIFY

7 Which of the following explains 'customer acceptance testing'?

a) A series of post-installation activities to ensure equipment and documentation is in accordance with requirements

b) Part of a pre-sales discussion to establish which of the additional-cost features will be required by the customer

c) Part of a periodic follow-up activity to assess that product quality and service are acceptable to the customer

d) A series of checks to ensure that a potential supplier is financially capable of delivering a high-cost contract

IDENTIFY

8 Which of the following explains the benefits of a 'Kanban' system?

a) It allows buyers to use the Internet to attract new suppliers

b) It automatically matches invoices to purchase orders

c) It reports detailed stock records over a time period

d) It provides a quick way of repeat ordering a specific item

IDENTIFY

9 An organisation has reported that it has a large value of stock regarded as 'redundant'. Which of the following describes redundant stock?

a) Stock classified by the organisation as ready for disposal as waste

b) Stock which has exceeded the stated 'use by' recommendations

c) Stock for which the organisation has no further use but is still usable by others

d) Stock volumes that are greater than immediately required

IDENTIFY

10 Which of the following best describes a typical total cost of ownership process?

a) Assessment of asset options, decisions based on all lifetime costs and monitoring through to end-of-life

b) Annual analysis of asset costs incurred, value for money assessment and replacement decisions based on latest requirements and timescale

c) Initial purchase, storage, financial and training costs analysis along with disposal costs if scrapped

d) Initial comparisons of purchase price against commercial benefit over the expected lifetime of the asset

11 Which of the following explains the term 'net present value'?

IDENTIFY

  a) The original purchase price less an allowance for the loss of value over time

  b) The difference between the price paid after negotiation with the list price

  c) The value of an asset at its 'end-of-life' which may be positive or negative

  d) The discounting of potential future financial benefits to reflect current values

12 Which of the following form the framework for typical risk assessments at the end-of-life of an asset?

IDENTIFY

  a) Sources of risk, probability of risk, impact, mitigation and control of risks

  b) Cost of disposal, risk of delays, contingency budget

  c) Details of decommissioning, dismantling and disposal

  d) Health and safety procedures, warning sign production and staff awareness

13 An organisation has commented that it recycles all packaging using specialist contractors which supply the packaging industry with the processed materials. This is an example of which of the following?

IDENTIFY

  a) Open-loop recycling

  b) Closed-loop recycling

  c) Socially responsible recycling

  d) Environmental recycling

Glossary

Aisles
Clear areas between racking or pallet stacks

Bill of materials
List of all the components, including the quantities required, to produce the required number of units of the end product

Book value
The notional value of stock as set down in a company's accounts; it is an estimate of value which may or may not be achieved or may indeed be exceeded

Bottleneck
A restriction inside a warehouse, store or stockyard that holds up or slows down activity. This may be caused by poor layout, access difficulties or simply the volume of picking or storage being handled

Brainstorming
A series of techniques used as part of creating a range of options to solve a problem or series of problems. The idea is to promote open and diverse ideas

Bullwhip effect
Distorted demand increasing up the supply chain

Business-to-business (B2B)
Commercial trade transactions between businesses (as opposed to business-to-consumer, B2C)

Capital expenditure
Money spent on acquiring and maintaining fixed assets bought by an organisation which are used within the organisation rather than bought for resale. (Typically, these assets are land, buildings and equipment)

Check digits
Numbers added to product codes which allow computer-based validation. These are usually created using specific number sequences and are designed to reduce the probability of errors

Circular economy
A principle of maximising reuse and value extraction of materials and products rather than disposal without consideration of outcome

Closing stock
The inventory held at the end of an accounting period; becomes the opening stock for the next period

Commodity markets
Raw material or part-processed product markets with established standards and trading allowing published prices reflecting demand and supply

Components
Manufactured items bought in to include in a larger final product, for example, exhaust systems for vehicles

Consignment stocking
A facility offered by a supplier to a buyer to allow a delivery of stock to the buyer with payment only after it is used or sold to a customer

Consignment stocking
A technique of acquiring stock from a supplier and only paying when sold or used rather than paying following a trade credit period

Consumables
Items which are typically required as part of a process, but which do not form part of a finished product. A machine may require cleaning products to maintain performance – the liquids and industrial wipes would be consumables

Cost benefit
A calculation that considers the benefits resulting from a specific cost or process. Some benefits may not have monetary values

Cross-docking
Activity in a warehouse or stockyard where a delivery is unloaded but then prepared for despatch without being stored. In some cases, a vehicle may be awaiting loading

Current assets
Accounting term used to describe stock items in an organisation which are routinely bought and sold. Accounting conventions also include cash and money the business is owed (debtors/receivables) as part of current assets

Delphi method
A structured forecasting technique using a panel of experts and a number of rounds of questioning. Responses are shared after each round and the experts encouraged to reconsider their own responses. It is intended to achieve a consensus view

Dependent demand
The requirement for a stock item which is directly related to and therefore dependent upon the rate of production (examples are: raw materials, components, energy)

Direct supplies
Supplies that are integrated into the finished product

Distribution centre
A storage facility, usually smaller than the organisation's main warehouse, that is geographically sited to serve a specific area

Distribution centres and distribution hubs
Warehouses that are intended to be a focal point for a specific activity for a geographic area

Docks
A feature of warehouse design – used for unloading and loading vehicles (i.e. loading and unloading bays)

Drum
Container for stock, which is usually cylindrical and can be made from a variety of materials. Contents are usually loose material or liquids

Ecological footprint
A technical term used to express the impact of activity in terms of the area of land and water usage required to support the activity and waste assimilation

EDI (electronic data interchange)
A computer-to-computer exchange of business documents in a standard format between different organisations

ERP (enterprise resource planning)
Business process management software that uses a system of integrated applications to manage the business and automate many back-office functions

Evergreen contract
A contract that is renewed automatically from year to year until cancelled by either party

Ex-works
The term given to a price for collection from the supplier's location rather than delivered to the buyer's site

Exponentially weighted average method (EWAM)
A statistical methodology which can be used give more importance to the most recent data

Finished goods
Products ready for sale and/or use

Fixed asset register
A document which typically details the fixed assets in the possession of an organisation, their date of acquisition, age, original cost and current cost. Some organisations also annotate maintenance costs and likely cost of disposal or current sale value

Fixed assets
Accounting term used to describe items which are in possession but not intended for routine sale. Typically, these include vehicles, fixtures and fittings, land, buildings and machinery. Most accounting standards have detailed rules on fixed asset requirements and descriptions

Fixed assets
An accounting term used to describe items acquired by an organisation which are not routinely sold but used within the organisation. Typical examples are land and buildings, fixtures and fittings, office and warehouse equipment. Fixed assets are also known as non-current assets

Flexible warehousing
Term used to describe any technique which allows the short-term ability to increase or decrease storage space

Flow
The ability of stock to be moved around a facility in the quickest and safest way. A poor flow makes movements slower and reduces efficiency

Forecasting
Decision-making tool used by businesses to help in budgeting, planning and estimating future growth

GRN (goods received note)
A document or electronic entry recording that goods have been received by an organisation. This is usually prepared after a visual inspection, although in some organisations formal acceptance testing may be required before the GRN is created

Guarantee
A commitment from the seller (or original equipment manufacturer) that should a product not meet a stated quality in a specified period then it will be repaired, replaced or refunded. There are likely to be terms and conditions. The guarantee is usually written

Hedge
A technique of taking a position either in current stock or future stock to offset potential losses should the price move. A hedge will have a cost of trading and may involve the use of technical financial contracts

Heijunka (schedule levelling)
Smoothing out production rates

Hire
A legal commitment with terms and conditions allowing the owner of an asset to charge fees to a renter. The period of rental is usually fixed, although some rentals can be 'open' until the return of the asset

Lease
A legal commitment with terms and conditions allowing the lessor (who owns the asset) to charge 'rental' fees to a lessee (who will be able to use the asset). The terms and conditions will detail the responsibilities for maintenance, insurance and end-of-contract rights and responsibilities

Holding costs/carrying costs
Costs associated with the storage and handling of physical stock

Independent demand
The requirement for a stock item which is not directly related to, and is therefore independent of, the rate of production (examples are: machinery spares, office equipment and consumables)

Indirect supplies
Supplies not incorporated in the finished product but which keep the business and factory operating

Inventory
Alternative term used for stock held in a facility or organisation

Inventory strategy
The overall approach to how stock is managed, including order points, quantities and values, physical placement of stock etc.

Just in time
A production methodology pioneered by Toyota where stock is acquired literally 'just in time' to be incorporated into the production process. It is a means of reducing stockholdings and reducing waste in production systems

Just in time (JIT)
A range of techniques which are dedicated to the systematic elimination of waste, including the elimination of delays and streamlining of processes

Kanban
The signal to move to the next process

Kitting
Activity in a warehouse or store of assembling groups of items that are to be used together – a 'kit of items' is created for a specific task

Lead time
The time delay between placing an order and the availability of the item in the required location. There may be an internal lead time in creating an order and another between receipt of goods and making them available to a user

Lean
Manufacturing system based on the minimisation of waste

Liquidity
The ease with which assets can be converted into cash. A firm with a high-value asset base but low liquidity may struggle to meet its debts on time

Mezzanine floor
A floor area typically inserted in a high-roofed building to create an elevated additional working or storage space

MRO inventory
Maintenance, repair and operations inventory; includes, for example, items such as cleaning equipment or office supplies

Net present value (NPV)
An accounting term for an amount in the future, adjusted to 'today's' value by a calculation. This allows a comparison between different projects on the same basis

Obsolescence
The process of becoming outdated

Opening stock
The inventory held at the start of an accounting period

Opportunity cost
A term from economics used to consider that funds used for one purpose could have been used for a different purpose with a better financial outcome

Pallets
Platform structures designed to support a load and be lifted using the forks typically seen on forklift trucks and other equipment. These are in a variety of standard sizes and can be made of many materials including plastic, resin, board or timber

Pareto principle (the 80/20 rule)
The theory that 80% of outcomes result from 20% of inputs, for example, 80% of sales are to the top 20% of customers; 80% of spend on inventory is accounted for by the top 20% of stock items

Picking
The activity of retrieving stock from storage

Purchase order lead time
The time period from placing an order to delivery of the goods

Purchasing card (procurement card)
Essentially a credit card owned by the company that enables an officer to make low-value purchases without the need for formal requisitions and purchase orders

Qualitative analysis
Analysis based on opinions and statements (which are often non-quantifiable) rather than numerical or statistical evidence

Quantitative analysis
Analysis based on numerical or statistical-based information rather than opinions and statements

Quarantine area
Area set aside for items which are awaiting inspection or testing. There may also be faulty items or items awaiting return to the supplier. The idea is that these items must not enter storage or be made available until cleared for use

Raw materials
The basic inputs to manufacturing a product, usually unprocessed or having had very little pre-processing, for example: metals, minerals, timber, fibres

Redundancy
The state of being no longer needed or surplus to requirements

Reorder point
The point either in time or in a process when the next order should be placed

Request for quotation
A standard document or electronic request from a buyer to a supplier detailing a requirement and requesting a quotation. Some also request other information which may include stock availability and technical detail

Return (or reverse) logistics
The storage, handling and movement of materials or products in the reverse direction from original supply. This may involve faulty goods, surplus goods or claims under guarantee. Some organisations offer a return of spare parts for recycling or reuse; end-of-life recycling or scrappage is also possible

RFID (Radio Frequency Identification)
Items which use radio technology for identifying itself and its location subject to having the appropriate hardware and software

Safety stock (buffer stock)
Stock held as a contingency or insurance against disruption or unexpected demand

Service level agreement (SLA)
This is a term used to describe a performance requirement. These are most typically expressed as contractual requirements. SLAs focus on measurable activities

Silo-working
Restricting information to the department that produced it

Single-piece flow
Situation in which products proceed, one complete product at a time, through various operations in design, order-taking and production, without interruptions, backflows or scrap (Womack and Jones, 2013)

Six Sigma
Statistical technique for measuring variations within production processes, with the aim of eliminating them. The Six Sigma premise is that variations create defects and other forms of waste

Stock keeping unit (SKU)
An identifiable item from stock. Organisations may assign individual SKU numbers of their own design or use industry or company standard numbers. Although an SKU relates to a single item, the item could be a box or pallet load rather than an individual item

Stock profile
The description of stock items in terms of value, rate of turnover, storage characteristics etc.

Stock turn/stock turnover (high or low)
How many times stock or inventory is being used/sold and purchased/replenished over a given time period

Stockout
Having no or insufficient materials to continue production or the finished goods to meet an order

Stocktake
An audit check of the stock physically held; this may be by amount or value, or both

Stockyard
An open area (which may have a canopy or some protection) often used to store bulky stock items, vehicles and appropriate materials

Stores
Small, local storage facility for immediate-use items

Supplier relationship management (SRM)
The strategic managing of all interactions with a designated supplier organisation

Tail spend
Spend that is not actively managed; it is a small proportion of total spend (10–20% under each spend category) but has a large number of suppliers accounting for it

Tender
A formal process of requesting a response to a detailed requirement from a buyer. The tender principle is designed to allow competitive bids with an evaluation of a number of supplier responses

Time bucket
The period of time specified

Time-series
A series of data points indexed (or listed or graphed) in time order

Total cost of ownership (TCO)
The total cost of an asset including its purchase price and operation costs over its whole life cycle

Total quality management (TQM)
Organisation-wide efforts to improve outputs through continuous improvement in internal practices

Tote box
Reusable storage box. These can be open or have lids or flaps to close them and come in a large variety of sizes and weight loadings

Triple bottom line (TBL)
The principle that organisations should not solely operate for a profit but also operate for a bottom line of people and planet. People and planet do not have an absolute financial or numeric result, but the care taken to optimise the end results still apply

Unit load
A term used to describe the grouping of different items into a convenient stack or stacks which make them easy to handle and store. Typically, this involves pallets and/or the plastic wrapping of a load

Warehouse
Large-scale storage facility – can be 'stand-alone' (for example, not connected to manufacturing, assembly, retailing) or 'integrated' (for example, on the same site products are either used or retailed)

Warranty
A commitment that the product will perform as stated for the specified period. The detailing of the warranty will determine the rights of the owner and responsibilities of the seller. A warranty for a period longer than the guarantee (or with enhanced rights) may be offered for an additional cost

Waste
Anything that does not add value to the product

'What if' analysis
Analysis-based scenarios exploring whether something will happen or not

Work in progress (WIP)
In inventory management the expression relates to stock part-way through a manufacturing process; in the services sectors the term is also used for anything between order and delivery

Working capital
A company's current assets minus its current liabilities; a measure of a company's ability to cover its short-term debts

Written off / to write-off
In relation to costs: accepting that they cannot be recouped (for example, through sale of the asset purchased); in relation to debts: accepting that they will not be paid; taking a potential 'asset' and marking its value down to zero in the accounts

Zoning
An arrangement in a stockyard, warehouse or stores facility where areas are determined based on requirements for different access, or the characteristics of different types of equipment or stock

Index

Issued under the authority of the Home Office
(Fire and Emergency Planning Directorate)

Fire Service Manual

Volume 1
Fire Service Technology, Equipment and Media

Physics and Chemistry for Firefighters

HM Fire Service Inspectorate Publications Section

London: TSO

Published by TSO (The Stationery Office) and available from:

Online
www.tsoshop.co.uk

Mail, Telephone, Fax and E-mail
TSO
PO Box 29, Norwich, NR3 1GN
Telephone orders/General enquiries: 0870 600 5522
Fax orders: 0870 600 5533
E-mail: customer.services@tso.co.uk
Textphone 0870 240 3701

TSO Shops
123 Kingsway, London, WC2B 6PQ
020 7242 6393 Fax 020 7242 6394
68-69 Bull Street, Birmingham B4 6AD
0121 236 9696 Fax 0121 236 9699
9-21 Princess Street, Manchester M60 8AS
0161 834 7201 Fax 0161 833 0634
16 Arthur Street, Belfast BT1 4GD
028 9023 8451 Fax 028 9023 5401
18-19 High Street, Cardiff CF10 1PT
029 2039 5548 Fax 029 2038 4347
71 Lothian Road, Edinburgh EH3 9AZ
0870 606 5566 Fax 0870 606 5588

TSO Accredited Agents
(see Yellow Pages)

and through good booksellers

ISBN 10 0-11-341182-0
ISBN 13 978-0-11-341182-5

Cover and half-title page photograph: Hampshire Fire and Rescue Service

Printed in the United Kingdom for TSO
N C2 8/06

Physics and Chemistry for Firefighters

Preface

In order to understand how fires behave and how they can be extinguished, it is necessary to understand some physics and chemistry. This book is divided into three parts which will introduce the reader to the relevant physical and chemical processes and then show how these work together in the phenomenon that we call fire.

Extinguishing fires is a matter of interrupting one or more of these processes so that burning cannot continue. Firefighters will appreciate that it is, therefore, important to acquire a good understanding of what happens in a fire, in order to be able to choose the best method available to extinguish it, and to avoid making it worse.

In the first part of this book, some of the physical properties of matter will be discussed. Some materials are heavier than others, bulk for bulk. Some heat up more easily than others. These and other properties greatly affect the way that materials behave when they are involved in a fire.

In the second part, the chemical processes relevant to fire will be discussed. Besides the burning process itself, the way that materials behave chemically in fire will also be discussed. It is hoped that firefighters will gain an understanding of the dangers that new materials present and the way the weapons they have to fight them work.

The third part of the book discusses fire extinction.

This book replaces: The Manual of Firemanship, Book 1 – Elements of combustion and extinction.

The Home Office is indebted to all those who assisted in the production of this book, in particular, Edinburgh University Department of Civil and Environmental Engineering, Dr. John Brenton and Dr. Dougal Drysdale.

Physics and Chemistry for Firefighters

Contents

Chapter 10 Other Combustible Solids   75

Chapter 11 Extiguishing Fires   79

Appendices   88

Further reading   93

Physics and Chemistry
for Firefighters

Physics and Chemistry for Firefighters

Chapter 1 – Physical properties of matter

Matter is the name given to all material things – anything that has mass and occupies space. Solids, liquids, gases and vapours are all matter. The amount of matter is known as the mass, and is measured in kilograms. In everyday life, the **mass** of a solid is measured in kilograms, although for liquids, gases and vapours, we are more accustomed to using **volume**, the amount of space occupied by a given substance, simply because it is easier to measure. Thus, we talk about litres of petrol and cubic metres of gas. However, gases, vapours and liquids also have mass which can be expressed in kilograms.

Density

> **Understanding density is extremely important for a firefighter.**

Understanding density is extremely important for a firefighter. For example, the density of a gas or vapour determines whether it will tend to rise or sink in air, and be found in the greatest concentrations at the upper or lower levels in a building. The density of a burning liquid partly decides whether it is possible to cover it with water to extinguish the fire, or whether the firefighter will need to use foam or other another extinguishing medium. However, another important factor is how well the burning liquid mixes with water, a property known as miscibility.

Imagine two solid rods, both the same length and width, one made of wood and one from iron. Though they are the same size, the iron rod weighs much more than the wooden rod. The iron rod is said to have a greater density than the wooden one.

The density of a material is defined as the mass of one cubic metre of material. One cubic metre is the standard "unit volume". A unit volume of iron has a greater mass than a unit volume of wood and is thus more dense.

Calculating values for the densities of different substances enables meaningful comparisons to be made. The density of a substance is calculated by dividing the mass of a body by its volume.

$$\text{Density} = \frac{\text{mass}}{\text{volume}}$$

$$\text{In symbols } D = \frac{M}{V}$$

$$\text{so } M = D \times V$$

$$\text{and } V = \frac{M}{D}$$

If mass is measured in kilograms (kg) and the volume in cubic metres (m^3), the "units" of density will be kilograms per cubic metre (kg/m^3). If mass is in grams (g) and volume in cubic centimeters (cm^3), density will be in grams per cubic centimetre (g/cm^3).

(Note: units should always be quoted, and care must be taken not to mix, or confuse, units.)

> **Water has a density of about 1000 kg/m^3 or 1 g/cm^3.**

Mercury has the very high density of 13 600 kg/m^3 or 13.6 g/cm^3 and is, therefore, 13.6 times as dense as water.

If the density of a substance is lower than the density of water, and does not mix with water, then that substance will float on water. To use our previous example, the density of wood is lower than that of water and the density of iron is higher, so wood floats and iron sinks.

> **If the density of a substance is lower than the density of water, and does not mix with (dissolve in) water, then that substance will float on water.**

The term specific gravity or relative density is sometimes used to give measure of density. The relative density of a substance is the ratio of the mass of any volume of it to the mass of an equal amount of water.

$$\text{Relative density} = \frac{\text{mass of any volume of the substance}}{\text{mass of an equal volume of water}}$$

$$= \frac{\text{density of that substance}}{\text{density of water}}$$

Relative density or specific gravity has no units as the units on the top and bottom of the equation are the same, so they cancel each other out when the one quantity is divided by the other.

1.1 Vapour density

Gases and vapours have very low densities compared with liquids and solids. At normal temperatures and pressures (e.g., 20°C and 1 atmosphere) a cubic metre of water has a mass of about 1000 kg and a cubic metre of air has a mass of around 1.2 kg.

We have previously mentioned that specific gravity is a ratio of the density of the substance in question compared with the density of water, so specific gravity is not a sensible thing to use for gases as their densities are so low: e.g., the specific gravity of air is 0.0013. For this reason, the density of a gas or vapour (vapour density, usually abbreviated to VD) is given in relation to the density of an equal volume of hydrogen, air or oxygen under the same conditions of temperature and pressure.

Hydrogen is often used as a comparison for calculating vapour density because it is the lightest gas. The vapour density of air compared with hydrogen is 14.4, meaning that a given volume of air is 14.4 times heavier than the same volume of hydrogen **at the same temperature and pressure**. For carbon dioxide the vapour density compared with that of hydrogen is 22, so a given volume of carbon dioxide is about 1.5 (that is 22/14.4) times as heavy as the same volume of air at the same temperature and pressure. (If the temperature and pressure are changed, the volume of the gas will change. This will be explained later.)

For fire service purposes it is much more convenient to compare the density of gases and vapours with that of air. The reference gas should always be given to avoid confusion: for example, the vapour density of methane is 0.556 (air = 1), or 8 (hydrogen = 1).

1.2 Liquids of different density

As we have said, the density of a burning liquid partly decides whether it is possible to cover it with water to extinguish the fire, or whether the firefighter will need to use foam or another extinguishing medium.

Consider water poured into two tanks (A) and (B) (Figure 1.1) which are standing on a flat, horizontal surface and are connected by a horizontal pipe as shown. The water will assume equal levels in each tank as, for the system to balance, there must be an equal "head" (or height) of water in each tank above the lowest point of the pipe. The "head" determines the water pressure at any depth: with interconnected tanks as in Figure 1.1, the levels adjust to ensure that the pressures at the level of the pipe are equal.

Figure 1.1 Diagrams showing the difference in density in liquids.

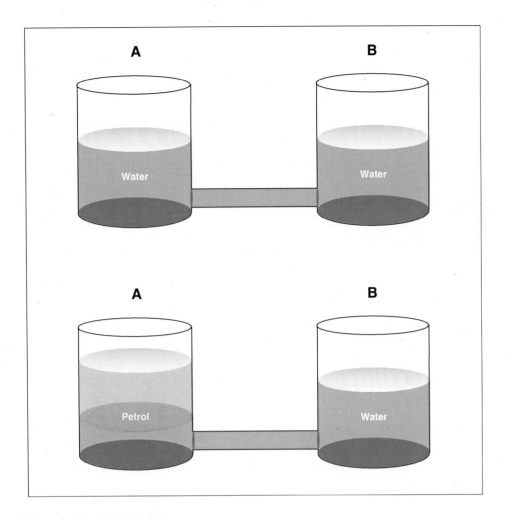

Problems are caused for the firefighter when water is used as an extinguishing agent when burning liquids are present.

As petrol and most other flammable liquids float on water, they cannot be smothered by water, so the addition of water to a fire involving burning liquids may cause the fire to spread further than it otherwise might have done.

Imagine now that petrol is poured into tank (A). As petrol has a specific gravity of about 0.75 and will not mix with water, it will float on the water. For the system to balance, the pressures created by the heads of liquid in each tank must be equal as before, but because petrol is less dense (lighter) than water, a greater "head" of petrol is required to produce the same pressure at depth. Consequently, the level of petrol is higher than the level of water. If water is added to tank (B), the water will raise the petrol in (A) and eventually the petrol will spill over, well before tank (B) is full.

1.3　Gases of different density

Unlike many liquids, all gases and vapours are completely miscible. However, differences in density will affect the way in which they mix. Thus, methane (the main component of natural gas) is a light gas with a vapour density of about 0.5 (air = 1). If it is leaking into a room from a faulty gas appliance, it will rise to the ceiling, entraining (mixing with) air as it rises to form a layer of methane and air mixture which will eventually descend to the level of the leak. (The concentration of methane in the layer will increase as the layer descends.) On the other hand, a leak of propane from a propane cylinder will produce a layer of propane/air mixture at low level in a similar fashion, as the vapour density of propane is roughly 1.5 (air = 1).

All heavier-than air gases, like carbon dioxide (VD 1.53, air = 1) and petrol vapour (VD 2.5, air = 1) will accumulate in low places such as wells and cellars, so creating dangers of asphyxia (suffocation) as well as of fire or explosion in the case of flammable vapours.

Differences in density can also be created by changes in temperature (see Chapter 4). Increase in temperature causes expansion, and a lowering of density. Understanding the consequences of this is extremely important: it can be compared with our example of the behaviour of petrol and water in interconnected tanks. As an example, we can consider the case of a chimney full of the hot products of combustion from an open fire.

The chimney and the rest of the building (Figure 1.2) act rather like our two tanks containing liquids of different densities, in that the chimney is effectively a tank full of hot light gas joined at the base to another tank full of cold, heavy gas, i.e. the sur-

rounding outside air. If we consider the hot, less dense gases inside the chimney and compare them to a column of cold, more dense air outside the chimney we have two volumes of gases of equal height but of different densities, and are thus unbalanced. The hot gases are said to be buoyant with respect to the cold air.

In order to restore the balance, cold air from outside flows into the base of the chimney and drives the hot gas out of the chimney. This would continue until the chimney is full of cold air, but in practice the fire at the base of the chimney continuously replaces the hot chimney gas which is driven from the top of the chimney.

If, however, the flow of hot gas from the chimney is prevented by a cover or damper, a pressure will develop at the top of the chimney, The weight of the column of lighter hot gas in the chimney is not enough to balance the weight of the heavier cold outside air. This unbalanced condition is responsible for a force which drives gas from the top of an open chimney. When the top is closed the force produces a pressure (which can be calculated if the densities of the hot and cold gases are known), and combustion products may escape from the fireplace into the room.

The same thing happens in a burning building. The air inside is heated by the fire and so becomes lighter. It rises and will escape through any available opening provided it can be replaced

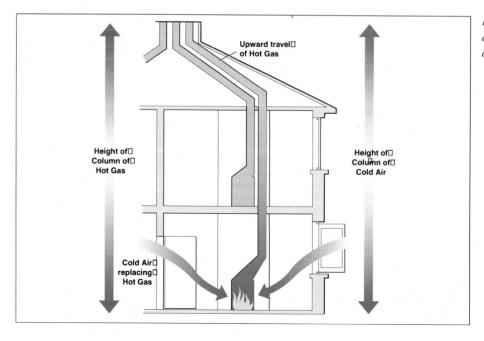

Figure 1.2 Diagram of a chimney showing the travel of convection currents.

Upward travel
of Hot Gas

Height of
Column of
Hot Gas

Height of
Column of
Cold Air

Cold Air
replacing
Hot Gas

by cold air entering at low level (compare with the fireplace). If there is no opening through which it can escape, a pressure will develop in the burning compartment and anyone opening a door or window into this space will release the pressure, which may cause an outrush of hot gases and possibly flames which could engulf them. (See Compartment Fires and Tactical Ventilation. Fire Service Manual Volume 2.)

When there are low and high level openings (e.g., broken windows and a hole in the roof), the building acts as an open chimney, with flames and the hot gases escaping at high level with cold fresh air entering from below. Under these circumstances, the fire will be very intense.

1.4 Matter and energy

Matter can exist in three states: **solid**, **liquid** or **gas**. Some substances are quite commonly found in all three states – for example, water is found as ice, liquid water and water vapour (steam) – but most substances are, at normal temperatures, found only in one or two of the states. For example, steel is solid up to its melting point of around 1400°C (the melting point varies according to the composition of the steel). Its boiling point, the point at which it turns into a vapour, is about 3000°C. Carbon dioxide is normally a gas, but under pressure it can be liquefied and if it is cooled sufficiently, it solidifies. Oxygen is normally a gas but it can be liquefied at very low temperatures (boiling point -183°C).

All matter is made up of extremely small particles called **atoms**. Atoms have a central core, or **nucleus** which contains smaller particles called **protons** and **neutrons**. Protons possess a positive electrical charge. The nucleus is surrounded by a system of **electrons**, which each carry a negative electrical charge. Atoms contain as many electrons as protons. As the number of protons and electrons are matched, and each proton possesses an equal and opposite charge to each electron, atoms are electrically neutral. The number and arrangement of electrons around the nucleus determines the chemical behaviour of the atom, that is to say, it determines which other atoms it will combine with. Chemical reactions take place when electrons move between atoms. An atom which has lost or gained one or more electrons in a chemical interaction will possess an electrical charge and is called either a positive or negative **ion**.

It now seems that it is not possible to get more than about 92 protons in a nucleus without it becoming so unstable that it falls apart. Otherwise, any number of protons is possible.

> **An element is a substance which contains atoms which are all of the same type.**

An element is a substance which contains atoms which are all of the same type: they all have the same number of protons. As there can be anything up to just over 92 protons in an atom, there are, just over 92 stable elements. Atoms of different elements can combine to form **molecules**.

Some molecules consist of two or more atoms of the same kind: for example, an oxygen molecule consists of two oxygen atoms (O_2). Other molecules consist of two or more atoms of different kinds: carbon dioxide consists of two atoms of oxygen and one of carbon (CO_2), water consists of two atoms of hydrogen and one of oxygen (H_2O). Carbon dioxide and water are chemical **compounds** and they can, by chemical means, be split into their component elements. This forms the basis of the science of chemistry, which is dealt with in Chapter 6.

Atom is a Greek word meaning 'indivisible': until about 70 years ago, it was believed that atoms could not be split into smaller particles. We know now that this is wrong and that atoms of one element can be "split" or combined with other particles to make new atoms of other elements. (The subject of atomic physics is discussed in the Manual of Firemanship, Part 6c, Chapter 45, Section 11.)

Energy is expended in doing work and may be in one of a number of different forms. **Heat, light** and **electrical energy** are well known from everyday

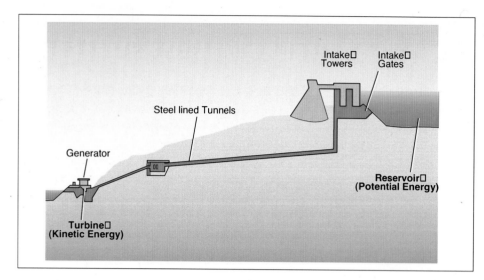

Figure 1.3 Diagram showing the conversion of potential into kinetic energy.

(Diagram: North Hydro)

experience. There is also **potential energy**, which is possessed by a body due to its position, for example by water stored in a hydroelectic dam, and **kinetic energy**, which is energy possessed by a moving body, for example by the water from the dam flowing through the turbines in the turbine hall). The potential energy is converted into kinetic energy as the water flows under gravity to the turbine hall, where it is then converted into electrical energy (Figure 1.3).

> **The faster something is moving, the more kinetic energy it has.**

For the vast majority of purposes we can say that energy cannot be created or destroyed – it can only be converted into another form of energy. (Note that when some radioactive processed occur, minute quantities of mass are "lost' and converted into large amounts of energy.)

The firefighter is mostly concerned with energy in the form of heat. Heat may be produced by a chemical change, such as combustion, in which we say that **chemical energy** is released as heat energy. Mechanical energy or kinetic energy can also be converted into heat energy by friction (e.g., frictional heating of brake pads).

We are familiar with the concept of temperature from everyday experience. **Temperature** is a

measure of how hot something is, and is related to how "fast" the constituent molecules are moving.

> **Temperature also determines which way heat will flow. Heat can only move from something at a high temperature to something at a lower temperature.**

The molecules which make up any substance, even a solid, are continually moving, although in a solid they vibrate around a fixed position. They also exert a force of attraction to each other, which becomes greater the closer they are together. The movement of molecules tends to spread them out while the attractive force, or force of cohesion, tends to bind them together.

If a solid is heated, heat energy is stored in the substance as the vibrational energy of the molecules. As more energy is stored, they vibrate faster and take up more space. At the same time, the temperature of the solid rises and thermal expansion occurs.

A temperature is reached when the molecules are vibrating so much that they break free of the rigid framework in which they have been held by the cohesive forces and become free enough to slide past each other, although they do not have complete freedom. At this point the solid melts and becomes a liquid.

Further heating causes the temperature to increase, and the energy is stored as kinetic energy of the molecules, which move with increasing rapidity until they are moving fast enough to overcome the cohesive forces completely. At this point, the liquid boils and turns into a gas (or more correctly, a vapour). If heat is taken away from a substance, kinetic energy of the molecules decreases and the reverse processes occur.

1.5 Melting, boiling and evaporation

The temperature at which a solid turns into a liquid is called the **melting point**. If we are considering a liquid turning into a solid, the temperature is called the **freezing point**, though these two temperatures are the same for the same substance under the same conditions. The temperature at which a liquid boils and becomes a vapour is the **boiling point**.

Since energy is required to overcome the forces of cohesion when a substance melts or boils, the heat which is supplied during these processes does not cause a rise in temperature of the substance. Conversely, when a vapour condenses or a liquid solidifies, it gives up heat without any fall in temperature so long as the change is taking place. So, melting or freezing, for a given substance at a given atmospheric pressure, take place at a certain temperature: for the transition between water and ice, at normal atmospheric pressure, this takes place at 0°C. Boiling, for a given substance at a given atmospheric pressure take place at another certain temperature: for the transition between water and steam, at normal atmospheric pressure, this takes place at 100°C.

Even at temperatures below boiling point, some molecules at the surface of the liquid may gain enough energy from colliding with other molecules for them to escape into the surrounding space as vapour. This process is **evaporation**.

Imagine a liquid in an enclosed space, where there is already air, such as water in a saucepan. Even if the pan is not heated, evaporation will take place.

The evaporating molecules build up a pressure known as the vapour pressure. At the same time, some molecules will re-enter the liquid. For any given temperature below the boiling point there is a definite vapour pressure at which the number of molecules which escape is just balanced by the number which are recaptured by the liquid.

Boiling occurs when the vapour pressure has become equal to the surrounding atmospheric pressure, the pressure of air. Vapour then forms not only at the surface of the liquid, but also in the body of the liquid, and we see bubbles.

If the external pressure is increased, the vapour pressure at which boiling will take place is increased and so the temperature must increase. If the external pressure falls, the reverse is true and the temperature at which boiling occurs will be lower.

Physics and Chemistry for Firefighters

Chapter 2 – Mechanics

> **This Chapter will discuss how things move and how the movement of objects is linked to their mass, the energy they possess and the forces which act on them.**

2.1 Motion

Imagine a body moving from a starting point A to another point B: for example a car moving between two cities.

The distance travelled by the car is the length of the line X. The average speed the car travelled at will be the distance travelled by the car divided by the time taken.

$$\text{Speed} = \frac{\text{distance travelled}}{\text{time taken}}$$

It has units of metres per second (m/s), or if distance is measured in miles, and time in hours, the units will be miles/hour (mph).

Although people tend to use speed and velocity interchangeably, there is a difference between them. Velocity has a direction associated with it: it is what we call a **vector** quantity.

The line Y shows the length of a straight line connecting the starting and finishing point. The length and direction of this line together give the **displacement** of the car from the starting point. Displacement is also a vector quantity.

Imagine a car journey from London to Bristol. Bristol is 200 km west of London, so at the end of the journey the car has a *displacement* of 200 km from London. However, the *distance* travelled will be longer than this though, as the roads tend to take convenient routes through the countryside rather than following perfectly straight lines. There may even be times when the car is travelling North-South rather than East West as it follows the road. At those times, the displacement of the car from London is not increasing, so although it has speed, its velocity is zero.

Figure 2.1 Car moving from A to B.

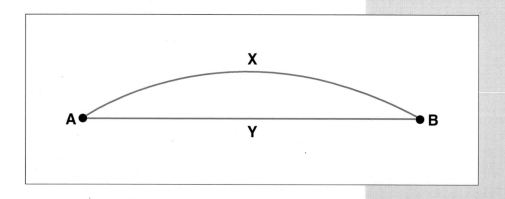

Speed is the rate of change of distance.

Velocity is the rate of change of displacement.

Acceleration is the rate of change of velocity.

The units of speed and velocity are m/s, while those for acceleration are m/s².

2.2   Momentum and force

Momentum is the product of mass and velocity

$$\text{Momentum} = \text{mass} \times \text{velocity}$$

So, a 2 kg object travelling at 10 m/s has a momentum of 20 kg.m/s

Force is the product of mass and acceleration

$$\text{Force} = \text{mass} \times \text{acceleration}$$
$$F = m\,a$$

The units are kg.m/s², which known as the **Newton (N)**.

Imagine that our 2 kg object is initially at rest, and then a force is applied which makes it accelerate at 10m/s². The applied force is equal to the body's mass times its acceleration.

$$F = ma$$
$$F = 2 \times 10 \text{ kg.m/s}^2$$
$$F = 20 \text{ N}$$

The "force of gravity" provides an acceleration which acts on everything. At the earth's surface, anything which is dropped will accelerate, under gravity, at 9.81 m/s² (this quantity is often referred to by the symbol g). It also determines the forces that are responsible for the movement of hot, buoyant gases in fires, and as described in Chapter 1.

The weight of a body is a measure of how strong the force due to gravity is on an object. In everyday speech, we usually use mass and weight interchangeably, but just as the words "speed" and "velocity" have different meanings, weight and mass also have different meanings.

Weight is the force due to gravity which acts on an object. The acceleration due to gravity that an object will experience is $g = 9.81$ m/s, so that a mass of two kilograms experiences a force due to gravity of

$$F = m\,a$$

$$\text{In this case } F = 2 \times 9.81$$
$$\text{i.e. the weight of the object is 19.62 N}$$

Giving definitions of weight and velocity which are different from those used in every day speech may seem like an unnecessary complication, but much science and engineering is only possible if every aspect of a problem is precisely defined, and every scientist or engineer everywhere knows exactly what is meant by each word.

2.3 Work, energy and power

Work is another every day term which has a rigid definition in science. If a body moves because a force acts on it, we say that work is being done on that object. Work is only being done if the object moves – if a force is being applied just to keep an object stationary, no work is done. The mathematical expression of work is:

$$W = F\,s$$

where W is the work done (in Joules), F is the constant force applied (Newtons) and s is the distance moved in the direction of the force (in metres). (The Joule (J) has units N.m, or $(kg.m/s^2).m$, i.e., $kg.m^2/s^2$: this illustrates the importance of ensuring that a consistent set of units is used.)

Taking our 2 kg mass, if this is raised vertically through 2 m, the work done *against gravity* will be

$$W = F\,s$$
$$W = 2 \times 9.81 \times 2$$
$$= 39.24\ J$$

Note that if the force acts in a different direction to the direction of travel, less work will be done. The interested reader should refer to the various text books on this topic.

If something is capable of doing work, it possesses energy. The energy that a body possesses by virtue of the fact that it is moving is called kinetic energy. The kinetic energy that a body possesses is equal to the amount of work that must have been done to it to increase its velocity from zero to whatever velocity it has. For a mass m moving with velocity v:

$$\text{Kinetic energy} = \frac{1}{2}\,mv^2$$

The units are $kg.m^2/s^2$, i.e., Joules.

Potential energy is the amount of energy that an object possesses because of its position or the arrangement of its components.

A body held above the ground has potential energy because it could do work while it is falling. Our 2 kg mass raised vertically through 2 m has a potential energy equal to the work required to raise it to that height, i.e., mass × acceleration × height (abbreviated as mgh), which as we have seen has the units of Joules. This is a consequence of the position of the mass in the earth's gravitational field. Other forms of energy are encountered, e.g., an electron in an electric field has electrical potential energy, while a stretched rubber band has elastic potential energy.

2.4 Friction

When an object moves or tries to move over a surface, both the object and the surface experience a frictional force along the common surface, each in a direction which opposes the relative motion of the surfaces.

Even on two very flat, well-polished surfaces, there are many microscopic imperfections which make the contact area much smaller than it would seem. These imperfections may interlock and, in the case of metal, may even weld together under very high local pressures.

We can see, then, that this locking and bonding will inhibit motion and that energy will be needed to overcome the frictional force. This energy appears as heat: when energy is expended on overcoming friction, heating occurs. This is the principle behind the rough strip on match boxes which provides the heat to start the chemical reaction in a match, and is also why brake blocks get hot on a car or bicycle.

Chapter 3 – Heat and Temperature

Some of the most destructive effects of fire are caused by heat, so it is obvious that the fire fighter should understand the effect of heat on materials. This chapter will discuss heat and temperature, how the two are linked and will lay the foundations for a discussion of the reaction of solids, liquids and gases to changes in temperature.

The amount of heat energy in a body cannot be measured directly. When heat energy is supplied to a body, it is true that the body's temperature will rise.

HOWEVER, temperature is just a measure of how hot a body is, NOT the amount of heat energy it contains.

In Chapter 1 and 2 it was stated that:

Energy

- is the ability to do work;

- can neither be created nor destroyed; and

- can exist in a number of different forms.

Heat is one form of energy. It can be produced by chemical means, for example by burning coal or oil, or by mechanical means, by friction. Passing a current through an electrical resistance also produces heat (e.g., an electric fire).

Heat can be converted into other forms of energy, for example into pressure energy in a steam boiler.

It is also possible to convert heat back into chemical energy or electrical energy.

Heat always flows from high temperature to low temperature. If a hot body and a cold body are placed in contact, the hot body (the one at the higher temperature) loses heat and the cold body (the one at the lower temperature) gains heat.

The fact that heat and temperature are not the same thing can be seen from a simple experiment. Imagine a piece of fine copper wire held in the flame of a match. After a couple of seconds, the wire will glow red hot, which tells us that the temperature of the wire has increased to 800 – 900°C.

Now imagine a similar match held under a kettle containing a litre of water. There would be no noticeable change in the temperature of the water, yet the amount of heat supplied to the wire and supplied to the water would be roughly the same.

The rise in temperature in a body to which heat is supplied is decided by three factors: the amount of heat supplied (or "transferred") to the body, the mass of the body and the *specific heat capacity* of the material from which the body is made.

The meaning of the term 'specific heat capacity' will be discussed later.

3.1　Measuring temperature

> **The human body cannot measure temperature, it can only make comparisons.**

The human body cannot tell reliably whether something is hot or cold, it can only compare what it is currently feeling with what it felt immediately beforehand. If you place one hand in a bowl of cold water and the other in a bowl of hot water and then, after an interval, both hands are placed in a bowl of tepid water, the hand which was in the bowl of cold water will feel that the tepid water is 'hot', while that from the hot water will feel that the tepid water is 'cold'.

Because it can only make comparisons, the human body cannot give a numerical value to temperature – people cannot step out into the street and reliably measure the air temperature just by the feel of the air on their skin.

Temperature can, though, be measured by making use of one of the effects of heat on materials. The commonest example is the use of the way that liquids expand as their temperature rises, the property of thermal expansion of a liquid. This is the principle behind the **thermometer** (Figure 3.1).

The thermometer consists of a narrow tube of fine bore with a small bulb at one end, and sealed at the other, containing a suitable liquid. The liquid is most commonly mercury, which has the advantages of a high boiling point (357°C), a uniform expansion coefficient and a low heat capacity; it is also opaque. However, its freezing point is about -39°C which makes it unsuitable for measuring temperatures greatly below the freezing point of water. Alcohol has a lower freezing point (-112°C) but also a much lower boiling point (78°C) than mercury. It can be is used for low temperatures work. Coloured water is sometimes used for rough measurement of temperatures between the freezing point and boiling point of water.

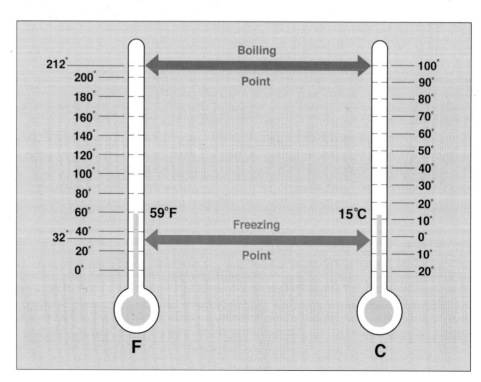

Figure 3.1 Diagram showing thermometer and a comparison between the Celsius and Fahrenheit thermometer scales.

3.2   Thermometric scales

Two scales are in common use
for measuring temperature:
the Celsius scale and
the Fahrenheit Scale.

Two fixed points are required for the construction of a thermometric scale. For the Celsius (or Centigrade) scale of temperature, the melting point of pure ice and the boiling point of pure water are taken as the fixed points *at standard atmospheric pressure.*

So, to fix the lower point of the scale, the bulb of the thermometer is placed in melting ice, while the upper fixed point of the thermometer is determined by placing the bulb in the steam above the surface of boiling water (at standard atmospheric pressure). If the pressure is different from the standard atmospheric pressure, a correction has to be applied to the upper fixed point. The level at which the liquid in the thermometer stands at each of the fixed points is marked on the stem of the thermometer.

Two thermometric scales are in common use:

3.2.1   The Celsius (or Centigrade) scale

On this scale the lower fixed point is marked 0. The upper fixed point is marked 100. The stem between these two points is divided into 100 equal divisions or degrees. These divisions are called Celsius degrees.

3.2.2   The Fahrenheit scale

The inventor of this scale used a freezing mixture to give him his lower fixed point, and the boiling point of water for the upper fixed point. The scale was divided into 212 equal divisions, which gave the freezing point of water as 32°F. There are 180 Fahrenheit degrees between the freezing point and the boiling point of water (at standard atmospheric pressure).

3.3   Other methods of measuring temperature

The 'liquid-in-glass' thermometer is not the only method of measuring temperature. There are several other methods, including the following:

3.3.1   The air or gas thermometer

Instead of using a liquid, a bulb containing air or some other gas can be used. In one such thermometer, the expansion of the gas causes a short thread of mercury to move along a scale. These thermometers are very sensitive, but may require correction to compensate for atmospheric pressure.

3.3.2   Using solids to measure temperature

The way that a solid expands when its temperature rises can be used for temperature measurement. The expansion may be used directly, or the differing expansion of two dissimilar metals may be used. This will be discussed further in the next Chapter.

3.3.3   Thermocouples

When the junction of wires of two different metals (for example iron and copper) is heated, an electrical potential (a voltage) appears at the junction. A calibration can be made between the potential and temperature, so that temperature can be measured indirectly by measuring the potential with a sensitive voltmeter. There are various types of thermocouple, some of which are capable of recording extremely high temperatures. (See Figure 3.2)

Thermocouples junctions can be made very small and so only take a short time to heat up or cool down. They are very good for following very rapid changes in temperature.

3.3.4   Electrical resistance

The electrical resistance of a wire increases with a rise in temperature and the change of resistance may be used to measure temperature. Platinum is normally used as it has a high melting point and a high 'temperature coefficient of resistance', so that a small rise in temperature produces a (relatively)

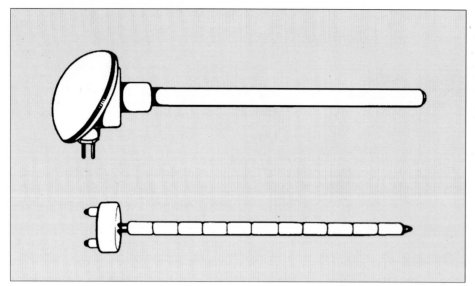

large rise in resistance. Platinum resistance thermometers can measure between -200°C and 1200°C. Their disadvantage is that they are large compared with thermocouples and so do not follow rapid changes in temperature very easily.

3.3.5 Thermistors

Thermistors are semiconductor devices, which have a negative temperature coefficient of resistance, so an increase in temperature produces a decrease in resistance. They are very robust and can be made very small and so can follow rapid changes in temperature. Their range is generally from -70°C to 300°C, but they are less accurate than resistance thermometers.

3.3.6 Comparison by brightness

At temperatures above about 750°C, objects start to glow, first a dull red, changing gradually to yellow and brightening as the temperature is raised to about 1250°C. Temperature measurements can be made by comparing the brightness of the object with the filament of an electric lamp whose brightness can be altered by varying the current flowing through it. If the current is too low, the filament appears darker than the object, while if it is too large, the filament appears brighter. When the filament "disappears" against the object, they have the same brightness *and* temperature. The latter can be found indirectly by measuring the current through the filament.

3.3.7 Infra-red

Infra-red cameras and other sensors detect heat in the same way that our eyes detect light. Light represents only one portion of the *electromagnetic spectrum* – a rainbow of different types of radiation which includes, in addition to visible light, radio waves, microwaves, ultra-violet radiation and X-rays.

Infra-red radiation is given off by bodies (and some gases) when they are hot. Infra-red sensors are sensitive to this type of radiation and can be designed to measure the temperature of an object by analysing the strength and the wavelength of the radiation.

Infra-red radiation behaves in exactly the same way as light, but it can pass through some things that light can't and it is blocked by some things that light can pass though. In particular, infra-red can pass through smoke at concentrations which block visible light. This is why infra-red cameras have become so valuable in search and rescue operations. The infra-red radiation emitted by an unconscious person lying in a cool environment can easily be detected.

3.4 The Kelvin scale of temperature

The Kelvin or 'Absolute' scale of temperature starts at -273°C, which has been found (theoretically and experimentally) to be the lowest temperature that it is possible to achieve. We have discussed before in the sections on melting and boiling, that the hotter a mass is, the faster the molecules that make up that body are moving. At -273°C, the molecules that make up a substance stop moving and it is not possible to cool the mass any further.

The Kelvin or absolute scale of temperature has its zero at -273°C. Degrees on this scale are the same size as Celsius degrees, and are denoted by the symbol K, so

Absolute temp. = Celsius temp. + 273
0 K = 273°C
273 K = 0°C
100°C = 373 K

Although the Celsius scale is the most widely used, the Kelvin scale must be used in certain circumstances – particularly when calculating how the volume of a gas changes with temperature and pressure (see Chapter 4). This will be discussed in more detail later, but Figure 3.3 shows how a given mass of gas will occupy a smaller volume as it cools (assuming that it does not condense into a liquid). For most purposes, it is possible to assume that the volume of this mass of gas is proportional to its temperature in *degrees Kelvin*. Therefore, if the temperature is doubled at a given pressure, its volume will double. Conversely, if the temperature is halved, the volume will halve. In principle, the volume would become zero at 0 K if it remained as

a gas. However, all real gases will condense to liquid or solid form at low temperatures.

Note that in equations, the symbol T is normally used for temperature, but great care must be taken in remembering which temperature scale is being used.

3.5   Units of heat

In the same way that length is measured in metres and temperature is measured in degrees, there are units which are used to measure the amount of energy in a body – what is colloquially called "heat". The concept of energy was introduced in Chapter 2, and discussed in the context of "work done". Energy can neither be created or destroyed, but can be converted from one form into another, e.g., potential energy into kinetic energy, or chemical energy into electrical energy. The conversion process is never 100% efficient, and some of the energy will appear in a different form, most commonly as "heat". Thus, some of the energy expended in bringing a moving car to rest is dissipated as heat generated by friction at the points of contact between the brake shoes and the brake drum.

3.5.1 The Joule (J)

The unit that scientists and engineers use to measure heat is the same as that used for energy, i.e., the **Joule**, which is named after a nineteenth century Manchester brewer who became interested in how much energy was needed to heat water. It is defined from mechanics; where energy is the

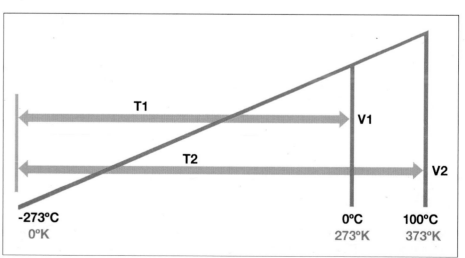

Figure 3.3 Graph showing the zero on the Kelvin or absolute scale.

ability to perform work, so work and energy are measured in the same units, as in Chapter 2. One Joule of work is done when the point at which a 1 Newton (1 N) force is applied moves through 1 metre in the direction of the force.

For convenience, to save writing strings of zeroes, larger units based on the Joule are used, the kilojoule and the megajoule:

1 kilojoule (1 kJ) = 1 000 J
1 megajoule (1 MJ) = 1 000 kJ = 1 000 000 J

In the same way that feet and inches were replaced by metres, there are older units which have now been replaced by the Joule. These will now be discussed briefly.

3.5.2 The calorie

This is defined as the quantity of heat required to raise the temperature of 1 gram of water through 1°C. The energy content of food is often measured in calories, though, confusingly the number of 'calories' we talk about in a bar of chocolate in everyday speech is actually the number of kilocalories.

1 kilocalorie = 1000 calories.
1 calorie = 4.18 joules.

3.5.3 The British thermal unit (Btu)

This is the quantity of heat required to raise the temperature of 1 lb of water through 1°F.

Another British unit is the **therm**, which is equal to 100 000 Btu (10^5 Btu).

1 Btu = 1 055 J
1 therm = 105 500 kJ.

3.6 Specific heat

As we have discussed, heat energy can only flow from a body at a higher temperature to one at a lower temperature. Heat transfer continues either until both bodies are at the same temperature (i.e. the initially hot body has cooled and the initially cold body has warmed), or until the two bodies are separated. Whatever, a certain amount of heat energy will have been transferred, which can be measured in Joules.

When heat is added to a body the temperature rises. The rise in temperature of the body depends on three things:

● the amount of heat energy supplied to the body;

● the mass of the body; and

● the specific heat capacity of the body.

The **specific heat capacity** of a material is the heat required to raise the temperature of one kilogram of the material by 1°C, and so is measured in Joules per kilogram per degree centigrade (J/kg°C). **In equations, the letter c is used as a symbol for specific heat capacity**.

Some texts may discuss the **heat capacity** of an object. This is the specific heat capacity of the substance it is made from multiplied by the mass. They are different quantities though easily confused. In general, the 'specific' is used when the value under discussion refers to a unit mass of material.

Imagine two containers, one containing water and the other containing the same mass of oil. Now imagine that a given amount of heat energy is supplied to each. This could be done by placing the containers on identical burners – ones that supply heat at the same rate – for the same amount of time.

Both containers are equipped with thermometers, so that the temperature rise can be observed.

Now, after 3 minutes, it is found that the temperature of the oil has risen by 10°C, but the temperature of the water has only risen by 5°C in the same time.

The masses of the oil and water are the same, and the amount of heat energy supplied to the oil and water was the same, so the difference in the temperature rise experienced by the two samples must be due to a difference in specific heat capacity.

The same amount of heat caused a greater rise in temperature in the oil than in the water. We know that specific heat capacity is a measure of how much heat it takes to bring about a one degree rise in temperature in a given material. Therefore, the water has a greater specific heat capacity than the oil as the water showed a smaller temperature rise for a given amount of heat supplied.

In summary:
The larger the specific heat capacity of a substance, the more energy it takes to raise the temperature by a given amount.

Table 3.1: *Specific heat capacities of some materials*

Material	c (J/kg°C)
Water	4200
Iron	460
Aluminium	900
Copper	400
Mercury	140
Glass (ordinary)	670
Ice	2100
Earth, rock, etc.	840
Carbon tetrachloride	850
Methylated spirit	2400
Benzene	1720
Glycerol	2560

The other side to this statement is that materials with a low specific heat capacity will heat up more rapidly in a fire situation than those of high specific heat capacity.

Water has an unusually high specific heat capacity: 4 200 J/kg per °C. There are very few substances which have a higher value than this, the most notable being hydrogen at constant volume, and mixtures of certain alcohols with water.

This is one of the reasons why water is good for fighting fire – a given mass of water can absorb a relatively large amount of heat energy.

Some values of specific heat capacities are shown in Table 3.1.

Substances such as petrol, alcohol and the like have low specific heat capacities. They are also readily vaporised and may produce hazardous vapours. In general, combustible materials with low specific heat capacities are of capable of promoting fire risks.

[It should also be noted that the *surfaces* of solids of low density, such as polyurethane foam, also heat up very rapidly when exposed to a heat transfer process (e.g. radiant heating from an electric fire). This is a result of low *thermal conductivity*. Instead of heat being rapidly transferred into the body of the solid by conduction, it "accumulates" at the surface, resulting in a rapid temperature rise. As a consequence low density combustible materials can be ignited very much more easily than materials of high density.]

3.7 Change of state and latent heat

By 'change of state' we mean the changes between the solid and liquid states (melting/freezing), liquid and gas states (boiling/condensation), and for a relatively few pure compounds, solid and gas states (sublimation). Freezing, melting, boiling, condensation and sublimation all cause a change of state.

3.7.1 Latent heat of vaporisation

When a kettle is put on to boil, heat enters the water from the kettle element and the temperature of the water rises until it reaches 100°C.

At this temperature the water boils, that is to say bubbles of vapour form at the bottom and rise to the surface where they burst and escape as steam. Once the water has started to boil, the temperature *remains constant* at 100°C – it doesn't get any hotter than 100°C. However, heat energy continues flow from the element into the water. This energy is not increasing the temperature of the water, but is being used to allow the water molecules to pull themselves apart from each other, converting the water from the liquid state to the vapour state, i.e. from liquid water into water vapour (steam).

Experiments show that 2 260 000 Joules (2.26MJ) are required to convert 1 kilogram of water at its boiling point into steam at the same temperature. This is known as **the specific latent heat of vaporisation** for water (latent means hidden – the latent heat is hidden heat because it doesn't cause a temperature rise). This extra heat goes into the vapour, but does not indicate its presence by producing a rise in temperature.

> It is this large amount of latent heat which makes water mists and sprays so effective in extinguishing flames – vaporisation of the water droplets helps cool the flame, and cause it to extinguish.

When steam condenses to form liquid water, the same amount of latent heat is given out. This is why steam can cause serious burns.

> **The specific latent heat of vaporisation of a substance is the amount of heat energy needed to change a unit mass of the substance from the liquid to vapour without a temperature change.**

All liquids besides water absorb latent heat when they are turned into vapour. For example, 860 000 J are required to convert 1kg of alcohol into vapour at its boiling point.

Latent heat is measured in Joules per kilogram (J/kg), although it is more usually expressed in kilojoules per kilogram (kJ/kg).

3.7.2 Effect of change of pressure on boiling point and latent heat

Water 'normally' boils at 100°C. By 'normally' we mean that it boils at 100°C when the external air pressure is the standard atmospheric pressure of or 1.013 bars where 1 bar = 10^5 N/m². This is the pressure of air which will support 760 mm of mercury in a mercury barometer, and so is sometimes written as "760mm mercury" or "760mm Hg".

> **If the external pressure is raised, the boiling point is raised, and if the external pressure is lowered, the boiling point is lowered.**

This effect is used in pressure cookers and in pressurised cooling systems for car engines, where the increased pressure raises the boiling point of the liquid in the system.

This behaviour is also used in the storage of "liquefied gases" such as propane and butane. At increased pressures, these gases liquefy at normal temperatures, and allow large amounts of "gas" to be stored in a relatively small volume (see Section 4.4).

Raising the boiling point increases the quantity of heat needed to raise the temperature of the cold liquid to the new boiling point, but it decreases the latent heat of vaporisation.

3.7.3 Latent heat of fusion

Just as latent heat is taken in when water changes to vapour at the same temperature, a similar thing happens when ice melts to form water. In this case, the latent heat is not so great. It requires 336 000 J (336 kJ) to convert 1 kg of ice at 0°C to water at the same temperature. Likewise, when water at 0°C freezes into ice, the same quantity of heat is given out for every 1 kg of ice formed. This is called the specific latent heat of fusion of ice. This is not confined to water alone; other substances absorb latent heat when they melt and conversely they give out latent heat on solidifying. This is the latent heat of fusion.

The definition of the specific latent heat of fusion of a substance is the quantity of heat required to convert unit mass of the substance from the solid to the liquid state without change in temperature. The same units (J/kg or kJ/kg, etc.) are used as for the latent heat of vaporisation.

3.7.4 Cooling by evaporation

Some liquids have a low boiling point and thus change from liquid to vapour quite easily at ordinary temperatures: these are called volatile liquids. Methylated spirit and ether are of this type. If you drop a little methylated spirit or ether onto your hand, it evaporates rapidly and your hand feels cold. Some local anaesthetics work in this way, 'freezing' the pain.

The cooling is brought about because, to change from liquid to vapour, the liquid absorbs heat energy from the hand to provide the latent heat of vaporisation of the liquid. The hand therefore feels cold. Water would also cause the hand to become cold but not so noticeably as methylated spirit. The spirit has a lower boiling point than water and so it evaporates more quickly at the temperature of the hand.

Physics and Chemistry for Firefighters

Chapter 4 – Thermal Expansion

In this Chapter we will discuss the practical problems and uses of thermal expansion and the ways in which we can calculate the degree of thermal expansion that a material will experience.

4.1 The thermal expansion of solids

As we have discussed in Chapter One and Chapter Three, a substance, whether solid, liquid or gas, will tend to expand when it is heated as long as it is not constrained by a container, a change of state or a change in chemical composition.

When a solid is heated, it expands in all three dimensions and, therefore, increases in length, breadth and thickness. The increase in length is often the most important, although the increase in area and volume due to thermal expansion can be readily calculated by considering the increase in each dimension

Within normal ranges of temperature, a solid which is "homogeneous" in structure, such as an iron bar, expands uniformly: the expansion of a bar in each direction is proportional to the rise in temperature.

"homogeneous": properties are the same in all directions

The expansion is also proportional to the length of the bar, but varies with the nature of the substance of which the bar is made.

4.1.1 Coefficient of linear expansion

The amount by which unit length of a substance expands when its temperature is raised by one degree is called the *coefficient of linear expansion* of the substance. The temperature scale must be stated. Thus we can say that the coefficient of linear expansion of a solid is the fractional increase in length of unit length when its temperature is raised by one degree Celsius.

To calculate the increase in length of a body:

Increase in = original × coefficient × temperature
length   length   of linear   rise
**   expansion**

This gives the *increase* in length. To find the *total* new length, the original length must be added.

For steel, the coefficient of linear expansion (denoted by the Greek letter α) is 0.000 012 per °C. Thus, a bar of steel 1 m long expands by 0.000 012 m for each °C rise in temperature; a 1 km bar expands by 0.000 012 km (12 mm) for each °C rise in temperature, and so on.

Some other typical values of the linear expansion coefficient, α, are:

Table 4.1 *Typical values of* α

Material	α (per °C)
Aluminium	0.000 023
Copper	0.000 017
Concrete	0.000 012
Steel	0.000 012
Invar steel	0.000 000 100
Common glass	0.000 009
Pyrex glass	0.000 003

4.1.2 Nickel-iron alloy (invar)

Invar is an alloy of iron and nickel (64 % iron, 36 % nickel) which has a coefficient of linear expansion of 0.000 000 1 per °C i.e., less than 1 per cent of that of steel. This is so small as to be negligible in most cases.

It is used for making measuring rods and tapes, watch and clock parts and other components which need must remain the same over a range of temperature.

> **Though there are many nickel-iron alloys, this very small coefficient of expansion applies only to this particular alloy which contains 36 % nickel.**

Figure 4.1 Forth Road Bridge. (Photo: The Royal Commission on the Ancient Historical Monuments of Scotland)

4.1.3 Allowing for expansion in large metal structures

Large metal structures, such as bridges, often experience large variations in temperature, so allowance must be made for the linear expansion of the parts.

In large bridges, this expansion is quite large itself. For instance, the Forth Road Bridge is a steel structure with a total length (l) of about 1960 m. The maximum temperature range between winter and summer is -30°C to +30°C, a range of △T = 60°C. Using the formula above, the difference between the maximum and minimum lengths of the roadway would be:

$$l \times \alpha \times \triangle T = 1960 \times 0\ 000\ 012 \times 60 = 1.41 \text{ m}$$

Figure 4.2 Main expansion joint at one of the main towers on the Forth Road Bridge.

(Photo: Forth Road Bridge Joint Board)

Even a bridge with a span of 20 m could change by 14 mm between the hottest and coldest temperatures. Allowance for this expansion is often made by fixing one end of the bridge and resting the other on rollers, or on a sliding bearing, so that the bridge may expand and contract without exerting a side load on its piers. Railway lines used to be laid in 45 or 60 ft (13.7 or 18.3 m) lengths, with gaps to allow for expansion and contraction, but modern methods now make it possible for the expansion to be taken up as a tension or compression in the rail, with expansion joints at distances of about 800 m.

In buildings, the normal range of temperature is not usually so great, since internal heating maintains a reasonable temperature in winter and the building fabric protects steelwork from excessive external temperatures. Nevertheless, some allowance has to be made for expansion to prevent the steelwork from distorting the walls of the building, even if the allowance is only made by leaving a small clearance between the steel frame and the brickwork. In a fire situation, however, the increase in temperature may be very great and the situation could arise in which a long beam could exert sufficient side load on a wall and cause it to collapse.

Problems of expansion are also encountered with materials which are poor thermal conductors. In a fire situation, heating the inner face of a tall brick wall will cause that face to expand, while the outer face remains cool. This may cause the wall to lean outwards at the top and can result in collapse of the structure.

4.1.4 Thermostats

Imagine two strips of different metals with different coefficients of linear expansion, of the same length, laid side by side. Imagine then that the temperature of the surroundings increase. As the strips warm up, each will increase in length according to its own coefficient of linear expansion.

If the same two strips were fastened together throughout their length, an increase in temperature would cause them to distort into a curve, forming the arc of a circle. As the strip cooled, it would straighten out again. Such a strip is known as a bi-metallic strip. (Figure 4.3).

If one end of a bi-metallic strip is fixed, a change in temperature will cause the free end to move.

Figure 4.3 Bi-metallic thermostat

Left
Above a specified temperature, the bi-metal strip will bend. This causes the electrical contact to be broken which results in the current being switched off.

Right
A fire alarm using a bi-metallic strip.

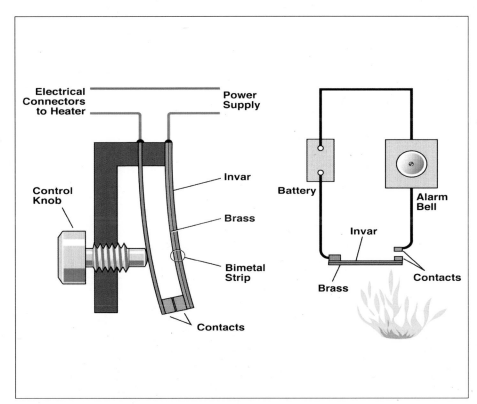

The movement of this free end can be made to open or close an electric circuit, to cause an alarm to be operated, or to switch off a heater. Such a device using a bi-metallic strip in this way is called a thermostat. (The principle is also used in rate-of-rise heat detectors.)

4.1.5 Coefficients of superficial and cubical expansion of solids

It can be shown mathematically that the coefficient of superficial (or area) expansion of a solid is twice the linear coefficient, and that of cubical expansion is three times the linear coefficient. Thus, the increase in volume $\triangle V$ of an object of volume V when the temperature is increased by $\triangle T$ is:

$$\triangle V = V \times 3\alpha \times \triangle T$$

so that the new volume will be V + $\triangle V$ (see Section 4.1.1 for the equivalent equation for linear expansion).

The expansion depends on the external dimensions of the solid and is not affected by any voids. The cubical expansion of a hollow metal box is the same as that of a solid block of the same metal of the same (external) volume as the box.

4.2   Thermal expansion of liquids

4.2.1 Cubical expansion

Since liquids have no definite shape and, therefore, no fixed dimensions other than volume, the only expansion which can be measured is that of cubical expansion.

Since a liquid has to be contained in a vessel, the apparent expansion of the liquid is affected by the expansion of the vessel, and the apparent expansion is, therefore, always less than the real expansion. However, the coefficient of cubical expansion of liquids is considerably greater than that of solids so (with the exception of water, which is dealt with below) the expansion of a liquid is always greater than that of its container.

Consider this comparison of the cubical expansion coefficients of glass, mercury and alcohol:

Material	Cubical expansion/°C)
Glass	0.000 024
Mercury	0.000 190
Alcohol	0.001 100

Thus, the thermal expansion of mercury is about 8 times that of glass, while that of alcohol is nearly 50 times that of glass. This is important in the design of thermometers.

The coefficient of cubical expansion of steel is 0.000 036/°C, and that of many liquids is of the order of 0 001/°C, i.e., about 30 times as much. Because of this, a sealed container (such as a storage tank) which is *completely* full of liquid may be a hazard in a fire situation (or even when exposed to strong sunlight) because of the internal pressures generated by expansion. If a pressure relief valve is fitted, this will allow the escape of liquid. The problem will be greatly reduced if the tank is not completely full, and there is an air space.

The so-called "frangible bulbs" used in many conventional sprinkler heads are sealed glass bulbs full of liquid. These break to operate and release water from the head when they are heated to a selected temperature, for example, when exposed to hot fire gases accumulating under the ceiling.

4.2.2 The effect of expansion on density

Since the density of a substance is the ratio of its mass to its volume, an increase of temperature results in a decrease of density; or conversely, the volume of a given mass of the substance increases as its temperature rises.

Water behaves in a peculiar way. Its expansion is not uniform: the expansion between 30°C and 50°C is double that between 10°C and 30°C. On cooling below 10°C, water contracts until its temperature reaches 4°C. On further cooling it expands until its volume at 0°C is 1.000 120 times greater than its volume at 4°C. It also expands further when it freezes. This means that water in ponds and lakes freezes from the top downward and, once the temperature on the surface has fallen to 4°C, further cooling of the lower level can only occur by conduction. This conduction is slow because water is a poor conductor.

4.3   The expansion of gases

4.3.1 Temperature, pressure, volume

Since a gas expands to fill all the available space, the volume of a gas may be changed by altering the volume of its container. If the volume is decreased, the pressure is increased.

This can be explained by saying that the same number of molecules of the gas occupy a smaller space and, therefore, collide with each other and with the container walls more frequently. The pressure is due to these collisions: more collisions, more pressure.

In a liquid, the molecules are much closer together to start with in than in a gas: the spacing of molecules in a liquid is comparable to that in a solid; though, because they are moving so quickly they do not remain in the regular structure of a solid. Because molecules in a liquid are so close together to start with, they cannot be compressed further. This is why gases can be compressed but liquids, generally, cannot.

Heating a gas increases the kinetic energy of the molecules which, therefore, move faster, and collide more frequently. So, heating a gas increases its pressure – provided its volume is unchanged. By increasing its volume as it is heated, the pressure can be kept constant.

We can see, then, that there are three variables which change with each other when dealing with a gas, namely **temperature**, **pressure** and **volume**. When dealing with a solid or a liquid, temperature and volume are important, but pressure is not so important.

4.3.2 The gas laws

There are three gas laws:

- Boyle's Law;

- Charles' Law; and

- The Law of Pressures.

These combine into the **General Gas Law**.

As we have seen, each solid or liquid will expand with rise in temperature by an extent determined by the coefficient of cubical expansion. However, all gases expand by the same amount for the same temperature rise.

Changes in volume of a gas depend on changes in temperature and pressure. To study the interaction between temperature, pressure and volume, one of these quantities is kept constant and the dependence of the other two on each other can then be studied. (Note: the mass of gas remains constant.)

This method of study provides the basis of the gas laws, the rules by which the behaviour of gases can be determined.

4.3.2.1 Boyle's Law

The change in volume of a gas caused by changes in pressure alone is the subject of the first of the gas laws, known as Boyle's Law. This states that:

> **Boyle's Law**
> **For a gas at constant temperature, the volume of a gas is inversely proportional to the pressure upon it.**

Experiments show that if the pressure applied to a given volume of gas is doubled, the volume is halved. If the pressure is trebled, the volume is reduced to one-third, provided the temperature is constant.

If we have a cylinder whose capacity is $1m^3$ it can contain 1 m^3 of a gas at 1 atmosphere, but if 120 m^3 of gas at atmospheric pressure are compressed and pumped into the same cylinder, the pressure will be 120 atmospheres (atm). If half of the gas is allowed to escape, then the pressure will fall to 60 atm.

This is why the pressure gauge on a breathing apparatus set is a measure of how much air there is in the cylinder.

Figure 4.4 Breathing Apparatus Compressor.
(Photo: Hamworthy Compressor Systems Limited)

In practice, when a gas is compressed – for example, when a breathing apparatus cylinder is charged, or a tyre in pumped up – heat is generated and the temperature increases: the valve gets warm. This heat is only generated by the pumping operation. If the pressure of the gas is measured before the temperature has returned to its original level, Boyle's Law does not hold, since the temperature of the gas is not the same as it was before it was pumped in: this is why the **'constant temperature'** part of the law is important – the calculations do not work if it is not fulfilled.

Mathematically, if V_1 and P_1 are the initial volume and pressure, and V_2 and P_2 are the final volumes and pressure, then

$$\frac{V_2}{V_1} = \frac{P_1}{P_2}$$

$$P_1V_1 = P_2V_2$$

So,

Initial pressure	×	Initial volume	=	Final pressure	×	Final volume

4.3.2.2 Charles' Law

Experiments show that all gases expand by 1/273 of their volume at 0°C for each 1°C rise in temperature, provided that they are maintained at constant pressure. Since the expansion for each 1°C rise in temperature is quite large, it is essential to take the initial volume at 0°C. These experiments were carried out by a French scientist named Charles at the beginning of the 19th century, and the law named after him states:

> **Charles' Law**
> **The volume of a given mass of gas at constant pressure increases by 1/273 of its volume at 0°C for every 1°C rise in temperature.**

As gases expand, their density decreases and they become buoyant. This is why hot air rises, how hot air balloons work and why hot smoke and fire gases collect at the top of rooms.

It will be seen from Figure 3.3 (page 17), which shows the change of volume of a gas with temperature, that the Kelvin (or Absolute) scale of temperature must be used, and that the relationship between volume and temperature is:

$$\frac{V_1}{T_1} = \frac{V_2}{T_2}$$

where V_1 and T_1 are the initial volume and absolute temperature and V_2 and T_2 are the final volume and absolute temperature (the Kelvin temperature, **NOT** the Celsius temperature). In other words, the volume of a given mass of gas is directly proportional to its absolute temperature, provided that its pressure is kept constant.

4.3.2.3 The Law of Pressures

The previous two laws lead to a third law concerned with the relationship between the pressure

Figure 4.5 Picture of smoke layer at top of room.

and temperature of a gas when the volume is kept constant. This is the case when a cylinder of gas, whose valve is closed, is heated, as could happen if it were in a fire.

Figure 4.6 Fire involving liquefied petroleum gas tanks.
(Photo: HM Fire Service Inspectorate)

This is expressed mathematically as:

$$\frac{P_1}{T_1} = \frac{P_2}{T_2}$$

4.3.2.4 The general gas law

The three gas laws can be combined into a single mathematical expression:

$$\frac{P_1 V_1}{T_1} = \frac{P_2 V_2}{T_2}$$

This general expression may be used for a given mass of gas when pressure, temperature and volume all change.

Remembering this law will allow you to remember all three – you can just remove the quantity which is being kept constant from both sides of the equation. For example, if volume is being kept constant, remove V_1 from the left-hand side and V_2 from the right hand side (because they are equal, they cancel), and insert the pressure and temperature values that you know.

It is important to remember that these gas laws are applicable to all gases provided that they *remain* as gases over the temperature and pressure range involved. When the temperature and pressure reach levels at which the gas liquefies, the gas laws no longer apply.

4.4 The liquefaction of gases

As has been noted previously, an increase in pressure raises the boiling point of a liquid.

Many substances which are gases at normal temperatures and atmospheric pressure can be compressed to such an extent that their boiling point is raised above atmospheric temperature and the gas liquefies (e.g., propane, ammonia).

Other gases cannot be liquefied at atmospheric temperature no matter how great a pressure is applied. These are the so-called 'permanent gases'. However, if the temperature is lowered sufficiently, it becomes possible to liquefy them by compression (e.g. methane, oxygen).

4.4.1 Critical temperature and pressure

For each gas, there is a **critical temperature** above which it cannot be liquefied by increasing the pressure alone. For example, carbon dioxide can be compressed to a liquid at 20°C, but at 40°C it will remain a gas.

Its critical temperature is in fact 31.1°C. Below this temperature it can be liquefied by increased pressure and it should properly be described as a vapour. Above this temperature it cannot be liquefied and is properly described as a gas, or, to emphasise the fact that it is above its critical temperature, **a true gas**.

The pressure required to liquefy a vapour at its critical temperature is called the **critical pressure**.

Some typical values of critical temperatures and critical pressures are shown in Table 4.2.

4.4.2 Liquefied gases in cylinders

Many materials such as fuel gases are liquified under pressure and stored and transported in cylinders.

Liquefied gases in cylinders do not obey the gas laws, since, below the critical temperature, any change in temperature, pressure or volume will result in either the liquefaction of gas or the evaporation of liquid. Thus the pressure in a cylinder of liquefied gas will remain constant as gas is drawn off (provided the temperature remains constant) since more liquid will evaporate to make up for the gas drawn off until all the liquid is evaporated.

For cylinders of liquified gas, the cylinder pressure is not any indication of the amount of gas in the cylinder.

A true gas will obey the gas laws and the pressure will fall as gas is drawn off. Thus the pressure in the cylinder is an indication of the quantity of gas it contains.

When liquefied gases are stored in cylinders, allowance must be made for expansion of the liquid in case the cylinder is heated beyond the critical temperature and the liquid turns into a vapour.

Table 4.2 *Critical temperatures, T_c and critical pressures, p_c for various substances*

	T_c (°C)	p_c (atm)
Water (steam)	374.0	-
Sulphur dioxide	157.0	219.0
Chlorine	144.0	78.0
Ammonia	132.0	77.7
Nitrous oxide	39.0	-
Carbon dioxide	31.1	73.1
Methane	-82.1	45.8
Oxygen	-119.0	50.0
Nitrogen	-147.0	33.7
Hydrogen	-240.0	12.9

This could lead to a substantial increase in pressure, with a risk of explosion. To minimise this danger, cylinders are never completely filled with liquid.

The amount of liquefied gas which may be charged into a cylinder is determined by its filling ratio, which varies from gas to gas and depends, among other things, on the density of the liquid.

$$\frac{\text{Filling}}{\text{ratio}} = \frac{\text{Weight of liquefied gas which may be charged}}{\text{Weight of cylinder completely full of water}}$$

The filling ratio for ammonia is 0.5, so that a cylinder capable of holding 10 kg of water may only be charged with 5 kg of ammonia. A cylinder of the same size could be charged with 12.5 kg of sulphur dioxide, for which the filling ratio is 1.25.

4.5   Sublimation

In the laboratory it is possible to produce such low pressures that the boiling point of water can be reduced to 0°C and lower. When this happens, ice does not melt to form water, but will vaporise completely as the temperature rises.

This direct change from solid to vapour without forming an intermediate liquid is given the special name of **sublimation**.

In order to achieve sublimation with water, extremely low pressures are required, but solid carbon dioxide sublimes at atmospheric pressure.

At higher pressures, carbon dioxide shows the normal sequence of melting followed, at a higher temperature, by boiling, so that under pressure – and only under pressure – it is possible to have liquid carbon dioxide.

Chapter 5 – Heat transmission

> As has been discussed earlier,
> heat always travels from
> high-temperature regions to
> low-temperature regions.
> In this Chapter, the ways in
> which heat energy can flow
> from hot bodies to cooler bodies
> will be discussed.

Heat energy always flows from regions of high temperature to regions of lower temperature. Heat will always flow when there is a temperature difference, no matter how small that temperature difference is.

There are three methods by which heat may be transmitted (Figure 5.1):

● conduction;

● convection; and

● radiation.

5.1   Conduction

Conduction may occur in solids, liquids or gases, although it is most clearly present in solids. In conduction, heat energy is passed on from each molecule to its nearest neighbour, with heat flowing away from the source of heat towards low temperature regions. The transfer of heat can be imagined to take place in much the same way as water in buckets being passed down a line of people in a 'bucket chain'. In the bucket chain each individual

will only move a very small distance to either side of their mean position; it is only the water which passes on. In conduction of heat, the molecules vibrate about a mean position and pass on heat energy by colliding with their neighbours.

Thermal conductivity, the ability to conduct heat varies between materials. Most metals conduct heat relatively easily and are, therefore, classed as good conductors though the ability to conduct heat varies between metals.

Figure 5.1 Diagram illustrating conduction, convection and radiation.

The best conductors of heat are silver and copper. Aluminium has about half the thermal conductivity of silver and iron about one-eighth. Non-metallic solids are poor conductors and, besides mercury, which is a metal, liquids and gases are very poor conductors of heat.

In fact, some solids and also liquids and gases are sometimes referred to as heat insulators because they are such poor conductors. In general good conductors of electricity (e.g., metals) are good conductors of heat, while poor conductors of electricity are good thermal insulators (e.g., most plastics).

Thermal conductivity can be measured experimentally and is usually denoted by the symbol K.

The flow of heat is measured in Joules per second (J/s) and this unit is the Watt (W). So:

1 J/s = 1 W

Thermal conductivity in the SI system of units is measured in Watts per metre per degree Kelvin (W/m K).

Thermal conductivity is important at most stages of a fire, but during the fully developed fire there is the danger of fire spread. As steel conducts heat very well, a steel girder passing through a fire wall may conduct sufficient heat through to the neighbouring compartment (room) to start a fire there. It is not necessary for flames to spread through the fire wall itself. (Figure 5.2).

Imagine a door built to separate rooms in case of a fire. If a fire occurs, a plain steel door will conduct heat rapidly to the other side, which could potentially cause the fire to spread outside the room.

Figure 5.2 Sketch showing how fire may be spread in a building due to the conduction of heat along an unprotected steel girder.

On the other hand, a wooden door, though it may burn, is initially a better barrier to heat as it is such a poor conductor. We can see then that the relative conductivity of building materials may be an important factor in the fire-resisting ability of a structure.

5.2 Convection

This occurs only in liquids and gases. It takes place for example, when a pan of water is heated (see Figure 5.3).

A pan full of water is heated from the bottom on a gas ring. As the water warms up, it expands and, therefore, becomes less dense, and so a given volume is lighter.

As the heated liquid is buoyant, it rises and colder, denser fluid takes its place at the bottom. This then becomes heated and so a circulation is set up. Heat energy is carried throughout the fluid by the molecules as they move until the water is the same temperature throughout. Compare this to conduction, in which the molecules do not move from their position: in convection it is the movement of the liquid or gas molecules through the mass of fluid which spread the heat energy around.

Convection is used in domestic hot water systems (Figure 5.4) and in many heating systems using so-

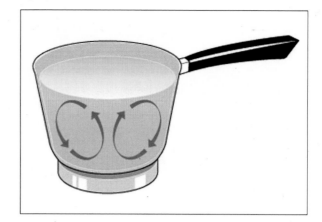

Figure 5.3 Convection in heated water.

called 'radiators'. Most of the heat from these radiators is in fact carried away by convection. It was also used in the 'thermo-syphon' system (now largely replaced by the pump-assisted system) of cooling motor engines.

Convection also causes the updraft in chimneys (see Figure 1.2). When a fire occurs in a building, convection currents can convey hot gases produced upwards through stairwells (Figure 5.5) and open lift and service shafts, thereby spreading the fire to the upper parts of buildings.

If the hot gas products escape from the upper levels, cool air must enter at low level to replaces them. This will, in addition, help to maintain the burning.

Figure 5.4 Small bore heating and hot water system.

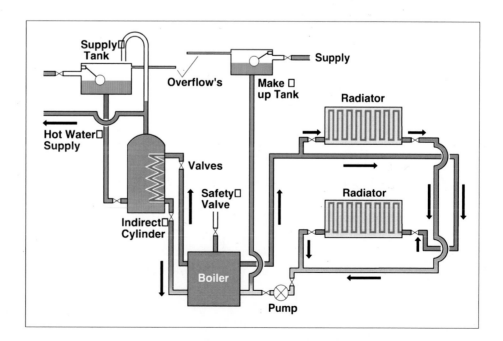

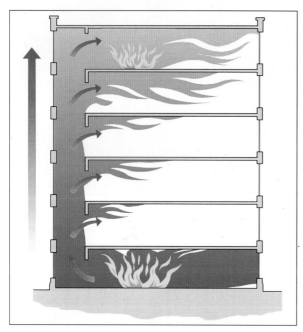

Figure 5.5 Sketch showing how fire on a lower floor can spread to upper floors by convection.

[The term "convective heat transfer" is used to describe the transfer of heat between a fluid (gas or liquid) and a solid. For example, a hot object in air loses heat partly by convection. The layer of air next to the hot surface becomes heated and, therefore, buoyant with respect to the surrounding cold air: it rises, carrying away the heat and is replaced by cold air. This in turn becomes heated, and a convection current is set up which cools the solid.]

5.3   Radiation

Heat may also be transmitted by a means which is neither conduction nor convection, nor requires an intervening medium. Energy from the sun passes through empty space to warm the earth. A radiant heater placed at high level in a room can be felt at lower levels, where neither conduction nor convection can carry it. This method of heat transmission is called *radiation* and does not involve any contact between the bodies which are providing and accepting the heat. To all intents and purposes, it behaves in the same way as light ("visible radiation") in that it travels in straight lines, will cast shadows, and will be transmitted through some materials and not others.

Heat is radiated as *infra-red* radiation, which is part of the spectrum of electromagnetic radiation.

Radio waves, microwaves, visible light and X-rays are all part of this spectrum; the only thing which makes one form of radiation different from another is the wavelength of the radiation. The following table shows how the different forms of radiation occupy the electromagnetic spectrum.

Radiation	Wavelength (m)
Radio waves (UHF to long wave)	10^{-1} to 10^{4}
Microwave	10^{-3} to 10^{-1}
Infrared	8×10^{-7} to 10^{-3}
Visible light: from red	8×10^{-7} red
to violet	4×10^{-7} violet
Ultraviolet	4×10^{-7} to 10^{-8}
X-rays	10^{-8} to 10^{-13}
γ (gamma)-rays	less than 10^{-13}

Different parts of the electromagnetic spectrum have been given different names simply for convenience. What we call "visible light" is so-called because energy in the interval 8×10^{-7} to 4×10^{-7} m can be detected by the eye. "Infra-red" radiation cannot be detected by the eye as it is beyond the "red" end of the visible spectrum. It also contains less energy than visible radiation, which in turn is less energetic that ultra-violet radiation. UV radiation causes damage to biological systems, but only a small amount reaches the surface of the earth from the sun as it is absorbed by the ozone layer in the upper atmosphere.

All types of electromagnetic radiation produce a heating effect when they are absorbed by a body. This will depend on the amount of energy absorbed. A proportion of the energy radiated from the sun is radiated as visible light. If a body is heated above ambient temperature, it will radiate heat in the infra-red region of the spectrum. These "energy waves" have wavelengths longer than those of visible light.

All forms of electromagnetic radiation travel in straight lines at *the speed of light*, 3×10^{8} m/s.

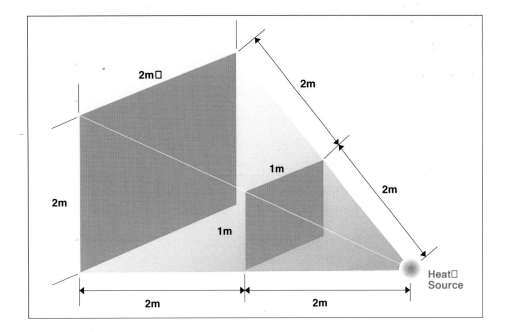

Figure 5.6 Diagram showing the inverse square law as it applies to radiation.

Radiation travels at this speed in a vacuum, but more slowly through matter such as air, water and glass.

The intensity of radiation – that is, how much energy reaches a surface of a given size – falls off inversely as the square of the distance from the source of radiation. This means that at twice the distance the intensity is one quarter; at three times the distance, the intensity is one-ninth, and so on. This inverse-square law is demonstrated in Figure 5.6.

The square with 1 metre sides placed at, say, 2 metres from the source will throw a shadow with 2 metre sides on a second sheet placed 4 metres from the source. Thus the energy falling on 1 m² is the same as that which would have fallen on an area of 2 m × 2 m = 4 m² at a distance of 4 m. So the energy per square metre at 4 m is one quarter that at 2 m, i.e. one quarter at twice the distance. This is important when considering the effect of radiation from a heat source such as a fire: a body of a given size and composition will heat up more slowly the further it is away from the radiation source.

When radiant energy (which, of course, includes infra-red radiation) falls on a body, there are three possibilities:

- **Transmission.** If energy passes through the body without warming it, it has been transmitted through the body. For example, 'transparent' materials transmit light.

- **Absorption.** The energy is absorbed by the body, whose temperature is raised; and

- **Reflection.** The energy may be reflected back from the surface in the way that light is from a shiny surface. Reflected energy does not enter the body, it just "bounces off" the surface.

Some substances absorb selectively: they allow some forms of radiation to pass, but not others. Glass, for example, allows light to pass but absorbs infra-red radiation – so glass may be used as a fire screen: the heat is stopped but the fire may be seen through it. However, for other reasons, such as its tendency to break under relatively low pressures and its behaviour at high temperatures, ordinary glass is not a good fire barrier.

Carbon dioxide and water vapour also exhibit this property. The sun's radiant energy, falling on the earth passes through the atmosphere and warms the ground, while the resulting infra-red radiation from the ground is absorbed by the atmosphere and so does not readily escape back into space. This is the cause of the 'Greenhouse Effect' – as industry, homes and transport have released more carbon dioxide into the atmosphere, the tendency to retain heat at the earth's surface has increased. It is believed that this may be producing a noticeable effect on the climate.

The ability of carbon dioxide and water vapour to absorb infra-red radiation in very narrow regions of the electromagnetic spectrum means that they also emit radiation in the same regions when they are hot. Radiation from small flames (e.g., at the early stage of a fire) is dominated by radiation from these gases, specifically at wavelengths of 2.8×10^{-7} and 4.4×10^{-7} m. Many infra-red detectors make use of this fact to distinguish between radiation from a flame and a hot solid object (such as a heating element) which emits over a wide range of wavelengths.

Some substances, such as pitch, transmit infra-red radiation, but absorb light.

The condition of the surface of a body affects its ability to absorb or reflect radiation. White or polished metal surfaces are the best reflectors and poor absorbers, while matt black surfaces are bad reflectors and good absorbers.

This is why white clothes, white-painted houses and cars, etc., are often used in hot climates. Snow and ice are poor absorbers of heat and reflect radiation very well. Because of this they melt slowly in direct sunlight. Melting will occur if the air temperature is raised, and heat is transferred by convection (Section 5.2).

Experiments have been carried out in which coal dust or other black powders have been spread on snow in order to accelerate melting. The sun's heat is more readily absorbed by the black powder, so its temperature rises and heat is transferred by conduction from the powder to the snow beneath.

Good reflectors of heat are also poor radiators. A polished silver teapot retains its heat better than a blackened teapot, in spite of silver being a good conductor. For the so-called radiators of a hot water system to radiate effectively they should be painted black, not a light colour as is usually the case. However, the principal way by which they warm a room is by heating the air immediately around them, which then rises, producing convection currents which spread heat throughout the room. The other side of the coin is that the heater is being cooled by convection.

Many fires have been caused by radiation – one of the most common is clothing being ignited by being placed too close to a source of radiation (Figure 5.7), as sometimes happens when people air clothes on a clothes horse placed too near a fire. Radiant heat from the sun passing through a glass window has sometimes been concentrated by an object inside the house which acts as a lens, such as a magnifying glass or a shaving mirror. The old-fashioned "bottle glass" used in windows will also concentrate the sun's rays and could, in principle, cause a fire, but a bottle, or pieces of broken bottle cannot.

Figure 5.7 Clothing may be ignited by radiation when placed too close to a source of radiated heat.

Chapter 6 – The Basis of Chemistry

The Chemistry of Combustion

Up to now, we have considered the physical properties of matter and heat, the properties that decide how bodies will behave when energy is supplied to them.

In the rest of this volume we will deal with the chemistry of combustion – the reactions by which energy is released in fires. Before discussing combustion in detail, it is necessary to talk about understand some of the basic concepts of chemistry.

Chemistry is a complicated subject bristling with long and difficult names to pronounce, and with intricate formulae used by the chemist. There are, of course, many text books available to the student on chemistry and, in presenting an opening to the study of fire-fighting techniques, it is difficult to decide exactly how much should be included. Many new processes and materials have become available in recent years. Firefighters are faced with so many new substances, particularly new building materials, during the course of their work, that they *must* have some idea how they will react when involved in fire. The particular hazards of many flammable materials and chemicals are dealt with separately in Parts 6b and 6c of the Manual of Firemanship. However, in this Part it is proposed to deal with those aspects of chemistry which applicable to the study of fire techniques, and to lead on to discuss some of the more hazardous chemical substances from a purely chemical point of view.

6.1 The basis of chemistry

Chemistry is the science of the composition of substances, their properties and reactions with each other. Substances may be solids, liquids or gases, in living or non-living systems, but all have one common factor – they consist of chemicals.

6.2 Atoms and molecules

Chemists recognise two distinct classes of substances; those which consist of a single chemical (elements and compounds) and those which are mixtures. A mixture may be separated into its constituents by some physical or mechanical means; for example, a mixture of salt and sand can be separated by dissolving the salt in water, leaving the sand behind. But to separate or change a single chemical substance, a chemical reaction is required.

Whether the substance is single or a mixture, it is made up from many millions of very tiny particles which the chemist calls molecules. (See Section 1.5) A mixture will contain more than one type of molecule, whereas a chemical compound contains only one type of molecule. Molecules of the same substance are all exactly alike in their properties and behaviour.

A molecule can be said to be the smallest particle of a compound capable of existing independently. The common substance chalk occurs in large quantities and in many different forms. For example, it is found in cliffs as lumps, or as a powder; it is, nevertheless, always recognisable as the same material, known chemically as calcium carbonate. This material is formed from innumerable calcium carbonate molecules. Each molecule is composed of even smaller particles called atoms. Every calcium carbonate molecule is exactly the same; each contains five atoms.

Molecules are formed from atoms. The number of different atoms comprising their molecules is relatively small. The molecules of all substances comprise various combinations of atoms, from approximately 90 different types of atom.

Atoms are the 'building blocks' of all substances. Unlike molecules, which can be broken down or changed during chemical reactions, atoms cannot be split *chemically* into anything smaller[1]. During chemical reactions the atoms rearrange to form different molecules, but the atoms themselves remain the same. They are the smallest particles to take part in chemical changes. Atoms are extremely small, their diameters being

between $\dfrac{1}{10000000}$ mm and $\dfrac{4}{10000000}$ mm

Substances formed entirely from one type of atom are called elements. There is an element corresponding to each different type of atom. Thus carbon, being formed entirely from carbon atoms, is an element. Similarly iron, containing only iron atoms, is another element. Elements may be composed of molecules made up from identical atoms joined together, or they may be composed of single atoms. The element oxygen consists of oxygen molecules, each molecule being two oxygen atoms joined together, whereas the element magnesium consists of single magnesium atoms. When we again consider the molecule of calcium carbonate (chalk) we find that it is composed of one atom of the element calcium, one atom of the element carbon, and three atoms of the element oxygen, all chemically bound together. A list of the names of some elements is given in Table 6.1; a full list is given in Appendix B.

6.2.1 Compounds and mixtures

When two or more atoms of different elements are chemically bound together to form molecules, all exactly the same, the substance formed is called a chemical compound. For example, each molecule of the compound calcium carbonate contains five atoms chemically bound together (one of calcium, one of carbon and three of oxygen). The compound formed from identical molecules can only be broken down or changed by a rearrangement of the atoms, known as a chemical reaction. A mixture (formed from two or more different sorts of molecules) can be separated by physical or mechanical means into the substances which make up the mixture.

---

1 They can be split by *nuclear* processes, which will be discussed elsewhere.

Table 6.1 *List of some elements with their atomic number, atomic mass and valency*

Name of element	Symbol	Atomic number	Atomic mass	Valency
Aluminium	Al	13	27.0	3
Bromine	Br	35	80.0	1
Calcium	Ca	20	40.0	2
Carbon	C	6	12.0	4
Chlorine	Cl	17	35.5	1, 3, 5, 7
Copper	Cu	29	63.5	1, 2
Fluorine	F	9	19.0	1
Gold	Au	79	197.0	1, 3
Helium	He	2	4.0	0
Hydrogen	H	1	1.0	1
Iodine	I	53	127.0	1, 3, 5, 7
Iron	Fe	26	56.0	2, 3
Magnesium	Mg	12	24.0	2
Mercury	Hg	80	201.0	1, 2
Neon	Ne	10	20.0	0
Nitrogen	N	7	14.0	3
Oxygen	O	8	16.0	2
Phosphorus	P	15	31.0	3
Potassium	K	19	39.0	1
Silicon	Si	14	28.0	4
Silver	Ag	47	108.0	1
Sodium	Na	11	23.0	1
Sulphur	S	16	32.0	2, 4, 6
Uranium	U	92	238.0	4, 6

> **Atoms are the smallest particles.**
>
> **Molecules are atoms chemically bound together.**
>
> **Elements contain only one sort of atom, either alone or grouped into molecules containing only one type of atom.**
>
> **Compounds are formed from one type of molecule which contains more than one kind of atom.**
>
> **Mixtures contain more than one kind of molecule.**

6.3 Symbols

Chemical symbols are used as a way of describing chemicals in terms of formulae, which are complete descriptions of molecules in terms of the constituent atoms. Symbols give as much information as possible, whilst still being simple and quick to use. Formulae may also be used to describe the way that atoms in a molecule are grouped together. This information may give clues to how one chemical compound may react with another.

Every element is assigned a symbol (see Table 6.1), which is different from that of all the other elements. A symbol may be one letter or two; in the latter case the convention is to write the second letter as a small letter. Thus the symbol for nickel is written Ni and not NI. NI would be interpreted as a molecule containing one nitrogen atom (N) and one iodine atom (I) (such a compound does not exist). In many cases the symbols are the first letter of the name of the element, often followed by a second letter taken from that name. However, there are several common elements whose symbols bear no relationship to their modern names, since they are based on the old Latin or Greek names. For example, the element sodium has the symbol Na which is derived from the Latin natrium, and lead has the symbol Pb, derived from plumbum (hence plumber, and plumb line).

6.3.1 Using symbols to write formulae

When a symbol is written it represents one atom of the element. Thus: H represents one atom of hydrogen; O represents one atom of oxygen.

A formula always represents one molecule of the substance and shows which atoms are present in the molecule and how many of them there are. Thus H_2O represents one molecule of water, containing two atoms of hydrogen and one atom of oxygen, bound together chemically. Similarly carbon dioxide has the formula CO_2, representing the molecule which contains one atom of carbon and two atoms of oxygen. If a molecule contains more than one atom of the same type, the number of similar atoms is written at the bottom right of the appropriate symbol:

Calcium carbonate
$CaCO_3$ 1 atom of calcium, one atom of carbon and 3 atoms of oxygen

Phosphorous pentoxide
PO_5 1 atom of phosphorus and 5 atoms of oxygen.

To represent more than one molecule we write a number in front of the formula: thus three molecules of water are represented by $3H_2O$. This group of three water molecules contain six hydrogen atoms and three oxygen atoms.

$2MgO$ represents two molecules of magnesium oxide (and, therefore, a total of two magnesium atoms and two oxygen atoms).

6.3.2 Radicals

Certain groups of atoms, common to families of related compounds, are known as radicals. **A radical can be defined as: 'a group of atoms present in a series of compounds which maintains its identity regardless of chemical changes which affect the rest of the molecule'.**

To show these radicals, formulae are often written with brackets enclosing the radical and with a number beyond the bracket to indicate how many of these radicals are in the formula.

Radicals are not complete molecules and have no independent existence. For example, the formula of one molecule of calcium hydroxide (slaked lime) is $Ca(OH)_2$, indicating that it contains one calcium atom and two hydroxyl (OH) radicals. The molecule contains two oxygen atoms and two hydrogen atoms, but they are always paired, as OH. Another common radical is NO_3, the nitrate radical. The formula for aluminium nitrate is written $Al(NO_3)_3$, indicating that the trivalent aluminium atom is combined with three monovalent nitrate radicals. Schematically:

$$Al \diagup \begin{matrix} NO_3 \\ NO_3 \\ NO_3 \end{matrix}$$

The meaning of valency will be discussed in Section 6.6. A list of common radicals is given in Table 6.2.

6.4   Atomic mass

The mass of one atom or one molecule is extremely small – of the order of 10^{-22} grams. It is of little practical value to quote the actual masses of atoms, but because atoms of different elements contain different numbers of protons and neutrons, knowing the mass is a big step towards identifying which element the atom belongs to.

It is, therefore, important to know how heavy one atom is in comparison with any other. The chemist, therefore, uses a relative atomic mass scale and not the actual masses of the atoms. Various scales have been proposed and, for technical reasons, the one most generally used is based on oxygen, which is given the atomic mass of 16.000. On this scale hydrogen has an atomic mass of 1.008. However, for normal purposes, the atomic masses can be rounded off, making hydrogen equal to 1.

We can then compare other atoms with hydrogen to see how many times heavier they are, so that we have the definition:

$$\text{Atomic mass} = \frac{\text{The mass of one atom of the element}}{\text{the mass of one atom of hydrogen}}$$

Table 6.2 *A list of common radicals*

	Name	Symbol
Valency 1	Ammonium	NH_4
	Bicarbonate	HCO_3
	Bromide	Br
	Chlorate	ClO_3
	Chloride	Cl
	Cyanide	CN
	Hydroxide	OH
	Iodine	I
	Nitrate	NO_3
	Nitrite	NO_2
	Perchlorate	ClO_4
Valency 2	Carbonate	CO_3
	Sulphate	SO_4
	Sulphide	S
	Sulphite	SO_3
Valency 3	Phosphate	PO_4

For example, the atomic mass of sodium is 23 (written Na = 23), meaning that an atom of sodium is 23 times heavier than an atom of hydrogen.

6.5   Molecular mass

In the same way, molecular mass is the mass of one molecule of the substance compared to the mass of one atom of hydrogen. For example, the molecular mass of water is 18 which means that one molecule of water is 18 times as heavy as one atom of hydrogen. Since a molecule consists of atoms joined together, the mass of the molecule is the sum of the masses of its component atoms. The molecular mass is found by adding together the atomic masses of those atoms present, thus: The molecular mass of sulphur dioxide (SO_2) is 64.

Molecular Mass $\;=\;$ atomic mass of sulphur $+$
$\qquad\qquad\quad$ 2 × atomic mass of oxygen
$\qquad\qquad\; =\; 32 + (2 \times 16)$
$\qquad\qquad\; =\; 64$

Similarly: nitric acid HNO_3, molecular mass 63;

Mol mass	= atomic mass H	+ atomic mass N	+ 3 × atomic mass O
	= 1	+ 14	+ (3 × 16)
	= 63		

6.6　Valency

When atoms combine to form molecules they do so in definite fixed ratios. For example, one sodium (Na) atom always combines with one chlorine (Cl) atom to give NaCl (common salt), but one magnesium (Mg) atom combines with two chlorine (Cl) atoms to give $MgCl_2$ (magnesium chloride). The 'combining power' of an atom depends on the arrangement and number of its electrons, but the mechanism of this is too complicated to discuss easily here.

The **valency** of an atom tells us how many chemical bonds the particular atom, or group of atoms (radicals) will form. Valencies are given in Table 3. When molecules are formed, the atoms or radicals generally combine in ratios in which the valencies are balanced. This property enables us to work out the correct formulae of many chemical compounds. For example, in magnesium oxide, Mg has a valancy of 2, and O has a valency of 2. To balance the valencies we need one Mg atom and one O atom; hence the formula MgO.

In potassium carbonate, potassium (K) has a valency of 1, while the carbonate radical has a valency of 2. Potassium carbonate requires two K atoms to combine with one carbonate radical, thus the formula is K_2CO_3.

In aluminium sulphate Al has a valency of 3, the sulphate radical has a valency of 2. To form the compound, two Al atoms are required to balance three SO_4 radicals (total number of "bonds" = 6), so that the formula for aluminium sulphate is $Al_2(SO_4)_3$.

6.6.1 Multiple valency

Several elements show more than one valency, including iron (Fe), copper (Cu) and nickel (Ni). The valency that the element shows depends on the particular circumstances – the other elements with which the element is combined, as well as on the conditions under which the reaction in which the compound is formed is carried out. More detailed knowledge of the chemistry of the element is required to predict which valency will be shown in any particular reaction. However, the names of the compounds formed are often adapted to help in deciding which valency state the element is in, in that particular compound, and hence to determine the correct formula.

6.6.2 Nomenclature

(1) -OUS and -IC
-OUS and -IC are used where an element shows two valencies.
-OUS always indicates the lower and -IC the higher valency. For example:

Iron
Ferrous: valency 2, e.g., $FeCl_2$ ferrous chloride.
Ferric: valency 3, e.g., $FeCl_3$ ferric chloride.
Tin
Stannous: valency 2, e.g., $SnBr_2$ stannous bromide.
Stannic: valency 4, e.g., $SnBr_4$ stannic bromide.

(2) Use of Roman numerals
A modern approach to the problem of multiple valency is to indicate which valency is being used by inserting the appropriate Roman numeral after the name or symbol of the element concerned, e.g.,
Iron (II) chloride $Fe(II)Cl_2$,
Iron (III) chloride $Fe(III)Cl_3$,
Tin (II) bromide $Sn(II)Br_2$,
Tin (IV) bromide $Sn(lV)Br_4$.

(3) -IDE
-IDE is used to indicate that a compound is made up of two elements only. By convention, metals are written before non-metals in names and formulae, thus:

Magnesium oxide MgO
(Mg valency 2; O valency 2).

Potassium sulphide K_2S
(K valency 1; S valency 2)

-IDE is also used exceptionally for a few radicals, e.g., -OH hydroxide. Thus:

Calcium hydroxide $Ca(OH)_2$
(Ca valency 2; OH valency 1).

(4) -ITE and -ATE

-ITE and -ATE are used where a compound contains more than two elements, one of which is oxygen. For two related compounds, that named -ITE always contains less oxygen than that named -ATE.

Sodium sulphite Na_2SO_3
(Na valency 1; SO_3 valency 2).

Sodium sulphate Na_2SO_4
(SO_4 valency 2).

Potassium nitrite KNO_2
(K valency 1; NO_2 valency 1).

Potassium nitrate KNO_3
(K valency 1; NO_3 valency 1).

The ending -ITE and -ATE are related to the ending -OUS and -IC where the latter are used in the names of acids. -OUS leads to -ITE and -IC to -ATE. For example:

Sulphurous acid H_2SO_3 gives sulphites $-SO_3$
Sulphuric acid H_2SO_4 gives sulphates $-SO_4$
Nitrous acid HNO_2 gives nitrites $-NO_2$
Nitric acid HNO_3 gives nitrates $-NO_3$

(5) Mono-, Di-, Tri-, Tetra-, Penta

Mono-, di-, tri-, tetra- and penta- are used in names to tell how many of a particular atom or radical are present.

Mono- 1 e.g., carbon monoxide CO,
Di-   2 e.g., carbon dioxide CO_2,
Tri-   3 e.g., sulphur trioxide SO_3,
Tetra- 4 e.g., carbon tetrachloride CCl_4,
Penta- 5 e.g., phosphorus pentachloride PCl_5.

(6) Per- always denotes that there is more oxygen present in the compound than would normally be the case:
Hydrogen oxide (water) H_2O,
Hydrogen peroxide H_2O_2,
Sodium chlorate $NaClO_3$,
Sodium perchlorate $NaClO_4$.

6.7   Simple equations

Consider a simple chemical reaction. When sulphur (a yellow solid element) burns in air, it combines with oxygen from the air, producing a colourless gas with a pungent choking smell. This gas is called sulphur dioxide (formula SO_2).

This can be stated simply as: "sulphur reacts with oxygen to form sulphur dioxide". A further simplification can be made by replacing 'reacts with' by "+" and 'to form' by an equals sign, "=". We then have:

Sulphur + oxygen = sulphur dioxide
     reacts with   to form

This statement can be simplified even further by replacing the names of the chemicals by symbols and formulae. (The molecules of oxygen, like those of most common elements that are gases, contain two atoms, but sulphur, like other solid elements, is assumed to consist of single atoms.) This gives:

$$S + O_2 = SO_2$$

This final statement represents the chemical equation for this reaction. It tells us that every sulphur atom involved reacts with one oxygen molecule to form one sulphur dioxide molecule.

> It should be noticed that each side of the equation contains the same number of each type of atom present. This must always be the case since a chemical reaction involves only a rearrangement of atoms – atoms do not appear or disappear – the equation must 'balance'.

Consider this other example. Magnesium (a metal) burns in oxygen to form magnesium oxide (a white powder). Magnesium reacts with oxygen to form magnesium oxide:

Magnesium + oxygen = magnesium oxide

$$Mg + O_2 = MgO$$

In this case, although there is the same number of magnesium atoms on each side of the equation, this is not true in the case of the oxygen atoms, where there are two on the left hand side and only one on the right hand side. This implies that oxygen atoms disappear during the reaction. The equation must be balanced before the equation is of any practical use – before it can tell us how the elements combine.

The equation above can be balanced by placing two molecules of magnesium oxide on the right hand side, thus:

$$Mg + O_2 = 2MgO$$

We now have equal numbers of oxygen atoms on each side of the equation, but the magnesium is 'out of balance'. By having two atoms of magnesium on the left hand side (instead of one):

$$2Mg + O_2 = 2MgO$$

the equation is now correctly balanced. Each side now contains equal numbers of each type of atom involved. It is of course possible to balance the equation by cheating. The equation:

$$Mg + O_2 = MgO$$

"balances" if we change the formula of magnesium oxide, thus:

$$Mg + O_2 = MgO_2$$

but MgO_2 does not exist. A chemical equation can only be balanced by changing the number of molecules present, not their formulae.

6.8 Use of chemical equations

The balanced equation: $2Mg + O_2 = 2MgO$ tells us that two atoms of magnesium react with one molecule of oxygen to produce two molecules of magnesium oxide.

These atoms and molecules have masses which are expressed in terms of their atomic and molecular masses (as described in Section 6.3). The atomic mass of magnesium is 24, that of oxygen is 16, and if we use this information together with the equation, we obtain:

2 Mg	+	O2	=	2MgO
2 x 24		2 x 16		2 (24 + 16)
48 units		32 units		80 units
Two magnesium atoms		Two oxygen atoms		Two MgO molecules each containing 1 magnesium and 1 oxygen atom

The 'units' are mass units, where one unit represents the mass of one hydrogen atom. Therefore, according to the equation, 48 units of magnesium will react with 32 units of oxygen to form 80 units of magnesium oxide. In other words the ratio:

$$\frac{\text{mass of magnesium}}{\text{mass of oxygen}} = \frac{48}{32}$$

An actual reaction between magnesium and oxygen will obviously involve millions of molecules of each substance. Suppose we 'scale up' this reaction until we have two million magnesium atoms instead of two. Then this number of magnesium atoms will react with one million oxygen atoms.

Two atoms of magnesium weigh 48 units, therefore, two million atoms of magnesium weigh 48 000 000 units.

Similarly, one molecule of oxygen weighs 32 units; therefore, one million molecules of oxygen weigh 32 000 000 units, so that the ratio:

$$\frac{\text{mass of magnesium}}{\text{mass of oxygen}} \text{ will again be } \frac{48}{32}$$

No matter to what extent the amounts of magnesium and oxygen are scaled up, the ratio will always be $^{48}/_{32}$. Therefore:

if 48 grams of magnesium are used, 32 grams of oxygen are needed. If 48 kg of magnesium are used, 32 kg of oxygen are needed, and 80g or 80 kg of magnesium oxide will be produced. For any other mass of magnesium, the masses of oxygen needed and magnesium oxide produced can be found by simple proportion.

6.9   Limitations of chemical equations

6.9.1 Reality

A chemical equation must be a summary of a known chemical reaction. For instance it is perfectly possible to write down the equation:

$$Cu + 2HNO_3 = Cu(NO_3)_2 + H_2$$
copper + nitric acid = copper nitrate + hydrogen

but such an equation is useless because it is found that when copper is placed in nitric acid, hydrogen is never produced. Therefore, the equation is not 'telling the truth', even though the sides balance.

6.9.2 Physical state

The equations we have been considering contain no information about the physical state of the chemicals, whether they are solids, liquids or gases, whether they are pure substances or are dissolved in water or some other solvent, or whether the solutions are dilute or concentrated. Sometimes it is important to specify the physical state. For example, the reaction of hydrogen and oxygen to form water vapour is associated with the release of a certain amount of heat. If the water vapour is allowed to condense, the latent heat of vaporisation is released. Thus, if we are quoting the amount of heat released by the reaction of hydrogen and oxygen, the physical form of the water must be stated. This can be done as follows:

$$2H_2 + O_2 = 2H_2O(g)$$
$$2H_2 + O_2 = 2H_2O(l)$$

where g and l refer to the gaseous (vapour) and liquid states respectively. As written, the second reaction releases more heat then the first, by an amount equal to the latent heat of evaporation of water.

6.9.3 Reaction conditions

Equations say nothing about the reaction conditions; whether heat must be used or pressure applied.

6.9.4 Heat

Equations do not tell us whether heat is given out or absorbed during a chemical reaction.

6.9.5 Rate of reaction

Equations say nothing about the rate of the reaction; whether it is slow, fast or inherently violent; or whether or not a catalyst[2] is necessary to make the reaction occur at a reasonable rate.

---

2 A catalyst is a substance that alters the rate of a chemical reaction, but does not itself undergo a chemical change.

Physics and Chemistry for Firefighters

Chapter 7 – Combustion

Flames are so much part of
our everyday experience that
it seems strange that there
is anything to write about
regarding their nature.
Certainly, every firefighter
knows what dangers flames
present, sees how they can
spread and is interested in how
they can be extinguished.
However, many people, if asked
what a flame actually is, would
find it difficult to produce an
answer. This section aims to
shed light on the nature of
flames, to give the reader an
insight into their make-up and,
especially, to highlight the
different types of flame.

7.1   The Fire Triangle

For combustion or burning to occur, oxygen, usually from the air, must combine with a fuel. A fuel may be in any one of the three states (gas, liquid or solid) initially, but for flaming combustion to occur, a solid or liquid fuel must be converted into a vapour, which then mixes with air and reacts with oxygen. Smouldering combustion, on the other hand, involves a reaction between oxygen (from the air) and the surface of the fuel: this is a complex process and in general only occurs with solid fuels which char on heating.

A flame is a region in which a sustained, heat-releasing reaction between a fuel in the vapour state and oxygen takes place. This region also emits light, usually with a strong yellow colour, though there are substances such as methanol which burn with a weak blue flame which cannot be seen in strong light.

One way of discussing burning is in terms of the triangle of combustion (Figure 7.1). For combustion to occur three things are necessary: heat, oxygen and fuel. Combustion will continue as long as these three factors are present. Removing one of them leads to the collapse of the triangle and combustion stops.

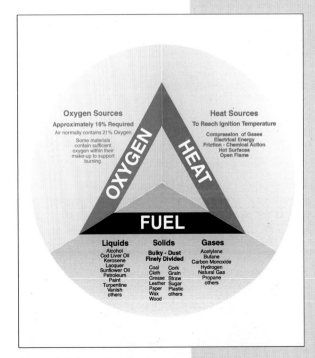

Figure 7.1 The triangle of combustion.

7.2 Heat of reaction and calorific value

All combustion reactions release heat energy and are therefore called **exothermic** reactions. The quantity of heat produced per unit weight of fuel can be calculated and is known as the **calorific value** of the fuel. For example, when 12 grams of carbon (the "gram atomic mass") are burned to carbon dioxide 392 920 Joules of heat are produced. This is the "heat of combustion", as tabulated in textbooks and handbooks: it refers to a standard amount of the fuel (the "mole") and has units kJ/mol. The calorific value for carbon is then:

$$\frac{392920}{12} = 32\ 743 \text{ Joules per gram (J/g)}$$

as one "mole" of carbon contains 12 g.

Besides calorific value, the rate of heat release is also important. For example, burning magnesium produces less heat than the burning of carbon, but when rates of reaction are considered, we find magnesium has a much higher rate of combustion than carbon so that the heat is released much more rapidly. **Heat release rate is now considered to be a major factor in whether a fire will spread over materials**, and a device called a Cone Calorimeter has been developed to measure this quantity for wall linings and building materials in general as part of the assessment of their flammability and suitability for their intended use.

7.2.1 Oxidation

An oxidation reaction is a reaction which involves combination with oxygen or other oxidising agents. The following reactions are typical examples of combustion:

(i) The oxygen may be supplied by the air.

$$2C + O_2 \rightarrow 2CO \text{ (carbon monoxide)}$$
$$2CO + O_2 \rightarrow 2CO_2$$
$$2H_2 + O_2 \rightarrow 2H_2O$$

(note that the oxidation of C to CO is not a flaming reaction: the others are).

(ii) The combustion may take place using oxygen which is contained within the burning material, the combustible material and the supporter of combustion being together in the same compound:

$$4C_3H_5(NO_3)_3 \rightarrow 12CO_2 + 10H_2O + 6N_2 + O_2$$
nitroglycerine

(iii) Oxygen may be provided by one of the materials in a mixture of compounds. The 'thermite reaction' illustrates this principle:

$$Fe_2O_3 + 2Al \rightarrow Al_2O_3 + 2Fe + \text{heat}$$
thermite mixture

(iv) Elements other than oxygen may be considered as oxidising agents; examples of these are chlorine and fluorine. "Combustion" may occur with these substances; for example, hydrogen will burn explosively with chlorine:

$$H_2 + Cl_2 \rightarrow 2HCl$$

Many organic materials (i.e., those based on carbon) will burn readily in halogen gases:

$$C_{10}H_{16} + 8Cl_2 \rightarrow 16HCl + 10C$$
turpentine

Nitrogen is not usually thought of as an oxidising agent or even a reactive element, but some metals will burn vigorously in this gas. Magnesium, aluminium and their alloys form nitrides in combustion reactions:

$$3Mg + N_2 \rightarrow Mg_3N_2$$
magnesium nitride

7.3 What makes a flame a flame?

There are two distinct types of flame: the premixed flame and the diffusion flame.

If a pool of paraffin is heated, its temperature will rise and combustible vapours will evaporate from the surface. When the temperature of the liquid surface reaches about 50 – 55°C (the firepoint, see Section 7.6.3), the rate of evaporation is high enough for the vapours to be ignited by a small flame, or spark, and support continuous flaming above the surface. After the paraffin has been burning for some time, the surface of the fuel will be close to its boiling point, supplying flammable vapours to the flame.

Once a flame has been established and flammable vapours are rising from the fuel surface, heat and what are called **chain carriers** are produced where the flame reactions are occurring. A proportion of these will pass into the next layer of gas and start the oxidation and heat release processes there, rather as in a relay race. Chain carriers are believed to be atoms or fragments of molecules known as **free radicals** which are extremely reactive. The type of chemical reaction which occurs in the flame is known as **a chain reaction**.

In fact, there are two distinct types of flame: the premixed flame and the diffusion flame. They have different properties, though both are familiar from everyday experience. Understanding that each behaves differently is important: under different circumstances fuel and air can combine in different ways to produce very different results.

7.4   Laminar flow and turbulent flow

Before we discuss flames, it is useful to define two types of gas flow: laminar flow and turbulent flow.

Laminar flow [Figure 7.2] is steady flow in which two particles starting at any given point follow the same path. Particles never cross each other's paths, so the particle paths are bunched together like uncooked spaghetti in a packet. At any given time, the velocities of all particles on one path are the same, but the velocities of particles in different paths might be different. Laminar flow is associated with slow flow over smooth surfaces.

In **turbulent flow**, [Figure 7.2] there are random changes in velocity and direction of the flow, although the flow as a whole is moving in a definite direction. If we consider wind blowing down a street on a windy day, leaves and litter may be blown up, down, across and around, revealing local changes in the flow, but the general direction of the wind is still down the street. Turbulent flow tends to occur in fast flows over rough surfaces and around obstacles.

Figure 7.2 Laminar and turbulent flow.

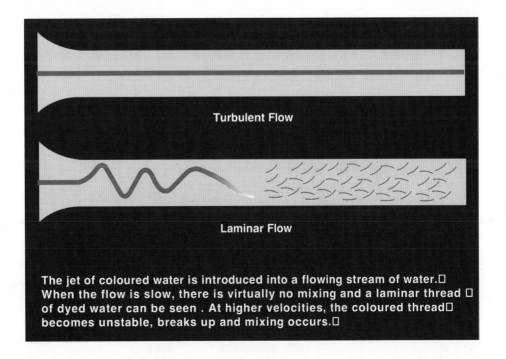

Turbulent Flow

Laminar Flow

The jet of coloured water is introduced into a flowing stream of water. When the flow is slow, there is virtually no mixing and a laminar thread of dyed water can be seen . At higher velocities, the coloured thread becomes unstable, breaks up and mixing occurs.

7.5 Premixed and diffusion flames

As we have seen, a flame is the region in which the chemical reactions take place which turn unburnt fuel vapours into burnt gases – the combustion products: for example, methane and oxygen react to give carbon dioxide and water vapour.

A certain amount of heat energy is required to start this reaction but more heat is produced by the reaction than it takes to initially start it, so the burning process is self-sustaining.

Premixed flames occur when a fuel is well-mixed with an oxidant, e.g., 10% methane mixed with air. For ignition to occur, energy must be supplied to the system in the form of a spark or small flame. A self-sustaining flame will then be established around the ignition source and propagate outwards in all directions.

The flame consists of a zone where cold unburnt gas (reactants) is transformed into hot burnt gas (products). The flame zone of a premixed flame may be less than 1 mm thick. As the volume of the hot burnt gas is greater than that of the same mass of cold unburnt gas, the flame front is pushed outwards from the ignition point, like the skin of an inflating balloon.

Not every mixture of air and fuel will burn. Depending on the type of fuel and oxidant involved (air or pure oxygen, for example), a mixture initially at room temperature and pressure will only burn

if the concentration of fuel lies between certain well-defined limits, called **flammability limits**. For example, mixtures of methane and air will only burn if the concentration of methane in air lies between 5% and 15%, whereas hydrogen will burn in air at concentrations between 4% and 75%.

The figures quoted for limits of flammability may vary as there are a number of factors which may slightly alter the value: pressure, temperature, dimensions of the test apparatus, direction of flame propagation and moisture content of the mixture all have some effect. (In general, the limits **widen** with rise in temperature.)

Within these ranges, there is an optimum mixture in which there is just sufficient fuel to use up all the oxygen. This is the **stoichiometric mixture**. Mixtures containing more fuel than the stoichiometric mixture are known as rich mixtures, and ones containing less fuel are lean mixtures. The stoichiometric mixture for methane is 9.4%. A 7% mixture is lean, while a 12% mixture is rich.

For each mixture of fuel and air between the flammability limits, there is a characteristic **burning velocity** at which a premixed flame will propagate through a stationary gas.

Burning velocities usually lie between 0.1 and 1.0 m/s. They tend to peak at the stoichiometric composition and fall away towards the flammability limits [Figure 7.3]. Burning velocity is dictated by the chemical processes involved – how quickly the fuel reacts with the oxygen. The methane and oxygen molecules do not simply combine instantaneously to form carbon dioxide and water vapour, but form free radicals and intermediates such as formaldehyde and carbon monoxide along the way to completing the reaction.

If the premixture flows into a flame with a laminar flow whose velocity is equal to the burning velocity of the mixture, the flame can be held stationary. This is how premixed flames on Bunsen burners, domestic gas rings etc., are held steady.

Local air currents and turbulence caused by obstacles can cause a flame to move at speeds much higher than the burning velocity. The speed at which a flame moves relative to an observer is the

Flammability Limits (% fuel/air by volume)

Gas	Lower limit	Upper limit
Hydrogen	4.0	75.0
Carbon monoxide	12.5	74.2
Methane	5.0	15.0
Butane	1.5	9.0
Ethylene	2.7	28.6
Acetylene	2.5	80.0

Figure 7.3 Flammability limits.

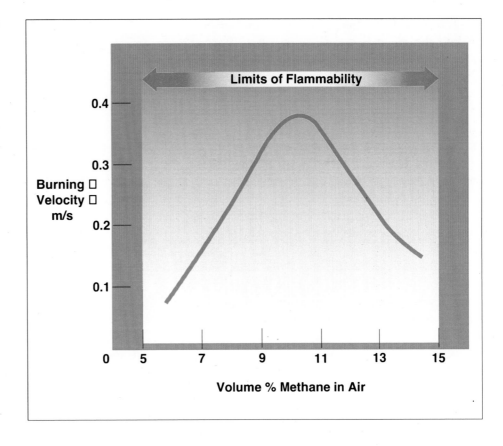

flame speed, which is different to the burning velocity. For example, the burning velocity of a stoichiometric methane-air flame is 0.45 m/s. If the unburnt gases are no longer stationary, the flame propagates at the local flow speed plus the burning velocity. As the flame gets faster, the flame front wrinkles as turbulence is produced in the unburnt gas, increasing the surface area of the flame front. This increases the reaction rate, increasing the rate at which burnt gas is produced, so pushing the flame front forward faster. In explosion situations, flame speeds of hundreds of metres per second can be achieved in gas-air mixtures, though the **burning velocity** of the mixture will be much lower than this. It is worthwhile making the distinction between these terms, as some older texts use flame speed to mean burning velocity. It is possible to achieve supersonic flame speeds, in which the combustion region is strongly coupled to a shock wave: this phenomenon is called **detonation**.

Diffusion flames occur at the interface where fuel vapour and air meet. Unlike premixed flames, the fuel vapour and the oxidant are separate prior to burning. The dominant process in the diffusion

flame is the mixing process. The fuel vapour and oxygen mix with each other by molecular diffusion, which is a relatively slow process, though the high temperatures associated with flames increase the rate at which diffusion occurs.

> Because diffusion flames exist only at the fuel-air interface, there is no equivalent of burning velocity, and no equivalent to rich or lean mixtures, or flammability limits.

Diffusion flames themselves fall into two broad types. In slow-burning diffusion flames, such as candle flames, the fuel vapour rises slowly from the wick in a laminar flow and molecular diffusion dominates. This type of flame is a **laminar diffusion flame**.

In industrial burners, fuel is injected at high velocity into the air as a spray or jet. Turbulence is induced at the interface where mixing takes place. This gives the flame an extremely large surface area in comparison to the relatively small surface area of the smooth fuel/air interface of the candle flame. In this turbulent case, it is the large interface area, rather than the rate of molecular diffusion, which determines the rate of mixing. This type of flame is a **turbulent diffusion flame**.

In a large fire (e.g., more than 1 m in diameter), the flames are turbulent diffusion flames, the turbulence generated by the strong buoyancy of the flames themselves. Inside the flame, there are regions of high temperature and low oxygen concentration where the fuel vapour is subjected to a mixture of pyrolysis (chemical decomposition in the absence of oxygen) and partial oxidation, leading to the formation of soot particles and products of incomplete combustion, in particular carbon monoxide (CO). These are the source of smoke, and of the gaseous species that render the fire products toxic.

7.6   Practical examples of premixed flames and diffusion flames

7.6.1 The Bunsen Burner

The Bunsen burner (Figure 7.4) should be familiar from school laboratories. It can produces both types of flame – premixed and diffusion. Gas is forced out of a jet at the base of the burner. If the air inlet collar at the bottom is open, air is entrained into the fuel flow and mixing occurs in the burner column. A pale blue conical flame is visible just above the top of the burner. This is a laminar premixed flame. When the air inlet to a Bunsen burner is closed, a yellow diffusion flame results.

7.6.2 A candle flame

When a match is held close to the wick of an unlit candle, the wax melts and rises up the wick by capillary action. There it evaporates, and a flame is established at the interface between the evaporating fuel and the surrounding air. The fuel and air are not mixed before burning, so this is a diffusion

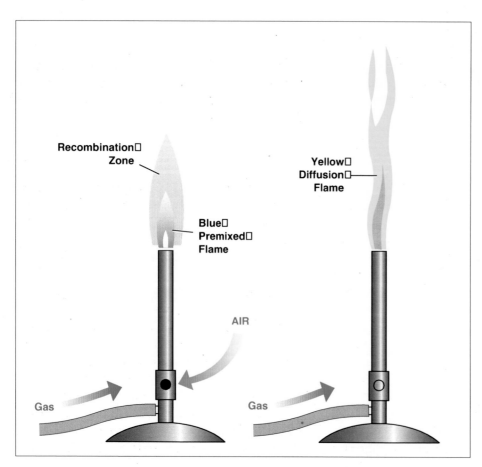

Figure 7.4 (a) Premixed flame on a Bunsen burner with full aeration; (b) diffusion flame.

flame. Once the flame is established, the process of melting, evaporation and burning is self-sustaining because heat is transferred from the flame back to the wick to sustain the melting and evaporation processes.

7.6.3 Flashpoint, firepoint and sustained fires

Imagine a dish of flammable liquid, such as paraffin. A region will exist above the liquid surface in which the evaporating fuel vapour is well mixed with air. If the paraffin is heated above about 40ºC, this well-mixed region will become flammable – that is, the vapour concentration in air is above its lower flammability limit. **The lowest temperature at which this occurs is called the 'FLASHPOINT', the liquid temperature at which application of an ignition source will cause a flame to flash across the surface of the liquid.** This is a premixed flame moving through the vapour/air mixture but, just above the flashpoint, it burns out, or self-extinguishes, because it has consumed all the vapour. If heating is continued, a temperature will be reached at which ignition of the vapours will lead to a "flash", followed by the development of a sustained diffusion flame at the surface flame. **This temperature is known as the 'FIREPOINT', the lowest temperature at which the rate of supply of fuel vapours (by evaporation) can sustain the flame.**

There are several types of apparatus for determining the flash point of a liquid. The most common is the Pensky-Martens "closed cup" test in which the vapours cannot diffuse away from the surface, but can achieve a uniform concentration in the head space above the liquid surface. The Abel apparatus is also a closed cup test. The Cleveland "open cup" test gives a slightly higher flashpoint than the Pensky-Martens, but can be used to determine the firepoint. Clearly, it is always necessary to quote the method and the type of apparatus used, and whether the result is an "open cup" or "closed cup" flashpoint. Note that the flashpoint is affected slightly by pressure: values quoted in handbooks, etc., are adjusted to normal atmospheric pressure. Corrections should be considered for high altitude applications.

The term "flash fire" is used to describe what happens if the temperature of the fuel is much greater than the firepoint and a flammable vapour/air zone exists at some distance from the liquid surface. This may happen if there is a spillage of petrol (firepoint approx. -40ºC) which forms a large pool. If an ignition source is introduced into the flammable zone, a premixed flame will flash back, igniting the fuel in the fuel-rich mixture above the liquid surface and giving rise to a large fire (turbulent diffusion flame).

In a sustained fire of this type, flames burn continuously above the surface until the fuel is consumed (or the fire is extinguished). In principle, combustible solids burn in the same way, although the formation of fuel vapours involves chemical decomposition of the solid which requires more energy than simple evaporation. For this reason, solids tend to burn much more slowly than combustible liquids.

7.6.4 Fireball

A fireball can occur when a mixture of vapour and mist droplets forms a cloud containing very little air, for example when a vessel containing pressurised liquid fuels, such as LPG, ruptures. The oxygen concentration within this cloud is far too low for premixed combustion to take place, but, if there is a source of ignition at the boundary between the fuel and the surrounding air, a premixed flame will flash through the flammable zone at the boundary, leading to the establishment of a diffusion flame. The fireball has then been established and will rise as it burns.

As burning progresses, instabilities are introduced in the surface of the flame increasing the surface area available for the reaction to take place. The fireball will increase in size until the fuel has been used up. Then it will shrink and extinguish.

7.6.5 Vapour cloud explosions

If a gas or vapour escapes under pressure from a rupture in a storage tank or pipeline, there is likely to be rapid mixing of the fuel with air, producing a cloud of fuel-air mixture, some of which will be of concentrations which fall between the flammability limits. If an ignition source is present in the cloud, a premixed flame will move outwards in all directions from the source. The flame will propagate through that region of the cloud which lies between the flammability limits.

After ignition, obstacles such as process vessels and pipework will introduce turbulence in the vapour/air mixture ahead of the flame, and cause wrinkling of the flame. This will increase the effective surface area of the flame, increasing the rate of burning, and the flame speed. This can generate overpressures which under severe conditions can cause blast damage. It is believed that this mechanism was responsible for the extensive damage caused at Flixborough in June 1974.

7.7   Ignition

For ignition to occur, sufficient heat energy is supplied to gaseous fuel and oxidant, either mixed to within flammability limits or at the interface between the fuel and the oxidant, to start a self-sustaining chemical reaction. This energy is generally supplied by a flame or a spark or a hot surface.

In this short section we will look at less obvious ways in which ignition can occur.

7.7.1 Spontaneous ignition temperature

This is the lowest temperature at which the substance will ignite spontaneously, that is the substance will burn without the application of a flame or other ignition source. This is sometimes referred to as the **auto-ignition temperature**.*

For some materials, the ignition temperature may be so low that there is a danger of them igniting under normal conditions, or in the range of temperatures that the material would experience during day-to-day use. Such materials are normally well documented and information available regarding their safe handling.

7.7.2 Self heating and spontaneous combustion

Certain materials may react with oxygen at room temperature. Compounds such as linseed oil which contain carbon-carbon double bands are very

---

* The auto-ignition temperature is not a true property of a material. It depends on how it is measured.

prone to this reaction, but any organic material stored in bulk quantities may be suspect, especially if it has been stored at an elevated temperature.

Imagine a pile of cloths soaked in linseed oil, which have been discarded after, for example a room has been decorated with paint or varnish containing a large proportion of linseed oil.

As the cloth is porous, oxygen in the air will be able to reach the centre of the pile. The linseed oil will oxidise slowly, even at room temperature, releasing heat. Because the centre of the pile is well insulated by the surrounding cloths, heat will build up and the temperature will rise. As the temperature rises, the reaction rate increases – roughly for every 10°C rise in temperature, the reaction rate doubles – so even more heat is given out and the temperature rises more quickly.

If heat is being produced more rapidly than it can escape, the temperature will continue to rise to a stage at which active combustion begins, usually well within the mass of material. Combustion will begin as a smouldering process, burning through to the surface of the pile where flaming combustion will be initiated.

Spontaneous combustion should be considered as a possible cause of a fire for which there is no obvious ignition source, but it is necessary to show that the material involved has the propensity to self heat, and that a sufficient quantity has been stored in such a way as to provide the necessary thermal insulation for the inside of the pile. A useful rule-of-thumb is that if the material does not produce a rigid char when it is heated, it is very unlikely to self-heat to ignition.

Sometimes the action of bacteria on certain organic materials can cause a rise in temperature eventually leading to active combustion (haystacks were prone to this). Powdered material, such as powdered coal used in power stations and some metals, can give rise to spontaneous combustion. Stocks of coal at power stations, if incorrectly stored in very large piles, can self-heat to ignition. In the manufacture of some plastics (e.g., polyurethane foams), the cross-linking process which creates the final molecular structure of the material is exothermic, and can lead to spontaneous combustion if slabs of foam are stored before the process is complete (see Chapter 10).

7.7.3 Smouldering

Smouldering only occurs in porous materials which form a solid carbonaceous char when heated. Paper, sawdust, fibreboard and latex rubber can all undergo smouldering.

Smouldering is the combustion of a solid in an oxidising gas such as air, without the appearance of a flame. The process is very slow, but smouldering fires can go undiscovered for a very long time and can produce a large amount of smoke. This is flammable, but it must accumulate and reach its lower flammablity limit before it can be ignited. This has been known to happen on a few, fortunately rare, occasions (e.g., the Chatham Dockyard mattress fire in November 1974).

Smouldering will undergo a transition to flaming under favourable conditions. The best documented examples involve cigarette ignition of upholstered furniture. The mechanism is not fully understood, and it is impossible to predict how long after the commencement of smouldering that the transition will occur.

7.8   Hazards of oxidising agents

Nearly all combustion reactions involve oxidation which in its most simple form is combination with oxygen, such as the combustion of hydrogen:

$$2H_2 + O_2 = 2H_2O$$

The oxygen in this case may be called an oxidising agent. The word oxidation also has a broader meaning where elements other than oxygen may be considered as oxidising agents. For example, most metals will react with chlorine, and other halogens: this is also a type of oxidation.

$$Mg + Cl_2 = MgCl_2$$

Here chlorine is the oxidising agent.

There are certain compounds which do not necessarily burn themselves but, on decomposition, release oxygen which can greatly assist a combustion reaction. Some of these compounds may be relatively stable at room temperature but at high temperatures they could be extremely hazardous.

Some of the more common oxidising agents are considered below.

7.8.1 Nitric acid and inorganic nitrates

Concentrated nitric acid is a very powerful oxidising agent and reacts vigorously with many organic compounds. Carbon itself reacts with the hot acid, in the following way:

$$C + 4HNO_3 = CO_2 + 4NO_2 + 2H_2O$$

When the concentrated acid mixes with carbonaceous (carbon-containing) material there is a violent reaction giving off a great deal of heat and nitrogen dioxide (nitrous fumes). Clearly, carbonaceous materials like sawdust and wood chippings must never be used to soak up a spillage of this acid. The nitrates (salts of nitric acid) are also good oxidising agents. They are used in large quantities in industry and agriculture. An example is the use of molten nitrate salt baths for the heat treatment of metals.

If they are strongly heated the nitrates of sodium and potassium give off oxygen and the metal nitrite:

$$2KNO_2 = 2KNO_2 + O_2$$

Most other metal nitrates form the metal oxide, giving off nitrogen dioxide ('nitrous fumes') and oxygen.

Ammonium nitrate is widely used as an agricultural fertiliser under various trade names. It is a white crystalline solid, very soluble in water (all nitrates are soluble in water). It does not burn by itself, but mixing it with a fuel (e.g., sugar) produces a powerful explosive. It decomposes violently when heated giving nitrous oxide and water:

$$NH_4NO_3 = N_2O + 2H_2O$$

Brown nitrous fumes (NO_2) are also given off on heating; decomposition is complex. These fumes of nitrogen dioxide will support combustion in a similar manner to oxygen.

Ammonium nitrate can detonate, but only large quantities, and under extreme conditions.

7.8.2 Permanganates

Of the permanganates, sodium ($NaMnO_4$) and potassium ($KMnO_4$) permanganates are the most common. They are powerful oxidising agents and may react violently with oxidisable organic materials. When mixed with glycerol (glycerine), spontaneous ignition occurs. With concentrated hydrochloric acid, permanganates produce the highly toxic chlorine gas as a result of oxidation.

7.8.3 Chlorates

Chlorates are often used as their sodium or potassium compounds. On heating, oxygen is released:

$$2KClO_3 \rightarrow 2KCl + 3O_2$$

Very violent reactions occur on contact with oxidisable materials and may occur merely by friction.

Potassium perchlorate ($KClO_4$) has a similar chemical formula, but is, in fact, stable. Anhydrous perchloric acid ($HClO_4$) is a powerful oxidising agent and will explode on heating. Sodium chlorate is used as a weed killer and has also been used in home-made explosives.

7.8.4 Chromates and dichromates

The most common compounds of this type are potassium chromate (K_2CrO_4) and potassium dichromate ($K_2Cr_2O_7$); these materials are yellow and orange respectively and are oxidising agents. They are soluble in water and will produce a highly combustible mixture with oxidisable substances.

7.8.5 Inorganic peroxides

Peroxides are a group of compounds which contain a higher proportion of oxygen than the 'normal' oxide. This extra oxygen is easily liberated, making these compounds good oxidising agents. Inorganic peroxides may be considered to derive from hydrogen peroxide (H_2O_2). Pure hydrogen peroxide is a clear viscous liquid with a specific gravity of 1.46 (at 0°C). It is soluble in water and is used at various concentrations. Above 70 per cent concentration in water it is a powerful oxidising agent and decomposes explosively:

$$2H_2O_2 \rightarrow O_2 + 2H_2O$$

This decomposition may occur on heating, but can also occur in by the presence of a catalyst: small traces of metallic dust, charcoal or even strong light may be sufficient. Concentrated solutions of hydrogen peroxide are often known as 'high test peroxide' (HTP).

Common metal peroxides, derived from hydrogen peroxide, are those of sodium (Na_2O_2) and barium (BaO_2). Sodium peroxide is a pale yellow solid which reacts vigorously with water, releasing oxygen:

$$2Na_2O_2 + 2H_2O \rightarrow O_2 + 4NaOH$$

A great deal of heat is released in this reaction and this could cause a fire in any nearby combustible material. The fire would be made worse by the oxygen evolved.

Sodium peroxide can absorb carbon dioxide, releasing oxygen as a product:

$$2Na_2O_2 + 2CO_2 \rightarrow 2Na_2CO_3 + O_2$$

7.8.6 Organic oxidising agents

When nitric acid reacts with organic compounds, two important types of substance are formed: organic nitrates ($-NO_3$) and nitro-compounds ($-NO_2$).

These compounds are oxidising agents and furthermore they carry oxidisable carbon-containing material within their own molecules. Consequently, both the organic nitrates and the nitro-compounds are highly flammable. Some that contain several nitrate or nitro groups in the molecule are explosive. Typical examples are glyceryl trinitrate (used in dynamite) and trinitrotoluene (TNT) – an important military explosive.

Most organic nitrates and nitro- compounds are toxic and many of them, including glyceryl trinitrate, may be absorbed through the skin.

7.8.7 Organic peroxides and hydroperoxides

These compounds have a structure similar to that of hydrogen peroxide (H_2O_2, arranged as H-O-O-H), with both hydrogen atoms replaced by organic groups, thus forming an organic peroxide. If only one hydrogen is replaced, a hydroperoxide is formed.

As would be expected peroxides and hydroperoxides are powerful oxidising agents and because there is a carbon-containing part of the molecule which can be oxidised, they are highly flammable. Some are explosive and sensitive to heat and mechanical shock. Because of this they are often diluted or 'damped down' with either water or stable esters.

Peroxides are extensively used as catalysts, especially in the plastics industry. They are toxic and are especially irritating to the skin, eyes and mucous membranes. Skin contact and breathing of vapours should be avoided. In all respects, organic peroxides and hydroperoxides should be treated with extreme caution.

Physics and Chemistry for Firefighters

Chapter 8 – Simple organic substances

Carbon forms a very large number of compounds, especially with hydrogen, oxygen, nitrogen and the halogens. It forms so many compounds that chemistry is divided into two branches:

- organic chemistry which deals with the chemistry of the carbon compounds; and

- inorganic chemistry which deals with the chemistry of all the other elements.

There are believed to be over a million stable carbon compounds, which explains why a separate branch of chemistry is necessary to study them.

Carbon atoms differ from almost every other type of atom in that they are able to link up with other carbon atoms and form chains and rings. Most other atoms only join with others of the same kind in twos or threes. In all these organic compounds the valency of carbon is always four.

Organic chemicals are divided into two classes:

- aliphatic compounds, which contain chains of carbon atoms; and

- aromatic compounds which contain a special kind of ring of six carbon atoms, known as a benzene ring.

Most organic chemicals are capable of burning. Our most important fuels, such as natural gas, petrol, paraffin and diesel oil are mixtures of organic compounds which contain carbon and hydrogen – the hydrocarbons.

8.1 Aliphatic hydrocarbons (paraffins or alkanes)

The aliphatic hydrocarbons are a series of compounds containing only carbon and hydrogen. The simplest member of paraffins, or alkanes, is methane, the main constituent of natural gas. It has the formula CH_4 and the structure of the molecule is conveniently represented as:

$$
\begin{array}{ccc}
 & H & \\
 & | & \\
H\!\!-\!\!\!\!&C&\!\!\!\!-\!\!H \\
 & | & \\
 & H &
\end{array}
$$

Methane, CH_4

The carbon atom uses each of its four valencies to join it to four hydrogen atoms which each have a valency of one. The CH_4 molecule can also be regarded as a combination of the group:

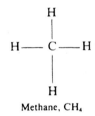

called a methyl group

with a hydrogen atom. Methane has well-defined chemical and physical properties. It is a relatively unreactive gas, although it is flammable and forms explosive mixtures with air at concentrations between 5% and 15% by volume. In common with other hydrocarbons, it burns completely to produce carbon dioxide and water:

$$CH_4 + 2O_2 = CO_2 + 2H_2O.$$

Larger molecules are built up by linking the carbon atoms together in chains. Hydrogen atoms are attached to the carbon atoms in accordance with the valency rules. For example:

Methane, CH₄ ... with an additional C atom becomes ... Ethane, C₂H₆

Ethane (C_2H_6) is another constituent of natural gas. Because the molecule is larger, the physical properties are different from methane. The boiling point, melting point and vapour density of ethane are higher than those of methane, whereas its spontaneous ignition temperature is lower.

Another increment in the chain length of the molecule results in propane (C_3H_8), a constituent of liquefied petroleum gas.

Ethane, C₂H₆ ... with an additional C atom becomes ... Propane, C₃H₈

Propane is chemically similar to ethane and methane, but once again, the physical properties differ (see Table 8.1).

In principle, the carbon chain can be extended indefinitely, until the chain consists of many thousands of carbon atoms, as in polyethylene (see Chapter 9). The longer the chain, the higher the boiling and melting points of the substance. Methane, ethane, propane and butane are all gases at room temperature and pressure, but heavier molecules, starting at pentane, C_5H_{12}, are liquids, and from hexadecane, $C_{16}H_{34}$ they are solids. Compounds near C_8H_{18} (octane) are found in petrol, those near $C_{10}H_{22}$, in paraffin, those near $C_{14}H_{30}$ in diesel oil, those near $C_{18}H_{38}$ in petroleum jelly (Vaseline) and those near $C_{25}H_{52}$ in paraffin wax. The following points may be noted concerning these compounds:

● they form a series in which each differs from the next by one -CH₂ unit;

● they have similar chemical properties; and

● their physical properties vary in a regular way.

As the number of carbon atoms increases:

● melting point, vapour density, boiling point and flash point **increase**; and

● solubility in water and spontaneous ignition temperature **decrease**.

8.2 Unsaturated aliphatic hydrocarbons

8.2.1 Olefines or alkenes

There is another series of aliphatic compounds known as the **olefins or alkenes**. The first member of the series is ethylene (C_2H_4), the formula for which is represented as:

where there is a double bond between the two carbon atoms. The carbon still has its valency of 4 and hydrogen that of 1, but each carbon atom uses two of its valency bonds to link to the other carbon atom. Compounds containing double bonds (and those with triple bonds) are known as **unsaturated** compounds.

Unsaturated compounds are much more reactive than the paraffins. Not only do they burn, but they react readily with chlorine, hydrogen chloride, bromine, and other reagents. For example:

(Ethylene) + Cl₂ → (Ethylene dichloride or dichloroethane)

The reactivity of ethylene makes it an important starting material in the production of plastics and other synthetic materials (see Chapter 9).

Table 8.1 *The Paraffins or Alkanes*

	Name	Formula	Structure	Vapour density (A = 1)	Melting point (°C)	Boiling point (°C)	Flash point (°C)	Flammable limits (% in air)	Self-ignition temperature (°C)
Gases	Methane	CH_4		0.554	–183	–161	Gas	5 to 15	538
	Ethane	C_2H_6		1.04	–172	–89	Gas	3.3 to 12.5	510
	Propane	C_3H_8		1.52	–187	–42	–104	2.4 to 9.5	510
	Isomers								
	n-Butane	C_4H_{10}		2.046	–138.6	–0.6	–60	1.5 to 9.0	466
	iso-Butane	C_4H_{10}		2.046	–160	–12	Gas	1.8 to 8.4	545
Liquids	n-Pentane	C_5H_{12}		2.48	–130	36	<–40	1.4 to 7.8	309
	n-Hexane	C_6H_{14}		2.97	–95.6	69	–7	1.2 to 7.4	260
	n-Hexadecane	$C_{16}H_{34}$		7.8	18	287	>100	–	205
Solids	n-Heptadecane	$C_{17}H_{36}$		8.33	22	303	–	–	200
	n-Octadecane	$C_{18}H_{38}$		8.81	28	308	–	–	200
	n-Heptacontane	$C_{70}H_{142}$		–	105	–	–	–	–

Other olefins can be obtained by progressively increasing the length of the carbon chain. As with the paraffins, the physical properties alter in a regular way as the size of the molecule increases (see Table 8.2).

8.2.2 Acetylenes, or alkynes

Acetylenes contain a carbon-carbon triple bond. The only important member is the gas acetylene (C_2H_2). It is an unsaturated compound and the only way of arranging the normal valency bonds of the carbon and hydrogen is:

H-C≡C-H
Acetylene

Here, each carbon atom uses three of the available valencies to make three bonds with the other. This triple bond makes acetylene very reactive: it can explode on exposure to heat or mechanical shock, even when air or oxygen are absent. Acetylene is

Table 8.2 *The Olefines or Alkenes*

Name	Formula	Structure	Vapour density (A = 1)	Melting point (°C)	Boiling point (°C)	Flash point (°C)	Flammable limits (% in air)	Self-ignition temperature (°C)
Ethylene	C_2H_4		0.98	−169	−103.9	Gas	2.7 to 28.6	450
Propylene	C_3H_6		1.5	−185	−48	Gas	2 to 11	495
The Butylenes	C_4H_8		1.93	about −185	about −6.3	<−80	1.7 to 10.0	384
Gases								

* The olefines are liquids from C_5H_{10} to $C_{16}H_{32}$, and then solids.

Table 8.3 *The Acetylenes or Alkynes*

Name	Formula	Structure	Vapour density (A = 1)	Melting point (°C)	Boiling point (°C)	Flash point (°C)	Flammable limits (% in air)	Self-ignition temperature (°C)
Acetylene	C_2H_2	H—C≡C—H	0.91	−81	−84†	−17.7	2.5 to 80	335
Methylacetylene	C_3H_4		1.38	−102.7	−23	Gas	1.7 to –	–
*Gases								

* The acetylenes are liquids from C_4H_6 to $C_{17}H_{32}$, and then solids.
† Sublimes

flammable and forms mixtures in air with wide flammability limits (2.5% – 89%). Some of its physical properties are given in Table 8.3. Acetylene is used in the manufacture of plastics (e.g., PVC), certain chemicals and in oxyacetylene welding. It is stored by dissolving it in acetone, which is absorbed on an inert porous material contained in cylinders.

8.3 Aromatic hydrocarbons

The simplest member of the aromatic hydrocarbons is benzene, C_6H_6. It has a unique structure, consisting of six carbon atoms arranged in a ring, apparently with alternating single and double bonds:

usually represented as

Benzene

However, the six carbon atoms are linked in a special way, and benzene does not behave like an olefin. In fact, the benzene ring is remarkably stable, so that aromatic compounds – those containing the benzene ring, such as toluene – are less reactive than olefins.

Benzene is a flammable liquid, but when it burns, the aromatic ring proves difficult to oxidise because of its stability: the high proportion of carbon in the molecule leads to the formation of a thick black smoke. It is no coincidence that the precursors of smoke in flames from any fuel have been found to have an aromatic structure. These are formed in the flame in regions where temperatures are high, but the oxygen concentration is low. If the fuel already contains an aromatic structure, it can be said quite categorically that it will burn with a very smoky flame.

Other aromatic compounds are formed by replacing the hydrogen atoms of benzene by other atoms or groups of atoms, such as methyl radicals. For example:

with one H atom replaced by a methyl radical, becomes

(Benzene, C₆H₆)

(Toluene, C₇H₈)

or

CH₃

Similarly:

CH₃

with a further H atom replaced by a methyl radical, becomes

(Toluene, C₇H₈)

CH₃ / CH₃
ortho-xylene
(o-xylene)

CH₃ / CH₃
meta-xylene
(m-xylene)

CH₃ / CH₃
para-xylene
(p-xylene)

Again, the physical properties of the members of this series vary in a regular way as the molecular weight increases, and the chemical properties remain similar. Some aromatic compounds, especially toluene and the xylenes are important solvents.

It is worth noting that hydrocarbons do not dissolve to any extent in water, but will float as their specific gravity is less than 1. Some aromatic compounds are toxic; benzene for example is highly toxic, both as a vapour and by skin absorption of the liquid. Many, more complex, aromatic compounds have been identified as carcinogens. Similar compounds are to be found in smoke.

8.4   Liquefied petroleum gases (LPG)

Propane (C_3H_8) and butane (C_4H_{10}) are gases at room temperature and pressure, but are easily liquefied using pressure alone. A very small amount of liquid will produce a great volume of gas and so by liquefying the gas a large amount can be stored in a small volume. As both gases are highly flammable and are widely used as fuel gases, installations containing the liquid gases are very widespread.

The important property for LPG is the critical temperature – the temperature above which it is impossible to liquefy a gas by pressure alone (see Section 4.4). For propane, the critical temperature is 96.7°C and for butane, 152°C. When in the right kind of container they will evaporate, increasing the pressure until there is no further net evaporation. Thus, inside each liquid gas container there is a liquid with pressurised vapour above it. As the gas is let out for use as fuel, more liquid evaporates to keep the pressure of the vapour at its original value.

As discussed, both propane and butane are highly flammable. If propane liquid escapes, it will quickly boil into a large amount of flammable vapour: 1 litre of liquid will produce 270 litres of vapour.

The vapours of both propane and butane are heavier than air and will seek lower ground; they are odourless and colourless, though very frequently, a stenching agent (mercaptan) is added.

When propane and butane evaporate they take heat from their surroundings. Propane has a boiling point of -42°C at atmospheric pressure, so at normal ambient temperatures and pressures, the liquid boils easily. This applies to vast majority of practical situations. However, butane has a boiling point of around -1°C, so that in winter conditions, the vapour pressure may be too low to provide a flow of fuel vapour. For this reason, "LPG" generally consists of a mixture of propane and butane.

> **In dealing with LPG it is vital to realise that above the critical temperature the substances can only exist as gases. Cylinders heated above this temperature are, therefore, likely to explode.**

Full details of the storage and fire-fighting techniques associated with liquefied petroleum gases will be found in the *Manual of Firemanship, Part 6c.*

8.5 Simple oxygen-containing compounds derived from hydrocarbons

There are many different types of organic compound which contain oxygen in addition to carbon and hydrogen. Some are reactive, and may be encountered in industrial processes (e.g., aldehydes) whereas others are relatively unreactive and are used as solvents (e.g., ketones). The more important types are discussed briefly.

8.5.1 Alcohols

The structure of the commonest alcohols is similar to that of paraffins, but with one of the hydrogen atoms replaced by a hydroxyl group O—H:

Methane, CH_4 with one H atom replaced by an O—H, group becomes Methyl alcohol CH_3OH (Methanol)

The whole series of alcohols is formed by adding -CH_2 groups to methanol:

- ethyl alcohol or ethanol (C_2H_5OH);

- n-propyl alcohol or n-propanol (C_3H_7OH); and

- n-butyl alcohol or n-butanol (C_4H_9OH).

As the molecular weight increases, there is a **general increase** in the:

- melting point;

- boiling point; and

- flash point.

This is accompanied by a **decrease** in the:

- solubility in water; and

- spontaneous ignition temperature.

The first few members of the series dissolve completely in water but members higher than butyl alcohol are only slightly soluble. All alcohols are less dense than water: the insoluble ones float.

Chemically the alcohols resemble each other. The first members of the series are highly flammable liquids. Ethyl alcohol is sometimes used as a fuel and is also used in rocket propulsion systems. Alcohols are also intermediaries in various chemical processes. Methanol and ethanol are widely used as solvents in industry and ethanol is the most important ingredient of beer, wines and spirits. Propanol and butanol are also used as solvents and some of the higher alcohols are used to make detergents. Nearly all alcohols are to a greater or lesser extent toxic according to type.

8.5.2 Aldehydes

These compounds all contain the group:

$$\equiv C \underset{\displaystyle O}{\overset{\displaystyle H}{<}}$$

attached to such organic groups as methyl (CH_3-), ethyl (C_2H_5-) and so on. The simplest member of the group is formaldehyde:

$$\underset{H}{\overset{H}{>}} C = O$$

with the formula CH_2O. Formaldehyde is a colourless, flammable gas with a pungent suffocating smell, though it is more usual to find it as a 4% solution in water, which also contains a little methanol. This solution is called formalin and gives off flammable vapour if heated above its flash point. This varies according to the formaldehyde and methanol concentration. The vapour is toxic. Formaldehyde is used in the manufacture of several plastics, as an antiseptic and as a preservative of anatomical specimens.

The next member of the series, acetaldehyde (CH_3CHO) has the structure:

$$H - \underset{\underset{\displaystyle H}{\displaystyle |}}{\overset{\overset{\displaystyle H}{\displaystyle |}}{C}} - C = O$$

and differs from formaldehyde by one CH_2 group. It is a colourless liquid with a strong fruity smell. The compound dissolves readily in water, is flammable and toxic and the vapour forms explosive mixtures with air. It is used as an intermediate in the manufacture of other chemicals and plastics.

The higher aldehydes (i.e. containing more than two carbon atoms) are rather less important. The physical properties of these materials vary in the usual way as the molecular weight increases.

8.5.3 Ketones

The simplest ketone is acetone [$(CH_3)_2CO$] which has the structure:

$$H - \underset{\underset{\displaystyle H}{\displaystyle |}}{\overset{\overset{\displaystyle H}{\displaystyle |}}{C}} - \underset{\underset{\displaystyle O}{\displaystyle ||}}{C} - \underset{\underset{\displaystyle H}{\displaystyle |}}{\overset{\overset{\displaystyle H}{\displaystyle |}}{C}} - H$$

Acetone is by far the most commercially important member of the series. It is a colourless, highly flammable liquid which is readily soluble in water and has a minty smell. It is toxic to the extent that high concentrations have an anaesthetic effect and the liquid dissolves the fats out of the skin, and so can give rise to dermatitis and skin irritations. Acetone is a very important industrial solvent for materials such as paint removers, cellulose acetate, fats, waxes and acetylene (see Section 8.2).

The next member of the series is methyl ethyl ketone (MEK):

$$\underset{CH_3}{\overset{C_2H_5}{>}} C = O$$

It is another important industrial solvent and closely resembles acetone, but with a higher flash-point, etc.

8.5.4 Carboxylic acids

The carboxylic acids or 'fatty acids' are a group of weak acids, related to the aliphatic hydrocarbons with a similar chain structure. They all contain the group:

which may be found attached to various organic groups such as methyl ($-CH_3$) and ethyl ($-C_2H_6$). The first member of the carboxylic acid series is formic acid, HCOOH:

Formic acid is a colourless liquid with a pungent smell. It is toxic and can cause burns on the skin. It is used in the textile industry, in electroplating and in the leather and rubber industries.

The next member of the series is acetic acid (CH_3COOH), which is present as a dilute solution in vinegar. It is flammable, dissolves readily in water and can burn the skin if concentrated. The vapour and the concentrated acid are toxic. It is used as a solvent in chemical manufacture.

The properties of some of these acids are given in Table 8.4.

8.5.5 Esters

The esters can be thought of as being derived from the carboxylic acids by the replacement of the hydrogen atom in the COOH group by a methyl or other radical. For example, "ethyl acetate" (see opposite).

Esters are flammable, colourless liquids or solids and are usually only slightly soluble in water, on which they float. They have fruity smells and are often found in fruit and in scents. The higher solid members of the series are found in beeswax. The esters are used as solvents, and in pharmaceuticals, perfumery and foodstuffs. Some properties of a few esters are given in Table 8.5.

8.5.6 Ethers

These all contain an oxygen atom -O- which joins two organic groups such as methyl or ethyl groups. The only one of commercial significance is diethyl ether ($C_2H_5-O-C_2H_5$). This substance is often referred to merely as 'ether'. It is a colourless, highly flammable, volatile liquid with a characteristic smell. It is less dense than water and immiscible in it. It is toxic in high concentrations and at lower concentrations has an anaesthetic effect.

Table 8.4 *Carboxylic acids*

Name	Formula	Structure	Vapour density (A = 1)	Melting point (°C)	Boiling point (°C)	Flash point (°C)	Flammable limits (% in air)	Self-ignition temperature (°C)
Formic acid	HCOOH		1.59	8	101	69	–	600
Acetic acid	CH_3COOH		2.07	16.6	118	45	4(lower)	566
Propionic acid	C_2H_5COOH		2.56	−22	141	54	–	–
n-butyric acid	C_3H_7COOH		3.04	−7.9	163.5	72	2 to 10	452

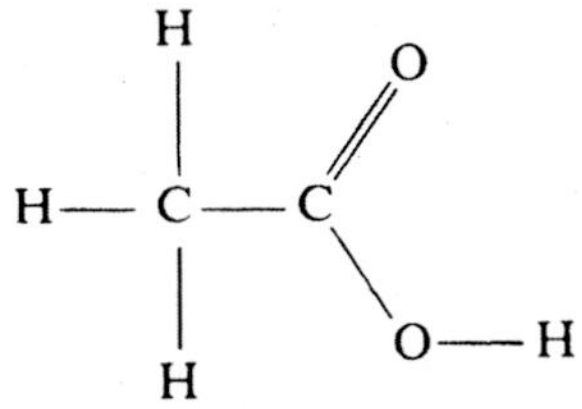

Acetic acid,
CH₃COOH

with the *H replaced by the ethyl radical C₂H₅, becomes

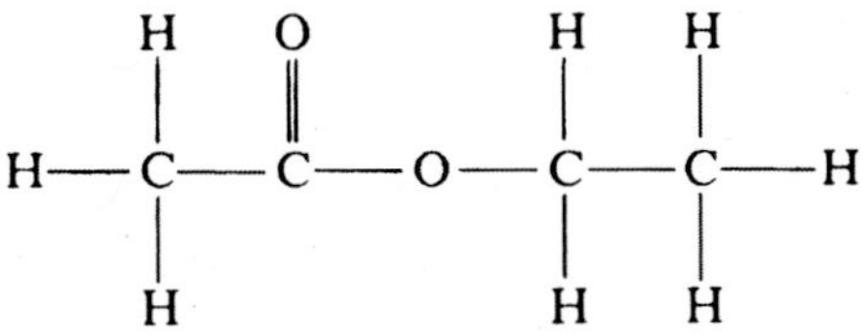

Ethyl acetate,
CH₃COOC₂H₅

Table 8.5 Esters

Name	Formula	Structure	Vapour density (A = 1)	Melting point (°C)	Boiling point (°C)	Flash point (°C)	Flammable limits (% in air)	Self-ignition temperature (°C)
Ethyl formate	HCOOC₂H₅	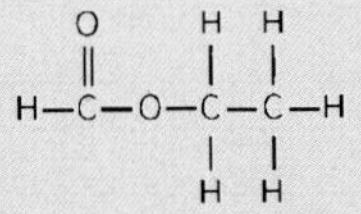	2.55	-79	-54	-20	28 to 16.5	455
Ethyl acetate	CH₂COOC₂H₅	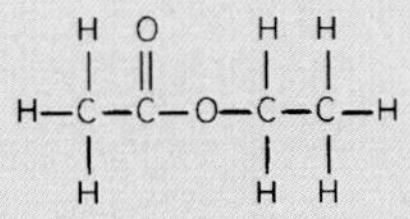	3.04	-84	77	-4	2 to 11.5	>427
Ethyl butyrate	C₃H₇COOC₂H₅	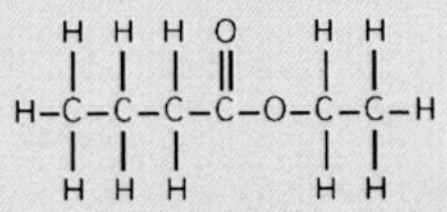	4	−93	121	25	–	463
Amyl acetate	CH₃COOC₅H₁₁	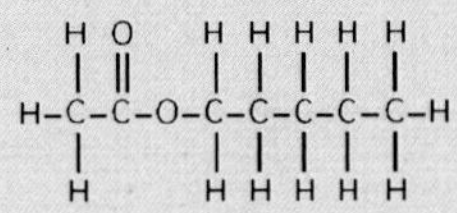	4.5	−78.5	148	25	1.1 to – 7.5	399

Diethyl ether has a boiling point of 34.5°C, a flash point of -4.8°C, flammable limits of 1.85 to 36.5% in air and a self-ignition temperature of 180°C. It may contain a substance known as ether peroxide which, if the ether is evaporated to dryness, can cause an explosion.

Physics and Chemistry for Firefighters

Chapter 9 – Polymers

9.1 Polymers

Many organic solids, including wood, plastics and rubbers, are polymers. This means that the molecules of which they are composed consist of very long chains of carbon atoms which can consist of many thousands of atoms.

For many years now, chemists have been able to create or synthesise polymer molecules in the laboratory. Many of these have passed into commercial use as plastics and synthetic rubbers. Polymers are formed by taking small molecules with two or more reactive groups and arranging for these to link up end to end and form long chains. For example in ethylene $H_2C=CH_2$, the double bond can be "opened" or broken to give:

$$H_2C \quad CH_2$$

which will very rapidly combine with other molecules of the same type to produce polyethylene:

$$-CH_2-CH_2-CH_2-CH_2-CH_2-CH_2-$$

which consists of a long chain of -CH$_2$- groups joined to each other. In a case such as this we call ethylene the **monomer**, polyethylene the resulting **polymer** and the process **polymerisation**.

Simple straight-chain polymers of this type are well known; many of them have small side groups attached to the chain, as in polypropylene:

$$\overset{\displaystyle CH_3}{\underset{\displaystyle |}{}} \quad \overset{\displaystyle CH_3}{\underset{\displaystyle |}{}} \quad \overset{\displaystyle CH_3}{\underset{\displaystyle |}{}}$$
$$-CH_2-CH-CH_2-CH-CH_2-CH-$$

or polystyrene:

$$-CH_2-CH-CH_2-CH-CH_2-CH-$$

Here the symbol:

stands for the benzene ring, which is the simplest aromatic structure (Section 8.3).

Polymers such as polyethylene, polypropylene and polystyrene soften and eventually melt at temperatures in excess of 100-150°C. Such materials are called **thermoplastics**.

Thermosetting plastics do not melt but break down and char on heating. In these plastics, the long chains are also linked together sideways by carbon-carbon bonds: the material is said to be **cross-linked**. Figure 9.1 illustrates this point, the lines representing polymer molecules and their cross-links.

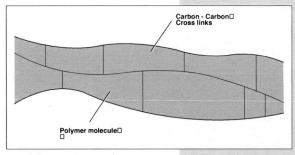

Fig. 9.1 The cross-links of polymer molecules of thermosetting plastics.

Industry uses the fact that thermoplastics soften or melt when they are processed. The same techniques can not be used in thermosetting plastics. These have to be processed as short chain molecules and then heated or a catalyst added to make the molecules cross-link.

Plastics often have other materials mixed into them to improve their properties or to make them cheaper:

- **Inert fillers** such as china clay, wood flour and carbon black, or, in laminated plastics, sheets of paper or glass-cloth;

- **Fire retardants**, to make the polymer more difficult to ignite;

- **Plasticisers**, mixed with some thermoplastics to make them more pliable (e.g., PVC insulation);

- **Stabilisers** to inhibit degradation due to atmospheric oxidation, attack by sunlight or decomposition under conditions of mild heating; and

- **Colouring materials**.

9.2   Fire hazards

> **Like any combustible material in a fire situation, plastics and rubbers may:**
>
> ● **give off toxic and corrosive gases; and**
>
> ● **give off large quantities of smoke, often in a very short space of time.**

However, many synthetic polymers produce much more smoke than "traditional" materials such as wood, and the rate of fire growth may be much greater, particularly if the material melts and drips, spreading fire as a burning liquid.

9.2.1 Toxic and corrosive gases

If plastics only contain the elements carbon and hydrogen, or carbon, hydrogen and oxygen, the main toxic gas to be expected is carbon monoxide (CO) which is formed when all organic materials are burned in quantity. The amount of CO produced increases if there is a relative shortage of oxygen. This gas is a well-known hazard to fire fighters. As it is odourless, colourless and produced in large quantities in fires in buildings, it is responsible for most of the fire fatalities. It can also cause the deaths of people who are confined to unventilated rooms with faulty gas heaters.

Many other toxic products are produced from plastics containing only carbon, hydrogen and oxygen. A whole range of toxic and corrosive species are produced under conditions of poor ventilation. Their nature depends on the structure of the polymer, and can include aldehydes and many other partially oxidised products.

Many plastics contain nitrogen in addition to carbon, hydrogen and oxygen. Plastics in this category include cellulose nitrate, nylon, polyurethane foams, melamine-formaldehyde plastics, urea-formaldehyde plastics, ABS (acrylonitrile-butadiene-styrene), some epoxy resins and nitrile rubbers. (Note that certain "natural polymers" such as wool and silk also contain nitrogen.) The fire products from these will contain nitrogen-containing species such as organic nitriles, hydrogen cyanide and NO_2. All of these are toxic. Intense, well ventilated burning will convert most of the original nitrogen into NO_2.

The class of material known as polyurethane foams (PUF) includes the "standard PUF" introduced in the 1970's as well as the newer "combustion modified foams" which began to appear in the 1980's. The standard foams have been extensively investigated and are known to produce appreciable amounts of CO and HCN in the fire gases. Other, highly toxic nitrogen-containing products may be produced, depending on the type of polyurethane foam and the conditions of burning.

Chlorine is present in polyvinyl chloride (PVC) and certain related co-polymers, in neoprene and in certain types of self-extinguishing fibre-glass polyester resin. In PVC fires, almost all the chlorine goes to form hydrogen chloride (HCl) gas in the fire gases. HCl is both toxic and corrosive, having a very sharp smell and forming a corrosive solution with water (hydrochloric acid). Apart from corroding many metals, the acid may cause long term changes in alkaline mortar. Ferroconcrete may be much less affected; nevertheless, copious washing after incidents involving PVC is desirable. Other chlorine containing polymers may also give hydrochloric acid gas and possibly other chlorine containing toxic compounds as well.

PTFE (poly-tetrafluoroethylene – 'Teflon') and some related materials, such as 'Kel-F' and some synthetic rubbers, sometimes known as 'vitons', contain fluorine.

If these materials are overheated, toxic fluorinated gases are produced. If these are inhaled through a lighted cigarette they become more dangerous. Toxic products from decomposing fluorinated materials should not be inhaled.

9.2.2 Smoke

Fires involving materials which contain the aromatic (benzene) ring structure (Section 8.3) will tend to produce large quantities of smoke. These include polyurethanes, phenol-formaldehyde resins, polystyrene (Section 9.1), polyesters, epoxy resins and polycarbonates.

If materials of this type ignite readily and burn rapidly in a fire (e.g. the early polyurethane foams), very large quantities of thick black smoke will be evolved in a very short period of time, and can lead to rapid smoke-logging of escape routes, etc.

Although PVC does not contain the aromatic structure, it produces large amounts of smoke in fires, because it decomposes in the solid phase to produce aromatic structures.

9.2.3 Burning tars or droplets

Thermoplastics melt on heating and so in a fire may form burning droplets which could help the fire to spread. Although polyurethane foams are not technically thermoplastics, they do give burning drops of tar in a fire. On the other hand PVC, which is a thermoplastic, does not give burning droplets, but merely forms a tarry coke-like product.

9.2.4 Exotherms

The polymerisation process may well produce heat. This is a problem for those manufacturers producing the raw plastics (normally in pellet form for thermoplastics), but there is a high degree of control of the processes involved, and it rarely causes a problem. However, the crosslinking or curing process involved in the manufacture of thermosetting materials may also be exothermic; for example, if blocks of polyurethane foam are stored before the exothermic curing process is complete, self-heating may occur, leading to spontaneous combustion (Section 7.7.2).

9.2.5 Catalysts

Various types of catalyst are used in polymerisation processes including acids, alkalis, complex organo-metallic compounds and organic peroxides.

Acids and alkalis present well known hazards. An organo-metallic catalyst may be in the form of a slurry in flammable solvents: some of these compounds, such as aluminium triethyl, react violently with water. Organic peroxides are oxidising agents and, therefore, present a considerable fire risk. **Under some conditions such materials can be explosive.**

9.2.6 Flammable solvents

Flammable liquids, such as acetone, methyl ethyl ketone, toluene, industrial alcohol and methyl alcohol are widely used as solvents in various processes and also as cleaning fluids, so may be present in fires on industrial premises. See also Chapter 8.

9.2.7 Dusts

Some processes produce fine plastic dusts. **These may present an explosion hazard if dispersed as a suspension in air.**

9.2.8 Self-extinguishing plastics

Many plastics are described as "self-extinguishing". While PVC and phenol-formaldehyde resins are naturally so, others may be made self-extinguishing by chemical changes in the polymer molecule or by the use of special additives.

The term 'self-extinguishing' means that, while a flame may (or may not) cause the material to burn, it will not continue to burn if the applied flame is removed. However, the term refers to the performance of plastics in a specific small scale test. In a fire situation, it will burn if surrounded by other burning materials, or perhaps on its own if a large enough area of the plastic has been ignited to produce flames which are self-sustaining.

> **'self-extinguishing' does not mean 'non-flammable' or 'non-combustible'.**

9.3 Monomer hazards

Monomers by definition are reactive compounds capable of polymerisation. Some, like ethylene, do not polymerise very easily and need exactly the right conditions of temperature and pressure, perhaps with a catalyst. Others, like styrene, may polymerise by accident, due to the presence of impurities, water, heat or other causes, and when this happens a great deal of heat may be given out. Some monomers have to be transported with a polymerisation inhibitor added to prevent the process occurring spontaneously.

As these monomers are mostly poor conductors of heat, the heat cannot get away easily, temperatures may rise and a fire may result. In addition to this problem, **monomers are flammable, and some are toxic.** It is also possible that some monomers in bulk quantities could start to polymerise in a fire with the ensuing added hazard of the heat given out by the polymerisation reaction.

Some of the more notable monomers used in the plastics industry are detailed below, but the number of monomers is very large and ever increasing, so the list cannot be considered as exhaustive.

Acrylonitrile

- colourless, partially water-soluble, flammable liquid with faint, pungent smell;

- polymerises explosively with some organic peroxides or concentrated caustic alkalis;

- highly toxic: can be absorbed through the skin and also through leather; and

- used as a starting material in the manufacture of ABS (acrylonitrile-butadiene-styrene) plastics and certain synthetic rubbers.

Butadiene

- vapour at room temperature and pressures, but easily liquefiable at room temperature;

- polymerises readily, especially in the presence of peroxide catalysts or air;

- flammable; and

- slightly toxic, narcotic in high concentration.

Epichlorhydrin

- used in the manufacture of epoxy resins;

- colourless, slightly water-soluble liquid with an irritating odour;

- polymerises exothermally with acids, bases and some salts; and

- highly toxic material and in fires may produce toxic gases including phosgene.

Methyl methacrylate

- clear liquid with acrid odour, used in the manufacture of acrylics (poly-(methyl-methacrylate));

- flammable;

- toxic;

- polymerises exothermally with peroxide catalysts; and

- normally stabilised, but heat accelerates the polymerisation.

Styrene

- used in the manufacture of polystyrene plastics and fibre-glass polyester resins;

- slightly yellow liquid, strong smell;

- normally stable, polymerisation greatly accelerated by heat or added peroxides;

- exothermic polymerisation: risk of fire and even explosion; and

- moderately toxic, vapour is an irritant to the eyes.

Vinyl acetate

- colourless, slightly water-soluble, flammable liquid, faint odour;

- polymerises with organic peroxides or when heated; and

- low toxicity, may act as an eye irritant.

Vinyl chloride

- sweet-smelling vapour at room temperature and pressure, easily liquefied;

- severe explosion hazard when exposed to heat or flame;

- moderately toxic acts as an anaesthetic in high concentrations;

- liquid may cause freeze burns due to rapid evaporation;

- flammable; and

- combustion gases contain hydrogen chloride which is both toxic and corrosive.

9.3.1 Intermediates and hardeners

Isocyanates

- used as intermediates in polyurethane foam manufacture;

- mostly brown liquids, slightly water-soluble, characteristic odour;

- skin irritants, may cause dermatitis, toxic by skin absorption;

- flammable – emit toxic gases when on fire;

- isocyanate vapours cause bronchial spasm repeated exposure may bring sensitisation;

- great caution should be exercised in dealing with them; and

- made harmless using special solutions of ammonia in water, to which an emulsifying agent has been added.

In manufacture dangerous exothermic reaction causing fires can readily occur where toluene di-isocynate (TDI-) based foams are produced, but is much less likely where the more extensively used diphenyl methane di-isocyanate (MDI) foams are made.

Chlorosilanes

- intermediates in silicone plastic manufacture;

- mostly fuming clear liquids;

- highly toxic;

- flammable; and

- react with water to produce hydrogen chloride gas – reaction is strongly exothermic in many cases.

Epoxides

- **Amine** hardeners – generally toxic. Some may cause dermatitis.

Chapter 10 – Other Combustible Solids

10.1 Wood

Wood is a complex polymeric material of natural origin. In spite of the widespread use of synthetic materials, wood still accounts for a high proportion of the combustible material which is used in buildings, not only as fittings and furniture, but also as structural members. The principal constituent of wood is cellulose, a polymer of D-glucose, which occurs in all higher plants.

There is a high water content in wood and the difference in moisture content between green and well-dried wood is significant in regard to fire risk. Considerable quantities of heat are required to dry timber, due to the high latent heat of vaporisation of water.

When wood is heated, decomposition starts at temperatures of around 170°C, forming char, with the evolution of carbon dioxide, carbon monoxide and water. The proportion of flammable vapours released at this stage is low. Above 300°C, the decomposition process which produces flammable vapours becomes the dominant pyrolysis reaction, but they will be mixed with some CO_2 and H_2O vapour from the char-forming process which still occurs, but no longer dominates. This mixture of gases and vapours is less flammable than the decomposition products from, for example, polyethylene which will be 100% hydrocarbon, undiluted by non-flammable gases. This, and the fact that there is always a significant amount of char produced which provides protection to the wood underneath, accounts for the remarkable fire properties of wood. For example, (i) thick sections of wood cannot burn in isolation and (ii) thick timber beams can survive longer in a fire than unprotected steel beams, because the char forms a protective layer around the sound timber below.

Many methods are available to reduce the combustibility of wood. The most successful involve impregnating the wood with chemicals (e.g., ammonium phosphates, etc.) which catalyse the char-forming reaction at the expense of the decomposition process which produces flammable vapours. The resulting vapours are of very low flammability (mainly a mixture of CO, CO_2 and H_2O) and will not support flame, or contribute significantly to a fire when other materials are burning.

10.2 Coal

Coal is a very complex mixture of carbon and a variety of resinous organic compounds. There are many varieties, with harder coal containing more carbon. Plates of inorganic, noncombustible materials are also found in coal: these consist of limestone and compounds of iron, magnesium and manganese.

In large heaps, such as those used for storage of coal at power stations, self-heating can occur, which may lead to spontaneous combustion (see section 7.7). The smaller the coal particles, the the greater the danger. It is promoted by moisture, and the greater the oxygen content of the coal, the greater the danger, so that coal, especially pulverised coal containing more than 10 per cent of oxygen, may be dangerous in storage. In addition, **coal dust can form an explosive mixture in air**.

Storage heaps must be kept as free as possible from excess of air and protected from external sources of heat. Coal is sometimes sprayed with a high flash-point mineral oil that reduces dustiness and protects coal surfaces against oxidation. Fires in coal stacks are dealt with in the Manual of Firemanship, Part 6c.

10.3 Metals

Three-quarters of all the elements are metals. To a chemist a metal is a substance which can lose electrons and form positive ions (ions are charged atoms or groups of atoms – see Chapter 1). In addition, metals tend to have a group of properties associated with them; if an element possesses most of them, we describe it as a metal.

10.3.1 Properties of metals

Metals will show most of the properties listed here, although there are exceptions to most of these. For example, most metals are malleable and ductile - can be hammered into shape and can be drawn out into wire – but antimony is very brittle and will shatter if hammered!

(i) all, except mercury, are solids at room temperature, though they have a wide range of melting and boiling points;

(ii) they form positive ions;

(iii) they are malleable and ductile;

(iv) they are good conductors of heat and electricity;

(v) they can form alloys;

(vi) the oxides and hydroxides are basic (and so can be alkali solutions in water); and

(vii) most dissolve in mineral acids, normally releasing hydrogen.

Metals show a wide range of chemical properties, and range from dangerously reactive metals such as sodium and potassium, to inert metals such as platinum and gold. Metals can be arranged in an 'Activity Series' (Table 10.1).

In this Table, the most reactive metals are at the top and the least reactive at the bottom. Whatever chemical property is considered, those metals at the top of the series react most vigorously, indeed often violently, and those at the bottom react slowly or not at all.

Table 10.1 *The activity series of metals*

Metal		Occurrence	Reaction with water
Potassium	K	Never found	React with
Sodium	Na	uncombined	cold water
* Barium	Ba	with other	to yield
Strontium	Sr	elements	hydrogen
Calcium	Ca		
Magnesium	Mg	Rarely found	Hot metals
Aluminium	Al	uncombined	decompose
* Chromium	Cr	with other	water and
Manganese	Mn	elements	Burning metals
Zinc	Zn		decompose
* Cadmium	Cd		steam
Iron	Fe		
Cobalt	Co		Very little
Nickel	Ni		reaction unless
Tin	Sn		at white heat
* Lead	Pb		
† HYDROGEN	H		
*Bismuth	Bi	Sometimes	Inactive with
Copper	Cu	found	water or steam
* Mercury	Hg	uncombined	
Silver	Ag	with other	
		elements	
Platinum	Pt	Found	
Gold	Au	uncombined	
		with other	
		elements	

* Indicates that breathing apparatus must be worn in an incident involving these metals.

† Although not a metal, hydrogen is included as it also forms a positive ion

Although hydrogen is not a metal, it is included in the Table as it also forms a positive ion. Many important metal reactions involve displacement of hydrogen either from water or from acids.

10.3.2 Reaction of metals with water or steam

It is obviously important for the firefighter to understand how these heated metals will react with water as, usually, water will be the most readily available firefighting medium. It will be shown that for some metals, though, the addition of water could be dangerous or disastrous.

● **Potassium to calcium**

These metals react immediately with water to release flammable hydrogen gas and leave a metal hydroxide. In some cases the hydroxide so formed is itself a corrosive alkali. In the case of potassium the reaction is so vigorous that the metal seems to ignite immediately on contact with water. A small piece of sodium will move rapidly over the surface of water and if prevented from doing so, will ignite. Larger pieces of these metals are in danger of explosion on contact with water. Calcium reacts steadily with cold water but vigorously with hot.

● **Magnesium to iron**

These metals react little with cold water, even when powdered. At higher temperatures, the reaction rate increases and a steady flow of hydrogen is produced by reaction with steam. If the metals are already burning the reaction with cold water becomes very fast, producing a lot of hydrogen which may lead to an explosion. Going down the series, the rate of reaction decreases until, with iron, there is little reaction unless the red-hot metal is exposed to steam.

● **Cobalt to lead**

Here the white-hot metals must be treated with steam before reaction will take place.

● **Bismuth to gold**

These metals do not react with water or steam as they are below hydrogen in the Activity Series.

10.3.3 Reaction with oxygen

Metals at the top of the Activity Series react most readily in air*. Sodium and potassium are so reactive that they are stored in paraffin oil to prevent oxygen reaching them. Many other metals will burn in air or oxygen with increasing difficulty going down the series. Even metals like tin and lead will burn at very high temperatures.

---

* Note that reaction in pure oxygen is always much more vigorous than in air.

When a metal is powdered, it presents a very large surface area compared with a block of the same mass. Combustion is made much easier as the powder or dust particles are so small and can be heated extremely rapidly to the temperature at which they will burn. **Some metallic dusts can burn or explode spontaneously when dispersed in air.** When this occurs at ordinary temperatures the material is said to be pyrophoric (e.g., "Raney Nickel", which is a finely divided form of Nickel, used as a catalyst).

Many flammable metal powders and dusts are pyrophoric, especially magnesium, calcium, sodium, potassium, zirconium, hafnium. Some metal powders will burn in carbon dioxide and nitrogen (e.g., magnesium) or under water. Metal powders when damp may also cause fires and explosions, even in the absence of air and often without warning, and in the absence of heat.

10.4 Sulphur

This is usually found either as a yellow powder (known as 'flowers of sulphur') or as yellow crystals, but it is sometimes produced as blocks or sticks. It burns with a blue flame to give sulphur dioxide:

$$S + O_2 = SO_2$$

Sulphur is used in the manufacture of rubber, in sulphur compounds, such as sulphur dioxide and sulphuric acid and in certain drugs. **It has a low toxicity, but the dust presents an explosion hazard.** Sulphur dioxide, however, is a highly toxic gas with a sharp pungent odour which can be easily liquefied under pressure at ambient temperatures. It has many uses, especially as a bleaching agent and as a food preservative.

Hydrogen sulphide (H_2S), which is also known as sulphuretted hydrogen, is formed as a by-product from many chemical processes, including the decomposition of organic sulphur compounds; for this reason it is frequently found in sewer gases. Hydrogen sulphide has a characteristic odour of rotten eggs and is highly toxic. **It is flammable and under certain conditions can produce an explosion risk.**

10.5 Phosphorus

The element phosphorus is extremely reactive and is found in nature combined with other elements, mostly as phosphates (compounds containing the PO_4 group). It is also present in all living matter. The pure element exists in two different forms: red phosphorus and white (or yellow) phosphorus. Their properties are itemised in the Manual of Firemanship, Part 6C, Section 16. White phosphorus is extremely dangerous as it will ignite in air at temperatures as low as 30°C giving dense white clouds of toxic fumes of phosphorus pentoxide:

$$4P + 5O2 \rightarrow 2P2O5$$

White phosphorus should never be touched with the bare hands as their warmth may cause ignition; moreover, phosphorus burns heal very slowly.

Red phosphorus is relatively safe if handled with care, and is used in making safety matches. The white form, because of its toxicity, is converted to phosphorus sulphide (P_4S_3) for use in non-safety matches.

Inorganic phosphates are crystalline solids which are normally safe unless one of the toxic metals is involved. Some are used as fertilisers.

Organic phosphates can be very toxic: some are used as pesticides and, for some of these, a few drops on the skin can prove fatal.

Physics and Chemistry for Firefighters

Chapter 11 – Extinguishing Fires

The ways in which burning can be stopped, and so the mechanisms which act when a fire is put out, have been dealt with in the previous chapters.

In this chapter, the various media used to put out different types of fire are examined.

The 'weapon' used against any given type of fire will depend upon the nature of the materials involved and the size and intensity of the fire.

11.1 Classification of fires by type

The current British/European Standard BS EN 2: 1992 *Classification of fires* defines four categories of fire, according to the type of material burning.

Class A
These are fires on solid materials, usually organic, leaving glowing embers. Class 'A' fires are the most common and the most effective extinguishing agent is generally water in the form of a jet or spray.

Class B
These are fires involving liquids or liquefiable solids. For the purpose of choosing effective extinguishing agents, flammable liquids may be divided into two groups: those that mix (are miscible) with water and those that do not (are immiscible).

Extinguishing agents are chosen according to whether the liquid fuel will mix with water or not. Agents which may be used include water spray, foam, light water, vaporising liquids, carbon dioxide and dry chemical powders.

Class C
These are fires involving gases or liquefied gases in the form of a liquid spillage, or a liquid or gas leak, and these include methane, propane, butane, etc. Foam or dry chemical powder can be used to control fires involving shallow liquid spills, though water in the form of spray is generally used to cool the containers.

Class D
These are fires involving metals. Extinguishing agents containing water are ineffective, and even dangerous. Carbon dioxide or dry chemical powders containing bicarbonate will also be hazardous if applied to most metal fires. Powdered graphite, powdered talc, soda ash, limestone and dry sand are normally suitable for Class D fires. Special fusible powders have been developed for fires involving some metals, especially the radioactive ones.

Electrical fires
Electrical fires are not treated as a class of their own, since any fire involving, or started by, electrical equipment must, in fact, fall into one of the other categories.

The normal procedure for dealing with an electrical fire is to cut off the electricity and use an extinguishing method appropriate to what is burning.

If this cannot be done with certainty, special extinguishing agents will be required which are nonconductors of electricity and non-damaging to equipment. These include vaporising liquids, dry powders and carbon dioxide. Very fine water mists have proven to be very effective at extinguishing fires using very little water, and their development has been hastened recently as they are seen to be an environmentally friendly replacement for halons. The rapid cooling that can be brought about by carbon dioxide extinguishers may affect sensitive electronic equipment - though it is the smothering effect of the gas, rather than the cooling which extinguishes the fire.

11.2 Classification of fires by size

To describe the size of a fire, the Central Fire Brigades Advisory Council has made the following recommendation:

Major fire   20–jets (or more)

Large fire   8–19 jets

Medium fire   3–7 jets

Small fire   1–2 jets, or 3 + hose reels

Minor fire   1–2 hose reels, or hand extinguishers.

11.3 Extinguishing fire: Starvation, smothering, cooling

We have seen from the *triangle of combustion* (see Figure 7.1), that three things are needed to allow burning to take place:

● a combustible material – fuel,

● oxygen, usually from the air, and

● enough heat to bring the material to a certain minimum temperature.

● **Starvation** – limiting fuel.

● **Smothering** – limiting oxygen.

● **Cooling** – limiting temperature.

Fire extinction is largely a matter of depriving the fire of one or more of these factors, so methods of extinguishing fire can be classified in terms of removing these factors:

In practice, fire extinguishing methods often use more than one of these principles, but it will be convenient to group them according to the main principle involved.

11.3.1 Starvation

Fires can be starved of fuel (Figure 11.1, top) in three ways:

1.   By removing potential fuel from the neighbourhood of the fire. For example, by:

● draining fuel from burning oil tanks;

● working out cargo at a ship fire;

● cutting trenches or creating fire breaks in, for example, peat, heath and forest fires, demolishing buildings to create a fire stop; and

● counter-burning in forest fires.

2.   By removing the fire from the mass of combustible material – for instance, pulling apart a burning haystack or thatched roof.

3.   By dividing the burning material into smaller fires which may be left to burn out or which can be extinguished more easily by other means. The beating out of a heath fire owes much of its effectiveness to this.

Figure 11.1 The triangle of combustion.
Top: starvation – or the limitation of the combustible material. Centre: smothering – or the
limitation of oxygen. Bottom: cooling – or the limitation of temperature.

11.3.2 Smothering

If the oxygen supply to the burning material can be sufficiently reduced, burning will cease (Figure 11.1, centre).

The general procedure in methods of this type is to try to prevent fresh air from reaching the to the seat of the fire and so to allow the combustion to reduce the oxygen content in the confined atmosphere until it extinguishes itself. This is less effective where, as in the case of celluloid, the burning material contains within itself in a chemically combined form the oxygen it requires for combustion.

Smothering is the principle behind snuffing out candles and capping oil well fires. The battening down of a ship's hold when a fire breaks out below decks will sometimes hold the flames in check until port is reached. Small fires, such as those involving a person's clothing, can be smothered with a rug, blanket, etc., while the use of sand or earth on a small metal fire is a further instance of the same principle.

Foam is an important practical smothering agent. Foams form a "blanket" over the burning surface and so separate the fuel from the air, thus preventing fuel vapours from mixing with air while at the same time shielding the surface from direct heat transfer from the flames.

Fires can be smothered with a cloud of fine dry powder, usually sodium bicarbonate, shot from a pressurised extinguisher, though research suggests that chemical interaction (inhibition) by the powder may be as important as the smothering action.

Another technique using the smothering principle is the use of **ternary eutectic chloride** powder for use on metal fires. This is applied using a gas cartridge pressurised extinguisher. The fusing temperature of the powder is in the region of 580°C, and it is applied to form a crust over the burning metal depriving it of oxygen from the air.

Inert gases such as nitrogen and carbon dioxide can be used to smother a flame temporarily. If these gases are vigorously discharged in the immediate vicinity of the fire, the oxygen content of the atmosphere may be reduced to such an extent that burning cannot be supported. Patented mixtures of inerting gases are now extensively used instead of halons in computer installations. "Total flooding systems" are used to protect special risks such as computer installations and rare book collections in libraries. This requires that the inerting gas is released into a closed space, as the appropriate inerting concentration must be reached following the discharge, and then maintained.

For larger fires, however, inerting agents aren't so useful, as the convection currents set up are sufficiently powerful to dilute the inert blanket before the extinguishing action can take effect. Strong winds may have the same effect. Applying inerting agents in a liquid form, which is then vaporised by the fire likely to be more effective, particularly as the burning region is also cooled by this. However, inerting gases can be used to great effect in enclosed environments such as electrical cabinets.

Very fine water mists have been shown to be able to extinguish fires using very small amounts of water. These have shown their worth in situations where halons would previously have been used and on offshore installations. They act mainly by inerting: a great deal of water vapour is created when water mist is discharged into a confined space with hot surfaces, and this smothers the fire. As the droplets are so small, they evaporate very quickly, and can rapidly smother the flames. Their small size which makes them such a good extinguishing agent also means, unfortunately, that they are easily swept away from the fire by opposing air movement and so are not suitable for fighting larger fires in unconfined spaces.

In the 1970's and 80's, halogenated hydrocarbons or **halons** were developed and used extensively as extinguishants. The first and probably the simplest of these was **carbon tetrachloride**, but it is toxic and its use was soon discontinued. A number of others of lesser toxicity were developed and found favour.

Many halons have been considered. They are identified by numbers which denote how many carbon and halogen atoms are in the molecule. The first digit gives the number of carbon atoms, the second gives the number of fluorine atoms, the third gives the number of chlorine atoms and the fourth gives the number of bromine atoms. A fifth digit may, or may not, be present which gives the number of iodine atoms. For example, bromochlorodifluoromethane has a formula CF_2ClBr, and so is known as Halon 1211.

These vaporising liquids act partly as inerting blankets similar to those mentioned in the preceding section, but mainly by chemical interference (inhibition) with the chain reactions in the flame, "mopping up" free radicals.

Although extremely effective, halons are no longer used except under some exceptional circumstances, as they are known to be very harmful to the earth's protective ozone layer. No more will be manufactured, though such as are already in stock will continue to be used in fixed installations where there is perceived to be a special risk, such as in certain military situations.

Fires can also be extinguished by separating the fuel from the flame by blasting it away. This is what happens when a candle is blown out and, on a larger scale oil well fires can be extinguished by the blast from exploding dynamite. This method does not work simply by depriving the flame of fuel, but also by making the flame unstable when air is supplied at high velocity in the vicinity of the fuel surface.

11.3.3 Cooling

If the rate at which heat is generated by combustion is less than the rate at which it is lost from the burning material, burning will not continue. (Figure 11.1, bottom).

So, to extinguish a fire by cooling, the rate at which heat energy is lost from the burning material must be increased by removing some of the heat energy. This reduces the temperature of the burning mass, reducing the heat release rate. Eventually, the rate at which heat is lost from the fire may be greater than the rate of heat production and the fire will die away.

Cooling the fuel is the main way in which water is used to extinguish fires. There are many variations: for example, a tank fire involving a high flashpoint oil (boiling point $>>$ 100°C) can be extinguished by a high velocity sprinkler spray which apparently produces a water-in-oil emulsion at the surface, thus causing rapid cooling. This neatly avoids the problem of water sinking to the bottom of the tank before it has had much effect on the temperature of the surface layer.

When it is applied to a fire, the extinguishing medium – water for example – itself undergoes changes as it absorbs heat from the fire:

(a)   its temperature will rise;
(b)   it may evaporate (boil);
(c)   it may chemically decompose (not water); and
(d)   it may react chemically with the burning material.

For the extinguishing medium to achieve maximum effect, it is clear that the quantity of heat energy absorbed when these changes occur should be as high as possible. That is to say that, referring to the points above in order, in a good coolant, the following properties should be as **high** as possible:

● the specific heat capacity;

● the latent heat of vaporisation; and

● the heat of decomposition.

The action of water depends predominantly on (a) and (b), the latter being far more important: it takes about six times as much heat to convert a given mass of water at its boiling point into steam as is required to raise the temperature of the same amount of water from the usual atmospheric value to its boiling point. Water is most efficiently used if it is applied to a fire in liquid form and in such a way that as much as possible is converted to steam. The smothering effect of the steam produced at the seat of the fire is thought to play a part in assisting in the extinguishing process.

In all fire-fighting operations where water is used it should be the aim to ensure that the proportion of water which escapes from the building in liquid form applied should be as low as possible.

When the heat of a fire is considerable, as in its early stages, the steam formed will not be visible, but as the temperature falls the steam will condense above the fire. This is widely recognised by experienced fire-fighters as a sign that a fire is being brought under control.

On the basis of thermal capacity and latent heat of vaporisation, water is an excellent fire extinguishant, since both figures are high. This fact, combined with its availability in large quantities, makes it by far the most useful fire extinguishant for general purposes. The role of decomposition is insignificant in the case of water, but certain substances, for example carbonates, absorb heat in this way (see the reference to dry powder extinguishers under Section 2, 'Smothering').

Water does not react with ordinary materials, but may prove dangerous with some fuels, evolving heat rather than absorbing it. Moreover, the reaction may result in the formation of a flammable product, thus adding fuel to the fire. The action of water on burning magnesium exemplifies both these effects, since it reacts with the metal exothermically (i.e., producing heat) with the formation of hydrogen, which is readily ignited. In the case of other media the reaction products may be undesirable in other senses, as in the case of the halons which can produce toxic gases which can be hazardous in enclosed spaces.

11.4 Fire extinguishing media

11.4.1   Water

Water is the most efficient, cheapest and most readily available medium for extinguishing fires of a general nature. It is used by fire brigades for the majority of fires, although the methods of application have undergone a number of improvements.

If more water is applied than is actually required to contain and extinguish the fire, the surplus will drain off and may seep through floors and perhaps cause more damage to goods and property than that caused by the fire itself. Accordingly, the method of applying water to a fire varies according to the size of the fire.

If only small quantities are required, portable water extinguishers or hand pumps may be sufficient. Hose reels are used for larger fires. These are fed from a tank on the appliance and water is pumped through the tubing on the reels by means of a built-in pump. For major fires, greater quantities of water are necessary: the built-in pumps driven by the vehicles' engines are often capable of pumping up to 4500 litres per minute, giving the water the necessary energy to provide adequate throw to penetrate deep into a building.

A variation in the application of water can be made using nozzles that produce jets or sprays ranging from large size droplets down to "atomised" fog. Judicious use of this type of application can not only cut down the amount of water used, minimising water damage, but also ensure that it is used to greatest effect. Atomised spray (fog) nozzles have become standard equipment on fire brigade appliances in the UK. They are quite effective when used in the correct situations, but their range is limited. Special pumps and ancillary equipment are used with high pressure fog, giving a greater range of application.

11.4.2 "Inert gas"

On cargo ships, a fire in a hold may be contained by "inerting" the space using the exhaust gases from the ship's engines to displace air. These gases have low oxygen and high carbon dioxide concentrations. (In the past, steam has been tried as a fire suppression agent to control fires in the petrochemical industry, but it is very expensive, requiring a fixed installation and an available source of high pressure steam.)

11.4.3 Foam

Firefighting foams have been developed primarily to deal with the hazards posed by liquid fuel fires.

Although water is used for most firefighting incidents, it is generally ineffective against fires involving liquid fuels. This is because water has a density that is greater than most flammable liquids so, when applied, it quickly sinks below their surfaces, often without having any significant effect on the fire.

Finished f... QS
consist of...
bination of...
trate and w...
These air f...
on the sur...
the foam b...
guish thes...

- by exc... surfac...

- by sep... surfac...

- by res... fro m...

- by for... help t... the fu... flamm...

- by coo... surfac... foam... which dilutes the oxygen around the fire;

The main properties of firefighting foams include:

- Expansion: the amount of finished foam produced from a foam solution when it is passed through foam-making equipment;

- Stability: the ability of the finished foam to retain its liquid content and to maintain the number, size and shape of its bubbles. In other words, its ability to remain intact;

- Fluidity: the ability of the finished foam to be projected on to, and to flow across, the liquid to be extinguished and/or protected;

- Contamination resistence: the ability of the finished foam to resist contamination by the liquid to which it is applied;

- Sealing and resealing: the ability of the foam blanket to reseal should breaks occur, and its ability to seal against hot and irregular shaped objects;

Knockdown and extinction: the ability of the finished foam to control and extinguish fires; and

Burn-back resistance: the ability of the finished foam, once formed on the fuel, to stay intact when subjected to heat and/or flame.

...amount of air added to the foam solution ...ends on the type of equipment used. Hand-held ...n-making branches generally only mix rela-...ly small amounts of air into the foam solution. ...sequently, these produce finished foam with ...expansion (LX) ratios, that is to say, the ratio ...he volume of the finished foam produced by ...nozzle, to the volume of the foam solution used ...produce it, is 20:1 or less. Other equipment is ...ilable which can produce medium expansion ...m (MX) with expansion ratios of more than ...1 but less than 200:1, and high expansion foam ...X) with expansion ratios of more than 200:1 and ...sibly in excess of 2000:1.

...ere are a number of different types of foam con-...itrate available. Each type normally falls into ...e of the two main foam concentrate groups, that ...is to say, they are either protein based or synthetic based, depending on the chemicals used to produce them.

Protein based foam concentrates include:

Protein (P);
Fluoroprotein (FP);
Film-forming fluoroprotein (FFFP); and
Alcohol resistant FFFP (FFFP-AR).

Synthetic based foam concentrates include:

Synthetic detergent (SYNDET);
Aqueous film-forming foam (AFFF); and
Alcohol resistant AFFF (AFFF-AR).

The characteristics of each of these foam concentrates, and the finished foams produced from them, vary. As a result, each of them has particular properties that makes them suitable for some applications and unsuitable for others.

Various types of surface active agents (or surfactants) are added to many firefighting foam concentrates. These are used to reduce the amount of fuel picked up by the finished foam on impact with fuel and to increase the fluidity of the finished foam. Surface active agents are also used as foaming agents because they readily produce foam bubbles when mixed with water.

In film-forming foam concentrates, surface active agents form an aqueous film of foam solution which, in certain conditions, can rapidly spread over the surface of **some** burning hydrocarbons to aid knockdown and extinction. This ability can make them ideal for use in certain firefighting situations such as aircraft crash rescue. However, the associated foam blanket tends to collapse quickly, so providing very poor security and resistance to burnback.

Water-miscible liquids, such as some polar solvents, mix freely with water and can quickly attack finished foams by extracting the water they contain. This rapidly leads to the complete destruction of the foam blanket. Fires involving these liquids can be extinguished by diluting them with large quantities of water. However, containment of the resulting mixture can cause problems and the application of sufficient quantities of water to achieve extinction can take a long time. Consequently, 'alcohol resistant' foam concentrates have been developed to deal with these particular types of liquid.

Further technical detail regarding foam will be found in the Fire Service Manual – Volume 1 – 'Fire Service Technology, Equipment and Extinguishing Media – Firefighting Foam' and details of operational use – in Volume 2 – Fire Service Operations – 'Firefighting Foam'.

11.4.4 Vapourising liquids

This category consists mainly of halons as discussed in Section 11.3.2. Halons have the property of vapourising rapidly when released from their pressurised container. The vapours are heavier than air, but when entrained into the flames, they inhibit the chain reactions and suppress flaming.

Due to environmental concerns, halons have largely been replaced with inerting gases (see Section 11.4.5) and fine water mists.

11.4.5 Carbon dioxide and inert gases

At normal temperatures, carbon dioxide is a gas 1.5 times as dense as air. It is easily liquefied and bottled in a cylinder, where it is contained under a pressure of approximately 51 bars at normal temperatures. When discharged from the cylinder, cold CO_2 vapour and some solid CO_2 are expelled from the "horn", which rapidly cools in the process. The solid quickly sublimes, and some of the liquid CO_2 evaporates to maintain the pressure in the cylinder. The gas, however, extinguishes by smothering, effectively reducing the oxygen content of the air. About 20 to 30 per cent is necessary to cause complete extinction, depending on the nature of the burning material. In fact, materials which have their own oxygen "supply" will continue to burn, as will any material that tends to react with the carbon dioxide, such as burning magnesium. Apart from these considerations, carbon dioxide is quick and clean, electrically non-conducting, non-toxic and non-corrosive. Most fabrics are unharmed by it.

For special risk situations, such as in transformer rooms and rare book collections in libraries, total flooding of the compartment may be required. For this, fixed carbon dioxide installations may be built in. However, although it is non-toxic, it is an asphyxiant at the concentrations necessary to extinguish a fire. The operation of total flooding CO_2 systems requires prior evacuation of all personnel.

Carbon dioxide is also available in bulk to fire authorities, by special arrangement with certain manufacturers who have agreed to supply tankers containing 10 tonnes of liquid to any fire on request.

11.4.6 Dry chemical powders

New problems have been produced for the firefighter by the use in industry of an ever widening range of risks and materials.

The rise of new plastics is one example of this, and the fabrication of reactive metals such as titanium, zirconium and beryllium is another. Sometimes, water cannot be used; on most fires involving burning metals, the result of applying water can be disastrous, often leading to an explosion. New methods of extinction have had to be evolved.

Chief among these are the dry chemical powders which are stored in cylinders under pressure, or which can be ejected by the release of gas under pressure.

The basis of most of these is sodium bicarbonate, which, with the addition of a metallic stearate as a waterproofing agent, is widely used as an extinguishant both in portable extinguishers and for general application in large quantities. Apart from stearates, other additives are sometimes used to decrease the bulk density and to reduce packing in the cylinder. Dry powder is very effective at extinguishing flame ("rapid knock-down"), and is particularly valuable in tackling a fire involving an incident in which someone's clothes have been soaked in flammable liquid, and ignited.

Dry chemical is expelled from containers by gas pressure and directed at the fire in a concentrated cloud by means of specially designed nozzles. This cloud also screens the operator from the flames and enables a relatively close attack to be made. Dry chemical powder can also be supplied in polythene bags for metal fires, as it is more effective to bury the fire under a pile of bags which melt and allow the contents to smother the fire.

Dry chemical powders are also tested for their compatibility with foam, as it was discovered that the early powders tended to break down foam. The two can complement each other on fires where foam is the standard extinguishant.

Ternary eutectic chloride powders have been developed for some metal fires, especially for the radioactive metals such as uranium and plutonium. These contain an ingredient which melts, then flows a little and forms a crust over the burning metal, effectively sealing it from the surrounding atmosphere and isolating the fire.

Some burning materials, such as metals, which cannot be extinguished by the use of water, may be dealt with by means of dry earth, dry sand, powdered graphite, powdered talc, soda ash or limestone, all of which act as a smothering agent.

Dry sand may also be used to prevent burning liquids, including paints and oils, from flowing down drains, basement lights, etc., and for confining shallow layers of such liquids, thus permitting the use of foam or spray branches. On no account should sand be used for extinguishing fires in machinery, such as electric motors, since its use may well necessitate dismantling the entire machine for cleaning, even though the fire damage is negligible.

11.4.7 Blanketing

Another fire extinguishing method is blanketing, which deprives the fire of oxygen. This is especially useful if someone's clothes are burning. The person should be laid down and covered or rolled in a rug, coat, jacket, woollen blanket, etc.

For dealing with fires in small utensils, such as those containing cooking fats, the best method is to smother the fire with a fire resisting blanket, or a cloth or doormat which has been wetted first.

11.3. Beating out

Small fires in materials, such as textiles, etc., may often be extinguished by beating them out, or by rolling and screwing up the burning material tightly to exclude the air. Beating is also the method normally employed to extinguish heath, crop and other similar fires in rural areas when water is not readily available.

Metrication

List of SI units for use in the fire service.

Quantity and basic or derived SI unit and symbol	Approved unit of measurement	Conversion factor
Length metre (m)	kilometre (km) metre (m) millimetre (mm)	1 mile = 1.609 km 1 yard = 0.914m 1 foot = 0.305m 1 inch = 25.4 mm
Area square metre (m^2)	square kilometre (km^2) square metre (m^2) square millimetre (mm^2)	1 mile^2 = 2.590 km^2 1 yard^2 = 0.836 m^2 1 foot^2 = 0.093m^2 1 inch^2 = 645.2 mm^2
Volume cubic metre (m^3)	cubic metre (m^3) litre (l) (= 10^{-3}m^3)	1 cubic foot = 0.028 mJ 1 gallon = 4.546 litres
Volume, flow cubic metre per second (m^3/s)	cubic metre per second (m^3/s) litres per minute (l/min= 10^{-3}m^3/min)	1 foot^3/s = 0.028 m^3/s 1 gall/min = 4.546 l/min
Mass kilogram (kg)	kilogram (kg) tonne (t) (1 tonne = 10^{3}kg)	1 lb = 454 kg 1 ton = 1.016 t
Velocity metre per second (m/s)	metre/second (m/s) International knot (kn) kilometre/hour (km/h)	1 foot/second = 0.305 m/s 1 Int. knot = 1.852 km/h 1 UK knot = 1.853 km/h 1 mile/hour = 1.61 km/h
Acceleration metre per second^2 (m/s^2)	metre/second^2	1 foot/second^2 = 0.305 m/s^2 'g' = 9.81 m/s^2
Force Newton (N)	kiloNewton (kN) Newton (N)	1 ton force = 9.964 kN 1 lb force = 4.448 N

Quantity and basic or derived SI unit and symbol	Approved unit of measurement	Conversion factor
Energy, work Joule (J) (= 1 Nm)	joule (J) kilojoule (kJ) kilowatt-hour (kWh)	1 British thermal unit = 1.055 kJ 1 foot lb force = 1.356 J
Power watt (W) (= 1 J/s = 1 Nm/s)	kilowatt (kW) watt (W)	1 horsepower = 0.746 kW 1 foot lb force/second = 1.356W
Pressure newton/metre^2 (N/m^2)	bar = 105 N/m^2 millibar (m bar) (= 10^2 N/m^2) metrehead	1 atmosphere = 101.325 kN/m^2 = 1.013 bar 1 lb force/in^3 = 6894 76 N/m^2 = 0.069 bar 1 inch Hg = 33.86 m bar 1 metrehead = 0.0981 bar 1 foothead = 0.305 metrehead
Heat, quantity of heat Joule (J)	joule (J) kilojoule (kJ)	1 British thermal unit = 1.055 kJ
Heat flow rate watt (W)	watt (W) kilowatt (kW)	1 British thermal unit/ hour = 0.293 W 1 British thermal unit/ second = 1.055 kW
Specific energy, calorific value, specific latent heat joule/kilogram (J/kg)	kilojoule/kilogram (kJ/kg) kilojoule/m^3 (kJ/m^3) joule/m^3 (J/m^3) megajoule/m^3 (MJ/m^3)	1 British thermal unit/ lb = 2.326 kJ/kg 1 British thermal unit/ft^3 = 37.26 kJ/m^3
Temperature degree Celsius (°C)	degree Celsius (°C)	1 degree centigrade = 1 degree Celsius

List of the elements with atomic number atomic weight and valency

Name of element	Symbol	Atomic number	Atomic weight	Valency
Actinium	Ac	89	227.0	3
Aluminium	Al	13	27.0	3
Americium	Am	95	243.0	3, 4, 5, 6
Antimony	Sb	51	122.0	3, 5
Argon	Ar	18	40.0	0
Arsenic	As	33	75.0	3, 5
Astatine	At	85	210.0	1, 3, 5, 7
Barium	Ba	56	137.0	2
Berkelium	Bk	97	249.0	3, 4
Beryllium	Be	4	9.0	2
Bismuth	Bi	83	209.0	3, 5
Boron	B	5	11.0	3
Bromine	Br	35	80.0	1
Cadmium	Cd	48	112.0	2
Calcium	Ca	20	40.0	2
Californium	Cf	98	251.0	
Carbon	C	6	12.0	2
Cerium	Ce	58	140.0	3, 4
Caesium	Cs	55	133.0	1
Chlorine	Cl	17	35.5	1
Chromium	Cr	24	52.0	2, 3, 6
Cobalt	Co	27	59.0	2, 3
Copper	Cu	29	63.5	1, 2
Curium	Cm	96	247.0	3
Dysprosium	Dy	66	162.5	3
Einsteinium	Es	99	254.0	
Erbium	Er	68	167.0	3
Europium	Eu	63	152.0	2, 3
Fermium	Fm	100	257.0	
Fluorine	F	9	19.0	1
Francium	Fr	87	223.0	1
Gadolinium	Gd	64	157.0	3
Gallium	Ga	31	70.0	2, 3
Germanium	Ge	32	73.0	4
Gold	Au	79	197.0	1, 3
Hafnium	Hf	72	178.5	4
Helium	He	2	4.0	0
Holmium	Ho	67	165.0	3
Hydrogen	H	1	1.0	1
Indium	In	49	115.0	3

Name of element	Symbol	Atomic number	Atomic weight	Valency
Iodine	I	53	127.0	1
Iridium	Ir	77	192.0	3, 4
Iron	Fe	26	56.0	2, 3
Krypton	Kr	36	84.0	0
Lanthanum	La	57	139.0	3
Lawrencium	Lw	103	257.0	
Lead	Pb	82	207.0	2, 4
Lithium	Li	3	7.0	1
Lutecium	Lu	71	175.0	3
Magnesium	Mg	12	24.0	2
Manganese	Mn	25	55.0	2, 3, 4, 6, 7
Mendelevium	Md	101	256.0	
Mercury	Hg	80	201.0	1, 2
Molybdenum	Mo	42	96.0	3, 4, 6
Neon	Ne	10	20.0	0
Neptunium	Np	93	237.0	4, 5, 6
Nickel	Ni	28	59.0	2, 3
Niobium	Nb	41	93.0	3, 5
Nitrogen	N	7	14.0	3, 5
Nobelium	No	102	253.0	
Osmium	Os	76	190.0	2, 3, 4, 8
Oxygen	O	8	16.0	2
Palladium	Pd	46	106.0	2, 4, 6
Phosphorus	P	15	31.0	3, 5
Platinum	Pt	78	195.0	2, 4
Plutonium	Pu	94	242.0	3, 4, 5, 6
Polonium	Po	84	210.0	2, 3, 4
Potassium	K	19	39.0	1
Praseodymium	Pr	59	141.0	3
Promethium	Pm	61	145.0	3
Protactinium	Pa	91	231.0	5
Radium	Ra	88	226.0	2
Radon	Rn	86	222.0	0
Rhenium	Re	75	186.0	2, 3, 4, 6, 7
Rhodium	Rh	45	103.0	3
Rubidium	Rb	37	85.5	1
Ruthenium	Ru	44	101.0	3, 4, 6, 8
Samarium	Sm	62	150.0	2, 3
Scandium	Sc	21	45.0	3
Selenium	Se	34	79.0	2, 4, 6
Silicon	Si	14	28.0	4
Silver	Ag	47	108.0	1

Name of element	Symbol	Atomic number	Atomic weight	Valency
Sodium	Na	11	23.0	1
Strontium	Sr	38	88.0	2
Sulphur	S	16	32.0	2, 4, 6
Tantalum	Ta	73	181.0	5
Technetium	Tc	43	99.0	6, 7
Tellurium	Te	52	128.0	2, 4, 6
Terbium	Tb	65	159.0	3
Thallium	T1	81	204.0	1, 3
Thorium	Th	90	232.0	4
Thulium	Tm	69	169.0	3
Tin	Sn	50	119.0	2, 4
Titanium	Ti	22	48.0	3, 4
Tungsten	W	74	184.0	6
Uranium	U	92	238.0	4, 6
Vanadium	V	23	51.0	3, 5
Xenon	Xe	54	131.0	0
Ytterbium	Yb	70	173.0	2
Yttrium	Y	39	89.0	3
Zinc	Zn	30	65.0	2
Zirconium	Zr	40	91.0	4

Suggestions for further reading

Books about Combustion, Flame and Fire
J.F. Griffiths and J.A. Barnard "Flame and Combustion". Blackie Academic and Professional.

"Thermal Radiation Monograph" The Institution of Chemical Engineers.

References
D.D. Drysdale "An Introduction to Fire Dynamics". John Wiley 1985.

J.F. Griffiths, J.A. Barnard "Flame and Combustion" Blackie Academic and Professional 1995.

G.B. Grant D.D. Drysdale "A Review of the Extinction Mechanisms of Diffusion Flame Fires". Fire Research and Development Group Publication Home Office 6/96.

Books about Physics
Muncaster "A-Level Physics". Stanley Thornes (Publishers) Ltd.
Nelkon and Parker "Advanced Level Physics". Heinemann Educational Books

Books about Chemistry
Open University Foundation Course in Science

General
I. Asimov, "Asimov's New Guide to Science". (Penguin Books, 1985).

"The SFPE Handbook of Fire Protection Engineering" (second edition). Society of Fire Protection Engineers, Boston, Massachusetts, USA.

Acknowledgement
The author would like to thank the Editor of the *Fire Engineers Journal* for allowing portions of the article "Flames in Fires and Explosions" by J. R. Brenton and D.D. Drysdale to be reproduced herein.